BX
1791

JUDICIAL DOCTRINES
OF RELIGIOUS RIGHTS
IN AMERICA

A Da Capo Press Reprint Series

CIVIL LIBERTIES IN AMERICAN HISTORY

GENERAL EDITOR: LEONARD W. LEVY

Claremont Graduate School

JUDICIAL DOCTRINES OF RELIGIOUS RIGHTS IN AMERICA

BY

WILLIAM GEORGE TORPEY

DA CAPO PRESS • NEW YORK • 1970

A Da Capo Press Reprint Edition

This Da Capo Press edition of
Judicial Doctrines of Religious Rights in America
is an unabridged republication of the first
edition published in Chapel Hill, North Carolina,
in 1948. It is reprinted by special arrangement
with the University of North Carolina Press.

Library of Congress Catalog Card Number 78-13228

SBN 306-70067-0

Copyright, 1948, by the University of North Carolina Press

Published by Da Capo Press
A Division of Plenum Publishing Corporation
227 West 17th Street, New York, N.Y. 10011

All Rights Reserved

Manufactured in the United States of America

JUDICIAL DOCTRINES
OF RELIGIOUS RIGHTS IN AMERICA

JUDICIAL DOCTRINES
OF RELIGIOUS RIGHTS
IN AMERICA

WILLIAM GEORGE TORPEY

Chapel Hill

THE UNIVERSITY OF NORTH CAROLINA PRESS

1948

PRINTED IN THE UNITED STATES OF AMERICA

BY THE SEEMAN PRINTERY, INC., DURHAM, N. C.

TO

My Mother

CONTENTS

CHAPTER   PAGE

I. HISTORICAL ANALYSIS...................   3

Religious situation in the Colonies—Spanish settlements—French settlements—English colonies—Early
state constitutions—The United States Constitution—
Article VI—First Amendment—State control—Revised state constitutions—Fourteenth Amendment—
Relation of Christianity to American law—Role of the
judiciary.

II. DELEGATED AND POLICE POWERS AS LIM-
ITATIONS UPON RELIGIOUS FREEDOM   37

Delegated power as a limitation upon religious freedom—Commerce power—Naturalization power—Postal power—Military power—Police power as a limitation
upon religious freedom—Public safety and order—
Sunday laws—Blasphemy—Fraud—Distribution of literature; solicitation—Health—Summary.

III. RIGHTS OF INDIVIDUALS IN THE FORMA-
TION AND TERMINATION OF RELIGIOUS
SOCIETIES............................   82

The nature of religious societies—Society and corporation distinguished—The acquisition of legal status—
Forms of incorporation—Liability of religious societies—
Powers of incorporated societies—Termination of the
life of a religious corporation—Merger of religious
societies—Associations of religious societies—Public aid—
Religious corporations distinguished from charitable and
educational corporations—Summary.

[vii]

IV. THE FINALITY OF ADMINISTRATIVE DE-
CISIONS OF RELIGIOUS SOCIETIES...... 118

The role of civil authority—Elements of a religious controversy—The agency having final ecclesiastical jurisdiction—Procedure—Relation of members to society—
Finality of ecclesiastical decisions involving property
rights—Temporalities not used in accordance with procedural rules of the society—Religious activity contrary
to civil law—Summary.

V. THE RIGHT OF RELIGIOUS ASSEMBLY..... 148

Legal status of the right of religious assembly—What
constitutes a disturbance—When assembly begins and
ends—Place of assembly—Number protected—Wilful
intent—Disturber need not be in church—Congregation
member may be disturber—Removal of disturber—
Secondary religious purpose—Commercial restrictions—
Summary.

VI. THE EXEMPTION OF CHURCH PROPERTY
FROM TAXATION...................... 171

Development of the concept of tax exemption—Strict
construction—What exemption includes—When exemption begins—Exclusive use—Primary religious use—
Primary secular use—Doctrine of divisibility—Ownership as test—Leased land—Private worship—Cemetery
lands—Special assessments—Summary.

VII. RELIGIOUS RIGHTS IN MARRIAGE AND
DIVORCE............................. 198

Early procedure—Validity of marriages—Polygamy—
Divorce procedure—Divorce for religious oppression—
Refusal to cohabit—Alienation of affections—Summary.

VIII. RELIGIOUS RIGHTS IN PARENTAL CON-
FLICTS OVER CHILD CONTROL......... 216

Historical background—Doctrine of co-equality—Limitation of the doctrine of co-equality—Supremacy of the
father in matters of religious belief—Non-interference

with state custody—Non-interference at age of discretion—Guardians as public officers—Antenuptial
agreements—Neglect of medical care—Summary.

IX. EDUCATIONAL PRACTICES INVOLVING
THE RIGHT OF RELIGIOUS FREEDOM.. 233

Non-sectarianism in public education—Public aid—
Reading the Bible in public schools—Compulsory flag
salute—Compulsory dancing lessons—Admission—
Wearing distinctive garb—Use of school for religious
purposes—Use of religious property for public school—
Excusing students for religious instruction—Teaching of
evolution—Teachers' views as to war—Vaccination—
Language restriction—Legality of sectarian schools—
Validity of private school regulations—Summary.

X. RELIGIOUS RIGHTS IN COURT TRIALS.... 277

Competency of witnesses—Credibility of testimony—
Witnesses in the federal courts—Children as witnesses—
Aspersions on religion of parties—Competency of
jurors—Dying declarations—Privileged communications—Summary.

XI. DEVISES AND BEQUESTS FOR RELIGIOUS
PURPOSES 307

Character of grants for religious purposes—Liberal construction favored—Indefiniteness of beneficiaries—
Purposes of trusts—Trusts contrary to public policy—
Effect of incorporation—Diversion of a trust—Bequests
for the saying of Masses—Restraints on religious practices—Peculiar religious beliefs of the testator as grounds
for avoiding a will—Summary.

XII. CONCLUSIONS AND SUGGESTIONS 326

BIBLIOGRAPHY 333

INDEX 373

JUDICIAL DOCTRINES
OF RELIGIOUS RIGHTS IN AMERICA

"ALMIGHTY GOD HATH CREATED THE MIND FREE. ALL ATTEMPTS TO INFLUENCE IT BY TEMPORAL PUNISHMENTS OR BURTHENS . . . ARE A DEPARTURE FROM THE PLAN OF THE HOLY AUTHOR OF OUR RELIGION . . . NO MAN SHALL BE COMPELLED TO FREQUENT OR SUPPORT ANY RELIGIOUS WORSHIP OR MINISTRY OR SHALL OTHERWISE SUFFER ON ACCOUNT OF HIS RELIGIOUS OPINIONS OR BELIEF, BUT ALL MEN SHALL BE FREE TO PROFESS AND BY ARGUMENT TO MAINTAIN, THEIR OPINIONS IN MATTERS OF RELIGION. I KNOW BUT ONE CODE OF MORALITY FOR MEN WHETHER ACTING SINGLY OR COLLECTIVELY."

—THOMAS JEFFERSON

I

Historical Analysis

In its broadest sense, religion includes all forms of belief in the existence of superior beings exercising power over humans and imposing rules of conduct with future rewards and punishments. History records the bitter clashes which have taken place in the world for centuries over the attempts of religious zealots and insistent sectarian groups to impose their religious ideas upon their fellow men by means of political assistance. Fresh imprints of the recurring conflict are still plainly visible upon European shores.

In America, however, the distinguishing characteristic of religion in its social aspects is its organization into a system of self-supporting and self-governing religious groups in a status of independence in so far as the civil government is concerned. This relationship between church and state is unique in the story of man's achievement. It is by far the most significant contribution America has made to the evolutionary development of religion. An appreciation of the American concept of church and state is fundamental to an understanding of our national life.

True religion and liberty are interdependent. Religion, being voluntary, cannot be forced upon anyone. The American theory of religious freedom guarantees complete liberty of religious thought, speech, and action within the limitations of the public peace and order. Religious freedom is impossible where the union of church and state exists because, of necessity, the one restricts the other. The separation of church and state in América sets up each power in an independent sphere. The church, as such, has no relation with the state except the duty of obedience to its law and the opportunity for improvement of its morals; the state has no relation to the church except the obligation to protect its liberty. Above all else, the state must be impartial as between all forms of belief and disbelief not inimicable to the public welfare.

For over a thousand years prior to the discovery of America, the Old World developed the concept of the union of church and state. The principle that the nation should legislate for the benefit of a system of religious beliefs, that the church should depend upon the state for support and defense, that the state should establish a particular church to be the representative of the only legally approved set of religious tenets, was established in European nations in which the faith of the Roman church prevailed as well as in those in which Lutheranism, Calvinism, and other anti-Roman beliefs existed. At the time when American exploration and colonization began there was practically uniform agreement that the prosperity of both church and state depended upon an intimate relationship between the two. It is not surprising, therefore, to find that the early colonizers on American shores were sympathetic toward the union of church and state.

Religious situation in the colonies.—The first settlers in what is now the United States were the Spanish. In 1493, after Christopher Columbus had discovered America and had made his return voyage to Spain, he appeared before King Ferdinand and Queen Isabella to tell them of his discovery. As a result of his journey Spanish explorers and settlers almost immediately set out for America. Through their efforts Spain built a vast New World empire. Spanish institutions were brought to the southeastern and southwestern parts of the United States and exerted great influence upon the life of the area, an influence which has been felt to the present day. The influence of the Spanish union of church and state was one of the principal civilizing forces in this region for over two centuries. This relation of sectarian to secular authority constitutes the beginning of the history of American church-state relations.

Spanish settlements.—In the sixteenth century the Spanish territory embracing Florida was a crown colony with a hierarchical system of government. The king was supreme. Viceroys directly dependent upon the crown ruled in his name according to the dictates of royal decree. Since the viceroyalties were extensive, they were partitioned into smaller districts ruled by governors. Further subdivisions for administrative purposes completed the hierarchical structure. In this political set-up was embodied the European theory of church and state.[1]

Ecclesiastics seeking to land in America without a license from the Spanish government were returned to Spain. After nomination by either church or local government officials, the higher ecclesiastical officers were appointed by the king and their names submitted to the Pope for pontifical approval.[2] The ecclesiastics receiving their appointments from the king could be removed by the king's order. The lesser clerics could be removed by a prelate with the assent of the viceroy.

Both ecclesiastical and secular courts existed in Spanish America. In the early history, ecclesiastical courts decided criminal and civil issues involving Catholics. However, as the territory expanded, the functions of the secular courts increased. Royal decrees soon permitted the common courts to assume jurisdiction in cases involving offenses committed both by Catholic laymen and by clerics. Jurisdictional disputes between ecclesiastical and secular courts were settled by the viceroy.

1. F. J. Hernaez, *Colección de bulas breves y otros documentos relativos a la iglesia de América y Filipinas*, I, 12-14; M. G. Zamora, *Regio patronato español e indiano*, pp. 299-300; Diego de Encinas, *Provisiones, cédulas, capitulos de orden anzas*, I, 122; J. Solorzano, *Política indiana*, Vol. IV.

2. *Recopilación de leyes de los reynos de las Indias* (2nd ed.), I, 38.

Church courts later were forbidden to entertain litigation arising out of the appointment of clerics to ecclesiastical office, even
when the questions involved were wholly religious in nature.[3]

Governmental approval was a prerequisite to the holding of
a church council or synod. The problems discussed usually dealt
with dogma, cult, and discipline. Decisions of provincial coun-
cils at which religious affairs constituted the principal order of
business had to be ratified by the king before the Pope could
publish them. Likewise, synodical decisions were submitted to
the viceroy for his inspection before promulgation.[4] If the
viceroy believed that there was a violation of royal sovereignty,
he sent the proposed decision to the higher secular body for final
appraisal.

Desire to prevent ecclesiastical interference in temporal matters prompted Spanish kings to control the admission into
America of papal bulls and documents through the Council of
the Indies. Local laws provided that the ecclesiastics in America should not obey pontifical documents which had not been
approved by the Council. Later, circulation within America
required, in addition, permission from the viceroy.[5]

It must be said that the Spanish kings zealously promoted
the spiritual and material prosperity of the Catholic church.
Viceroys had a duty to punish any irregularities of a neglectful
cleric. They also possessed the power to expel recalcitrant
clerics from their viceroyalties. Any reprimands were secretly
administered so as not to exert an undue influence on the Indians. At the institution of the Inquisition in America, Protestants and Catholics who were accused of heresy were subjected
to punishment. The civil court inflicted civil penalties upon
those convicted. Only Indians were excused because of their
immaturity. The multitude of religious institutions set up in
the New World was concrete evidence of the faithful execution
of the religious trust placed in the Spanish government.

3. Solorzano, *op. cit.*, Nos. 1-6.   4. Diego. *op. cit.*, p. 136.
5. D. V. Sarsfield, *Relaciones del estado con la iglesia en la antigua
América española.*

In the area of Spanish territorial expansion within the North American continent religion was not forgotten. The conjunction of the religious with the secular is illustrated by an official communication made by a Spanish viceroy to Tristan de Luna, the explorer, upon the occasion of his famous expedition: "What I charge and command you in his royal name is that you should have principally before your eyes the service of God and of his majesty, the welfare, conversion, and good treatment of the natives, and of the religious and the Spaniards who go in your company, keeping them in peace and justice."[6] This expedition, but one typical chapter in the history of the endeavor of Spain to enlarge its colonial holdings, is thus characterized by a distinct respect for religion.

A scholar of Spanish-American affairs[7] has aptly summarized the close church-state relationship which existed in America during the sixteenth and seventeenth centuries as follows: The secular government had legal power

1. To give permission for the erection of churches
2. To control by license the movements of clergy traveling to America
3. To appoint bishops and other ecclesiastics
4. To determine the geographical limits of bishoprics
5. To reprimand clerics
6. To collect taxes
7. To control religious communications
8. To settle disputes

By the exercise of these powers, the Spanish kings directly influenced religious affairs. The authority of the church was confined principally to matters of dogma.

The Spanish state thus became a convenient vehicle for the introduction and expansion of the first formal religious creed in the New World. The missionary, as a religious and political agent of the Spanish government in the conquest of America,

6. H. I. Priestly, ed., *The Luna Papers*, I, 36.
7. J. G. Icazbalceta, *Biografía de don Fr. Juan de Zumarraga,* p. 127.

influenced the development of the southern United States up to and after the arrival of the English in this region in 1763.

French settlements.—French settlements in North America were stimulated in 1603 when Champlain explored the St. Lawrence region. Gradually the French expanded their territory from the basin of the Great Lakes to the basin of the Mississippi. A series of forts extending from the St. Lawrence through the Mississippi Valley to New Orleans constituted the foundation of a French Empire in America. Like the Spanish, the French brought their customs and social ideals to the New World.

Although the primary purpose of the French Empire was fur trading, the Christianizing efforts of French missionaries, such as Jacques Marquette, were an important factor in the life of the inhabitants. The benevolent attitude of co-operative French national and colonial governments toward the Roman religious orders gave further stability to the union of political and religious forces. As in the South, the religious regulations of the Mississippi Valley were bound up with the civil administration. The transfer of the French Empire to the English in 1763 tended to dissolve the established political-religious relations.[8]

A review of the French situation is significant. It reveals that, as in the Spanish settlements, early American settlers and colonizers in areas controlled by the French sought to perpetuate a religious system already established in Europe, a system in which secular control was dominant and religious freedom strikingly lacking. Religious freedom is a concept rather than a characteristic of the physical environment. Its realization became a practical matter only after centuries of American experience. Religious freedom is an American creation.

English colonies.—A consideration of life in England in the seventeenth century indicates that the correlation of the religious

8. M. M. Besson, *Histoire des colonies françaises;* G. L. Jaray, *L'empire français d'Amérique.*

with the civil administration was a natural development in the English settlements in America. The Puritans, for example, set up a theocracy, that is, a civil government based on church membership. The resultant administration was exceptionally intolerant. In fact, toleration of dissenters from the established state religion was seditious in seventeenth-century Massachusetts. Colonial literature is replete with illustrations reflecting the dominant religious viewpoint. Denunciation of those who failed to follow the tenets of the dominant sect is typified by the opinion of President Oakes of Harvard College, who once stated: "I look upon unbounded Toleration as the first-born of all abominations."[9] Individuals who did not conform to Puritan dogma were expelled from the colony. Often persons were hanged because they insisted upon worshiping according to divine revelation as they themselves understood it. The direct effect of such religious control upon the early history of New England is clearly discernible.

The colonists in Virginia established a civil state in which conformity to the established church was an indication of good citizenship. The Puritan wanted his neighbor to conform because he desired to make the state religious and preserve his set of religious beliefs. The Virginian sought conformity to the established church because the church was a department of the state, and religious dissent was a sign of civil disorder. It may be noted that the Puritan experiment illustrated that one result of the union of church and state was heterodoxy, whereas the Virginia program indicated that insistence upon conformity promoted disorder.[10]

Rhode Island denied the religious objectives of both Massachusetts and Virginia by erecting an insurmountable barrier between church and state and by reserving to the individual conscience and to voluntary association all matters of religious import. Roger Williams maintained that the civil government

9. J. B. Felt, *Ecclesiastical History of New England*, p. 29.
10. S. H. Cobb, *The Rise of Religious Liberty in America*, chaps. IV-V.

should not interfere with religious belief, and consequently he fostered a settlement in Rhode Island in which church and state were completely separated. There were no religious restrictions on citizenship. No questions as to one's belief or disbelief were permitted. The civil law of the colony did not distinguish between Jew or Christian, atheist or Congregationalist, Catholic or Protestant, Methodist or Presbyterian. Never before was there a more perfect equality of religion before the law.[11]

Into some one of these three types of civil-religious systems the remaining colonies may be grouped. In the Massachusetts category fall Plymouth, New Hampshire, Connecticut, and New Haven. At Plymouth the Pilgrims sought freedom to worship, but the supposition that they desired to establish general religious liberty is far from the truth. Their concept of religious freedom was liberty for themselves, although it should be understood that they were much more lenient toward dissenters than were their Massachusetts neighbors. New Haven was similar to theocratic Massachusetts in the severity of its regulations.[12] Connecticut and New Hampshire were more liberal in their administration of religious rules.

To the Virginia group North and South Carolina must be added. The Church of England was established in each at the outset and continued to have legal status until the American Revolution. In New York, New Jersey, Maryland, and Georgia popular opinion toward the Church of England changed during the seventeenth century. In New York and New Jersey the English sought to force the Church of England on a group who had been members of the Reformed Church of Holland. The Dutch Reformed Church was removed from its favored

11. For the full significance of the role of Roger Williams, see: A. B. Strickland, *Roger Williams—Prophet and Pioneer of Soul-Liberty; Letters and Papers of Roger Williams;* S. H. Brockunier, *The Irrepressible Democrat;* C. Smyth, *Roger Williams and the Fight for Religious Freedom.*

12. Such regulations pertained to disqualifications from voting, holding office, etc. See Cobb, *op. cit.,* chap. 14.

position in these two colonies, but an attempt to introduce the English Church, which caused much bitterness, was unsuccessful. The English Church never became the legally established institution in either colony.

In Maryland, religious freedom prevailed at the outset. Lord Baltimore permitted both Catholics and Protestants to settle in his colony. The Maryland legislature protected from molestation every person who professed belief in Christ as long as the individual was obedient to the civil government. Later, the religious life of the colony was conditioned by local events. Rivalry of the Puritan and the Cavalier and subsequent political changes modified the protective legislation. Eventually the Church of England was given legal preference.

Georgia's charter guaranteed freedom of worship to the citizens of the colony. However, after the nullification of this charter by the crown, the Church of England was established by royal decree and by legislative enactment.

In the seven colonies mentioned above,[13] the Church of England was supported by local civil rule through favorable legislation. Frequently Anglican bishops resident in England used a religious society as the chief medium for extending Anglicanism in the New World. Religious societies recruited missionaries and schoolmasters, fixed their rates of pay, and regulated removals. Nearly all business affecting the interests of the Church of England in the colonies passed through standing committees of the societies. To facilitate the program of the political-religious societies, the English bishop often exerted his influence upon the secular administration of the realm.

In these colonies the Anglican Church benefited by the sympathetic attitude of the executive and judicial branches of the colonial governments. On the other hand, colonial assemblies were often hostile to the English church. Especially did an antagonistic feeling prevail in those colonies where dissenters

13. Virginia, North Carolina, South Carolina, New York, New Jersey, Maryland, and Georgia.

were numerous. Against the passage of acts unfavorable to their interests, English clergymen and religious societies protested— both before the colonial legislatures and before the British Parliament. Nevertheless, on the whole the Anglican Church benefited in the seventeenth and eighteenth centuries by a high degree of co-operation from many colonial governments.[14]

Pennsylvania and Delaware were similar to Rhode Island. In each of these colonies no church was ever established. Pennsylvania and Delaware, however, were not so liberal as Rhode Island. In them the Quakers did not extend civil privileges to infidels. To that extent religious freedom was limited. Although the distinction as to belief or non-belief in the existence of God was clearly written into the fundamental law of each colony, the precaution appears to have been an expression of opinion instead of a practical rule of exclusion. No instance of actual interference with an individual on account of his alleged atheistic opinion is found in the records.

By 1700, however, the voting privilege in most colonies depended upon conformity to a state-approved sect. Events, such as the hanging of persons in Salem, Massachusetts, for witchcraft, would occasionally indicate a sharp victory for the forces of theocracy. As a general rule, a definite union of church and state meant that the church received pecuniary assistance from the state; church membership became a prerequisite for voting or for holding office; church attendance was made compulsory by law.[15]

Progress toward religious freedom was a very slow process. Each colony had its own internal problems bound up with the religious issues. Sometimes only the passage of time could soften the clashes between conformists and nonconformists. Nevertheless, in America, the concept of the union of church

14. H. L. Osgood, *The American Colonies in the 17th Century*, III, 82, 243, 390.

15. E. F. Humphrey, *Nationalism and Religion in America*, particularly chap. VIII.

and state gradually passed into oblivion during the eighteenth century.

The factors leading to the establishment of the American principle of religious freedom were many. Over a period of time, the methods, claims, and arrogance of the Church of England generated rebellion in the hearts of the great majority of Americans. The unwillingness of the established religion to permit any other form of worship often meant that many people living in sparsely populated areas could not enjoy the benefit of any legal church. The frequent indifference of church officials to the spiritual good of the people, as well as the corruptness of some of the clergy, prompted the colonists to place an unfavorable valuation on an established church as a civil institution. A sense of the injustice of taxing people for the support of a sect not of their own choosing developed among the colonists. Ridiculous persecutions kept the religious issue alive in many sections of the country. Periods of colonial reawakening strengthened the voice of the dissenters, especially in the Middle and Southern colonies.

Two other factors assisted in making America a fruitful place for the growth of the principle of religious liberty. Titles to many of the colonial settlements were conveyed originally by proprietary grant. By this legal arrangement, the government as well as the land was under the control of an individual or of a small group. To encourage individuals to settle in particular areas, inducements in the form of guaranteed civil rights were often extended to persecuted groups in Europe, and there were many sectarian groups who came to insist upon the fulfillment of these promises. In the second place, a great number of colonists near the end of the colonial period did not belong to any church whatsoever. Lack of interest in the established church was a prime reason for a proportionate decline in church membership. It was logical for non-church members to oppose the exercise of special privileges by any particular sect. It may be significant to point out that two of the chief political leaders

of the century favoring the separation of church and state
were Thomas Jefferson and James Madison, both non-church
members.

With the dawn of the American Revolution practically all
of the colonies had reached the stage where the separation of
church and state could be made legally complete. Although
each colony had its own specific experience, there was a growing
feeling that it would be desirable to adopt some greater degree
of religious liberty, to be protected, but not hampered, by the
civil government. Although there were no specific religious
issues involved in the Revolution, the dominant political and
social thought of the period, coupled with the necessity for the
creation of new state governments to take the place of the out-
moded colonial political institutions, furnished an opportunity
for the incorporation of the developing principle of religious
freedom into the states' fundamental laws. The resultant state
constitutions were to a great extent merely a formulation of
what had already been made a practical matter.[16]

Early state constitutions.—That the early state constitutions
displayed a tendency to separate church and state in order that
there might be qualified enjoyment of individual religious freedom is evident from a survey of early fundamental laws. To
many eighteenth-century Americans the theory of democracy
meant individual freedom in the determination of their affairs,
spiritually as well as materially. Judge Cooley states that "the
American people came to the work of framing their fundamental laws, after centuries of religious oppression and persecution, sometimes by one party or sect and sometimes by another,
had taught them the utter futility of all attempts to propagate
religious opinions by the rewards, penalties, or terrors of human
laws. They could not fail to perceive, also, that a union of
Church and State, like that which existed in England, if not
wholly impracticable in America, was certainly opposed to the
spirit of our institutions, and that any domineering of one sect

16. J. T. Adams, *Dictionary of American History*, IV, 444-445.

over another was repressing to the energies of the people, and must necessarily tend to discontent and disorder."[17]

Experience had demonstrated to the colonists the truth of John Locke's statement that no man or society of men had any authority to impose their opinions or interpretations on any other, since, in matters of religion, every man must know, and believe, and give an account for himself. His ideas exerted an immense influence on American legal theory of the period.[18]

The necessity of conformance to a state-approved sect as a condition of voting was gradually recognized as undesirable, prior to the Revolution. Therefore, in the formulation of early state constitutions, requirements of membership in specific sects as prerequisites to suffrage were generally omitted.[19] The exception was the South Carolina Constitution of 1778, which stated that "the qualification of electors shall be that every free white man, and no other person, who acknowledges the being of a God, and believes in a future state of rewards and punishment . . . shall be deemed a person qualified to vote."[20] This provision, however, was eliminated in the revised South Carolina Constitution of 1790.[21]

The separation of church and state, however, was not complete in the first state constitutions. Legal favoritism for particular types of Christianity persisted in some form in the early documents.[22] The Constitution of New Jersey (1776) required belief in a Protestant sect as a qualification of office-holding. Pennsylvania (1776) compelled state officers to believe in a Supreme Being. Maryland (1776) stipulated "a declaration of a belief in the Christian religion" as a prerequisite for its

17. T. M. Cooley, *A Treatise on the Constitutional Limitations* (8th ed.), p. 960.

18. P. W. Ward, *A Short History of Political Thinking*, p. 66.

19. F. N. Thorpe, *American Charters, Constitutions and Organic Laws, 1492-1908*, Vols. I-VII.

20. Article XIII.

21. K. H. Porter, *A History of Suffrage in the United States*, pp. 1-21.

22. Humphrey, *op. cit.*, chap. 1.

public leaders. The Constitution of Delaware (1776) required state officers to believe in the Scriptures.

Other constitutions contained similar provisions. Citizens of North Carolina (1776) who doubted the existence of God or the truths of the Protestant faith were incapable of holding office. (The word "Protestant" was not changed to "Christian" until 1835.) Only Protestants could hold the more important offices in Georgia under the Constitution of 1777. A Christian sectarian religion was established as a state religion in South Carolina (1778). Massachusetts (1780) required its governor and high state officials to be Christians. Vermont's Constitution (1788) suggested that her citizens "ought to observe" the Sabbath.

Sanford H. Cobb compiled the following statistics relative to religious qualifications for officeholders in the first thirteen state constitutions:[23]

Two (Virginia, Rhode Island) conceded full freedom.

Six (New Hampshire, Connecticut, New Jersey, Georgia, North Carolina, South Carolina) specified Protestantism.

Two (Delaware, Maryland) insisted on Christianity.

Four (Pennsylvania, Delaware, North Carolina, South Carolina) required agreement in the divine inspiration of the Bible.

Two (Pennsylvania, South Carolina) required belief in Heaven and Hell.

One (Delaware) required a declaration of faith in the doctrine of the Trinity.

Three (New York, Maryland, South Carolina) excluded ministers from civil office.

Two (Pennsylvania, South Carolina) required belief in one Supreme Being.

Toleration in many states thus meant only the separation of some specific sect of Christians, and not Christianity itself, from civil institutions. Usually some form of the Christian religion was recognized. In fact, certain acts, such as expressing

23. Cobb, *op. cit.*, p. 501.

disregard for the Lord, which in a Mohammedan or Pagan nation might be unnoticed, were made obnoxious by statute. The criminal laws of every state reflected public sentiment as to what was proper and permissible. Consequently, actions regarded as harmful when measured by Christian standards were punished as crimes against society. Nevertheless, the trend toward a complete separation of church and state was well under way.

Congress, under the Articles of Confederation, accentuated the tendency. By the Ordinance of 1787, providing for the government of the territory northwest of the Ohio River, the national legislature assured complete religious liberty but displayed an appreciation of religion as an essential element of national prosperity. Article I of the act stated that "no person demeaning himself in a peaceable and orderly manner shall ever be molested on account of his mode of worship or religious sentiments in the said territory." Article III, on the other hand, encouraged the establishment of schools, on the assumption that religion, morality, and knowledge were necessary to good government. It remained a task for the framers of the Constitution, however, to develop further safeguards for religious liberties.

The United States Constitution.—The legal basis of American religious freedom in its relation to the national government is the Constitution of the United States. This noteworthy document, framed after the establishment of national independence, and after valuable experience under the Articles of Confederation, is the supreme law of the land. James Madison once said of the framers that "there never was an assembly of men, charged with a great and arduous trust, who were more pure in their motives, or more exclusively or anxiously devoted to the object committed to them, than were the members of the Federal Convention of 1787, to the object of devising and proposing a constitutional system which should best supply the defects of that which it was to replace, and best secure the permanent liberty and happiness of their country."[24]   The delegates did their job well; the importance of their product, the Constitution, as a bulwark of religious liberty and as an incentive to parallel state action can hardly be overestimated.

The Constitution itself has been said to be Christian in substance.   Justice and humanity, attributes of Christianity, predominate.   To the extent that it provides for an official oath from the President and the legislative, executive, and judicial officers—both of the national and state governments—the document gives recognition to a Supreme Being.   Exemption of Sunday from the days during which a President may legally consider the signing of a bill tends to promote Sunday observance.   The conclusion of the Constitution, beginning with the words "in the year of our Lord," gives recognition to the chronology which makes the life of Christ the turning point of history.

An analysis of the American theory of religious freedom, however, is more concerned with specific legalities than with implications.   For that reason reference will be made immediately to the Sixth Article, the only section of the original document directly related to religious freedom.

Article VI.—Article VI, Section 3, of the United States Constitution declares that all senators and representatives of the United States and the members of the several state legislatures, and all executive and judicial officers of the United States and of the states, shall be bound by oath or affirmation to support the Constitution, but that "no religious test shall ever be required as a qualification to any office or public trust under the United States."   The effect of the last clause has been to exclude discrimination for or against any specific sect in the matter of elective and appointive officers.   Ecclesiastical control of the affairs of government was thus rendered an effective blow.

24. Jonathan Elliot, *Debates in tne Several State Conventions on the Adoption of the Constitution* (2nd ed.), V, 122.

Charles Pinckney of South Carolina proposed the religious clause to the Constitutional Convention. Roger Sherman, another delegate, believed it unnecessary because he considered the prevailing liberality a sufficient guarantee against the use of such tests. Other delegates desired to require a belief in the existence of a Deity, or in a state of future rewards and punishments, as a legal sanction upon the officials of the new national government. English experience with religious tests, however, moved the majority at the convention to denounce test laws as provocative of arrogance and hypocrisy. The net result of such laws, it was pointed out, was to exclude from office conscientious qualified men.[25] The framers of 1787, by their action in adopting the Pinckney proposal, indicated their determination to guard against religious oppression.[26]

Joseph Story pointed out that the religious clause had the double purpose of satisfying the scruples of respectable persons who were opposed to any religious test and of cutting off any alliance between the church and the national government. The founding fathers were sensible of the dangers inherent in such an association, he believed, and they were aware that bigotry and intolerance were always ready to terrorize and eliminate those doubting a particular dogma. In the history of the parent country, evidence of the pains and penalties of nonconformity had been written in unequivocal language, he asserted.[27] It was Supreme Court Justice Iredell who on one occasion stated that the clause sought to promote religious liberty by placing all religious groups on the same plane.[28]

The state conventions which met in 1787 and 1788 to consider the ratification of the Federal Constitution revived, among other legal differences, the contrasting viewpoints then held relative to the feasibility of banning religious tests. The forum

25. David Hutchison, *The Foundations of the Constitution*, pp. 280-281.
26. Elliot, *op. cit.*, V, 498.
27. Joseph Story, *Commentaries on the Constitution of the United States*, p. 690.
28. Elliot, *op. cit.*, II, 118.

for the debate on this question was simply shifted from the floor of the Constitutional Convention to the legislative chambers of the various state capitols. An appreciation of this struggle is fundamental to an understanding of American religious freedom.

The exclusion of religious tests as a qualification for office-holders in the government was strongly frowned upon in those jurisdictions which already required such tests for state offices. These states expressed fear that without such tests the national government might be controlled by Catholics, Jews, and infidels. Massachusetts, where Congregationalism was the established church, voiced strong disapproval of the abolition of the religious tests. One delegate to the Massachusetts state convention "shuddered at the idea that Romanists and pagans might be introduced into office and that Popery and Inquisition may be established in America."[29]

Defense of the abolition of the tests was warmly upheld in the Bay State convention by one Reverend Backus, who argued that "nothing is more evident, both in reason and the Holy Scriptures, than that religion is ever a matter between God and individuals; and therefore, no man or men can impose any religious test without invading the essential prerogative of our Lord. . . . Imposing of religious tests has been the greatest engine of tyranny in the world. . . . Some serious minds discover a concern lest if all religious tests should be excluded the Congress would hereafter establish Popery or some other tyrannical way of worship. But it is most certain that no such way of worship can be established without any religious tests."[30] The religious article formed but one part of the proposed Constitution. However, the sharp diversity of political thought may be seen in the fact that the state convention ratified the Constitution by a vote of 187 to 168.

In the North Carolina convention similar fear was expressed that, without religious tests, Jews, Catholics, and infidels might

29. *Ibid.*, p. 148.
30. *Ibid.*, p. 149.

obtain control of the political processes.   Mr. Iredell represented the true American spirit by pleading that America set
herself before the rest of the world as an illustration of general
religious liberty.   "Happily," he commented, "no sect here is
superior to another.   As long as this is the case, we shall be
free from those persecutions with which other countries have
been torn."[31]   In spite of his efforts, North Carolina did not
approve the Constitution until November 21, 1789, exactly seventeen months after ratification by the nine states necessary for
the adoption of the new government.

On the other hand, Virginia desired a more definite guarantee against the establishment of a state religion than was implied
in Article VI.   Experience had tempered the attitude of Virginia; the Church of England had been disestablished there
only after an intense struggle.   Popular resistance to political
control of religious beliefs had been succinctly expressed as
recently as four years before the submission of the Federal
Constitution to the states.   In 1784, the Virginia legislature
considered a proposal to provide for teachers of the Christian
religion out of state funds.   After debate, the lawmakers directed that the bill be published and distributed so that the
citizenry might indicate its attitude on the measure.[32]   Protests
designed to halt passage of the measure were made to the legislators.   James Madison, in his *Memorial and Remonstrance*,
emphatically wrote that the control of religion was not within
the jurisdiction of civil government.[33]   The proposal failed to
pass the Virginia House of Delegates at its next session.

Moreover, in Virginia complete liberty had been guaranteed
to all forms of religious belief by a state law sponsored by
Thomas Jefferson and enacted in 1785.[34]   Unique at that time

31. *Ibid.*, p. 130.
32. Cobb, *op. cit.*, pp. 482-511.
33. Hutchison, *op. cit.*, p. 288.
34. For a clear understanding of the part played by Thomas Jefferson in
the quest for religious liberty, see J. Schouler, *Thomas Jefferson*; S. E. Forman, *The Life and Writings of Thomas Jefferson*; F. W. Hirst, *Life and*

for its liberality, the statute provided: "No man shall be compelled to frequent or support any religious worship, place, or ministry whatsoever, nor shall be inforced, restrained, molested, or burthened in his body or goods, nor shall otherwise suffer on account of his religious opinions or belief; but that all men shall be free to profess, and by argument to maintain their opinions in matters or religion, and that the same shall in no wise diminish, enlarge, or affect their civil capacities."[35]   In the light of these events, Virginia's objection to an allegedly inadequate religious guarantee can be readily understood. Without stronger modes of protection, nevertheless, the Federal Constitution was ratified in Virginia by a vote of 89 to 79.

That the religious clause embodied in Article VI of the Constitution was received by the states with varied degrees of favor or disfavor is thus a matter of record. As a counter proposal, some states recommended that Congress amend the Constitution to secure religious freedom more adequately. Virginia, for example, suggested, among other amendments, the following proposal: "That religion, or the duty which we owe to our Creator, and the manner of discharging it, can be directed only by reason and conviction, not by force or violence; and therefore all men have an equal, natural, and unalienable right to the free exercise of religion, according to the dictates of conscience, and that no particular religious sect or society ought to be favored or established, by law, in preference to others."[36]   This amendment, incidentally, is substantially the sixteenth article of Virginia's *Declaration of Rights* which had been adopted by the legislature of the state in 1776.[37]

North Carolina favored an addition to the Federal Constitution which read: "That religion, or the duty which we owe

Letters of Thomas Jefferson; M. W. Trumbell, *Thomas Jefferson, Father of American Democracy;* C. G. Bowers, *Jefferson and Hamilton: The Struggle for Democracy in America.*
   35. W. W. Hening, *Collections of Laws of Virginia*, XII, 84.
   36. Elliot, *op. cit.*, III, 659.
   37. Hening, *op. cit.*, IX, 111.

to our Creator, and the manner of discharging it, can be directed only by reason and conviction, not by force or violence; and therefore all men have an equal, natural, and unalienable right to the free exercise of religion, according to the dictates of conscience; and that no particular religious sect or society ought to be favored or established by law in preference to others."[38] The similarity of this proposal to the Virginia suggestion is apparent.

Like Virginia, New York had already abolished the union of church and state. Disestablishment of the Episcopal Church from the state occurred in 1777 when the New York Legislature repealed those of its laws which might be interpreted as supporting any particular sect. The opposition to the adoption of the Federal document was able to muster 27 votes out of the 57 cast on the question of ratification. The New York Convention then recommended the adoption by the national amendatory process of the following declaration: "That the people have an equal, natural, and unalienable right freely and peaceably to exercise their religion according to the dictates of conscience, and that no religious sect or society ought to be favored or established by law in preference to others."[39] While considering ratification of the new constitution, New Hampshire proposed an amendment to specify that "Congress shall make no laws touching religion, or to infringe the rights of conscience."[40]

After a vigorous minority in Pennsylvania failed to check ratification of the Federal Constitution, the dissenting delegates proposed to the nation a guarantee of religious freedom reading as follows: "The right of conscience shall be held inviolable, and neither the legislative, executive, nor judicial powers of the United States shall have the authority to alter, abrogate, or infringe any part of the constitutions of the several states, which provide for the preservation of liberty in matters of religion."[41]

38. Elliot, *op. cit.*, IV, 244.
39. *Ibid.*, I, 328.   40. *Ibid.*, I, 326.
41. L. Carey, *American Museum*, Vol. II, No. 5, p. 536.

Rhode Island prefaced her approval of the Federal Constitution with the declaration that "religion, or the duty which we owe to our Creator, and the manner of discharging it, can be directed only by reason and conviction, and not by force and violence; and therefore all men have a natural, equal, and unalienable right to the exercise of religion according to the dictates of conscience; and that no particular religious sect or society ought to be favored or established, by law, in preference to others."[42]

Although the Constitution was finally ratified by the required nine states within approximately nine months after submission, the variety of suggestions for amendment to strengthen religious liberty and the vigorousness with which the proposals were accompanied made it evident that the first Congress would have to consider suggestions of this character.

First Amendment.—The first session of the first Congress of the United States under the Constitution met on March 4, 1789. On June 8, James Madison moved, in the House of Representatives, to consider the amendments to the Constitution which had been proposed by the states, among them being suggestions for greater religious guarantees. After lengthy debates on the issue, Madison made a motion for the appointment of a special committee to report desirable amendments. He believed that "the great mass of the people who opposed the Constitution disliked it because it did not contain effectual provisions against encroachments on particular rights, and those safeguards which they have been long accustomed to have interposed between them and the magistrate who exercises the sovereign power; nor ought we to consider them safe, while a great number of our fellow-citizens think these securities necessary."[43] Consequently, he proposed to Congress the insertion of the following: "The civil rights of none shall be abridged on account of religious belief or worship, nor shall any national religion be established, nor

42. Elliot, *op. cit.*, I, 334.
43. J. Gales, *Annals of Congress*, I, 440.

shall the full and equal rights of conscience be in any manner, or on any pretext, infringed."[44]

After Madison's motion had passed, and after a special committee appointed to consider the amendments had reported, the House of Representatives, and later the Senate, approved twelve amendments, encompassing a range of state suggestions for national constitutional improvement.[45] The preamble introducing the proposals explains their source: "The conventions of a number of states having, at the time of their adopting the Constitution, expressed a desire, in order to prevent misconstruction or abuse of its powers, that further declaratory and restrictive clauses should be added; and as extending the ground of public confidence in the government will best insure the beneficent ends of its institution, resolved . . . ."[46] The third proposal contained a prohibition against a national religion and a guarantee of the free exercise of religious beliefs.

Upon submission to the states, ten of the twelve proposals were approved by the necessary three-fourths of the state legislatures and became effective in 1791. Among the ten finally adopted as part of the fundamental law was the guarantee of religious liberty found in Amendment I, providing: "Congress shall make no law respecting an establishment of religion, or prohibiting the free exercise thereof; or abridging the freedom of speech or of the press; or the right of the people peaceably to assemble and to petition the government for a redress of grievances." The inclusion of this further safeguard of religious liberty was thus due directly to the efforts of the states of Virginia, North Carolina, New Hampshire, New York, Rhode Island, and the minority in Pennsylvania—all of which recommended such a guarantee in substantially the same words.

The First Amendment is really the Magna Carta of religious liberty. It positively prohibits the establishment by Congress of any specific national church. It guarantees to all religious

44. *Ibid.*, p. 440.   45. Elliot, *op. cit.*, I, 338-339.
46. *Ibid.*, p. 338.

societies freedom of religious exercise. Congress may not interfere with this liberty. Constitutionally, religious liberty is regarded as one of the inalienable rights of national citizenship,
on a legal equality with liberty of press, speech, assembly, and
petition.

English history reveals the gradual recognition of such
rights as trial by jury, the right to bear arms, freedom of speech
and press, the right of assembly and petition, and others equally
important. However, it was for America to abolish the possibility of a national conjunction of church and state and to secure
a most sacred right for all, namely liberty of religion and the
free exercise thereof. It was this liberty, creating a wall of
separation between the church and the federal government,
which Thomas Jefferson subsequently deemed one of the "essential principles of our government."[47]

State control.—The Federal Constitution and the Bill of
Rights did not nullify the union of church and state which
existed in a few instances in 1789. Neither did they forbid any
state to establish a religion or to assist a specific sect. The First
Amendment forbids only Congressional action. The Bill of
Rights does not apply to state action.[48]

In fact, the framers had no intention of interfering with the
religion of the citizens of the several states. By virtue of the
Tenth Amendment, "The powers not delegated to the United
States by the Constitution, nor prohibited by it to the States, are
reserved to the States respectively, or to the people." Hence,
under our federal system, the power over religion was left exclusively to the states,[49] to be exercised according to their own
constitutions and ideas of justice. The United States Supreme

47. *The Writings of Thomas Jefferson* (P. L. Ford, ed.), VIII, 5; for an
analysis of the historical setting of the First Amendment, see majority and
dissenting opinions in *Everson v. Board of Education of the Township of
Ewing*, 330 U. S. 1, 67 Sup. Ct. 504, 91 L. Ed. 472 (1947); see also *Thomas
v. Collins*, 323 U. S. 516, 65 Sup. Ct. 315, 89 L. Ed. 430 (1945).

48. Hutchison, *op. cit.*, p. 286; for references to cases, see p. 321.

49. *Hale v. Everett*, 53 N. H. 9 (1868).

Court once summarized the situation by declaring that "the Constitution makes no provision for protecting the citizens of the respective States in their religious liberties; this is left to the State constitutions and laws; nor is there any inhibition imposed by the Constitution of the United States in this respect on the States."[50]

As has been mentioned previously,[51] in two states, New York and Virginia, the union of church and state had been abolished before the meeting of the Philadelphia Convention. But in other jurisdictions official relationships between church and state remained for decades after 1787. Connecticut, for example, taxed her citizens for supoprt of the Congregational Church until 1818; Massachusetts did likewise until 1833. Atheists were long excluded from public office in Pennsylvania, North Carolina, South Carolina, Tennessee, Maryland, and New Jersey. Clergymen were constitutionally disqualified from civil office because of their ecclesiastical duties in Delaware, Kentucky, Maryland, and Tennessee.[52]

Revised state constitutions.—State constitutions revised since the first part of the eighteenth century, as well as those formulated by new states preparatory to entering the Union, have emphasized a complete separation between church and state. Religious provisions of the present state constitutions are to be construed with an understanding of the history of religious intolerance and with reference to the laws and customs prevailing at the time of the adoption of the constitution in the particular state.[53] The guarantees apply alike to individuals of all religious beliefs and disbeliefs. Under their protection anyone may hold any religious opinion he pleases and even may form a religion embracing such opinion as long as he does not disturb the public peace and order.[54]

50. *Permoli v. First Municipality,* 44 U. S. 589, 3 How. 589, 11 L. Ed. 739 (1845).
51. Pp. 21-23, *supra.*   52. Cobb, *op. cit.,* chap. 4.
53. *People v. Stanley,* 81 Col. 276, 255 Pac. 610 (1927).
54. *Glover v. Baker,* 76 N. H. 261, 83 Atl. 916 (1912).

American state constitutional provisions respecting religious freedom take the form of prohibitions against: (1) the establishment of a religion by the state; (2) the compulsory support of religious institutions; (3) compulsory attendance at religious worship; and (4) unlimited restraints upon the expression of religious belief.   In some jurisdictions the constitutional provisions apply only to legislative action.   For example, in Pennsylvania in 1911 a prisoner was compelled by a jailer to attend religious services held in jail.   The prisoner believed that his religious freedom had been curtailed and sued for trespass. Determining that there was no cause of action, a county court ruled that the State Bill of Rights guaranteeing freedom of conscience did not apply to compulsion exercised by one person over another except so far as it might be claimed that the compulsion was authorized by law.[55]   In other states the constitutions forbid the compulsion of religious practices exercised by one person over another in a non-governmental capacity.   As an illustration, compulsory church attendance by a student upon the insistence of the authorities of a private military school was held illegal by a New York court.[56]

Fourteenth Amendment.—While formerly state governments were restricted in the enactment of religious laws only by the limitations of their own constitutions, recently the protection of the Fourteenth Amendment of the United States Consitution, originally adopted in 1878, has been extended to insure the citizenry against possible religious tyranny by state rule. The pertinent section of the amendment reads: "No State shall make or enforce any law which shall abridge the privileges or immunities of citizens of the United States; nor shall any State

55. *Merrick v. Lewis*, 40 Pa. Co. 290 (1911); for a federal case in which no cause of action was found to exist against a private person who allegedly abridged another's right to freedom of religion, see *McIntire v. William Penn Broadcasting Company of Philadelphia*, 151 F. (2d) 597 (C. C. A., 1945); certiorari denied 327 U. S. 779, 66 Sup. Ct. 530, 90 L. Ed. 1007 (1946).

56. *Miami Military Institute v. Leff*, 220 N. Y. 799, 129 Misc. 481 (1926).

deprive any person of life, liberty, or property, without due process of law, nor deny to any person within its jurisdiction the equal protection of the laws."

In 1923, the United States Supreme Court declared that the liberty guaranteed by the Fourteenth Amendment includes the right to worship God according to the dictates of one's own conscience.[57] In 1934, the same tribunal considered the relation of the same amendment to the protection of religious liberty.[58] At that time, Mr. Justice Butler further defined the scope of the amendment by stating: "The 'privileges and immunities' protected are only those that belong to citizens of the United States as distinguished from citizens of the States—those that arise from the Constitution and laws of the United States as contrasted with those that spring from other sources. . . .

"There need be no attempt to enumerate or comprehensively to define what is included in the 'liberty' protected by the due process clause. Undoubtedly it does include the right to entertain the beliefs, to adhere to the principles and to teach the doctrines on which these students base their objections."[59] The importance of the above quotation lies in its reference to the right of religious belief.

In a concurring opinion in the same case, Mr. Justice Cardozo assumed that the religious liberty protected by the First Amendment against invasion by the nation was protected by the Fourteenth Amendment against invasion by the states. He was further of the opinion that "the First Amendment, if it be read into the Fourteenth, makes invalid any state law 'respecting an establishment of religion, or prohibiting the free exercise thereof.' "[60] But nowhere in Mr. Justice Cardozo's opinion was there a conclusive statement of the effect of the Fourteenth Amendment on religious liberty.

57. *Meyer v. Nebraska*, 262 U. S. 390, 43 Sup. Ct. 625, 67 L. Ed. 1042 (1922).
58. *Hamilton v. Regents of the University of California*, 293 U. S. 245, 55 Sup. Ct. 197, 79 L. Ed. 343 (1923).
59. *Ibid.*, p. 261.   60. *Ibid.*, p. 266.

The liberalized Court of 1940 accentuated and made effective the parallels between the First and Fourteenth Amendments. In a decision declaring a state statute invalid[61] because it deprived certain individuals of their liberty without due process as conceived in the Fourteenth Amendment, Mr. Justice Roberts, speaking for the majority of the Court, specifically ruled that the fundamental concept of liberty embodied in the Fourteenth Amendment included the liberties protected by the First Amendment. The First Amendment had nullified Congressional legislation establishing religion or prohibiting its free exercise, he held; hence, the Fourteenth Amendment had made the state legislatures as incapable as Congress of enacting such laws.[62]

The constitutional prohibition on state legislation applicable to religion was revealed by Mr. Justice Roberts in a twofold aspect. "On the one hand, it forestalls compulsion by law of the acceptance of any creed or the practice of any form of worship. Freedom of conscience and freedom to adhere to such religious organization or form of worship as the individual may choose cannot be restricted by law. On the other hand, it safeguards the free exercise of the chosen form of religion. Thus the amendment embraces two concepts—freedom to believe and freedom to act. The first is absolute but, in the nature of things, the second cannot be."[63] Because individual actions continue to be subject to regulation for the protection of society, freedom to act must be appropriately defined in order to preserve the enforcement of the protection. But the authority to regulate must be so exercised as not to infringe unduly the freedom thus protected.

This opinion was the first Supreme Court decision squarely

61. *General Statutes of Connecticut,* sec. 6294, as amended by sec. 860 d of the 1937 supplement.

62. *Cantwell v. Connecticut,* 310 U. S. 296, 60 Sup. Ct. 900, 84 L. Ed. 1213 (1940); see also *State v. Barlow,* 107 Utah 292, 153 P. (2d) 647 (1944); appeal dismissed 324 U. S. 829, 65 Sup. Ct. 916, 89 L. Ed. 1396 (1945).

63. *Cantwell v. Connecticut,* 310 U. S. 296, 303, 60 Sup. Ct. 900, 903, 84 L. Ed. 1213, 1218 (1940).

holding that freedom of religion is protected against state interference by the Fourteenth Amendment.[64] Judicial analysis has thus broadened the scope of the protection of the Fourteenth Amendment to include the sphere of religious liberty.

Relation of Christianity to American law.—The constitution of every one of the forty-eight states exhibits directly or indirectly a profound respect for religion.[65] It has been said that Christianity is a part of the law of the land.[66] In a limited sense, this assertion is correct. Christianity has been regarded as a part of the common law in legal practice.[67] Under this theory, the states adopted a common law recognition of Christianity, rejecting those portions of the English law on the subject which were not suited to their institutions. Hence, freedom for the exercise of Christian beliefs has antedated freedom for the exercise of any belief and freedom for lack of belief.

Chancellor Kent of New York stated that "the people of this State, in common with the people of this country, profess the general doctrines of Christianity, as the rule of their faith and practice. . . . The case assumes that we are a Christian people, and the morality of the country is deeply ingrafted upon Christianity and not upon the doctrines or worship of those impostors [atheists]."[68] A constitutional declaration of religious liberty, it was there said, was never intended to withdraw religion in general, and with it the best sanctions of moral and social obligations, from all consideration of the law.

The Supreme Judicial Court of Maine once declared: "It is farthest from our thought to claim superiority for any religious

64. Note, "Constitutional Law—Fourteenth Amendment—Religious Liberty" (1940) 40 *Columbia Law Review* 1067-1071.

65. *Church of the Holy Trinity v. United States*, 143 U. S. 457, 12 Sup. Ct. 511, 36 L. Ed. 226 (1892); Julius H. Miner, "Religion and the Law" (1943) 21 *Chicago-Kent Law Review* 156-180.

66. Philip Schaff, "Church and State in the United States," *Amer. Hist. Assn. Papers* (1887), Vol. II, No. 4, p. 440. See: R. K. Morton, *God in the Constitution.*

67. *Vidal v. Girard's Executor*, 43 U. S. 127, 2 How. 127, 11 L. Ed. 205 (1844).

68. *People v. Ruggles*, 8 Johns. (N. Y.) 290, 293 (1811).

sect, society, or denomination, or even to admit that there exists
any distinct, avowed connection between church and state in
these United States or in any individual state, but, as distinguished from the religions of Confucius, Gautama, Mohammed,
or even Abram, it may be truly said that, by reason of the number, influence, and station of its devotees within our territorial
boundaries, the religion of Christ is the prevailing religion of
this country and of this state."[69]

Mr. Justice Brewer of the United States Supreme Court
wrote that there are many evidences of the fact that this is a
Christian nation. Among them he named the form of oath universally prevailing, concluding with an appeal to the Almighty;
the custom of opening legislative sessions and political conventions with a prayer; laws respecting the observance of the Sabbath; the closing of the courts, legislatures, and similar public
assemblies on that day; and the multitude of charitable organizations existing under Christian auspices.[70]

Judge Story maintained that the general sentiment of the
nation at the time of the adoption of the First Amendment was
that "Christianity ought to receive encouragement from the
state so far as was not incompatible with the private rights of
conscience, and the freedom of religious worship."[71] An attempt
to level all religions and to hold each in utter indifference as a
matter of state policy would have created universal disappro-
bation, if not universal indignation, he added. In his opinion,
the original intent of the First Amendment was not to promote
infidelity or any non-Christian belief by prostrating Christianity.
Rather, it was to exclude all rivalry among Christian sects and
to prevent any national ecclesiastical establishment.

Efforts have been made to rivet tenets of Christianity into
the Constitution itself by the amendatory process.[72] Thus dur-

69. *State v. Mockus*, 120 Me. 84, 93, 113 Atl. 39, 42 (1921).
70. *Church of the Holy Trinity v. United States*, 143 U. S. 457, 12 Sup.
Ct. 511, 36 L. Ed. 226 (1892).
71. Story, *op. cit.*, p. 698.
72. For an analysis of proposed U. S. Constitutional amendments pertain-

ing the Civil War period of American history, when the religious sensibilities of the nation were deeply stirred, an organization entitled the "National Association to secure certain religious amendments to the Constitution" was formed. Its purpose was to secure Congressional passage of an amendment to the preamble of the United States Constitution which would recognize faith in God. The amended preamble would have read: "We, the people of the United States (humbly acknowledging Almighty God as the source of all authority and power in civil government, the Lord Jesus Christ as the Ruler of all nations, and his revealed will as the supreme law of the land, in order to constitute a Christian government, and) in order to form a more perfect union, establish justice, ensure domestic tranquility, provide for the common defence, promote the general welfare, and secure the (inalienable rights and) blessings of (life), liberty, (and the pursuit of happiness) to ourselves and our posterity (and all the inhabitants of the land), do ordain and establish this Constitution for the United States of America."[73] Two conventions of the association, one in Cincinnati in 1872 and the other in New York in 1873, sought to focus national attention on the Christianization problem. Formal proposals to carry out the purpose of the association were introduced in Congress in 1894, 1895, 1896 and four times during the period 1908-1910.[74]

To have been effective, however, an addition to the powers of Congress giving the national lawmaking body authority, by appropriate legislation, to obtain the stated objective of creating a Christian government and to forbid the public participation in non-Christian religions would have been a necessary concomitant

---

ing to religion, see H. V. Ames, *The Proposed Amendments to the Constitution of the U. S.* (Annual Report, American Historical Association, 1896), II, 277-278 and M. A. Musmanno, *Proposed Amendments to the Constitution* (House Document 551, 70th Congress, 2nd Session, 1929), pp. 131-135, 182-185.

73. Schaff, "Church and State in the United States," *loc. cit.*, p. 420.
74. Musmanno, *op. cit.*, pp. 184-185.

of this proposal. Obstacles to legislative approval were tremendous. Besides, the assumption of the Association that the original document is hostile to religion was false. The Constitution is neither hostile nor unfriendly to any religion; it is silent because religion is outside the sphere of the national government.[75]

By way of opposition to the program of the Association was the attempt of the Liberal League in 1873 to remove every trace of Christianity from the Constitution. As published in its literature, the objectives of the League were mainly that churches and other ecclesiastical property be no longer exempt from public taxation, that the employment of chaplains in governmental activities be discontinued, that public appropriations for sectarian institutions cease, that executive officials of both the state and nation cease the proclamation of religious festivals, that the judicial oath of the court be abolished, and that Sunday laws be abolished.[76] To effectuate the program of the Liberal League it would have been necessary to revolutionize the public sentiment of the time and to alter the constitutions of the states and the nation. Neither the Liberal League nor the National Association was able to enforce its program. Consequently, the judiciary never had the opportunity to consider the proposals.

Nevertheless, the fact of the matter is that Christianity cannot be considered the official religion of the state as established by law.[77] A command of the Bible will not be enforced by a civil power. No one can be punished for rejecting Christianity as a system of religious beliefs. The law takes cognizance of offenses against the Supreme Being only when they become offenses against man and his temporal security.[78] In any event the courts cannot render judgments based upon Christianity unless its precepts have been incorporated into positive law. In the sense that civil institutions are based upon Christian precepts,

75. *Ibid.*, p. 421.   76. Humphrey, *op. cit.*, p. 502.
77. *Lindenmuller v. People*, 33 Barb. (N. Y.) 548 (1861).
78. *State v. Chandler*, 2 Harr. (Del.) 553 (1837).

Christianity may be regarded a part of our jurisprudence.[79]   But in so far as Christianity connotes doctrinal compulsion upon all citizens, Christianity does not make up part of our law.   The point to be emphasized is that the people of the states and of the United States as a political entity have no creed.

Role of the judiciary.—In America, the religious convictions of an individual are placed beyond the scope of political control. Promotion of religious faith, whether in church or shrine, mosque or synagogue, tabernacle or meeting house, tent rally or camp meeting, is protected, as is the propagation of disbelief. American constitutions also assure immunity from penalties to the individual who in the legitimate exercise of his own religion offends the religious ideas of others.

An individual's activities, however, may result in a clash of his conception of religious duty with the secular interests of society.   "When does the constitutional guarantee compel exemption from doing what society thinks necessary for the promotion of some great common end, or from a penalty for conduct which appears dangerous to the general good?   To state the problem is to recall the truth that no single principle can answer all of life's complexities.   The right to freedom of religious belief, however dissident and however obnoxious to the cherished beliefs of others—even of a majority—is itself the denial of an absolute.   But to affirm that the freedom to follow conscience has itself no limits in the life of a society would deny that very plurality of principles which, as a matter of history, underlies protection of religious toleration."[80]   How should the two opposites be reconciled?

Constitutions do not ordinarily define "religion" nor describe what is meant by "religious freedom."   Constitutional explanation of the meaning of the "free exercise of religion" is noticeably absent from the documents themselves.   The exact

79. H. C. Black, *Handbook of American Constitutional Law* (4th ed.), p. 514.

80. *Minersville School District v. Gobitis*, 310 U. S. 586, 593, 60 Sup. Ct. 1010, 1012, 84 L. Ed. 1375, 1378 (1940).

meaning of other phrases associated with religious liberty is frequently unclear. Certainly such words as "religious freedom" and "free exercise of religion" do not connote the absolute. There must be a limit to religious, as there is to other, liberty when it manifests itself in public acts. Liberty is not lawlessness. Democratic philosophers agree that no man has the liberty to do wrong or to create injury to his neighbor, or to jeopardize public welfare. Liberty in its very nature is limited by the supreme law of self-preservation which inheres in a state as well as in an individual. Exactly what are the limits in each instance?

Legislatures sometimes have contravened constitutional mandates respecting religious liberty. Infrequently, under pressure of a forgetful or dangerous minority, legislators have sought to nullify the protection inherent in the concept of religious freedom. On the other hand, individuals sometimes have sought to camouflage their civil or criminal faults under a cloak of religious expression. In each case the question becomes, "What is the practical application of the American theory of religious freedom?"

In such situations it has been the American judiciary which has been called upon to balance the secular with the sectarian demands and to make realistic the American ideal. It will be our purpose to examine concrete situations in which the question of religious liberty has been posed for judicial determination and to delineate a significant series of legal principles which have arisen therefrom.

II

Delegated and Police Powers as Limitations upon Religious Freedom

---

Delegated power as a limitation upon religious freedom.— Although limited by the positive restraints imposed by the Constitution, the federal government possesses delegated power, that is, authority specifically conferred upon it by the Federal Constitution. In the exercise of its delegated power, Congress has had occasion to make laws which have allegedly contravened religious freedom. In each instance, however, regardless of the arguments to the contrary, the courts have upheld the particular federal statute in question.

(1) *Commerce power.*—Article I, Section 8, clause 3 of the United States Constitution provides that Congress shall have power to regulate commerce with foreign nations, among the states, and with the Indian tribes. By virtue of this clause the national lawmakers have passed immigration laws excluding various groups of individuals from entry into the country.

The Immigration Act of 1903[1] increased the number of classes of aliens who were to be excluded from admission into the United States. Among these additional prohibited classes were anarchists. In the same year an immigration board of special inquiry decided that a particular person was an anarchist and held him for deportation. In an application for habeas corpus to discharge the alien the contention was set up that the

1. Act of March 3, 1903, 32 *Stat.* 1214, c. 1012, 40 *U. S. C.* sec. 191.

law was unconstitutional.[2] Among other grounds, it was argued that Article I of the Constitution (providing that Congress shall make no law prohibiting the free exercise of religion) was contravened. The Court denied the allegation with the comment: "It is difficult to understand upon what theory the exclusion of an alien who is an anarchist can be held to be a prohibition of the free exercise of religion."[3]

The effect of the First Amendment upon the commerce power was further illustrated by a case in the United States District Court in California. In that case the refusal of federal authorities to admit an alien anarchist into the United States was held not to contravene Article I because the guarantees of free worship apply only to residents legally in the United States.[4]

(2) *Naturalization power.*—Article I, Section 8, clause 4 authorizes Congress to establish a uniform rule of naturalization. The Naturalization Act of 1906[5] requires an applicant for citizenship to declare under oath that he will support and defend the Constitution and laws of the land. Section 382 provides that the naturalization court must be satisfied that, after the five years of residence preceding an application, an applicant must be well disposed to the good order and happiness of the United States. Included in a series of questions to be answered by prospective citizens for the information of the court was the following: "If necessary, are you willing to take up arms in defense of this country?" (Question 22.)

To this query Rosita Schwimmer in 1929 replied: "I would not take up arms personally." She broadened her response by stating that she did not care "how many other women fight, because I consider it a question of conscience." The United States Supreme Court ruled that although pacificism in one sense is in harmony with the policy of the United States government and with the Constitution, such an attitude should not

2. *United States v. Williams*, 126 Fed. 253 (C. C., 1903).
3. *Ibid.*, p. 255.
4. *United States v. Parson*, 22 F. Supp. 149 (D. C., 1938).
5. Act of April 3, 1906, 34 *Stat.* 596, c. 3592. 8 *U. S. C.* sec. 381.

hinder a person from fighting for his nation in an emergency. The Court concluded that an individual without a sense of nationalism is not held by ties of affection to any government and is likely to be incapable of the attachment to our constitutional principles which are required of aliens seeking naturalization. Consequently, Mrs. Schwimmer was denied the privilege of citizenship because of her stated refusal to bear arms at some possible future time of need.[6] The importance of the Schwimmer case in an analysis of religious freedom lies in the fact that the Supreme Court later referred to the Schwimmer decision in a situation in which the religious issue was more prominent.

A year after the Schwimmer decision, Douglas Macintosh, a Yale University professor of theology, filed a petition for naturalization. At a preliminary hearing before a naturalization examiner he submitted a memorandum explaining his answers. In answer to Question 22, he wrote: "Yes, but I should want to be free to judge of the necessity." From a stipulated statement of facts it appeared that he was ready to give the United States as much allegiance as he could ever give to any country, but that he could not place his allegiance to the government before his allegiance to the will of God. In view of his qualified answer, the naturalization court ruled adversely upon his petition. Upon appeal a United States Circuit Court decided that Question 22 was merely informative. Although a citizen has a duty to defend his country, the appellate court held that a person does not lack a sense of nationalism or affection for his government if he conscientiously requests to be excused from bearing arms. His qualified response was believed by the Court to have been intended merely to preserve his right of exemption from military service in a future war. The Circuit Court, consequently, held the qualified answer no bar to compliance with the naturalization regulations.[7]

6. *United States v. Schwimmer*, 279 U. S. 644, 49 Sup. Ct. 80, 73 L. Ed. 558 (1929).
7. *Macintosh v. United States*, 42 F. (2d) 845 (C. C. A., 1930).

On appeal to the United States Supreme Court the opinion of the Circuit Court was reversed.[8] Naturalization is a privilege to be withheld as Congress may determine, the majority of the Supreme Court declared. An alien may claim it only upon compliance with the statutory terms. The Court said that the professor's statement in the case indicated that he was unwilling to take the oath of allegiance except with his own qualification; that he would do what he deemed in the best interests of the nation, but only in so far as he thought his actions would not contravene the best interests of humanity; and, moreover, that he would assist in defending his country by bearing arms and by extending his moral support only if he believed the war to be morally justified. While the professor did not anticipate engaging in propaganda against a war considered justifiable by his government, it was pointed out that he preferred to make no promise even as to that. His position was thus explained to be the only one he could take consistently with what he understood to be the moral principles of Christianity. The Court held that the Schwimmer decision was controlling. The majority ruled: "When he speaks of putting his allegiance to the will of God above his allegiance to the government, it is evident, in the light of his entire statement, that he means to make his own interpretation of the will of God the decisive test which shall conclude the government and stay its hand. We are a Christian people, according to one another the equal right of religious freedom, and acknowledging with reverence the duty of obedience to the will of God. But, also, we are a Nation with the duty to survive; a Nation whose Constitution contemplates war as well as peace; whose government must go forward upon the assumption, and safely can proceed upon no other, that unqualified allegiance to the Nation and submission and obedience to the laws of the land, as well those made for war as those made for peace, are not inconsistent with

8. *United States v. Macintosh*, 283 U. S. 605, 51 Sup. Ct. 570, 75 L. Ed. 1302 (1931).

the will of God."[9]   So interpreting the naturalization process, the Supreme Court denied the petition for citizenship.

A vigorous dissent from the prevailing opinion was written by Mr. Chief Justice Hughes. He said that the question was not whether Congress had the authority to fix conditions upon which the privilege of naturalization is granted or to exact a promise to bear arms as a condition of its grant of naturalization. Assuming Congress had this power, he believed that the issue was whether Congress had exacted such a promise. "The question is whether that exaction is to be implied from certain general words which do not, as it seems to me, either literally or historically, demand the implication."[10]   He thought the requirement should not be implied, because such a construction is directly opposed to the spirit of our institutions. The Chief Justice analyzed the oath requirement for officeholders and concluded that our historic struggle for religious liberty and the presence of many citizens who have been unwilling to sacrifice their religious beliefs made it impossible for him to reach the conclusion that conscientious objectors are disqualified for public office because of the oath. He regarded the oath for officeholders and for naturalization to be the same in substance. Refusal to take the oath for conscientious reasons in either instance he believed to be legal. Upon the assumption that a duty to a moral power higher than the nation has always existed, he concluded that there is opportunity to enforce the authority of law and to maintain the theory of supremacy of the law necessary to orderly government without compelling applicants for citizenship to assume by an oath an obligation to subordinate their duty to God to their duty to secular power. In his opinion the Schwimmer judgment rested upon the special facts of that case.

(3) *Postal power.*—Article I, Section 8, clause 7 gives Congress power to establish post offices and post roads. Directly by statute and indirectly through administrative officers, Congress has evolved a set of postal rules under which the mails

9. *Ibid.*, p. 625.   10. *Ibid.*, p. 627.

are carried. Such regulations cannot be disregarded on the ground that they may violate constitutional provisions regarding religious freedom.

A postal law of 1888[11] prohibits the use of the mails for the transmission of obscene literature. An individual was later indicted and found guilty of depositing a lewd paper in the mails, contrary to the law. Upon appeal to a Circuit Court of Appeals, the defendant suggested Amendment One as a bar to prosecution. The Court pointed out, however, that the constitutional guarantees of religious freedom had nothing to do with the statute involved, and that these guarantees could not be made a shield for a violation of criminal laws which are not designed to restrict religious worship but to protect society against immoral practices. The conviction was upheld.[12]

Another postal statute[13] forbids the use of the mails to defraud. The validity of an indictment under the statute was questioned as contravening constitutional guarantees of religious freedom. The defendant allegedly believed that he had attained a supernatural state of self-immortality which he contended he could transmit to others for cash. Nevertheless, the court decided that there had been a violation of a legal postal statute. The Court reasoned that by the indictment the government did not seek to prevent an honest entertainment of religious belief. Instead, what the government did was to prevent a defendant from pretending to possess views for the fraudulent purpose of obtaining money by the use of the mails.[14]

In another action to prosecute certain individuals for using the mails to defraud, the indictment charged a scheme to defraud through representations, involving defendants' religious beliefs, which were alleged to be false and known by the defendants to be false. The trial judge withdrew from the jury

11. Act of June 18, 1888, 25 *Stat.* 187, 18 *U. S. C.* sec. 353.
12. *Knowles v. United States,* 170 Fed. 409 (C. C. A., 1909).
13. Act of March 2, 1889, 25 *Stat.* 873, c. 393, 39 *U. S. C.* sec. 255.
14. *New v. United States,* 245 Fed. 710 (C. C. A., 1917).

the question whether the alleged religious experiences had in fact occurred, but submitted to the jury the single issue whether the defendants honestly believed the religious experiences had occurred. The Circuit Court of Appeals reversed a judgment of conviction on the ground that the trial judge's restriction of the issue to one of good faith was erroneous. However, the United States Supreme Court upheld, as a course required by the First Amendment, the district judge's action in withholding from the jury all questions concerning the truth or falsity of the religious beliefs of the defendant.[15]

(4) *Military power.*—Article I, Section 8, clauses 11, 12, 14 enable Congress to declare war, to raise armies, and to make rules for the land and naval forces. On the strength of these powers Congress has required military service on the part of American citizens. Draft laws have excluded ordained clergymen and theological students from compulsory training. Members of certain enumerated sects, whose tenets oppose the moral right to engage in war, have been relieved of combatant duty and instead have been subjected to various non-combatant duties.

The Selective Draft Act of 1917[16] proposed to raise a national army by subjecting all male citizens between the ages of twenty-one and thirty years to duty in the national army for the period of the emergency. To carry out its purposes, the act made it the duty of those liable to the call to register. The act exempted from subjection to the draft regularly ordained ministers and theological students. Members of enumerated sects whose tenets excluded the moral right to engage in war were relieved from military service in the strict sense of the word.

An individual who failed to register was prosecuted for violation of the law. One ground for his defense was that the act violated Article I of the Constitution. The reasoning was as follows: Exemption of members of recognized churches who

15. *United States v. Ballard*, 322 U. S. 78, 64 Sup. Ct. 882, 88 L. Ed. 1148 (1944).
16. Act of May 18, 1917, 40 *Stat.* 76, c. 15, 50 *U. S. C.* sec. 226.

hold certain beliefs, and the holding to service of persons not members of such churches who hold the same beliefs, was an act of establishment of religion, because benefits conferred upon some would be refused others if they were not members of those particular churches. The argument continued that exemption of the clergy and divinity students was a direct move in the establishment of religion. The defendant contended that the law recognized the clergy as a class exempt from certain duties of other citizens and was a direct legislative support of recognized churches by bestowing an immunity upon their leaders. The court held, however, that the law was not one respecting the establishment of religion in the sense in which those words were used in the Amendment. For this reason, the Draft Act was not unconstitutional.[17]

Certain other individuals who failed to register and who, consequently, were charged with violation of the Selective Draft Act argued before the United States Supreme Court that the exemption of certain religious groups had the effect of establishing a national religion. The Court readily discounted their contention.[18] The Court commented: "We pass without anything but statement the proposition that an establishment of a religion or an interference with the free exercise thereof repugnant to the First Amendment resulted from the exemption clauses of the act to which we at the outset referred, because we think its unsoundness is too apparent to require us to do more."[19]

Section 5 (d) of the Selective Training and Service Act of 1940[20] exempted a regular or duly ordained minister of religion from training and service, but did not exempt him from registration. If a registrant was deemed by a local draft board to be a minister of religion, he was classified IV-D, exempt from com-

17. *United States v. Stephens,* 245 Fed. 956 (D. C., 1917).
18. *Selective Draft Cases,* 245 U. S. 366, 38 Sup. Ct. 159, 62 L. Ed. 349 (1918).
19. *Ibid.,* p. 389.
20. Act of Sept. 16, 1940, 54 *Stat.* 885, c. 720, 50 *U. S C.* sec. 301.

batant and non-combatant service. If the local board determined that the registrant was not a minister of religion but had conscientious scruples against war, he was classified as a conscientious objector, IV-E, and made subject to induction for work of national importance under civilian direction. Differences of opinion over the meaning of the term "minister of religion" prompted registrants to appeal from their classifications and led to allegations of denial of religious freedom.[21]

It was judicially stated that the term "minister of religion," as used in the Selective Training and Service Act, must be interpreted according to the intention of Congress, and not according to the meaning attached to it by members of any particular group.[22] A "minister of religion" was defined to be one who (1) has followed a prescribed course of study of religious principles, (2) has been consecrated to the service of living and teaching that religion through an ordination ceremony under the auspices of an established church, (3) has been commissioned by that church as its minister in the service of God, and (4) generally is subject to control or discipline by a council of the church by which he was ordained.[23]

In defense of prosecutions for failure to report for induction, certain Jehovah's Witnesses claimed that they were entitled to a IV-D classification because they were ministers of religion. Applying the above definition, courts refused exemption from training and service to Jehovah's Witnesses who spent only a

21. Note, "Constitutional Law—Freedom of Religion—Exemption of Conscientious Objectors from Military Service" (1943) 43 *Columbia Law Review* 112-114.

22. *United States v. Mroz*, 136 F. (2d) 221 (C. C. A., 1943); see also *United States ex rel. Trainin v. Cain*, 144 F. (2d) 944 (C. C. A., 1944); certiorari denied 323 U. S. 795, 65 Sup. Ct. 439, 89 L. Ed. 635 (1945); *United States v. Pitt*, 144 F. (2d) 169 (C. C. A., 1945); *Van Bibber v. United States*, 151 F. (2d) 444 (C. C. A., 1945); for a discussion of the scope of the review of a selective service classification in the instance of a claim to classification as a minister of religion, see also *Cox v. United States*, U. S. ——, —— Sup. Ct. ——, —— L. Ed. ——, decided November 24, 1947.

23. *Buttecali v. United States*, 130 F. (2d) 172 (C. C. A., 1942).

portion of their time in distributing religious literature, while devoting the major part of their time to secular activity[24] such as that of a storekeeper,[25] a joiner in a shoe company,[26] a helper in a paper mill,[27] a coal miner,[28] a freight traffic clerk,[29] or a carpenter.[30] Exemption was also denied the reader of a Christian Science Church, an attorney, who could show no earnings from his religious practice.[31]

The classification of a registrant as a conscientious objector subject to induction for work of national importance under civilian direction, instead of as a minister of religion exempt from combatant and non-combatant service, was deemed not to contravene the guarantees of the First Amendment.[32] Limiting a registrant to the exercise of his religion only in a conscientious objectors' camp was held not to be an illegal denial of religious freedom.[33] A draft board which classified a registrant as a minister of religion, exempt from service, had a right to reclassify him subsequently so as to make him liable for service.[34]

Police power as a limitation upon religious freedom.—State

24. *Checinski v. United States*, 129 F. (2d) 461 (C. C. A., 1942).
25. *Rase v. United States*, 129 F. (2d) 204 (C. C. A., 1942).
26. *United States v. Mroz*, 136 F. (2d) 221 (C. C. A., 1943); on petition to Supreme Court for writ of certiorari, appeal dismissed in *Mroz v. United States*, 320 U. S. 805, 64 Sup. Ct. 23, 88 L. Ed. 486 (1943).
27. *United States v. Domres*, 142 F. (2d) 477 (C. C. A., 1944).
28. *Goodwin v. Rowe*, 49 F. Supp. 703 (D. C., 1943).
29. *Ex parte Stewart*, 47 F. Supp. 415 (D. C., 1942).
30. *Buttecali v. United States*, 130 F. (2d) 172 (C. C. A., 1942).
31. *In re Rogers*, 47 F. Supp. 265 (D. C., 1942).
32. *Checinski v. United States*, 129 F. (2d) 461 (C. C. A., 1942); see also *Roodenko v. United States*, 147 F. (2d) 752 (C. C. A., 1945); certiorari denied 324 U. S. 860, 65 Sup. Ct. 867, 89 L. Ed. 1418 (1945); *United States v. Brooks*, 54 F. Supp. 995 (D. C., 1944); affirmed 147 F. (2d) 134 (C.C. A., 1945); certiorari denied 324 U. S. 878, 65 Sup. Ct. 1027, 89 L. Ed. 1430 (1945); *United States ex rel. Zucker v. Osborne*, 54 F. Supp. 984 (D. C., 1944); affirmed 147 F. (2d) 135 (C. C. A., 1945); certiorari denied 325 U. S. 881, 65 Sup. Ct. 1574, 89 L. Ed. 1997 (1945).
33. *Rase v. United States*, 129 F. (2d) 204 (C. C. A., 1942).
34. *United States v. Domres*, 142 F. (2d) 477 (C. C. A., 1944); for legality of use of theological panels in evaluating claims to exemption, see *Eagles v. United States ex rel. Samuels*, 329 U. S. 304, 67 Sup. Ct. 313, 91 L. Ed. 252 (1946) and *Eagles v. United States ex rel. Horowitz*, 329 U. S. 317, 67 Sup. Ct. 320, 91 L. Ed. 260 (1946).

statutes have been passed for the purpose of restraining individual actions which tend to injure the public welfare. Such laws do not contravene constitutional guarantees of religious liberty, although the individual actions which they prohibit may have been done pursuant to what was believed, or allegedly believed, to be a religious duty at the time of commission. By the exercise of the police power, states have legally curbed assertedly religious practices.

(1) *Public safety and order.*—Laws to promote the safety, peace, and order of society have been judicially approved. A member of a religious society (for example, the Salvation Army) may not, on the basis of religious guarantees, claim exemption from an ordinance requiring a license before participation in a street parade. In such instances, enforced obedience to municipal regulations constitutes no invasion of religious freedom.[35] A Massachusetts court enunciated the general rule: "The provisions of the constitution which are relied on, securing freedom of religious worship, were not designed to prevent the adoption of reasonable rules and regulations for the use of streets and public places; a religious body, however earnest and sincere, cannot avail itself of these provisions, as an authority to take possession of a street in a city, in violation of such rules, for the purpose of public worship therein. The fact that there is no actual disturbance or breach of the peace on the particular occasion is immaterial."[36]

Typical of the precedence given to public safety regulations is a Michigan situation. An ordinance[37] of the city of Grand Rapids prohibited any person or persons from marching, parading, or riding upon the city streets with musical instruments, banners, flags, or torches without having first obtained the consent of the mayor or common council. A member of the

35. *State v. White*, 64 N. H. 48, 5 Atl. 828 (1886); *Marshburn v. City of Bloomington*, 32 Ill. App. 243 (1889).

36. *Commonwealth v. Plaisted*, 148 Mass. 375, 381, 19 N. E. 224, 226 (1889).

37. *Grand Rapids Ordinance of September 13, 1886*, sec. 2.

Salvation Army was arrested for an alleged violation of the ordinance because he paraded without municipal consent. Pointing out that no one can lawfully stretch his own liberty to interfere with that of his neighbors, the court sustained a conviction.[38]

A Massachusetts law[39] required a license for street parading. A member of the Salvation Army who played a cornet in a street parade without a license defended his behavior on the ground that his action was done as religious worship. Even though he created no disturbance, he was found guilty of violating the law. The Court added that in public demonstrations the Salvation Army has the same rights in law and is subject to the same restrictions as any secular body employing similar practices.[40]

A 1927 ordinance[41] of a Kentucky municipality forbade persons from appearing on the streets wearing masks or other disguise to conceal their identity. Several individuals were tried on a warrant charging violation of the law. The defense set up the plea, among others, of denial of freedom of religious worship. The Court of Appeals of Kentucky answered, however, that obviously the ordinance did not limit the right to worship according to the dictates of one's conscience. The constitutionality of the ordinance was upheld.[42]

The Public Service Commission of Pennsylvania refused a certificate of public convenience necessary for the transportation of persons by public vehicles on call.[43] Appeal to a Pennsylvania court from the Commission's order was predicated upon the assumption that the refusal of the certificate denied orthodox Jewry their religious freedom. The appellant insisted that the vehicle for which a certificate had been denied could thus not be used as a common carrier to convey a particular group of individuals to religious rites, such as funerals. The appellant

38. *In Matter of Andrew Frazee*, 63 Mich. 396, 30 N. W. 72 (1886).
39. *Massachusetts Statutes of 1885*, c. 323.
40. *Commonwealth v. Plaisted*, 148 Mass. 375, 19 N. E. 224 (1889).
41. *Kentucky Statutes of 1927*, sec. 3490.
42. *City of Pineville v. Marshall*, 222 Ky. 4, 299 S. W. 1072 (1927).
43. Application Docket No. A-4516-1921.

further testified that there were no other Jewish taxicab operators in the community and that the Hebrew religion requires all people of that religion to patronize a member of their own religion on various occasions. From the evidence the Court concluded that no rule of Jewish faith required that in conducting funerals the deceased or the mourners be conveyed in a vehicle operated as a common carrier. Further, it was pointed out that a certificate was not necessary to furnish a hearse or vehicle for mourners by the method of individual bargaining. The Superior Court of the state significantly said that the appellant seeks to engage in a business, not a religious exercise. Because religious liberty cannot be broadened to interfere with regulations enacted for the good order and general welfare of the people, the refusal of the Public Service Commission to issue the certificate was upheld.[44]

A municipal ordinance[45] protecting the public peace by banning excessive noise at night was allegedly violated by a colored pastor who conducted religious services in his church. Throughout the religious services in question, at various intervals, the preacher shouted "Amen," "Praise God," and "Glory Hallelujah" in such a tone that his voice was audible for at least two blocks. In fact, a few witnesses who entertained great respect for his vocal powers testified that his shouts could be heard a distance of six blocks. In the trial court the preacher was convicted of public disturbance. Although such manifestations of religious emotionalism might seem unnecessary, if not ridiculous, and to many might even be offensive, the appellate court maintained that such an unusual illustration of overzealous worship does not justify criminal action. The Court pointed out that its conclusion was not founded upon the premise that the occupation of the defendant entitled him to rights not held by others.

44. *Halperin v. Public Service Commission,* 81 Pa. Super. 591 (1923).
45. Ordinance of the city of Louisiana, Missouri; case does not report citation of law.

Rather it was an example of a bona fide religious practice. The decision of the trial court was reversed.[46]

For the purpose of preserving the public peace, the legislature of New Hampshire prohibited any person from addressing any derisive or annoying word to any other person lawfully in any street or other public place, or from calling such person by any offensive name.[47] During the course of distributing religious literature, a member of Jehovah's Witnesses used offensive language while addressing another person. He was thereupon indicted for violation of the statute. In defense, he claimed that the satute contravened his freedom of religion. After conviction in a state court, he subsequently appealed to the United States Supreme Court. The statute and the conviction were upheld,[48] the court observing, "We cannot conceive that cursing a public officer is the exercise of religion in any sense of the term."[49]

The Mississippi legislature in 1942 passed a law prohibiting, among other actions, any person from giving information which reasonably tended to create an attitude of stubborn refusal to salute or respect the flag of the United States.[50] Two Jehovah's Witnesses were convicted for distributing printed matter reasonably tending to create such an attitude. They appealed their conviction to the Supreme Court on the ground that their rights guaranteed by the Fourteenth Amendment were denied. The United States Supreme Court held that the Fourteenth Amendment prohibits the imposition of punishment for urging that, on religious grounds, citizens refrain from saluting the flag. The convictions were reversed.[51]

46. *City of Louisiana v. Bottoms,* 300 S. W. 316 (1927).
47. *Public Laws of New Hampshire II* (Codification of 1926) c. 378, sec. 2, p. 1470; Act of August 28, 1885.
48. *Chaplinsky v. New Hampshire,* 315 U. S. 568, 62 Sup. Ct. 766, 86 L. Ed. 1031 (1942).
49. *Ibid.,* p. 571.
50. *General Laws of Mississippi* (1942), c. 178.
51. *Taylor v. Mississippi,* 319 U. S. 583, 63 Sup. Ct. 1200, 87 L. Ed. 1600 (1943).

A Massachusetts statute prohibited minors from selling on the streets or in other public places any newspapers, magazines, periodicals, or other articles of merchandise.[52] The statute also made it unlawful for any person to furnish to a minor any article which he knew the minor intended to sell in violation of the law and for any parent or guardian to permit a minor to work in violation of the law. A guardian, a member of Jehovah's Witnesses, furnished religious literature to her minor ward, a nine-year-old niece, also a Jehovah's Witness, and permitted the minor to distribute it on the streets. After conviction for violating the law had been sustained in the highest court of the state, appeal was made to the United States Supreme Court. The appellant contended that the child's freedom of religion (specifically, her freedom to preach the gospel by public distribution of religious magazines) and the aunt's claims to parental right were infringed.

The United States Supreme Court observed that although the custody, care, and nurture of a child resided first in the parents, the family itself was not beyond regulation in the public interest, as against a claim of religious liberty. Emphasizing that the state's authority over children's activities was broader than over like actions of adults, the Supreme Court, by a five to four decision, held that the rightful boundary of the state's power had not been crossed in this case, and therefore sustained the conviction.[53]

(2) *Sunday laws.*—Although at common law an Englishman was not prohibited from ordinary labor on Sunday, all Sunday work not necessary or charitable was forbidden in England in 1678. Every craftsman, artificer, workman, laborer, or other person was prohibited from engaging in worldly labor on the Lord's Day.[54] Regulations governing the conduct of people on

52. *Massachusetts General Laws* (Ter. Ed.), c. 149, as amended by Acts and Resolves of 1939, c. 461.
53. *Prince v. Massachusetts,* 321 U. S. 158, 64 Sup. Ct. 438, 88 L. Ed. 645 (1944); see also *City of Portland v. Thornton,* 149 P. (2d) 972 (1944).
54. See *Elden v. People,* 161 Ill. 296, 43 N. E. 1108 (1896).

the first day of the week were among the first enactments of every American colony except Rhode Island. After the Revolution Sunday observance was enforced in the original thirteen states.[55]

Some form of Sunday law has been copied and perpetuated in every state of the union.[56] Laws providing for the cessation of labor on Sunday have been frequently challenged on religious grounds. The effect of such statutes has been to limit the scope of legally permissible activities on the day observed as holy by Christian sects. Analysis of court decisions indicates a practically unanimous judicial approval of such laws.[57]

In early American adjudication, Sunday laws were upheld as the exercise of a prerogative of free Christian people seeking to preserve public order and to promote the Sabbath as a day of voluntary worship.[58] The New York Supreme Court in 1861, for example, observed that at common law every malicious act tending to bring religion into contempt might be punished; the Christian Sabbath, as an institution of Christianity, might be protected from desecration by such laws as the lawmaking body might consider necessary to guarantee the privilege of undisturbed worship. The court further commented that outward respect and observance of Sunday might be deemed essential to maintain the peace and good order of society and to preserve religion from open contempt.[59]

Gradually the state police power has become the chief foundation upon which the validity of Sunday laws rests. Judge Cooley wrote: "There can no longer be any question, if there ever was, that such laws may be supported as regulations of police power."[60] That the public peace and welfare are greatly

55. Alvin W. Johnson, "Sunday Legislation" (1934) 23 *Kentucky Law Journal* 131-166.
56. See *State v. Barnes*, 22 N. D. 18, 132 N. W. 215 (1911).
57. 16 *Corpus Juris Secundum* 603; 60 *Corpus Juris* 1033, note 52.
58. 25 *Ruling Case Law* 1414.
59. *Lindenmuller v. People*, 33 Barb. (N. Y.) 548 (1861).
60. Cooley, *op. cit.*, p. 1281.

dependent upon the protection of the religions of the country and upon the prevention of acts which are subversive of them has often been judicially stated. The opinion of Mr. Justice Field of California has repeatedly been approved by courts of last resort in many states: "In its enactment, the legislature has given sanction of law to a rule of conduct, which the entire civilized world recognizes as essential to the physical and moral well-being of society. . . . The legislature possesses the undoubted right to pass laws for the preservation of health and the promotion of good morals, and if it is of opinion that periodical cessation from labor will tend to both, and thinks proper to carry its opinion to a statutory enactment on the subject, there is no power, outside of its constituents, which can sit in judgment upon its action."[61]

With respect to the selection of a particular day in each week as the day of rest for all of the people, religious views admittedly have played a controlling influence. But this consideration is not destructive of the police nature and character of the Sunday law. There has been held to be a wide difference between keeping a day holy for religious observance and prohibiting labor in one's ordinary vocation on that day. It is discretionary with the legislature to select not only the day but also the length of the interval during which rest shall be taken.[62]

Some courts have cited other factors in upholding Sunday laws. It has been suggested that respect should be rendered the Sabbath because Christianity is the predominant religion.[63] Sunday statutes protect the observance of the Christian Sabbath as a civil institution.[64] Although with the adoption of the state constitutions freedom of conscience has been guaranteed, the opinions of the great mass of citizens have been respected in order to promote the sanctity of Sunday.[65]

61. *Ex parte Newman,* 9 Cal. 502, 520 (1858); see cases listed in 25 R. C. L. 1416.
62. *Elliott v. State,* 29 Ariz. 389, 242 Pac. 340 (1926).
63. *Lindenmuller v. People,* 33 Barb. (N. Y.) 548 (1861).
64. *Rosenbaum v. State,* 131 Ark. 251, 199 S. W. 388 (1917).
65. *Pirkey v. Commonwealth,* 134 Va. 713, 114 S. E. 764 (1922).

Courts have frequently declared that constitutional prohibitions of compulsory worship are not contravened by the enactment of Sunday laws.[66] By the enactment of such laws no religious ceremony is imposed upon anyone. No one is required to attend any form of worship. One who deems another day more suitable for religious observances may select that day for his ceremony.[67] Sunday laws do not interfere with the religious scruples of any individuals, therefore, because the wills and consciences of all people are left free in this respect.

Laws prohibiting the running of railroad trains on Sunday have been generally construed to be valid, provided the statutes were passed in good faith for the welfare of the people.[68] Typical is a Georgia law[69] which forbade the running of freight trains on any railroad in the state on Sundays. The superintendent of a railroad company was convicted of causing a freight train to be run contrary to the Georgia law. The Georgia Supreme Court upheld the statute as a regulation of internal police power.[70] Upon appeal to the United States Supreme Court the constitutionality of the law was upheld.[71] Mr. Justice Harlan, speaking for the majority of the court, considered it a civil regulation prescribing a rule of conduct within the territorial jurisdiction of a state, not a religious statute. He remarked: "It is none the less a civil regulation because the day on which the running of freight trains is prohibited is kept by many under a sense of religious duty. The legislature having, as will not be disputed, power to enact laws to promote the order and to secure the comfort, happiness and health of the people, it was within its discretion to fix the day when all labor, within the limits of the State, works of necessity and charity excepted,

66. 25 *R. C. L.* 1418.

67. *Komen v. City of St. Louis*, 316 Mo. 9, 289 S. W. 838 (1926).

68. 25 *R. C. L.* 1429, 1430. So held in North Carolina, Virginia, Georgia, and West Virginia.

69. *Georgia Code of 1882*, sec. 4578.

70. *Hennington v. State*, 90 Ga. 396, 17 S. E. 1009 (1892).

71. *Hennington v. Georgia*, 163 U. S. 299, 16 Sup. Ct. 1086, 41 L. Ed. 166 (1896).

should cease."[72]   A Missouri law[73] requiring at least one train each day each way over all lines of railroads was attacked as violating the employees' right of religious freedom.   The Supreme Court of Missouri sustained the regulation with the statement that any employee may accept or refuse employment on Sunday, with the choice of staying home or attending religious worship.   No more compulsion was deemed present in his service on Sunday than on any week day.[74]

Although Sunday laws may make no exemption for persons observing another day of worship, they are nevertheless valid. A Pennsylvania court summarized the situation by explaining: "If from the choice falling on the first day of the week, the Jew and the Seventh-day Christian suffer the inconvenience of two successive days of withdrawal from worldly affairs, it is an incidental worldly disadvantage, temporarily injurious, it may be, to them, but conferring no superior religious position upon those who worship upon the first day of the week.   The law intends no preference.   The command to abstain from labour is addressed to every citizen, irrespective of his religious belief."[75]

The City of St. Louis passed an ordinance[76] requiring bakeries to close after nine o'clock in the morning on Sundays.   A defendant baker argued that he and his patrons were orthodox Jews; that the bakery products were in accordance with the requirements of that faith; that he and they observed Saturday or Jewish Sabbath as a day of worship; that the ordinance discriminated against them and violated their religious freedom. The Supreme Court of Missouri, however, declared that a law which permits a person believing in a different observance to worship on his day cannot be said to interfere with freedom of

72. *Ibid.*, p. 304.
73. *Missouri Laws of 1907*, p. 180.
74. *State v. Chicago, B. & O. Railroad Co.*, 246 Mo. 512, 143 S. W. 785 (1912).
75. *Specht v. Commonwealth*, 8 Pa. 312, 313 (1848).
76. *Ordinances of the City of St. Louis*, No. 31353.

religious belief. The St. Louis ordinance was judged to contain nothing to sustain the assumption that it was directed against any cult or creed.[77]

The prohibition of the playing of baseball on Sunday is a legal exercise of the police power. Judicial consideration of the game itself has held that it is attendant with many loud outbursts which have become objectionable to those who look upon Sunday as a day of peace and quiet. While there are many enjoyments consistent with the proper observance of the day, court opinion holds that the tendency to commercialize the day should be resisted. The use of the police power to preserve the public peace is suggested by the judicial remark that although baseball in itself is harmless, injunctions may be issued to restrain the playing on Sunday. The ground for these court orders is the fact that noises disturb the quiet of the persons in the neighborhood.[78] A Baltimore, Maryland,[79] ordinance banning ballplaying in a secluded part of a park where no residents could be disturbed and where no admission was charged was upheld.[80] The allegation of a breach of religious freedom was answered as follows: "It is hard to conceive how the ordinance can be said to infringe any guaranty of religious liberty. We have never heard of a religious denomination which declared as an article of faith that it was the duty of its members to play baseball on Sunday."[81] Athletic games on Sunday are not unlawful unless specifically declared so by legislative enactment.[82]

On the other hand, the application of a Sunday law to a situation which bears no reasonable relation to the public morals, peace, or welfare is illegal. In one instance, a member of a Bible association rented a theater and showed a film entitled

77. *Komen v. City of St. Louis*, 316 Mo. 9, 289 S. W. 838 (1926).
78. *Hiller v. State*, 124 Md. 385, 92 Atl. 842 (1914).
79. *Maryland Laws of 1898*, c. 123, sec. 906.
80. *Hiller v. State*, 124 Md. 385, 92 Atl. 842 (1914).
81. *Ibid.*, p. 390.
82. 25 *R. C. L.* 1427. So held in Missouri, Kansas, New Mexico, Texas, Nebraska, Indiana.

"Photo Drama of Creation" on a Sunday. Expenses incurred in showing the movie were obtained through a voluntary contribution from those present. The purpose of the movie was to instruct the audience. The association which exclusively controlled the theater for the day permitted no applause. Nevertheless, the member who rented the building was arrested for violation of a law[83] banning the exhibition of movies on Sunday. The judiciary of the state concluded from the evidence that the law should not be construed to apply in this case. The exercises were not conducted merely in the guise of religion as a pretense for covering acts criminal in nature, the court stated. To declare the use of the movie machine for religious purposes illegal is an improper use of the police power.[84]

A Sunday law may conflict with constitutional provisions respecting equal protection of the laws. If the statute treats all general business alike, valid objections will not be entertained. An ordinance, however, prohibiting the opening on Sundays of stores in certain lines of business and allowing others to open has been held not a general Sunday closing ordinance, with reasonable exceptions for works of necessity and charity. A law[85] of a town in Arizona, for example, was deemed to give special privileges to certain businesses and to deny them to others without legal excuse.[86] A discriminatory classification by the legislature will cause the judiciary to nullify a Sunday regulation.[87]

If the judiciary believes that the primary purpose of a Sunday law is to compel religious observance, the statute will be nullified. In other words, while the legislature may impose civil obligations, it may not prescribe obligations of a strictly religious nature.[88] A situation in point occurred in Maryland.

83. *Revised Code of Idaho*, sec. 6825, as amended by *Session Laws of 1911*, p. 342.
84. *State v. Morris*, 28 Idaho 599, 155 Pac. 296 (1916).
85. *Ordinances of the Town of Somerton* (Arizona), No. 37.
86. *Elliott v. State*, 29 Ariz. 389, 242 Pac. 340 (1926).
87. 25 R. C. L. 1420.
88. See *State v. Baltimore & Ohio Railroad Co.*, 15 W. Va. 362 (1879).

A Sunday law[89] sought to enforce the observance of that day as a religious obligation. An individual who had been arrested on a charge of working on Sunday contrary to the law attacked its constitutionality on the ground that it violated guarantees of religious freedom. The court explained the general rule: Laws prohibiting labor on Sunday are usually upheld on the theory that they prescribe a rule of civil duty for all persons on Sunday. That the first day of the week is the one invariably selected as a day of rest in legislation of this character has no legal significance. The court noted that it is not the policy of the law to enforce compliance because of Sunday observance by the Christian world. Rather, the court simply enforces a law requiring cessation from labor on one day in seven. The court thought that the Maryland law in question sought to enforce observance of the Sabbath as a religious obligation. The law was declared invalid.[90] Usually, however, laws relating to Sunday observance have been uniformly recognized as being within the right of the legislature to enact for the purpose of promoting public order and morals and to secure the comfort, happiness, and health of the people.[91] While the overwhelming majority of the people are adherents of the Christian faith, the rules apply to the whole group.

(3) *Blasphemy.*—Blasphemy is the malicious reviling of God or religion.[92] Under the common law, blasphemy against the Deity in general, or a malicious and wanton attack against Christianity in particular for the purpose of exposing its doctrines to contempt, was punishable as a secular offense. Although early cases revealed that a written publication of the blasphemous words increased the seriousness of the offense, it was immaterial whether the offense was oral or written.[93] Christianity is not considered a part of the law of the land; nevertheless, the

89. Act of Maryland of 1723, c. 16.
90. *District of Columbia v. Robinson*, 30 App. D. C. 283 (1908).
91. *Ex parte Ferguson*, 70 P. (2d) 1094 (1937).
92. 11 *C. J. S.* 357.
93. See *State v. Chandler*, 2 Harr. (Del.) 553 (1838).

fact that it has been the popular religion of the country has rendered derogation of it indictable as directly tending to disturb the public peace.[94] Blasphemy, a crime at common law, was not abrogated by state constitutions.[95]

The significance of laws against blasphemy was emphasized in the Mockus case,[96] the leading blasphemy case in recent years. The Maine Supreme Court stated that "from the dawn of civilization, the religion of a country is a most important factor in determining its form of government, and that stability of government in no small measure depends upon the reverence and respect which a nation maintains toward its prevalent religion."[97] Blasphemy is a temporal offense. Violation of religious precepts will not be punished as such. Punishment follows because such attacks tend to destroy the peace of society. Religions other than Christianity may be attacked without liability to prosecution.[98]

Although remarks intended to disparage the Supreme Being are illegal, free inquiry into religion, including controversial issues, has been held permissible.[99] Anti-blasphemy statutes do not prohibit free religious discussion for any honest purpose or prevent the simple disavowal of belief in the existence of God. Differentiation between the lawful and unlawful discussion of religious subjects is based on the motive with which the discourse is carried on and the intent with which the words are spoken. If one speaks maliciously with the purpose of ridiculing the Divinity, punishment legally follows. Intent is the essential element.

Depending upon the precise statute involved, the offense of blasphemy may be committed either by using profane language

94. *Updegraph v. Commonwealth*, 11 Serg. & R. (Pa.) 394 (1832).
95. See *People v. Ruggles*, 8 Johns. (N. Y.) 290 (1811); also Leon Whipple, *The Story of Civil Liberty in the United States*, pp. 38-41.
96. *State v. Mockus*, 120 Me. 84, 113 Atl. 39 (1921).
97. *Ibid.*, p. 93.
98. 11 C. J. S. 358, note 17; B. H. Hartogensis, "Denial of Equal Rights to Religious Minorities and Non-Believers" (1930) 39 *Yale Law Journal* 676-677.
99. *Commonwealth v. Kneeland*, 20 Pick. (Mass.) 206 (1838).

against God, or by reproaching Him, His creation, His rule, His final judgment, the Holy Ghost, the Holy Scriptures, or by ridiculing any of the above.[100] Declaring that the Holy Scriptures are a mere fable and that they contain a great many lies,[101] and cursing and denying a belief in God and His creation with the intent to impair the reverence in which He is held,[102] have been punished. A transgressor may not shield himself behind vestments when he is accused of having used improper language.[103] Incidentally, laws making it a crime to blaspheme do not deny freedom of speech.[104]

(4) *Fraud.*—Statutes seeking to prevent fraud have been upheld in spite of allegations that they deny religious liberty or extend religious preferences.[105] Thus, an Indiana law[106] prohibited the wearing by non-members of the badge of a secret society. A non-member of an incorporated secret society was charged with unlawfully wearing its badge and emblem. The statute was attacked on the ground that it gave undue regard to a religious sect. The contention was denied by the judicial declaration that, although no law could extend preferences to any religious society or mode of worship, the constitutional restriction on legislative preference for any creed had no reference to benevolent or fraternal organizations. Since the court believed that the society in question was of the latter type, a religious preference was denied. The court went on to uphold the validity of the Indiana regulation on the theory that it was a police regulation directed against false impersonation.[107]

Kosher laws punish the selling or exposing for sale with

100. *State v. Mockus,* 120 Me. 84, 113 Atl. 39 (1921); *Zeisweiss v. James,* 63 Pa. 465 (1870).
101. *Updegraph v. Commonwealth,* 11 Serg. & R. (Pa.) 394 (1832).
102. *Commonwealth v. Kneeland,* 20 Pick. (Mass.) 206 (1838).
103. *Delk v. Commissioner,* 166 Ky. 39, 178 S. W. 1129 (1915).
104. *State v. Mockus,* 120 Me. 84, 113 Atl. 39 (1921); *Zeisweiss v. James,* 63 Pa. 465 (1870); see T. A. Schroeder, *Constitutional Free Speech.*
105. 16 C. J. S. 555, 556.
106. *Indiana Acts of 1891,* p. 340, c. 132.
107. *Hammer v. State,* 173 Ind. 199, 89 N. E. 850 (1909).

intent to defraud any meat falsely represented as having been prepared under orthodox Hebrew requirements. Such laws protect, rather than violate, constitutional guarantees of religious freedom. It has been held that a statute of this type is aimed at a form of fraud, the victim of which is probably a person of a specific religious sect. Such protection as the law offers has been deemed to be in distinct accord with constitutional provisions which forbid the interference with the free exercise and enjoyment of religious worship. Defense of violations of kosher laws based on religious scruples, consequently, have been fruitless.[108]

Laws prohibiting the practice of telling fortunes and predicting the future, for a remuneration, cannot be challenged on the theory that they infringe religious guarantees. Justifying violations of the regulations designed to prevent fraud by appeals to religious beliefs does not find favor with the courts. Thus, the president of a county spiritualist society was convicted of being a disorderly person[109] because she prophesied the future for remuneration. She insisted she had simply given advice to the complaining witness. She contended that the power which mediums of the society possessed was not exercised for personal gain but was compensated only by the societies. The court remarked that witches have been in ill repute in all jurisdictions since 2,000 B.C. but, bad as they were, they were preferable to fortunetellers. The claim that the defendant simply gave advice was insufficiently supported to prevent a conviction.[110] The court held: "This modern attempt to excuse violations of lawful salutary police regulations, enacted for the protection of the community by appeals to constitutional rights and religious beliefs, does not find favor with the courts."[111]

A law of the State of Washington[112] defined as a vagrant

108. See *People v. Goldberger*, 163 N. Y. S. 663 (1916).
109. *New York Code of Criminal Procedure*, sec. 899, subd. 3.
110. *People v. Ashley*, 172 N. Y. S. 282, 184 App. Div. 520 (1918).
111. *Ibid.*, p. 285.
112. *Washington Rem. & Bal. Code* sec. 2688.

one who practiced fortunetelling. Although a defendant in an action was an ordained minister of the National Astrological Society, and the principles of religion as laid down by that society included horoscope reading, practicing for cash constituted a violation of the law.[113] The defendant vainly sought to show that his right to pursue a calling had been impaired because the casting of horoscopes, the drafting of a map of the heavens at the time of one's birth, and the interpretation of horoscopes by tracing the movements of the planets to ascertain their relative positions at a given date and the aspects resulting therefrom constituted a legal vocation. The point emphasized by the court was that the accused's guilt or innocence was not affected by his status. Harmful practices arising from any source were punishable.

A law[114] of St. Louis, Missouri, prohibited the pursuit or practice of the art of telling and revealing information of a secret or hidden nature pertaining to the past or future of another's life. Under the law, a charge was made that a person distributed cards describing himself as possessing supernatural powers. Conviction was sustained on evidence that he was engaged in telling fortunes; no abridgement of freedom of religion resulted from a conviction. The court emphasized that freedom of religion is not violated by banning practices inconsistent with peace and order.[115]

An interesting case interpreting the role of mediums was decided in Oklahoma in 1922. A law of 1915[116] made it unlawful to pretend to tell fortunes for money by the use of any subtle craft or means, either by palmistry or otherwise. Nevertheless, for a fee of one dollar, a spiritualistic reading was made by a medium allegedly in a state of trance, which purported to convey information to a person from the spirit of Minnehaha,

113. *State v. Neitzell,* 69 Wash. 567, 125 Pac. 939 (1912).
114. *Rev. Code of St. Louis* (1914), sec. 625, p. 975.
115. *City of St. Louis v. Hellscher,* 295 Mo. 293, 242 S. W. 652 (1922).
116. *Oklahoma Session Laws of 1915,* sec. 1, chap. 59

the legendary Indian girl of Longfellow's *Hiawatha.* The feminine recipient of the message was told that she was going to marry a wealthy man, and she was informed of other allegedly future events. The feminine customer was a policewoman who caused the arrest of the medium for violation of the law. Upon trial the defendant contended that as a member of the National Spiritualist Association she was licensed to give spiritual advice and that the tenets of her religion involved the practice of communicating with departed spirits. The court at the outset remarked that, whether or not religious in nature, beliefs in spiritualism constituted a system of speculative philosophy characterized by superstitious credulity and tinged with hypocrisy. Assuming that such beliefs formed a religion, the court went on to say that religious liberty does not comprehend the right to carry out every scheme a person desires to claim as a part of his religion. The court jocularly commented that it would be well worth a dollar of any girl's money to receive the benefit of the advice of the romantic spirit of Minnehaha (if one could be sure of the latter's identity), but seriously ruled that, regardless of the merits of religions, the duty of the judiciary was to decide the law as it related to the facts of the situation. The gist of the judicial determination was the statement that fanatic philosophers and religious zealots, like other people, must conform to wholesome police regulations.[117] In a separate concurring opinion another judge of the same court upheld the conviction because the medium who allegedly carried on communication with the spirit world had never filed her rates with the State Corporation Commission!

But the practice of spiritualism in a church whose charter permitted the teaching of spiritualism was held not to violate an anti-fortunetelling law of New Jersey.[118] The evidence in the case revealed that a medium in a spiritualist church acted as a message bearer and predicted the future to those present.

117. *McMasters v. State,* 21 Okla. Crim. 318 (1922).
118. *New Jersey Laws of 1898,* Act of June 14th.

A collection, notice of which had been posted, was taken, amounting to twenty-five cents per person in attendance. The medium was paid for her services. A judge held that the offense alleged was in fact participation in religious services. The medium was consequently freed.[119]

(5) *Distribution of literature; solicitation.*—Municipal ordinances requiring prior consent from a local administrative officer for those who would distribute literature, books and other articles, whether sold or given free, have been attacked as unconstitutional when applied to individuals attempting to disseminate religious literature. Since local laws of this nature are usually passed for the purpose of eliminating fraud, the authority to enact them emanates from the police power.[120]

Judicial opinion had held that the general regulation of solicitation could not be attacked on constitutional grounds if the regulation did not include any religious test and did not unreasonably obstruct the collection of money. This rule has been upheld even if the collection was for religious purposes.[121] The Supreme Court said that such regulation in itself would not be a forbidden check on the free exercise of religion.[122] Hence, persons who offered for sale books containing interpretations of the scriptures were guilty of violating such ordinances requiring a license, even though the purpose was not to make money but to spread religious teachings. The Arkansas Supreme Court once said: "It is true, as argued, that appellants were prompted to sell and deliver the books on account of religious convictions or from religious motives, but the convictions or motives inspiring their acts are not controlling in determining them peddlers or hawkers. The purpose of the ordinance was to require all parties engaged in the business of peddling or

119. *State v. Delaney*, 122 Atl. 890 (1923).
120. 16 *C. J. S.* 602.
121. See *Maplewood v. Albright*, 176 Atl. 194 (1934); *State v. Hundley*, 195 N. C. 377, 142 S. E. 330 (1928).
122. *Cantwell v. Connecticut*, 310 U. S. 296, 60 Sup. Ct. 900, 84 L. Ed. 836 (1940).

hawking to pay a license."[123] In Massachusetts, in 1930, the fact that the religious books offered for sale without a license, contrary to law,[124] contained the religious ideas of the defendant was immaterial as a defense to a prosecution.[125]

A local law[126] banning soliciting without a permit from the superintendent of city police was upheld as a police measure. The court added that a solicitor was free to worship God according to his own conscience, but that other persons were protected from having someone else thrust his religious tenets upon them against their will.[127]

A local ordinance[128] of Griffin, Georgia, required the written permission of the city manager before there might be a legal distribution of circulars, handbills, advertising, or literature of any kind, whether delivered free or offered for sale. One Spencer Coleman was charged with violation of the ordinance by giving out religious literature and soliciting orders without a permit. However, he stated that he was sent by Jehovah to do this work. Specifically, he testified that "under the authority of Jehovah I am a duly ordained and authorized minister of the gospel, and it is incumbent upon me, in obedience to God's law, to preach the gospel. I worship Jehovah God by obeying His commandments. God's work, the Bible, commands all who worship Him in spirit and in truth to go from place to place and tell others about Him and His Kingdom. At the time I was arrested I was going from house to house in obedience to His word, and according to the dictates of my own conscience. I did not ask for a permit from the police department because I am sent by Jehovah to do His work."[129] The Court of

123. *Cook v. Harrison,* 180 Ark. 546, 548, 21 S. W. (2d) 966, 967 (1929).
124. *General Laws of Massachusetts,* c. 101, sec. 14.
125. *Commonwealth v. Anderson,* 272 Mass. 100, 172 N. E. 114 (1930).
126. *Pittsburgh Ordinances Series of 1921,* Ordinance Book, XXXII, 128.
127. *City of Pittsburgh v. Ruffner,* 134 Pa. Super. 192, 4 A. (2d) 224 (1939).
128. *Local Ordinances* (Griffin, Georgia), sec. 1.
129. *Coleman v. City of Griffin,* 55 Ga. App. 123, 125, 189 S. E. 427, 428 (1936).

Appeals of Georgia ruled that since the ordinance was directed against the acts and not the beliefs of a citizen, a violation could not be defended by the assertion that it interfered with religious thought. There being no deprival of his right to worship, the prohibition as stated in the ordinance was upheld.[130] An appeal from the decision of the highest court in the state to the United States Supreme Court was dismissed for want of a substantial federal question.[131]

Contrary to the same ordinance, one Alma Lovell distributed a pamphlet and magazine in the nature of a religious tract describing the gospel of the "Kingdom of Jehovah." She did not seek a permit because she regarded herself sent by Jehovah, and because such an application would have been, in her belief, an act of disobedience to the Lord. Upon trial, she contended that the ordinance prohibited the free exercise of her religion by denying the right to distribute religious literature. Conviction in a recorder's court led to a sentence of fifty days' imprisonment in default of a fifty-dollar fine. The Superior Court of the county refused to review the case; the Court of Appeals of the state approved the decision of the Superior Court; and the state's Supreme Court denied an application for certiorari.[132] In 1938, on appeal, the United States Supreme Court believed a federal question had been properly presented and assumed jurisdiction. The Court at the same time noted that in the previous (Coleman) case the federal question had not been properly presented. Grounding its judgment upon the fundamental rights of freedom of speech and press, the Court explained that the ordinance was not limited to literature which was obscene or offensive to public morals or provocative of unlawful conduct. The comprehensiveness of the ordinance covered every sort of circulation. Because the ordinance prohibited the distribution of

130. *Ibid.*
131. *Coleman v. City of Griffin,* 302 U. S. 636, 58 Sup. Ct. 23, 82 L. Ed. 495 (1937).
132. *Lovell v. City of Griffin,* 55 Ga. App. 609, 191 S. E. 152 (1939).

literature of any kind at any time at any place and in any manner without a permit from the city manager, it was held invalid on its face. Legislation of this type would restore the system of license and censorship in its worst forms, said Mr. Chief Justice Hughes. The judgment of the recorder's court was, in effect, reversed.[133]

In 1939, the United States Supreme Court accepted jurisdiction in a similar case. An ordinance[134] of the Town of Irvington, New Jersey, required a written permit from the chief of police before any distribution of material from house to house could be legally carried out. Persons who delivered articles in the regular course of business to the premises of individuals ordering or entitled to same were exempt. A member of the Watch Tower Bible and Tract Society and one who as such was certified by the Society to be one of Jehovah's Witnesses called in this capacity at various houses in the town and displayed an identification card of the Society. The card stated that the bearer was an ordained minister sent by the Society organized to preach the gospel of God's kingdom. The member then left, or offered to leave, booklets with the occupants of the house. Conviction of a violation of the ordinance was had in a recorder's court and affirmed in the Supreme Court of New Jersey. Judicial approval of the ordinance prohibiting solicitation rested upon the ground that it was aimed at protecting occupants from annoyance and at preventing unknown strangers from visiting houses by day and by night.[135] The State Court of Errors and Appeals upheld the Supreme Court and said that "a municipality may protect its citizens against fraudulent solicitation and, when it enacts an ordinance to do so, all persons are required to abide

133. *Lovell v. City of Griffin*, 303 U. S. 444, 58 Sup. Ct. 666, 82 L. Ed. 949 (1938); J. R. S., "Constitutional Law—Freedom of Press—Distribution of Handbills" (1940) 25 *Washington University Law Quarterly* 611-614.

134. Citation of law not given in case either in state or federal courts.

135. *Town of Irvington v. Schneider*, 120 N. J. Law 460, 200 Atl. 799 (1938).

thereby. The ordinance in question was evidently designed for that purpose."[136]

The United States Supreme Court, however, held that the municipal regulation was not merely the common type of municipal regulation necessitating some form of registration of hawkers, nor was it a general ordinance to prohibit trespassing. Instead, it banned "unlicensed communication of any views or the advocacy of any cause from door to door" and permitted "canvassing only subject to the power of a police officer to determine, as a censor, what literature 'might' be distributed from house to house and who 'might' distribute it."[137] In effect, one's liberty to communicate with town residents at their homes depended upon the exercise of administrative discretion. Conceding that fraudulent appeals might be made under the guise of charity, Mr. Justice Roberts, speaking for the Court, concluded that a municipality could not, on this account, require prior administrative approval for those who wished to disseminate their ideas. Although it was pointed out that commercial soliciting might be subjected to some degree of regulation in the public interest, the ordinance in question was void.

A statute[138] of Connecticut restricted soliciting for alleged religious, charitable, or philanthropic causes unless the project was approved by the secretary of the public welfare council. The secretary, upon determining that the cause was a bona fide one, was given authority to issue a certificate of approval. Three men, members of Jehovah's Witnesses, went singly from house to house. Each was equipped with a bag containing books, pamphlets on religious subjects, a portable phonograph and a set of records, each of which, when played on the phonograph, introduced and described one of the books. Upon being per-

136. *Town of Irvington v. Schneider*, 121 N. J. Law 542, 543, 3 A. (2d) 609, 610 (1939).

137. *Schneider v. State*, 308 U. S. 147, 163, 60 Sup. Ct. 146, 152, 84 L. Ed. 155, 166 (1939).

138. *General Statutes of Massachusetts*, sec. 6294, as amended by sec. 860 d of the 1937 supplement.

mitted by the person who responded to his call to play the record, each member asked the person to buy the book described. If permission to play the record was refused, the solicitor asked for a contribution toward the publication of the pamphlets. If a contribution was obtained, a pamphlet would be given upon the promise that it would be read. One record included an attack upon a particular religion and was played in a neighborhood where approximately ninety per cent of the residents were members of the attacked religion. Other evidence showed that one of the defendants received permission from two men to play this record. Tried for violation of the statute, the three solicitors were held to have solicited illegally within the purview of the law. The State Supreme Court declared the legislation constitutional as an effort by the state to protect the public against fraud and imposition in the obtaining of funds for alleged religious, charitable or philanthropic purposes. Conviction also was upheld on another count charging commission of the common law offense of inciting a breach of the peace.[139]

The United States Supreme Court, however, found that the statute as applied deprived the defendants of their liberty without due process of law. Granting that a state may by general and non-discriminatory legislation regulate the times, places, and manner of soliciting and safeguard the peace and order of the community by other means, the Court noted that the law required an application to the secretary of the public welfare council, who was entrusted with authority to determine whether the cause was religious, and that the issuance of the certificate depended upon his affirmative action. Such censorship, the Court believed, was a denial of religious liberty. Mr. Justice Roberts further held that the conduct of the defendant in playing the record for the men after permission had been granted did not constitute a breach of the peace. Although an individual might resort to exaggeration and vilification to persuade others, our national history was interpreted as regarding freedom of religion

139. *State v. Cantwell*, 126 Conn. 1, 8 A. (2d) 533 (1939).

and speech as essential to enlightened public opinion. Thus there was no menace such as would render a person liable for breach of the peace.[140]

The City of Fredericksburg, Virginia, attempted to require Jehovah's Witnesses to pay a license fee for selling their pamphlets or offering them for sale, but the State Supreme Court held that the ordinance as applied was invalid. The court believed that the requirement of payment of the tax would have the effect of suppressing two religious publications of the sect.[141]

The constitutionality of ordinances of three municipalities located in Alabama, Arkansas, and Arizona imposing license taxes upon the sale of printed matter was brought before the United States Supreme Court in 1942. Under the terms of an ordinance of the City of Opelika, Alabama, a license fee of $10 per annum was levied on book agents. A member of Jehovah's Witnesses sold books without a license and was subsequently convicted of a violation of the ordinance in disregard of his claim of interference with religious freedom. The Supreme Court of Alabama sustained his conviction. Similar decisions were made by the highest courts of Arkansas and Arizona. Appeal from each decision was taken to the United States Supreme Court.

The United States Supreme Court contrasted the regulations involved in the Lovell case,[142] the Schneider case,[143] and the Cantwell case[144] with the ordinances involved here by stating that differences between censorship and complete prohibition either of subject matter or individuals participating on the one hand versus regulation of the conduct of individuals in the time,

140. *Cantwell v. Connecticut*, 310 U. S. 296, 60 Sup. Ct. 900, 84 L. Ed. 836 (1940); for the constitutionality of an ordinance regulating soliciting for charitable purposes but exempting soliciting for religious purposes, see *Gospel Army v. City of Los Angeles*, 27 Cal. (2d) 232, 163 P. (2d) 704 (1945) and Note, "Freedom of Religion—Regulation of Solicitation of Charitable Funds by Religious Organization" (1946) 15 *Fordham Law Review* 113-117.

141. *McConkey v. City of Fredericksburg*, 179 Va. 556, 19 S. E. (2d) 682 (1942).

142. P. 66, *supra*.   143. P. 67, *supra*.   144. P. 68, *supra*.

manner, and place of their activities on the other, are decisive. The Court explained that when proponents of religious theories used the ordinary commercial methods of sale of articles to raise propaganda funds, it was a natural and proper exercise of the power of the state to charge reasonable fees for the privilege of canvassing. Because the Supreme Court viewed the sales of books as partaking more of the nature of commercial than religious transactions, the Court in June, 1942, held, in a five-to-four decision, that the ordinances were valid even though the licensing authority could revoke them without notice. Thus the principle was enunciated that a city ordinance which required that licenses be procured and reasonable taxes paid for the conduct of various businesses (including the selling of books and pamphlets on streets or from house to house) and which was general in its incidence did not infringe the free exercise of religion when applied to a member of a religious organization who was engaged in selling the printed propaganda of his sect.[145]

Subsequently, an ordinance of the City of Jeannette, Pennsylvania, provided that all persons canvassing, soliciting orders for wares or merchandise of any kind, or delivering such articles, must procure a license to transact such business at a fee depending upon the length of time for which the license was sought. Without obtaining a license, eight Jehovah's Witnesses solicited people to purchase and on occasion gave away free certain religious books and pamphlets. In connection with these activities the Witnesses played a phonograph record expounding certain of their views on religion. The eight were convicted and fined for violation of the ordinance. Appeal was ultimately made to the United States Supreme Court.

Prior to its determination of the constitutionality of the Jeannette ordinance, the Supreme Court, in March, 1943, had ordered a reargument of the Jones case decided in 1942. On

---

145. *Jones v. Opelika*, 316 U. S. 584, 62 Sup. Ct. 1231, 86 L. Ed. 1691 (1942); see Victor W. Rotnem and F. G. Folsom, "Recent Restrictions upon Religious Liberty" (1942) 36 *American Political Science Review* 1053-68.

the same day that the Court announced its decision concerning the Jeannette ordinance, the Court also reversed its previous judgment in the case of *Jones v. Opelika*.[146]

The United States Supreme Court narrowed the problem of the Jeannette case into a single issue, namely, the constitutionality of an ordinance which, as construed, required religious colporteurs to pay a license tax as a condition to the pursuit of their activities. The hand distribution of religious tracts was described by the court to be an age-old form of missionary evangelism, occupying the same high estate under the First Amendment as did worship in churches and preaching in pulpits, and having the same claim to constitutional protection as the more orthodox and conventional exercises of religion. Pointing out that the alleged justification for the ordinance was that the religious literature was distributed with a solicitation of funds, under circumstances similar to those in *Jones v. Opelika*, the Supreme Court reasoned that the mere fact that religious literature was sold by itinerant preachers rather than donated did not transform evangelism into a commercial enterprise. An itinerent evangelist was judged not to become a mere book agent by selling religious tracts to help defray his expenses or to sustain him. Although the problem of drawing the line between purely commercial and religious activity may be difficult, it could not be plainly said, the Court held, that the eight Witnesses were engaged in a commercial rather than a religious venture. In a five-to-four decision, the Supreme Court held that the tax imposed by the ordinance was a flat license tax, the payment of which was a condition of the exercise of constitutional privileges, and was therefore void.[147]

Freed from the controlling precedent of the Jones case,

146. *Jones v. Opelika*, 319 U. S. 103, 63 Sup. Ct. 890, 87 L. Ed. 1290 (1943).

147. *Murdock v. State*, 319 U. S. 105, 63 Sup. Ct. 870, 87 L. Ed. 1292 (1943); Norman L. Stamps, "Constitutional Law—Freedom of Speech and Religion—City License as a Prerequisite to Distribution of Religious Literature" (1943) 11 *University of Kansas City Law Review* 230-233.

vacated that day, Mr. Justice Douglas, in the majority opinion, stated that "we can restore to their high, constitutional position the liberties of itinerant evangelists who disseminate their religious beliefs and the tenets of their faith through distribution of literature."[148]

In 1944, the question of the constitutionality of a similar ordinance was again before the Supreme Court. A town ordinance in South Carolina provided that a license on a business, occupation, or profession must be obtained by persons carrying on such activity and fixed the fee for agents selling books at $1 per day or $15 per year. A Jehovah's Witness, who was also an ordained minister of the sect, went from house to house, without a license, distributing certain books. He obtained his living from the money he thus received and had no other source of income. He refused to obtain a license on the ground that the ordinance restricted his freedom of worship, in violation of the First Amendment. Nevertheless, he was found guilty in the Mayor's Court, whose judgment was subsequently affirmed by a county court and the State Supreme Court.

On an appeal to the United States Supreme Court, Mr. Justice Douglas, speaking for the majority of the court, declared that the ordinance was in all respects the same as the ones involved in the Opelika and Murdock cases. The Supreme Court accepted as bona fide the appellant's assertion that he was preaching the gospel by going from house to house presenting the gospel of the kingdom in printed form. In response to the question whether a flat license tax as applied to one who earns his livelihood as an evangelist or preacher in his home town is constitutional, the court replied in the negative, with the comment that the protection of the First Amendment is not re-

148. *Ibid.*, p. 117; see also *Busey v. District of Columbia*, 138 F. (2d) 592 (D. C., 1943); 78 App. D. C. 189, conforming to mandate of 319 U. S. 579, 63 Sup. Ct. 1277, 87 L. Ed. 1598 (1943); certiorari granted in 319 U. S. 735, 63 Sup. Ct. 1154, 87 L. Ed. 1695 (1943).

stricted to orthodox religious practices. The conviction was reversed.[149]

By the decisions in the Murdock case and in the rehearing of the Opelika case, the distribution of religious literature in return for money, when done as a method of spreading the distributor's religious belief, is an exercise of religion within the First Amendment and therefore immune from interference by the requirement of a license. By the decision in the Follett case, there is no difference between an itinerant distributor and a person who remains in one general neighborhood or between one who is active in distribution part time and another who is active all of his time.

An unusual limitation was placed on the distribution of religious literature by a municipality in Ohio. An ordinance made it unlawful for any person distributing handbills, circulars, or other advertisements to ring a door bell, sound a door knocker, or otherwise summon the inmate of any residence to receive such material. A Jehovah's Witness went to the homes of strangers, knocked on doors, and rang doorbells in order to distribute leaflets advertising a religious meeting. She was convicted in a mayor's court for violation of the ordinance in spite of her defense that the ordinance violated her rights of freedom of press and of religion. After her conviction was upheld by the Supreme Court of Ohio, she appealed to the United States Supreme Court. The United States Supreme Court stated that "freedom to distribute information to every citizen wherever he desires to receive it is so clearly vital to the preservation of a free society that, putting aside reasonable police and health regulations of time and manner of distribution, it must be fully preserved." The prohibition contained in the ordinance was judged by the court to serve no purpose except that for-

149. *Follett v. Town of McCormick,* 321 U. S. 573, 64 Sup. Ct. 717, 88 L. Ed. 938 (1944); Louis B. Boudin, "Freedom of Thought and Religious Liberty Under the Constitution" (1944) 4 *Lawyers Guild Review* 9-24.

bidden by the Constitution, namely, the restriction of the dissemination of ideas. The ordinance was held invalid.[150]

The legal protection accorded a person in connection with his distribution of religious literature has recently been broadened to include the actions of an individual distributing such literature in a company-owned town and in a federally-owned and operated village. An Alabama law[150a] making it a crime to remain on another's premises after being warned not to do so was held to abridge freedom of the press and of religion when applied to a member of Jehovah's Witnesses distributing religious literature on a company-owned sidewalk in a business block in a suburb owned by a ship-building corporation. In holding the Alabama statute void, the United States Supreme Court stated that persons living in company-owned towns are free citizens of their state and country, just as residents of other towns.[150b] A Texas law[150c] making it an offense for a peddler wilfully to refuse to leave premises after notice by the owner to do so was deemed unconstitutional as applied to a minister of Jehovah's Witnesses who refused a village manager's request to discontinue his religious activity and leave a federally-owned and operated village constructed for defense workers. The United States Supreme Court reasoned that the only difference between this case and the Alabama case was that in this case the Federal Government owned and operated the village. Neither Congress nor federal agencies acting pursuant to Con-

150. *Martin v. City of Struthers*, 319 U. S. 141, 63 Sup. Ct. 862, 87 L. Ed. 1313 (1943).

150a. *Code of Alabama*, 1940, Tit. 14, sec. 426.

150b. *Marsh v. Alabama*, 326 U. S. 501, 66 Sup. Ct. 276, 90 L. Ed. 265 (1946); W. E. Aulgur, "Right of Jehovah's Witnesses to Distribute Religious Literature upon Street of Company Town" (1947) 12 *Missouri Law Review* 61-65; G. D. Ernest, "Right of Jehovah's Witnesses to Distribute and Sell Their Literature Upon the Streets of an Unincorporated Privately-Owned Community" (1946) 6 *Louisiana Law Review* 707-711; J. O. Jarrard, "Freedom of Speech, Press and Religion" (1946) 14 *University of Kansas City Law Review* 112-116; A. R. Solie, "Freedom of Speech and Religion Versus Property Rights—Jehovah's Witnesses in Company Town" [1947] *Wisconsin Law Review* 121-125.

150c. *Penal Code of Texas*, 1925, Art. 479, chap. 3.

gressional authority may abridge the freedom of press and religion safeguarded by the First Amendment, the Court concluded.[150d]

(6) *Health.*—Various laws have been passed by state legislatures to promote the public health. In this area of activity conflicts with allegedly religious practices have arisen. Laws restricting the use of intoxicating liquors have often been framed on the theory that they were an exercise of the police power to protect the public health. Since these laws frequently permit religious sects to obtain sacramental wine, they have been attacked as violative of the guarantees of religious liberty, but to no avail. It has been held that state prohibition acts do not give undue preference to religious sects by permitting them to obtain sacramental wine.

For illustration, an Illinois prohibition law[151] forbade the transportation of intoxicating liquor over a public highway in the state. Legitimate uses of intoxicating liquor were expressly exempted from the application of the act; the manufacture, transportation, and sale of intoxicating liquor for sacramental purposes were free to all persons and all religious denominations to the same extent as before the passage of the act. One Harvey Marquis, a truck driver, was arrested on a charge of violating the statute after he was found asleep in the cab of a truck loaded with bottled beer. On trial, defense counsel argued that the statute violated the Illinois constitutional provision[152] prohibiting the giving of any preference to any religious denomination or mode of worship because its prohibition did not extend to intoxicating liquors for sacramental purposes. It was further said that since some religious organizations use wine for such purposes and others do not, the act gave a preference to those using wine and granted a special privilege to them. The defend-

150d. *Tucker v. Texas,* 326 U. S. 517, 66 Sup. Ct. 274, 90 L. Ed. 274 (1946).
151. *Illinois Laws of 1919,* p. 930.
152. *Illinois Constitution,* Art.II, sec. 3.

ant was convicted, however, and the Illinois Supreme Court sustained the conviction. The court held that the right to use intoxicating liquors for religious purposes existed for all religious groups. Specifically, the court stated: "It is not a special privilege in those exercising the right because others who also have the right do not exercise it."[153]

A prohibition law[154] of South Dakota permitted a clergyman to obtain intoxicating liquor for sacramental purposes upon an order from any sheriff. A law enforcement agent having a search warrant visited the home of an orthodox Jew who was suspected of possessing liquor contrary to the state prohibition law. Upon finding two kegs of alcoholic beverages, the state brought action against the suspect for unlawful possession of the liquor. The defendant contended that the liquor found in his possession was used for sacramental purposes and, consequently, was not being held in violation of law. Further, he claimed that his constitutional right to worship God according to the dictates of his conscience had been infringed. The court was not impressed by his arguments. Granting that the defendant was the priest of his own family, as he alleged, and assuming that there was a necessity for wine for sacramental purposes as specified by his religious sect, the court reasoned that the wine could have been obtained in a lawful manner. A conviction in the lower court was upheld.[155]

A Wisconsin law[156] required any male applying for a marriage license to file a certificate that he was free from any venereal disease. One Alfred Peterson presented himself to four physicians for an examination to determine whether he had a venereal disease. Each time he tendered the statutory fee of $3.00; each physician refused to make the examination because the physician believed the fee to be insufficient compensation for making the test. Peterson thereupon renewed his application

153. *People v. Marquis*, 291 Ill. 121, 123, 125 N. E. 757, 759 (1919).
154. *South Dakota Rev. Code of 1919*, sec. 10333.
155. *State v. Kramer*, 49 S. D. 56, 206 N. W. 468 (1925).
156. *Wisconsin Statutes of 1913*, sec. 2339 m.

for a marriage license without the medical certificate. After being refused the license, he brought suit to compel the issuance of a marriage license. Among other grounds, he challenged the law on the theory that it violated the religious freedom of applicants. The court was unimpressed by the claim. The court upheld the law and observed: "We have not been able to appreciate the force of the contention that the law interferes in any respect with religious liberty. We know of no church which desires its ministers to profane the marriage tie by uniting a man afflicted with a loathsome disease to an innocent woman."[157]

The enforcement of reasonable regulations in the practice of medicine, as commonly provided for by state statutes enacted under the police power as essential for public health, does not oppose guarantees of religious liberties.[158] A state license is a legal prerequisite for one who desires to furnish medical advice for a fee. Any persons, individually or collectively, any minister or congregation, may resort to prayer for the healing of the sick at any time they desire. This religious right, however, does not mean that a person, under the cloak of religious belief or religious exercise, may heal commercially for hire, using prayer as the curative agency. It is the commercial venture of healing by prayer practiced as a money-making scheme that constitutes the practice of medicine forbidden by law.

If one practices medicine without a license, he is none the less guilty because in so doing he also practices his religion. For example, the Alabama legislature made it a misdemeanor[159] for any person to treat or offer to treat diseases of human beings by any system of treatment whatever without a license. An individual who treated a person for a fee without a license from the State Board of Examiners was charged with a violation of the law. The Alabama Supreme Court ruled that the law did

157. *Peterson v. Widule*, 157 Wisc. 641, 643, 147 N. W. 966, 971 (1914). 158. 16 *C. J.* 602.
159. *Alabama Code* (1907), Vol. III, c. 27c, sec. 7564, p. 835; Act of Aug. 9, 1907, amending Acts of March 9, 1877, and Feb. 18, 1891.

not interfere with the exercise of religious liberty. Instead, it merely was a police regulation, safeguarding the life and health of the public.[160]

In one instance a preacher of the Divine Scientific Healing Mission was arrested for practicing medicine without a license, contrary to law.[161] He testified in court that the members of the mission believed in healing the sufferings of humanity by placing the hands on the body. This process was considered to be a gift of the divine spirit. In reply to this argument that his treatment was a gift from the Almighty, the judge held that the nature of the defendant's business, not his tenets, was the point in controversy. Because the evidence showed that he was practicing medicine within the meaning of the statute and did not have a license, he was found guilty [162]

In another case an individual who held a certificate to teach as a clergyman in the Church of the Illumination gave medical advice for a charge without having a state license.[163] The tenets of the church were that there is a purpose for our existence on earth, and that "this soul or divine spark which is the soul in the human body, is there for a purpose." The body was considered a sort of specialized soil to receive it, in which it grew and developed. In their teachings the members emphasized healing the ailing and the sick and bringing them to bodily perfection. The members believed in a "four fold development: that is, taking care of the body, mind, spirit, and the soul." Upon trial for violation of the statute, the defendant claimed that he was practicing his religious beliefs rather than practicing medicine. According to his testimony (in harmony with the tenets of his church), the bringing of the body to a normal condition was interwoven with the spiritual problem. Further evidence was adduced to show that the congregation believed that

160. *Fealy v. City of Birmingham*, 73 So. 296 (1916).
161. *Colorado Rev. Stat. of 1908*, c. 127, sec. 6069.
162. *Smith v. People*, 51 Col. 270, 117 Pac. 612 (1911).
163. *Washington Rem. Comp. Stat.*, sec. 6145.

the pastor should assist those who were sick as a matter of health and Christian obligation. Nevertheless, conviction for the violation of the medical statute was upheld by the Supreme Court of the State of Washington.[164]

On prosecution for practicing medicine without a permit,[165] a defendant alleged that his practices were a science called Naturopathy, and were a part of the religious creed to which he subscribed. The fact that the title of doctor had been used, and drugs prescribed, was another matter for court consideration. Stating that it was immaterial whether the defendant could prove that his practices were in accordance with the tenets of some religious organization, the State Supreme Court of North Dakota approved a conviction for violation of the medical law.[166] A judge in another case commented on the unfair competition with qualified physicians which is offered by unlicensed individuals who combine faith with patent medicines.[167]

Summary.—In only a comparatively few cases has the decision been reached that the exercise by Congress of a delegated power contravenes guarantees of religious freedom. Laws based on the commerce, naturalization, postal, and military powers have been attacked on religious grounds. In many of the instances cited the alleged violation of religious liberty has been a remote factor in the situation. In each case, however, the Federal Courts have consistently refused to impede the administration of the national laws.

Many state laws based upon the police power have allegedly conflicted with constitutional guarantees of religious liberty. Laws insuring public safety and order may legally include in their scope the activities of religious societies and their members. Sunday laws apparently discriminate in favor of Christianity. They have, however, been upheld on the theory that a state

164. *State v. Verbon*, 167 Wash. 140, 8 P. (2d) 1083 (1932).
165. *North Dakota Revised Code*, sec. 463.
166. *State v. Miller*, 59 N. D. 286, 229 N. W. 569 (1930).
167. *People v. Vogelgesang*, 221 N. Y. 290, 111 N. E. 977 (1917).

may designate a day of rest. Legally, the fact that this day of rest coincides with a Christian holiday is a mere coincidence. Likewise, laws punishing blasphemy are valid because they tend to preserve the peace of society, although in reality only derogation of the Christian religion is forbidden.

References to religious freedom in defenses to the charge of fraud have often been far-fetched. States may punish for fraudulent practices without fear of judicial disapproval. Health laws have been consistently deemed a valid exercise of the police power, even though they restrict the practices of individuals who would combine spiritual and physical healing for a fee.

Comprehensive laws limiting solicitation and restraining the distribution of literature may contravene religious freedom as conceived by the American judiciary. The courts will not permit administrative discretion to abrogate an individual's right to circulate his own religious ideas. It should be noted in this connection, however, that the rights of freedom of speech and freedom of the press are closely associated in cases of this type.

Evidence indicates that state laws passed in pursuance of the police power generally have been upheld by the courts. The fact that the concept of religious liberty is applicable to thought, but not necessarily to action, renders an appeal to constitutional guarantees ineffectual in such instances. The welfare of the state remains paramount to the activities of particular individuals.

III

Rights of Individuals in the Formation and
Termination of Religious Societies

The nature of religious societies.—A church may be defined
as a body of believers having the same creed, acknowledging
the same spiritual authority, and observing the same religious
practices. Implicit in the term "church" is the idea of an organization for religious purposes.[1] The objectives of a church
organization have been judicially described as the holding of
religious exercises, the maintenance and support of the ministry,
the provision of the conveniences of a church home, and the
promotion of the growth and efficiency of the work of the general church of which it may form a component part.[2]

Conceptual definitions of religious societies rendered by the
American judiciary exhibit a great deal of similarity. Typical
is the idea that a religious society consists of a voluntary association of individuals, united for the purposes of having a common place of worship and of providing a proper teacher who
instructs them in religious doctrines and duties and administers
the rites of the church.[3] The Supreme Court of Nebraska significantly described a church society as a voluntary organization
"formed for the advancement of the spiritual welfare of its
members, by counsel, admonition, and example, and to enable

1. *In re Douglass' Estate,* 94 Neb. 280, 143 N. W. 299 (1913).
2. *First Presbyterian Church v. Dennis,* 178 Iowa 1352, 161 N. W. 183
(1917).
3. *Baptist Church v. Witherell,* 3 Paige (N. Y.) 296 (1832).

the society to employ and pay a pastor to look after not only the welfare of that particular organization, but many charitable objects requiring aid, and to promote, as far as possible, with the means at hand, the welfare of the race."[4] The scope of the term "religious society" is important, as there is an unquestioned right to organize voluntary religious associations to assist in the expression and dissemination of any religious doctrine, and to create tribunals for the decision of controverted questions of faith within the association, and for the ecclesiastical government of all the individual members, congregations and officers within the general association.[5]

Early religious societies in America were unincorporated. The simplicity of procedure did not necessitate the adoption of corporate forms. Further, religious corporations, as they were known at common law, were not looked upon with favor by the early inhabitants of America. In their minds religious corporations were associated to a great degree with the idea of a union of church and state. Therefore the disposition was to give no recognition to them in law. As a practical matter, early religious societies existed for nearly all of the purposes for which they later were incorporated.

Nevertheless, in order to enable religious societies to enjoy the privileges of legal entities competent to deal with the civil courts in a recognized manner, the right of religious societies to incorporate was gradually recognized. American legislatures began over a century ago to pass special acts granting charters to religious societies. As in the case of early attempts of other private groups to secure charter privileges, a proposed act to incorporate church societies was often subject to the whims and jealousies of politically minded legislators. Consequently many societies did not apply for a charter.

Public reaction set in against the legislative procedure of granting special charters. Ultimately, constitutional amend-

4. *Jones v. State*, 28 Neb. 495, 499, 44 N. W. 658, 659 (1890).
5. *Watson v. United States*, 80 U. S. 679, 20 L. Ed. 666 (1871).

ments and new and revised incorporation laws were passed. By the terms of the amendments, legislators were often prohibited from granting special charters. General statutory specifications were laid down, upon compliance with which the individuals seeking a charter were declared incorporated by an administrative officer, often the Secretary of State. General incorporation laws applicable to religious societies have been amended from time to time. It is now legally possible for such societies to become incorporated either under general laws or under special statutory enactments in all states except Virginia and West Virginia. In these two states, the incorporation of religious societies is prohibited by their respective state constitutions.[6]

Society and corporation distinguished.—The distinction between a religious society and a religious corporation is frequently emphasized.[7] The religious society is the group of communicants who attend divine services at a church. The religious corporation is an inanimate person possessing exclusively temporal powers. The members of the corporation are individuals who are entiled to vote in corporate elections; otherwise they are inactive. The corporation owns the temporalities, the management of which is directed by the trustees. Although generally the case, it is not always necessary that members of the corporation and all of the trustees be communicants of the church. Likewise, a member of the religious society is not necessarily a member of the corporation. It is clear that membership in the corporation and membership in the society are not necessarily concomitant.[8]

Judicial opinion has held further that "the corporation was the legal entity which held the title to the real and personal estate used for worship and other religious purposes in the absence of express provision to the contrary. The church was the body of communicants gathered in the church membership

6. *Constitution of Virginia*, Art. IV, sec. 59; *Constitution of West Virginia*, Art. VI, sec. 47.
7. 23 *R. C. L.* 424.
8. *Fiske v. Beaty*, 201 N. Y. S. 441, 206 App. Div. 349 (1923).

for the celebration of the Lord's Supper and for mutual support and edification in piety, morality and religious observances. The corporation and the church, although indissolubly associated, were nevertheless separated by this distinct line of demarcation."[9] A church society, by incorporation, therefore, does not lose its existence or become wholly merged in the new corporation. However, the practical result has been that in cases of disagreement between corporation and church, the power of the corporation has prevailed.

The acquisition of legal status.—Sometimes unincorporated religious societies performed functions for which legal sanction had not been obtained. When the question of status arose after a period of years and no charter could be produced, the practice of using the common law rule of prescription frequently prevailed.[10] Under the presumption that a charter had been originally granted, the religious group was held legally able to make contracts and to enjoy, in general, the benefits accruing to bona fide incorporated societies. Thus in an action for breach of contract a court has held that it was not necessary for the plaintiff to prove that the defendant religious society had formally accepted its act of incorporation and was duly organized under it. Since the evidence showed that the defendant had acted like a corporation for thirty-six years, the judge held that the defendant could not avoid the legal consequences of its contract by disputing its legal capacity to make the contract. The plaintiff recovered damages.[11]

Usually, however, affirmative action has been held necessary to effectuate compliance with the incorporation law. Laws do not make it obligatory upon all voluntary religious societies to become incorporated; instead they merely prescribe the mode

9. *McNeilly v. First Presbyterian Church of Brookline,* 243 Mass. 331, 337, 137 N. E. 691, 694 (1923).
10. 23 R. C. L. 426.
11. *Whitmore v. Fourth Congregational Society of Plymouth,* 68 Mass. 306 (1854); *Federal Savings and Loan Insurance Corporation v. Strangers Rest Baptist Church,* 156 Kans. 205, 131 P. (2d) 654 (1942).

of incorporation. For that reason judicial analysis suggests that to presume incorporation would be to carry the presumptive evidence doctrine too far. Unless the legislatures impose the same restrictions on unincorporated societies that they do on incorporated ones, the courts have declared their unwillingness to do so.[12]

Statutory regulations must be at least substantially complied with and all of the specific requirements generally observed before the corporate status can attach.[13] The usual method of incorporating is to assemble the members of the society at a designated time and at the place where worship usually is held. The appropriate papers are signed, a name is chosen, and officials are selected. The filing of the papers and the certification by an administrative official usually completes the process of incorporation. Sometimes, in order to become organized, a religious society must elect officers and trustees and keep a record of its proceedings which relates, among other items, the purpose of organization and the affirmative action of the society.[14] Members of a church have incorporated independently of any superior ecclesiastical body.[15] The provisions of the church constitution adopted by the group are binding on the members unless contrary to law or to public policy.[16] "It is a well recognized principle of law that a church society may adopt for its government a constitution, and that, unless its provisions are in conflict with the statute or contrary to public policy, it will be binding upon the members of the church."[17]

12. *Alden v. St. Peters Parish,* 158 Ill. 631, 42 N. E. 392 (1895). See also 23 *R. C. L.* 426.
13. 23 *R. C. L.* 425; 54 *C. J.* 11; *Ferraria v. Vasconcelles,* 23 Ill. 403 (1860); *People v. Peck,* 11 Wend. (N. Y.) 604 (1834); *In re Application for Charter,* 55 York (Pa.) L. R. 186 (1942).
14. 23 *R. C. L.* 436; see especially, *Gullet v. First Christian Church of Meridian,* 154 Miss. 516, 122 So. 732 (1929).
15. *Parish of Immaculate Conception v. Murphy,* 89 Neb. 524, 131 N. W. 946 (1911).
16. *Geiss v. Trinity Lutheran Church,* 119 Neb. 745, 230 N. W. 658 (1930).
17. *Ibid.,* pp. 749-750.

A court may not approve a proposed religious corporation which might possibly tend to glorify qualities which are the antithesis of religion. Although the purpose of a particular proposed corporation was to establish churches, an aim on its face harmless, the fact that the churches so founded were dedicated to Aphrodite, Greek goddess of love and beauty, led a court to withhold approval, because Aphrodite, according to history, possessed questionable qualities of character. On a later rehearing, the certificate of incorporation was approved after the judge was shown that the proposed corporation was not being organized for any other purpose than the worship of a religious conception of love and beauty and that no precepts of the church would glorify any qualities antagonistic to religion.[18]

In one case, a court refused to approve a proposed religious corporation because of its title. Approval of a certificate of incorporation as "Church of God World Headquarters, Inc." was sought by a group of coreligionists. The application for incorporation was denied because, the court held, the appellation "Church of God" is a generic term which the group could not arrogate to their exclusive use.[19]

In a Pennsylvania case Christian Scientists were refused a charter on the ground that the church body which sought to incorporate was primarily interested in the treatment of cases, rather than in the propagation of a system of religious beliefs. The court differentiated between religion and the law as follows: "We are not to consider the matter from either a theological or metaphysical standpoint, but only in its practical aspects. It is not a question as to how far prayer for the recovery of the sick may be efficacious. The common faith of mankind relies, not only upon prayer, but upon the use of means which knowledge and experience have shown to be efficient; and when the

18. *In re Long Island Church of Aphrodite*, 14 N. Y. S. 763, 171 Misc. 1032 (1939).

19. *In re Church of God World Headquarters, Inc.*, 46 N. Y. S. (2d) 545 (1944).

results of this knowledge and experience have been crystallized
into legislative enactments, declarative of what the good of the
community requires in the treatment of disease, and of the
qualifications of those who publicly deal with disease, anything
in opposition thereto may fairly be taken as injurious to the community. Our laws recognize disease as a grim reality, to be met
and grappled with as such."[20] Inasmuch as the Christian Science
principle tended to oppose the law, the court refused to approve
a legal status for the organization.

Legislatively imposed conditions precedent to corporate organization must now be performed without the use of judicial
dispensatory power.[21] However, liberality in the exercise of
court discretion is perceivable in a group of nineteenth-century
cases in which religious societies were judicially conceived as
incorporated in spite of a lack of strict compliance with incorporation laws. In one instance the articles of association were
not signed by the persons who adopted them. Supposing themselves legally organized, the members of this religious society
exercised the functions of a regularly incorporated society, and
for a long period bought and sold church property. Later,
when the failure to sign the articles was brought to the attention
of the court, the judge remarked that even though the articles
had not been properly signed, the records revealed an honest
effort of the organization to administer its affairs. The benevolent attitude of the court helped to save the society from a
verdict of legal nonexistence.[22] Corporate status has also been
conferred upon societies although they were organized under
unconstitutional statutes,[23] and although there was no sufficiency
of notice of the meeting of incorporators.[24] The fact that the

20. *In re First Church of Christ Scientist,* 205 Pa. 543, 546, 55 Atl. 536,
539 (1903).
21. 23 *R. C. L.* 426.
22. *Trustees of the First Congregational Church of Ionia v. Webber,* 54
Mich. 571, 20 N. W. 542 (1884).
23. 54 *C. J.* 11.
24. *East Norway Lake Lutheran Church v. Froislie,* 37 Minn. 447, 35
N. W. 260 (1887).

certificate of incorporation had not been sealed,[25] lacked proper acknowledgment[26] or was not sworn to[27] did not preclude corporate existence.

Forms of incorporation.—A study has revealed five distinct classes or forms of church corporations in American history, three of which prevail at present.[28] Two early forms were the *territorial parish* and the *corporation sole.* Under the *territorial parish* form, every town was considered to be a parish; religious duties were a function of the town. Under the *corporation sole,* the legal entity was composed of only one person to whom and to whose successors belonged legal perpetuity. Both of these early forms have disappeared. American church societies today fall into one of three types: the *corporation aggregate* for congregational types of churches; the *revised corporation sole* for monarchical types of churches; and the *trustee corporation* for intermediate churches.

In the *corporation aggregate* the church members are the corporators. Rules and regulations are made by them as a body. Each local body is a self-governing, independent democracy. Trustees are only officers carrying out the mandate of the membership. One court remarked that it was the ecclesiastical society constituting the church, not the persons who signed the articles of incorporation, which became a legal entity with power to transact religious business; the trustees were spoken of as agents in its behalf.[29]

The *revised corporation sole,* or the prelacy type, permits bishops and higher ecclesiastics of various denominations to man-

25. *Stoker v. Schwab,* 1 N. Y. 425, 56 Super. 122 (1888).
26. *Franke v. Mann,* 106 Wisc. 118, 81 N. W. 1014 (1900).
27. *Baltimore Railroad Co. v. Washington Fifth Baptist Church,* 137 U. S. 568, 11 Sup. Ct. 185, 39 L. Ed. 784 (1891).
28. Carl Zollman, *American Civil Church Law,* chap. 2; Carl Zollman, "Classes of American Religious Corporations" (1915) 13 *Michigan Law Review* 566.
29. *Sanchez v. Grace Methodist Episcopal Church.* 114 Cal. 295, 46 Pac. 2 (1896); *Drozda v. Bassos,* 260 A. D. (N. Y.) 408, 23 N. Y. S. (2d) 544 (1940).

age the temporalities. In religious organizations patterned after the revised corporation sole there is no local sovereignty.[30] The local trustees cannot authorize the diversion of the temporalities of the church from the purposes to which they were devoted by the founders. Property is dedicated for use in conformity with the canons of the superior church organization.[31]

In the *trustee corporation,* or presbyterian type, the powers of government rest in the body of believers but are exercised through representatives in a hierarchical fashion. The local church is subordinated to the control of the supreme governing body in the hierarchy.[32] Specifically, the local governing body is the church session. A district presbytery embraces representatives from the sessions in the district. Delegates chosen from the congregations make up a synod which includes a number of presbyteries. At the top of the pyramidical structure is the general assembly composed of clergy and ruling elders chosen by each of the presbyteries.[33]

The trustee corporation was devised to give permanence and responsibility to a system previously characterized by instability and irresponsibility. Such an arrangement overcame the objectionable decisions to the effect that, upon the death of the trustee, the trust reverted to the original owner,[34] or to the heirs of the testator,[35] and that the existence of the old board of trustees might be terminated.[36] Trustees of a religious corporation are officers, similar to the directors of a railroad company.[37]

Liability of religious societies.—The common law rule of liability is that a voluntary association not formed for profit,

30. *Smith v. Bonhoof,* 2 Mich. 115 (1851); *Searle v. Roman Catholic Bishop of Springfield,* 203 Mass. 493, 89 N. E. 809 (1909).
31. *Parish of Immaculate Conception v. Murphy,* 89 Neb. 524, 131 N. W. 946 (1911).
32. *Ramsey v. Hicks,* 174 Ind. 428, 91 N. E. 344 (1910).
33. 54 *C. J.* 7.
34. *Morgan v. Leslie,* 1 Wright (Ohio) 144 (1832).
35. *Cahill v. Bigger,* 47 Ky. 211 (1848).
36. *Lee v. Methodist Episcopal Church,* 193 Mass. 47, 78 N. E. 646 (1906).
37. *Robertson v. Bullions,* 11 N. Y. 243 (1854).

like a church organization, is not liable as such on its contracts because it has no legal status.[38] The typical judicial viewpoint has been that a certifying officer is liable in an individual capacity for debts of an unincorporated religious society, unless authority from the whole membership had been delegated. Application of this rule made a building committee of an unincorporated religious group, through whom materials for the construction of a church structure had been purchased, liable although at the time of sale the seller had charged the material in the name of the society and had been informed at the time of purchase by the committee that the money was to be raised by subscriptions, fairs, and other similar methods.[39] Trustees of an unincorporated society signed a note to pay a fire insurance premium issued to the trustees; in a later action they were held liable on the contract because the church society was not a responsible principal.[40] Deacons of an unincorporated society who, in their official capacity, had signed a note in payment for church furniture were declared individually liable for payment.[41] The chairman of a building committee of an unincorporated religious sect signed a contract to purchase seats and thereby made himself responsible.[42] A contract engaging the services of an organist as the agent of a board of stewards of an unincorporated society was later treated as binding on the board of stewards jointly and severally, not on the congregation for whose benefit the arrangement had been formulated.[43]

Recently the status of an unincorporated religious society has been viewed differently with respect to legal remedies. Judicial

38. 54 *C. J.* 17.

39. *Clarke v. O'Rourke*, 111 Mich. 108, 69 N. W. 147 (1896); *Sheehy v. Blake*, 77 Wisc. 394, 46 N. W. 537 (1890).

40. *Phoenix Insurance Co. v. Burkett*, 72 Mo. App. 1 (1897).

41. *Burton v. Grand Rapids School Furniture Co.*, 10 Tex. Civ. App. 270, 31 S. W. 91 (1895).

42. *Summerhill v. Wilkes*, 63 Tex. Civ. App. 456, 133 S. W. 492 (1910).

43. *Forsberg v. Zehm*, 150 Va. 756, 143 S. E. 284 (1928); *Congregation of St. Augustine R. C. Church v. Metropolitan Bank of Lima*, 32 N. E. (2d) 518 (1936); Note, "Religious Societies—Liability of Board of Stewards" (1928) 15 *Virginia Law Review*, 98-99.

reasoning suggests that a voluntary association may sue or be sued in its association name; that an unincorporated church society has inherent power to authorize its trustees to sign contracts and notes on behalf of the association; and that, when sued thereon, the trustees may offer the defense that they signed in a representative capacity.[44]   Under such a doctrine, prior authorization removes the individual liability that formerly was attached to trustee action.

A trend of recent decisions is to acknowledge the fact that associations of men, organized for common objectives, possess a personality which the courts may in some instances recognize. Although the theory still prevails that in the absence of legislative authority the courts may not properly confer a legal status upon such a society, it is becoming clearer that the dividing line between incorporated and unincorporated societies is so indefinite that sharp differentiations may not be possible.[45]   In *United Mine Workers v. Coronado*[46] the United States Supreme Court made reference to positive legal recognition of the existence, and provisions for protection of, unincorporated groups.   The court commented upon the influence of equity procedure by which the designating of one person for many in a suit is permitted.   As a result of its analysis, the suable character of unincorporated groups has been judicially accepted.   This opinion of the highest court of the land indicates "a natural development in the law by which the ancient rule was brought into conformity with modern needs that in various ways had been formally recognized

---

44. *Mercantile Commerce Bank and Trust Company v. Howe.* 113 F. (2d) 893 (C. C. A., 1940); *Bahr v. Evangelical Lutheran St. John's Society of Poynette,* 236 Wisc. 490, 295 N. W. 700 (1941); *Slaughter v. Land,* 194 Ga. 156, 21 S. E. (2d) 72 (1942); *Chester Housing Authority v. Ritter,* 344 Pa. 653, 25 A. (2d) 72 (1942); *Davidson v. Church of Christ of Parrish,* 245 Ala. 203, 16 S. (2d) 179 (1943); E. M. Dodd, Jr., "Dogma and Practice in the Law of Associations" (1929) 42 *Harvard Law Review* 977-1014.

45. 23 *R. C. L.* 425-426.

46. *United Mine Workers v. Coronado Coal Co.,* 259 U. S. 344, 42 Sup. Ct. 570, 66 L. Ed. 975 (1922).

in the litigation and statutes of the country."[47] Elsewhere the Supreme Court has considered unincorporated groups as legal entities liable for damages.[48]

An unincorporated society, in a congregational meeting which had been duly called in conformity with the rules of the church, was held legally able to enter into a contract for the necessary labor and materials for a church building. In a suit to enforce a lien on the property of a church society for the balance of the compensation due for labor performed in connection with the erection of the building, the lien was upheld, since the sum agreed upon had not been paid. The court ruled that the church structure should be rented or sold in order to discharge the debt. The conclusion that the authorization by an unincorporated society rendered the lien enforceable led to an overruling of precedent to the contrary.[49] In another case it was held that a resolution of an unincorporated group empowering the trustees to sign for the membership in the purchase of an organ relieved the trustees of individual liability.[50]

In a suit for damages brought by a discharged clergyman against the trustees of an unincorporated religious society in Texas there was no evidence that the society had authorized the trustees to employ the clergyman. Although judgment could not be obtained against the trustees in their official capacity, or against the religious society, or against church property, the implication remained that the society would have been liable for breach of contract had the society's authority been given.[51]

47. *Hawthorne v. Austin Organ Co.*, 71 F. (2d) 945, 950 (C. C. A., 1934).

48. *Burkwaggoner Association v. Hopkins*, 269 U. S. 110, 46 Sup. Ct. 48, 70 L. Ed. 183 (1925); *Hempkill v. Orloff*, 277 U. S. 537, 48 Sup. Ct. 577, 72 L. Ed. 978 (1928).

49. *Cain v. Rea*, 159 Va. 446, 166 S. E. 478 (1929); *Mitterhausen v. South Wisconsin Conference Association of Seventh Day Adventists*, 245 Wisc. 353, 14 N. W. (2d) 19 (1944).

50. *Hawthorne v. Austin Organ Co.*, 71 F. (2d) 945 (C. C. A., 1934); see also *Bailey v. Washington*, 236 Ala. 541, 185 So. 172 (1938); Note, (1935) 48 *Harvard Law Review* 674-675.

51. *McCall v. Capers*, 105 S. W. (2d) 323 (1937).

In a few cases, the members of an unincorporated religious society have been held liable on contracts on the theory that the members were joint partners.[52] However, the majority of the cases in which the partnership aspect has been considered have opposed this theory, because in such societies profit has not been the objective.[53] As a general rule, a member of an unincorporated religious group is not individually liable for church debts unless he authorized the obligation or subsequently approved it through direct action.[54] One effect of incorporation is the abolition of the individual liability of members of the society for debts incurred by the society or by its agents.[55] The creditor of a religious corporation has no right of action against individual members as such.[56] The incorporated religious society is liable only for the acts of its officers done within the scope of their authority.[57]

That a religious corporation is like a charitable organization in the sense that, for injuries caused by the negligence of its servants or agents, it is not liable for damages, has generally been the rule.[58] The principle upon which charitable corporations were held not liable for the acts of their servants involved

52. *Wilkins v. Wardens of St. Marks Protestant Episcopal Church*, 52 Ga. 352 (1874); *Jones v. Watson*, 63 Ga. 680 (1879); *Thurmond v. Cedar Rapids Baptist Church*, 110 Ga. 816, 36 S. E. 221 (1900); *Goesele v. Bimeler*, 55 U. S. 589, 14 L. Ed. 554 (1852).

53. *Burke v. Roper*, 79 Ala. 138 (1885); *Shradi v. Dirnfield*, 52 Minn. 465, 55 N. W. 49 (1893); *Phoenix Insurance Co. v. Burkett*, 72 Mo. App. 1 (1897); *In re Maguire's Estate*, 13 Phila. 244 (1887).

54. *Mood v. Methodist Episcopal Church, South*, 289 S. W. 461 (1926); W. A. Sturges, "Unincorporated Associations as Parties to Actions" (1923) 33 *Yale Law Journal*, 383-405.

55. 54 *C. J.* 28.

56. See *Allen v. North Des Moines Methodist Episcopal Church*, 127 Iowa 96, 102 N. W. 808 (1905).

57. *Haas v. Missionary Society of the Most Holy Redeemer Church*, 26 N. Y. S. 868, 6 Misc. 281 (1893); Joseph Stodola, "Religious Societies" (1931) 6 *Notre Dame Lawyer* 387-388.

58. 61 *C. J.* 34; *Northwestern University v. Wesley Memorial Hospital*, 125 N. E. 13 (1919); *Lawson's Estate*, 264 Pa. 77, 107 Atl. 376 (1919); *Zoularian v. New England Sanatorium*, 230 Mass. 102, 119 N. E. 686 (1918); *Burgie v. Muench*, 65 Ohio App. 176, 29 N. E. (2d) 439 (1940).

considerations of public policy. But some courts have decided that public buildings operated by religious corporations must now be maintained in as safe a condition as any other building.[59] In these states a religious society owes an invitee on its premises a duty of reasonable care. Hence, failure to light a building when dark and in use may constitute failure to maintain such place in a safe condition. In such circumstances, the religious corporation may be sued for damages as compensation for the injuries sustained.[60]

In another case a communicant, while ascending the rectory steps, was struck by the outward swing of the rectory door. In an action for injuries suffered, the complaint was dismissed as to both defendant pastor and defendant church society. Upon appeal the dismissal of the complaint against the defendant pastor was upheld, but a new trial was ordered on the charges against the defendant society. In other words, the society did not enjoy immunity from a negligence suit.[61]

Powers of incorporated societies.—Courts generally permit a religious corporation to do that which reasonably promotes its ecclesiastical objectives.[62] Judicial approval of the extent of power inherent in a religious corporation is indicated by the statement that "there is a wide range within which benign purposes of the founders of the society may be accomplished and there should be no paring down of the authority bestowed unless

59. *Green v. Church of Immaculate Conception,* 288 N. Y. S. 769, 248 App. Div. 757 (1936); *Goldberg v. Agudath B'Nai Israel Congregation,* 66 Ohio App. 379, 34 N. E. (2d) 73 (1940); 23 R. C. L. 459. So held in Ohio, Michigan, Washington. Massachusetts, New York, and Wisconsin.

60. *Wilson v. Evangelical Lutheran Church of the Reformation,* 230 N. W. 708 (1930); *Weigel v. Reintjes,* 154 S. W. (2d) 412 (1941); F. J. Graham, "Negligence: Religious Societies, Charities" (1930) 15 *Marquette Law Review* 54-55.

61. *Anderson v. Christ Church of Bay Ridge,* 287 N. Y. S. 403, 248 App. Div. 584 (1936).

62. 23 R. C. L. 458; see *Sherman v. American Congregation Association,* 113 Fed. 609 (C. C. A., 1902); *Pelter v. Sacred Heart Catholic Church,* 186 Okla. 45, 96 P. (2d) 24 (1939).

a particular act is clearly violative of that authority."[63] Within its "wide range" a religious corporation may utilize only such powers as are expressly granted or are necessarily implied for the purpose of executing the powers which are expressly granted.[64]

The legal rights of religious corporations vary in the several states.[65] All states, except Virginia and West Virginia, confer power upon religious corporations to manage property, to draw up contracts, and usually to make by-laws.[66] In Virginia and West Virginia, where church societies cannot be incorporated, statutes provide for the appointment of trustees to hold title to the permanent property for the group. The powers of such trustees are limited by the law authorizing their appointment.[67] In any event a religious corporation may engage in its specified activities only after authorized action has been taken by the trustees as a board, and upon an affirmative vote of the number of trustees required by statute. The individual action of a board member will not bind the corporation.[68]

The authority of a religious corporation to establish a missionary school has been challenged. On one occasion an appellant claimed that neither the establishment of missions nor the general diffusion of Christianity would be facilitated by the creation by a religious society of an institution of higher education. Granted that a religious corporation possessed the first two powers, did it impliedly have the third? Explaining that the missionary society had not been able to secure an adequate num-

63. *Boardman v. Hitchcock*, 120 N. Y. S. 1039, 1043, 136 App. Div. 253, 257 (1910).

64. 54 C. J. 10; see especially *Lenoux v. Annual Alabama Conference of Methodist Episcopal Church, South*, 236 Ala. 529, 183 So. 672 (1938); *Goodhope Colored Presbyterian Church v. Lee*, 241 Ala. 195, 1 So. (2d) 911 (1941).

65. Zollman, *American Civil Church Law*, p. 80.

66. For a discussion of the power of a religious corporation over its members, see chap. V, *infra*.

67. *Globe Furniture Co. v. Trustees of Jerusalem Baptist Church*, 103 Va. 559, 49 S. E. 657 (1905).

68. *In re McCanna's Estate*, 230 Wisc. 561, 284 N. W. 502 (1939).

ber of clergymen to meet the needs of foreign lands and that the missionary schools had been established to teach converts with the motive of carrying out the aims of corporate organization, the court typically held that the purpose of such schools was not to offer secular education but to prevail upon the people to accept the Lord. The creation of such religious schools was approved.[69]

Whether the ownership of property and the management of business enterprises in connection therewith in furtherance of one or more tenets of religious faith constitutes an illegal exercise of corporate powers is not a settled question. One line of decisions pleads for a broad interpretation of power so that the interpretation will avoid prosecution of any person and protect all in the free exercise of religious faith.[70]

An Iowa case illustrates the point. The Amana Society was incorporated under a state law[71] permitting the incorporation of religious societies. Later the Society engaged extensively in agricultural pursuits and in business and manufacturing enterprises for financial gain. The county attorney filed a petition claiming the society had exceeded its corporate powers and sought the dissolution of the corporation and the forfeiture of its privileges. The Iowa Supreme Court upheld the Amana Society by ruling that under a free government every citizen should be allowed to follow that mode of life that is dictated by his conscience. The court stated: "Where the ownership of property and the management of business enterprises in connection therewith are in pursuance of and in conformity with an essential article of religious faith, these cannot be held, in the absence of any evidence of injurious results, to be in excess of the powers conferred by the law upon corporations. We have discovered no decision touching the question decided; but, in

69. *Boardman v. Hitchcock*, 120 N. Y. S. 1039, 136 App. Div. 253 (1910).

70. 23 *R. C. L.* 443; 54 *C. J.* 33, note 44. So held in Pennsylvania, New Jersey, and Iowa.

71. *Acts of Iowa Seventh General Assembly*, chap. 131.

view of the spirit of tolerance and liberality which has pervaded our institutions from the earliest times, we have not hesitated in giving the statute an interpretation such as is warranted by its language and which shall avoid the persecution of any and protect all in the free exercise of religious faith, regardless of what that faith may be."[72]

Another set of decisions holds that no society, religious or otherwise, has a constitutional right to incorporate and carry on secular activity.[73] To illustrate, in South Dakota in 1922 thousands of acres of land and thousands of dollars of personal property owned by a communistic religious corporation were devoted to agricultural and industrial activities. The state attorney brought action to have the corporation adjudged to have forfeited its corporate rights. The state maintained that the corporation was not organized for religious purposes but for business and profit. After an adverse decision in the trial court, the state attorney appealed to the South Dakota Supreme Court. That court decided that the society had acted *ultra vires* by pursuing secular activities and amassing wealth not devoted to religious or educational purposes. The court ruled that the trial judge should have decreed a vacation of the articles of incorporation and a dissolution of the corporation. The opinion stated that "the principal business of the corporation is secular, viz. the engaging in farming and other industrial pursuits for the purpose of the sustenance of its colonies, that next in order the business of the corporation is political, viz. the government of its members; and that lastly and secondarily the objects of the corporation are religious, and, to a very limited degree, educational. For this reason we cannot conclude that it was the legislative intent that this corporation was organizable as a religious corporation."[74]

72. *State v. Amana Society.* 132 Iowa 304, 318, 109 N. W. 894, 899 (1906).

73. 23 *R. C. L.* 458; 54 *C. J.* 33, note 43. So held in Georgia, Ohio, and South Dakota.

74. *State v. Hutterische Bruder Gemeinde,* 46 S. D. 189, 211, 191 N. W. 635, 643 (1922).

The power of religious corporations to construct buildings or make improvements of any kind has been restricted to such buildings as are directly or indirectly appropriate to the advancement of religion and to such improvements as are essential to increase the comfort of the members of the society and of others who may associate with the members in the religious exercises. Applying the theory that the incidental powers of a religious corporation permit it to carry out the powers expressly granted and can in no manner enlarge the express powers, courts have held that religious corporations may not hold real estate beyond what is necessary for the transaction of specific corporate purposes.[75] Thus, an incorporated society has been denied the right to build a business block,[76] and to purchase a real estate site for speculation.[77]

Other activities of religious corporations have been held *ultra vires.* The holding as an investment of national bank stock obtained by a will has been held to be invalid.[78] The carrying on of a business of commercial printing for the general public had no reasonable relation to religious objectives.[79] A religious corporation has been prohibited from transporting passengers for hire.[80] An Ohio religious corporation established a savings bank and engaged in the business of banking by receiving deposits and by circulating bank paper, among other activities. An Ohio court declared the creation of such a bank illegal.[81] In one instance a corporation formed for the promotion of literary advancement and a study of the Bible operated a garage and advertised as "Pocono Pines Garage, Gasoline, Oil, etc." A court stopped this activity on the request of a

75. 23 *R. C. L.* 445-446.
76. *First Methodist Episcopal Church v. Dixon,* 178 Ill. 260, 52 N. E. 887 (1889).
77. *Thompson v. West,* 59 Neb. 677, 82 N. W. 13 (1900).
78. *Haight v. First Baptist Church of Camillus,* 42 F. Supp. 925 (D. C., 1942).
79. *State v. Southern Publishing Association,* 84 S. W. 580 (1904).
80. *Harriman v. First Bryan Baptist Church,* 63 Ga. 186 (1879).
81. *Huber v. German Congregation,* 16 Ohio St. 371 (1865).

neighboring businessman.[82]   Under the by-law of a religious
society, a standing committee had authority "to manage business
of the society, expending only such sums as the society shall
place at their disposal." The committee, however, had no
authority to employ counsel on the credit of the society.[83]

Under a charter giving a group the power to advance the
cause of religion, to supply preachers and to encourage the reading of religious books, action by the corporation in establishing
an orphans' home was nullified in Maryland. Such a power
was so foreign to the stated purposes of the charter that the
court refused to deem it as granted by implication.[84]   An Alabama corporation which was authorized to receive and hold
property for the promotion of religion and education was without power to indorse and become liable for the payment of
bonds issued by a memorial hospital. The fact that the hospital
was a subsidiary of the incorporated body was immaterial.[85]

Like other charters, the charter of a religious corporation is
subject to the police power of the state. The right of the state
so to limit religious activities has been upheld even when the
state did not reserve the right to amend the original charter.
A New York case involved the authority of the state to limit
the powers contained in the charter of a church corporation to
control land for cemetery purposes. Certain land had been
acquired by the corporation. On the basis of a subsequent
municipal charter, the use of the land for cemetery purposes
was prohibited by the city officials. Upon protest by the corporation a court held that the society was entitled to be protected against the impairment of its contract (charter) under
the principle of the Dartmouth College case, but that regardless
of the provisions of the charter the society was subject to the
police power of the state. It was pointed out that the state may

82. *Pocono Pines Assembly v. Miller*, 229 Pa. 33, 77 Atl. 1094 (1910).
83. *Child v. Christian Society*, 144 Mass. 473, 11 N. E. 664 (1887).
84. *Curtis v. Maryland Baptist Union Association*, 5 A. (2d) 836 (1939).
85. *Lenoux v. Annual Alabama Conference of Methodist Episcopal Church,
South*, 236 Ala. 529, 183 So. 672 (1938).

regulate the use of land for burial purposes in order to protect the public health. The action of the government in modifying the original charter was judged valid.[86]

Termination of the life of a religious corporation.—The life of a religious corporation may be terminated by diverse methods.[87] The charter may contain provisions relating to its own expiration.[88] Inactivity for a long period of time[89] or abuse of corporate powers[90] may be a cause for dissolution. A voluntary motion to disband, accompanied with the approval of a civil court, may legally terminate corporate life in certain jurisdictions.[91] One judge described the process as follows: "[The members] voted and resolved that they would no longer endeavor to maintain the appearance of a visible church; that they declared the same dissolved and extinct; and that the said vote and resolve were entered on the records of said church. This seems to the court to have been a dissolution of the church, so that it thenceforth ceased to be a visible church in any sense, legal, or ecclesiastical."[92]

Legislative authority[93] whereby the trustees of an incorporated religious society may dissolve a religious organization and transfer the property to a new religious corporation has been voided when applied to a society patterned on the congregational type of organization, because the consent of the congregation has not been obtained upon proper notice.[94] A religious corporation which by its nature is perpetual has been deemed

---

86. *Moritz v. United Brethren Church of Staten Island,* 278 N. Y. S. 342, 244 App. Div. 121 (1935).

87. 54 *C. J.* 96-97.

88. *First Society in Irving v. Brownell,* 5 Hun (N. Y.) 464 (1875).

89. *Scott v. Curle,* 48 Ky. 17 (1848); *Sosna v. Fishman,* 154 S. W. (2d) 398 (1941).

90. *People v. Volunteer Rescue Army,* 262 App. Div. (N. Y.) 237, 28 N. Y. S. (2d) 994 (1941).

91. See *Easterbrooks v. Tillinghast,* 71 Mass. 17 (1855).

92. *Ibid.,* p. 21.

93. *New Jersey Laws of 1914,* chap. 150.

94. *St. John the Baptist Greek Catholic Church v. Gengor,* 121 N. J. 349, 189 Atl. 113 (1937).

to continue in a legal sense until dissolved by affirmative action. A Missouri religious corporation transfered its property to another church and suspended its religious services. Since it had not formally dissolved, but instead had retained the right to the property in the event of the termination of the transferee church, the corporation was later adjudged competent to accept a legacy.[95]

The dissolution of an incorporated church by a presbytery was held not to dissolve the corporation as such.[96] The connection of every member of the congregation was cut and the trustees became extinct by virtue of the ecclesiastical order; nevertheless, by statute,[97] the civil corporation remained, although it was without the power to act or to administer property for the purposes for which it was obtained.

Merger of religious societies.—The identity of an original religious corporation may also be lost by merger with another corporation. Religious societies have often exercised a right to combine with other sectarian groups. Early legislative approval of the desire of societies to consolidate was expressed by New York in 1784, and other states followed in due course. In the process of joining forces, the actions of the religious sects have prompted a series of judicial inquiries.[98]

Legislative assent usually must be given, prior to the time of consolidation, usually by general statute.[99] There being no authority at common law for merger, corporations have no inherent ability to make such an arrangement.[100] A Wisconsin

95. *Pearson v. First Congregational Church of Joplin,* 106 S. W. (2d) 941 (1937).

96. *Westminster Presbyterian Church v. Presbytery of New York,* 127 N. Y. S. 836, 142 App. Div. 855 (1911).

97. *New York Laws of 1880,* chap. 167.

98. 23 R. C. L. 427; *Terpening v. Gull Lake Assembly of Michigan Conference of Methodist Protestant Church,* 298 Mich. 510, 299 N. W. 165 (1941); *Purcell v. Summers,* 34 F. Supp. 421 (D. C., 1940); see also *Purcell v. Summers,* 145 F. (2d) 979 (C. C. A., 1944).

99. *Chevra Bnai Israel v. Chevra Bikur Cholim,* 52 N. Y. S. 712, 24 Misc. 189 (1898).

100. *Agoodash Achim of Ithaca v. Temple Beth El,* 263 N. Y. S. 81, 147 Misc. 405 (1933).

jurist has approved the idea that "legislative authority is just as essential to a valid consolidation or merger of existing corporations as it is to the creation of a corporation in the first instance. It follows that an agreement between two or more corporations to consolidate, in the absence of legislative authority, is *ultra vires,* and will not be enforced even though it may have been partly performed. This applies to religious as well as other corporations."[101]

Strict compliance with the statutory mandates is generally required.[102] In one case a law[103] provided that an agreement by two religious corporations to consolidate must be approved by the bishop and standing committee of the diocese and by the supreme court of the state. A lower court enjoined two church organizations from merging as the statute allowed. Upon appeal the lower court was rebuked by the appellate judge, who ruled that a court of equity was not at liberty to assume jurisdiction of a question which already had been remitted to a competent authority by law.[104] In another case it was stated that, although the action of a society in voting to merge had been unanimous, the members themselves were powerless to do what the trustees themselves could not legally do.[105]

The consolidated church corporation becomes subject to all provisions of the consolidation law.[106] Usually the statute provides that the property of both original societies becomes vested in the consolidated group. Under these circumstances the former societies as such cease to have any right of ownership.[107]

101. *Evangelische Lutherische St. Thomas Gemeinde v. Congregation of the German Evangelical Lutherische St. Matthews Church of Milwaukee,* 191 Wisc. 340, 345, 210 N. W. 942, 944 (1926).

102. 54 *C. J.* 93.

103. *New York Laws of 1876,* chap. 176.

104. *MacLaury v. Hart,* 121 N. Y. 636, 24 N. E. 1013 (1890).

105. *Agoodash Achim of Ithaca v. Temple Beth El,* 263 N. Y. S. 81, 147 Misc. 405 (1933).

106. 54 *C. J.* 94; see also *Westminister Presbyterian Church v. Presbytery of New York,* 127 N. Y. S. 836, 142 App. Div. 855 (1911).

107. 54 *C. J.* 96; *Bennett v. St. Paul's Evangelical Lutheran Church,* 137 Md. 341, 112 Atl. 619 (1921).

In order to legalize an actual merger which had existed for years, a court decided that a special legislative act, changing the name of the meetinghouse association and augmenting its power, was necessary.[108] Application of the doctrine of strict compliance resulted in a judicial conclusion that a particular mission was incompetent to consolidate with a sectarian church corporation.[109] The mission was judicially recognized as a benevolent society, a group to which the consolidating statute[110] made no reference. Likewise, two congregations were prevented from combining for certain purposes while retaining a separate existence for other affairs. The attempted consolidation was denied, with the judicial reminder that the essential characteristic of merger was collective unity of the whole body in all property and other external relations. Among other things, the court concluded, this theory necessitated that the ownership of all corporate property and the right of contracting be located in the new corporation. No parceling of activities was permissible.[111]

The question whether an unincorporated and an incorporated religious society may consolidate has not been uniformly answered. In New York, merger has been judicially forbidden to two such groups because, among other reasons, the court held that the consolidating bodies must have been organized previously under the religious corporations law.[112] The court interpreted the statute permitting consolidation of two or more corporations as applying exclusively to those of a similar nature.[113] In Minnesota, however, when an unincorporated and an incorporated religious society sought to combine, the court approved the action. Corporations *de facto* were held to possess the same rights and privileges and to exercise the same functions

108. *Wheaton v. Cutler*, 84 Vt. 476, 79 Atl. 1091 (1911).
109. *Selkir v. Klein*, 100 N. Y. S. 449, 50 Misc. 194 (1906).
110. *New York Rev. Stats. of 1813*, chap. 60.
111. *In re German Lutheran & Reformed Wyomissing Church*, 9 Pa. Co. Ct. 12 (1871).
112. *New York Laws of 1896*, chap. 56.
113. *Chevra Bnai Israel v. Chevra Bikur Cholim*, 52 N. Y. S. 712, 24 Misc. 189 (1898).

as corporations *de jure.* The Minnesota Supreme Court reasoned as follows: "One is entitled to incorporate under it [the law]; the other to reincorporate under it. Why may they not combine and form a single corporation, the one becoming incorporated, the other reincorporated in the new organization? However this may be, the two societies in question have created what is at least a *de facto* consolidated corporation which includes both, and has succeeded to the property of both."[114]

Unincorporated religious societies may consolidate, subject only to the limitations of their own constitutions, rules, and discipline, the limitations of any trusts under which they may hold property, and the limitations of statutes.[115] That every unincorporated church group possesses an implied power of union, emerging from the purpose for which all are constituted, has been judicially stated. If two such organizations reach the conclusion that they can better serve their fundamental aim by union, and they can agree on points of difference previously separating them, the court did not see why they should remain separated. Another court pointed out that to nullify such combinations led to the absurd conclusion that the law compels the perpetuation of divisions.[116]

As a general practice the American judiciary has looked favorably upon religious consolidation.[117] Judicial opinion inclines to the view that denominational differences were not intended to be permanent and that independent groups were not essentially meant for perpetuity. In Christian thought unity has been deemed more desirable than division. Denominational groupings have as their primary objective the spreading of the faith, and the individual advancement of each group contributes to the general cause. Therefore, one judge concluded that a

114. *Mabel First Lutheran Church v. Cadwallader,* 172 Minn. 471, 481, 215 N. W. 845, 849 (1927).
115. 54 *C. J.* 93; *Housing Authority of New Orleans v. Merritt,* 196 La. 955, 200 So. 311 (1941).
116. *McGinnis v. Watson,* 41 Pa. 9 (1861).
117. 54 *C. J.* 93-94.

union with another church organization might be considered progress toward a common goal.[118]

Associations of religious societies.—In contrast to a merger, an association of religious societies may be formed as a federation for some specific purpose. In an association there is no change in the identity of the individual groups. By becoming a member of an association for a limited time, a religious society does not forfeit its property rights unless ecclesiastical regulations prevail to the contrary.[119] Thus, when a majority of a congregation, properly having possession of the church structure, united with other faiths in the locality under the name of "Community Church" as a matter of expediency, the independent status and property rights of each society remained the same. The court pointed out that the name "Community Church" did not indicate a religious association which had distinctive doctrines, but rather a federation of two or more churches, and that such federations are not uncommon.[120] In another instance, a congregationally governed church withdrew from membership in an association. The validity of a subsequent attempt by the association to determine which of the two groups constituted the true local congregation was denied by the Supreme Court of Alabama. The court held that although the association could exclude any church from its membership for specified reasons, the action of the association had no effect on the local church beyond exclusion.[121]

The enjoyment of a trust fund by a religious society is not disturbed by the society's becoming a member of an association. In one instance a congregation united with another of a different denomination to secure a regular pastor and a fixed place for services. Under the agreement each church was to retain its

118. *First Presbyterian Church v. First Cumberland Presbyterian Church,* 245 Ill. 74, 91 N. E. 761 (1910).
119. 5 *C. J.* 1334.
120. *Christian Church v. Crystal.* 78 Cal. App. 1, 247 Pac. 605 (1926).
121. *Caples v. Nazareth Church of Hopewell Association,* 245 Ala. 656, 18 So. (2d) 383 (1944).

own organization, receive and dismiss its own members, remain true to its own denomination, and contribute to its own denominational projects as each might choose. Each society continued to own its own building and parsonage. For convenience, community services were held in one church in summer, in the other in winter. After this arrangement had been in effect for a time, one of the religious groups used part of a bequest in connection with the maintenance of the community organization. Trustees of the will then brought action to stop the benefits of the fund on the ground of alleged diversion of the bequest by the religious group. A court ruled that the bequest did not depend upon the support of a doctrinal minister or upon a considerable attendance of members at the church services. As long as there were sufficient members of adequate zeal to maintain public worship according to the forms of the sect, the benefaction would continue. There was no evidence that the tenets of the religious society required separation from other Christian worship. The court commented that there should be no bar to joint worship of two Christian groups while each maintained its own distinct doctrinal characteristics. The trust fund was continued.[122]

The judiciary has protected the rights of a minority denomination in an agreement whereby each sect has been guaranteed the use of the common property at different times. In one case several religious denominations contributed to the expense of building a church and keeping it in repair with the understanding that the building was to be used by all without interference from each other. The particular denomination which contributed most was to have the preference as to the time of use. When one sect was denied the use of the building, the Pennsylvania Supreme Court ruled that the privilege of using the property was a legal right of each denomination and issued an order accordingly.[123]

122. *Jepperson v. Advent Christian Publication Society*, 83 N. H. 387, 142 Atl. 686 (1928). For a general discussion of trusts, see chap. XI, *infra*.
123. *Williams v. Concord Congregational Church*, 193 Pa. 120, 44 Atl. 272 (1899).

A society may sever at will its voluntary ecclesiastical connection with another group. The termination does not affect the character of the original societies.[124]

Public Aid.—State constitutions frequently prohibit the legislatures from giving public aid to religious societies, incorporated or unincorporated. The common provisions specify that public money shall not be appropriated to assist any church or sectarian purpose. Land grants for the benefit of religion are also forbidden. It is the duty of the judiciary to hold strictly to the fundamental law and to prevent any disregard of it, either by way of a direct legislative act or by way of an indirect process whereby an administrative agency might apportion public money to sectarian groups.[125]

The Pennsylvania legislature once appropriated a sum of money for the use of a sectarian hospital for charitable purposes.[126] Five taxpayer suits were instituted to restrain the payment of the money appropriated. The judiciary interpreted the state constitution[127] as forbidding state aid directly or indirectly to any sect, even in the sphere of public charity and education. Regardless of the worthiness of the purpose, the court refused to permit public funds to be placed under sectarian administration.[128] Later the legislature of the same state appropriated one million dollars for the use of the state welfare department to pay for the treatment of indigent sick or injured in hospitals not owned by the state.[129] One section of the law stated that no hospital should receive any payment for services rendered in excess of the actual cost of the service. Payment to an allegedly sectarian hospital was challenged as violating Article III of the state constitution. The State Supreme Court

124. *Duessel v. Proch,* 78 Conn. 343, 62 Atl. 152 (1905); *Lawson v. Kolbenson,* 61 Ill. 405 (1871); *Organ Meeting House v. Seaford,* 16 N. C. 453 (1830).
125. 23 *R. C. L.* 422; 54 *C. J.* 52; see also constitutional provisions.
126. *Pennsylvania Appropriation Act of 1919.*
127. *Pennsylvania Constitution,* Art. III, sec. 18.
128. *Collins v. Kephart,* 271 Pa. 428, 117 Atl. 440 (1921).
129. *Pennsylvania Appropriation Act of April 13, 1925.*

held void a financial arrangement which had been entered into by a sectarian hospital and the state welfare agency. The court imagined a situation in which the welfare administrator might select only hospitals of his faith, and after facilities of such institutions became geared to continue the work, a new administrator might be appointed who through bigotry or otherwise would choose hospitals of another faith and deny money to the original hospitals. Chaos would result. Whether the institution was to receive profits plus costs or only cost of services was immaterial. The fact remained that the hospital, to the extent that it received any money, was enabled to function as a sectarian institution.[130]

Contracts between a political subdivision and an ecclesiastical body, under which the latter receives remuneration for services rendered, have been held invalid. A municipal appropriation[131] payable monthly to a sectarian hospital for city patients and for free patients with contagious diseases was enjoined by a Georgia judge. In a taxpayer's action, the city aldermen were deemed to have violated their duty to hold money in trust to be spent only in a lawful manner.[132]

An ordinance[133] of a city council provided that the city enter into a contract with the Salvation Army. The latter would assume the charity work of the city and render an itemized bill each month for its services, the cost not to exceed seventy-five dollars per month. In a taxpayer's action seeking an injunction to prevent the city from paying a sum under the contract, the ordinance was held void. The judge commented that when the city contracted with the Salvation Army, even at actual cost of the service, a substantial advantage was given to the society in the furthering of its religious purposes. The giving of loaves and fishes, concluded the court, was a powerful instru-

130. *Collins v. Martin*, 290 Pa. 388, 139 Atl. 122 (1927).
131. *Savannah, Georgia, Ordinance* of January 9, 1924.
132. *Richter v. Savannah*, 160 Ga. 178, 127 S. E. 739 (1925).
133. *La Grange, Georgia, Ordinance* of May 2, 1921.

mentality in the successful prosecution of the work of a sectarian institution.[134]

An Act of Congress of 1897[135] appropriated $30,000 for the construction of two buildings, to be erected at the discretion of the Commissioners of the District of Columbia. The Commissioners made an agreement with a private hospital for the construction of an isolating ward on the hospital grounds, for the receipt therein of poor patients sent there by the Commissioners, and for payments by the District on the account of the hospital. A suit in equity was begun to enjoin the District Commissioners from paying certain money to the hospital. The action was brought on the ground that members of the corporation, a private eleemosynary entity, belonged to a monastic order, and, since the institution was conducted under the auspices of a church, it was allegedly sectarian. The United States Supreme Court, however, held that, assuming that the hospital was a private eleemosynary corporation, the fact that its members were members of a monastic order or sisterhood and that the hospital was conducted under the auspices of a sectarian organization, was wholly immaterial. The possibility that a particular church might exert a powerful influence over the members of a nonsectarian and secular corporation, incorporated for a certain defined purpose and with clearly-stated powers, was judged not sufficient to convert such a corporation into a religious body. Analysis of the charter itself indicated that it did not limit the exercise of the corporate powers to the members of any particular religion. The court decided that the act of Congress revealed nothing sectarian in the corporation and that the agreement at issue was a legitimate exercise of power.[136]

Another case involved a grant from Congress to a church organization of Wyandotte Indians. The law[137] appropriated

134. *Bennett v. La Grange*, 153 Ga. 428, 112 S. E. 482 (1922).
135. Act of March 3, 1897, 29 *Stat.* 665, c. 387.
136. *Bradfield v. Roberts*, 175 U. S. 291, 20 Sup. Ct. 121, 44 L. Ed. 168 (1899).
137. Act of July 28, 1866, 14 *Stat.* 309, c. 295; 19 *U. S. C.* sec. 54.

a sum of money to the trustees and stewards of the Indian group, to be applied to a building program. In a suit for possession of the fund, its legality was upheld by virtue of the responsibility resting upon the federal government for Indian protection. The court specified that such an appropriation was not a grant to a denomination to aid missionary work but to the church as an Indian church, and hence valid.[138]

Permission for a religious denomination to construct an edifice on publicly owned property for the convenience of inmates of a public institution has been adjudged not to violate the constitutional principle of non-public support of religious societies. The board of commissioners of a county poor farm by a resolution[139] set aside a plot for a chapel, to be used for religious worship and funeral services by a religious society. Construction of a religious structure, one hundred and thirty-eight feet by sixty-six feet, was begun by the church group. By an arrangement between the county and a bishop, the use of the public land was given to the church free; the cost of the structure was to be paid for by the society. Objection was raised that the plan constituted a grant to the church for sectarian purposes. An injunction against the erection of the building on county grounds was sought. The court analyzed the situation as follows: the county parted with nothing but acquired a building; the church acquired nothing but received a license to erect a building. The constitution prohibited the county from giving land to the church, but there was no prohibition against the church giving the building to the county. The latter situation was said to prevail by virtue of the resolution. It was further held that the constitution did not prohibit poor persons, who were unable to earn a livelihood and whose care the county had assumed, from meeting together for religious worship in a building on a poor farm. In return for the care given the body, the state should not exact the surrender of all care for the soul, the court

138. *Sarahass v. Armstrong*, 16 Kans. 192 (1876).
139. *Cook County Resolution* of February 20, 1911.

commented. Thus it was not a violation of the constitution for
the county, at no expense to itself, to permit a clergyman to
pray at a funeral or to allow a poor person to have a burial with
a religious ceremony. The court concluded: "No person can be
required to attend or support any ministry or place of worship
against his consent; and no preference can be given by law to
any religious denomination or mode of worship. This does
not mean that religion is abolished. . . . No one can be obliged
to attend or to contribute; but no one has a right to insist that
the services shall not be held."[140]   The man of no religion had
a right to act according to his absence of belief. However, he
had no right to insist that others have no religion.

*Religious corporations distinguished from charitable and
educational corporations.*—Religious corporations do not have
the same rights and privileges as charitable and educational corporations. For example, considerations of public policy have
frequently resulted in legal limitations upon the extent of ownership of real estate applicable to corporations formed for public
worship. The civil courts have been called upon to draw legal
distinctions between various types of benevolent corporations.[141]

Primarily, the character of a corporation is to be judged by
the objects of its creation as expressed in its charter. Tuscaloosa
Institute, an unincorporated association for educating young colored men in academic, collegiate, and theological studies, received a bequest in real estate. Later, the Institute became
incorporated. Action was brought to determine title to the
property on the assertion that the Institute could not take land
because it was a religious corporation, barred as such from holding land by the Missouri Constitution.[142]   The court ruled, however, that a corporation formed for purely academic purposes
was not a religious entity, even though it was for the training

140. *Reichwald v. Catholic Bishop*, 258 Ill. 44, 47, 48, 101 N. E. 266,
267 (1913).
141. 23 *R. C. L.* 425; 54 *C. J.* 33.
142. *Constitution of Missouri*, Art. II, sec. 8.

of colored youths in theological studies. The court emphasized that if the school had been incorporated solely for the purpose of educating young men for the ministry it would have been a religious corporation. Since the contrary was true, the Institute was under no religious disability to hold title to real estate.[143] Consequently, an incidental right to impart religious instruction does not necessarily render a corporation religious.

The fact that a corporation is under the control of members of a particular church does not necessarily make it a religious corporation. An educational institution established to teach literature, arts, and sciences was held not to be a religious entity in spite of the fact that its control was in the hands of the synod of a church. The constitution of the state at that time forbade the formation of a religious corporation. The court remarked that, if colleges may be incorporated by men having no religious views but not by men having religious views, the discrimination against religious people would be contrary to the best interests of the state. To the argument that the selection of the teachers and the management of the curriculum of the college enabled a religious society to inoculate its students with its creed, the court replied that this was an incidental effect of which the law takes no account. The court said that the corporation was not chartered to teach religion. If, while obtaining an education, one was influenced by a particular sect, the law had no concern. A suit by a tax collector to recover an assessment against certain real estate was fruitless.[144]

Section 8 of the Bill of Rights of the Missouri Constitution provides that no religious corporation can be established except under general law for the purpose only of holding title to such real estate as may be prescribed by law for church edifices, parsonages, and cemeteries. In an action by a resettlement corporation against a stockholder, the defense was that the corpora-

143. *Wyatt v. Stillman Institute,* 303 Mo. 94, 260 S. W. 73 (1924).
144. *State v. Trustees of Westminster College,* 175 Mo. 52, 74 S. W. 990 (1903).

tion was a religious society organized for the purpose of holding land other than for church edifices, parsonages, and cemeteries and was therefore illegal. The court decided that the association formed for the purpose of establishing settlements of persons of a particular religious sect was not a religious corporation. From an examination of the articles of incorporation, the primary object of the association was colonization, not propagating religion. Granting that the arrangement was confined to one sect, nevertheless the court found nothing in the constitution which would prevent persons of one faith from settling together.[145]

There is a marked distinction between a religious society and other organizations acting auxiliary thereto. Missionary societies have been recognized as exempt from statutes restricting religious congregations from holding more than a definite amount of land.[146] The United States Supreme Court explained that the reasons of public policy which restrict religious societies in their ownership of property "do not apply at all, or if at all, only with diminished force, to corporations which have no ecclesiastical control of those engaged in religious worship, and cannot prescribe the forms of such worship."[147] While missionary boards are important agencies in the aid of general religious work, they are thus not societies formed for religious worship.

A fraternal beneficiary society founded by, and limited to membership in, a church is not a religious corporation. No one is brought into membership except by his own free will nor restrained if he wishes to withdraw. By expulsion or suspension no one is deprived of a right which he holds independent of the society, or which was not created by the society itself and is contractual, depending for its enjoyment upon the observance of the agreement. In a suit to recover on a life insurance policy

145. *St. Louis Colonization Association v. Hennessy,* 11 Mo. App. 555 (1882).

146. See *Stump v. Sturm,* 254 Fed. 535 (C. C. A., 1918).

147. *Gilmer v. Stone,* 120 U. S. 586, 594, 7 Sup. Ct. 689, 693, 30 L. Ed. 734, 737 (1887).

issued by a society to the plaintiff's father, a court said that a fraternal beneficiary society was not formed to teach or propagate the religious faith, but to cultivate the spirit of fraternity among its members, who were of that faith, and incidentally to provide a pecuniary benefit for them and their families. The corporation did not thereby become a propagator of religious dogma. It only secured to its members that exclusive congenial association which it promised. The attempt to nullify the legal existence of the fraternal group was dismissed.[148]

Incorporation of the trustees of the general assembly of any religious society does not violate a constitutional prohibition against religious corporations; the assembly itself is recognized as not constituting a church society.[149] In Illinois the Young Men's Christian Association has been considered to be a nonreligious organization because it did not exercise any ecclesiastical control over its members, or prescribe any form of worship for them, or subject those who fail to conform to its rules to ecclesiastical discipline.[150] Likewise a benevolent business, incorporated to maintain a charitable home primarily for indigent members of a certain religious sect, was not deemed a religious entity.[151]

A Georgia court believed that the Salvation Army was a religious corporation. The court commented that it is a church on wheels, whose work is primarily directed to spiritual and moral reform. It is sectarian because it preaches a gospel and seeks to disseminate Christian truth.[152]

Summary.—A religious society comprises a voluntary group of individuals who join together for purposes of religious worship. The society itself may be unincorporated or incorporated.

148. *Franta v. Bohemian A. C. C. Union,* 164 Mo. 304, 63 S. W. 1100 (1901).
149. See *General Assembly of the Presbyterian Church v. Guthrie,* 86 Va. 125, 10 S. E. 318 (1889).
150. *Hamsher v. Hamsher,* 132 Ill. 273, 23 N. E. 1123 (1890).
151. *Jordan's Administrator v. Richmond Home for Ladies,* 106 Va. 710, 56 S. E. 730 (1907).
152. *Bennett v. La Grange,* 153 Ga. 428, 112 S. E. 482 (1922).

Although most societies were unincorporated over a century ago, today the reverse is true. Incorporation, however, is not a prerequisite to religious worship. Courts have consistently guarded the rights of individuals in the formation of religious societies.

In order to enable religious societies to exercise certain rights and privileges, legislatures have provided for their incorporation. At first special laws pertaining to the incorporation of particular societies were passed, but after abuses occurred general incorporation laws gradually superseded special legislative acts. General incorporation laws for religious societies now are found in all states except Virginia and West Virginia. Although the courts have adopted in some instances a lenient attitude toward the efforts of a religious group to incorporate, statutory regulations must be substantially met.

Religious corporations at present are of three types: the corporation aggregate, the revised corporation sole, and the trustee corporation. Each type is a counterpart of a method of internal church administration. The adoption of any of these types enables a society to carry on its temporal affairs more effectively. In general, courts have permitted a religious corporation to do that which reasonably promotes its ecclesiastical objectives.

One fundamental difference between unincorporated and incorporated religious societies has been the matter of liability of the membership. Under the common law the religious society in its unincorporated form was not liable on its contracts. As a result, trustees who entered into agreements often were subject to damages on unperformed contracts. Lately, many jurists have insisted that a voluntary association of individuals may sue or be sued in its association name. Under this theory the personal liability of the trustee acting in an official capacity is removed.

A religious corporation may be terminated by provisions of its own charter, by inactivity, by appropriate resolution, or by merger. Compliance with civil law is essential in any event.

The judiciary has been favorably disposed toward consolidation of religious societies. Religious societies may federate for a particular purpose. In contrast to a merger, the courts have permitted religious societies to retain their independent status while joined in a federation.

State constitutions frequently prohibit public assistance for religious societies through any form of appropriation, either direct or indirect. As a general rule, the courts have prevented overzealous legislators from violating such prohibitions. The problem of distinguishing between religious corporations and those closely related either in respect to control or motive has frequently been brought to the judiciary for settlement. The courts have consistently adhered to a strict interpretation of corporate laws and charters, thereby discounting many claims to bona fide religious status.

IV

The Finality of Administrative Decisions of Religious Societies

The role of civil authority.—Freedom of religious worship cannot be maintained if the civil courts invade the domain of the religious society, construe its canons, dictate its discipline, and regulate its trials. That a church without discipline must become, if it is not already, a church without religion is a truism. It is as much a delusion to confer religious liberty without the right to make and enforce religious rules as it is to create government without authority to punish offenders. If religious rules do not conflict with civil rules, and if civil rights are not involved, the exercise of religious freedom in a democracy must be determined as each sect sees fit. Civil authority may protect but it cannot interfere to destroy.[1]

Elements of a religious controversy.—A fundamental principle of American religious freedom is that secular courts have no jurisdiction over religious controversies and will not question any decision of a church tribunal relating to its internal affairs, in the absence of an interference with civil or property rights. Generally, matters of discipline, excision, faith, and practice are regarded as subjects of purely ecclesiastical cognizance. In such matters the religious tribunal is not only supreme, but it is wholly outside the realm of secular inquiry.[2]

1. John W. Patton, "The Civil Courts and the Churches" (1906) 54 *American Law Register* 391-423.
2. 23 R. C. L. 429; 54 C. J. 79.

The record of a clergyman in Illinois who signed a one-year contract with a local church board is illustrative. Before the expiration of the year the license of the clergyman was revoked by a district council of the church after charges had been preferred against him. He later sued in a civil court for the remainder of his salary and was awarded a judgment of six hundred and eighty dollars. The case was appealed. The evidence showed that the clergyman had been tried according to church law by a properly constituted ecclesiastical body and that his right to continue in the ministry of the church had been properly terminated. The appellate court pointed out that his contract was made subject to the rules of the church. The promise to pay was, as a necessary condition, contingent upon his remaining a duly licensed minister, and was subject to the suspension of his right to exercise ministerial functions within the sectarian group. The trial court had thus erred in not dismissing the petition for a judgment; the decision of the civil court of original jurisdiction was reversed.[3] The principle that the parties are bound by the decision of an appropriate church council, unless its action is set aside by a higher religious tribunal, was held to conclude the case.

In another case a clergyman who was charged with an ecclesiastical offense because he had omitted the word "regeneration" from baptismal ceremonies appealed to a civil court. He contended that the alleged omission was not an offense against church law. The civil court refused jurisdiction with the remark that the church should make and enforce its own rules without secular interference. As usual, the court stated that decisions of ecclesiastical courts determining what constitutes an offense against the laws of the religious society are final.[4]

The purposes of a charter of a Maryland religious corporation were to organize a German Evangelical Lutheran Church in accordance with Lutheran doctrine and the fundamental doc-

3. *Marsh v. Johnson*, 259 Ky. 305; 82 S. W. (2d) 345 (1935).
4. *Chase v. Cheney*, 58 Ill. 509 (1871).

trines of the unaltered Augsburg Confession, and to conduct services only by ministers who were members in good standing in an Evangelical Synod and who held the unaltered Augsburg Confession as a rule of faith. The articles of incorporation also stated that religious services should always be said in the German language as long as the congregation included one male member who should so desire it. An amendment to the charter required that the ministers should also believe in the Symbolical Books of 1580. Later, the trustees allegedly abandoned the fundamental form of worship and prevented members from holding services in accordance with the Augsburg Confession and the Symbolical Books. It was also claimed that the trustees permitted worship by ministers who denied the validity of the Symbolical Books and that they terminated the use of the German language for services. The court, however, denied that it possessed the power to decide spiritual affairs. An injunction to prevent the practices was refused.[5] The ruling of the court is typical.

The courts have refused to decide the abstract truth of various religious doctrines,[6] to determine whether the sacraments have been administered property,[7] and to adopt theological standards.[8] Civil authority will not enforce spiritual obligations,[9] nor determine the fitness of a clergyman to continue his duties,[10] nor compel church officers to perform their religious duties.[11] The decision of a church court pertaining to the election of a deacon was considered binding by the Michigan Supreme Court.[12] A civil court has refused to inquire into

5. *Shaeffer v. Klee*, 100 Md. 264, 59 Atl. 850 (1905).
6. *Trustees of East Norway Lake Evangelical Lutheran Church v. Halvorsen*, 42 Minn. 503, 44 N. W. 663 (1890).
7. *Colden v. Bradford*, 8 Cowen (N. Y.) 456 (1826).
8. *State v. Ancker*, 2 Rich. Law (S. C.) 245 (1846).
9. *Congregation of the Roman Catholic Church v. Martin*, 4 Rob. (La.) 62 (1843).
10. *Warren v. Pulitzer Publishing Co.*, 336 Mo. 184, 78 S. W. (2d) 404 (1934).
11. *Ferraria v. Vasconcelles*, 31 Ill. 25 (1863).
12. *Attorney-General v. Geerlings*, 55 Mich. 562, 22 N. W. 89 (1885).

alleged irregularities in the removal of officers or in the diversion of funds[13] and has refrained from investigating the ecclesiastical teachings of the pastor.[14] Whether the pastor, and the deacons supporting him, should be permitted to use a church building after they had been excluded at an election was held to be an ecclesiastical question not for the determination of the civil courts.[15]

The agency having final ecclesiastical jurisdiction.—What particular agency has final ecclesiastical jurisdiction depends upon the type of governmental organization used by the sect. In the monarchical type final discretion rests with the spiritual leader. The supreme governing body of the intermediate type exercises final jurisdiction over religious matters. In the congregational type of church organization the majority of the society decides. When the majority decision of a Congregational or Baptist society has been duly expressed in the regular and appropriate manner, it is final. Otherwise, a disagreeable minority might seriously hamper the stability of a church organization by objecting to such trivialities as the color the church building is about to be painted, the interior decorations, the heating system, and other matters of business management. To permit these hindrances would place religious property upon such a precarious basis that the society would be thwarted in seeking to acquire essential materials.

The majority of a congregation in Illinois, at a meeting conducted in compliance with the provisions of the church constitution, voted for the removal of a church building to another location. The minority, who preferred to remain at the old site, sought a court decree to have the property sold and the proceeds divided. Both sides had consistently adhered to the doctrines, tenets, and modes of worship adopted by the society. The minority in a religious organization having the congrega-

13. *Thomas v. Lewis*, 224 Ky. 307, 6 S. W. (2d) 255 (1928).
14. *Reichert v. Sarembi*, 118 Neb. 404, 213 N. W. 584 (1927).
15. *Grantham v. Humphri* . 185 Miss. 496, 188 So. 313 (1939).

tional form of government could not, the court said, because of disagreement with the majority operating within the constitution and rules of the society, withdraw from the religious group and compel a partition. The decree was denied.[16]

In another case the rules of a religious society of the congregational type provided that, in the event of a division of membership, the majority should be the proper group to retain the property and, further, that meetings of the congregation should be called by the minister. After a split had occurred in the congregation, the minister, who sided with the minority faction, refused to call a meeting at which the question of the disposal of the property could be decided. Although the required formal notice by the clergyman was not given, the majority gave both sides notice of a meeting, held the meeting without the minister, and sold the property. Upon an appeal to the Wisconsin Supreme Court the majority was upheld in its action, even though the minority did not attend the meeting. The court reasoned that the sale was made in good faith by the majority, who succeeded to the title of the property because of the division.[17]

Unless there is a specific trust dedicated to the propagation of those particular doctrines which were held by the society at the time the trust was obtained, the members of a congregational type of society who adhere to the acknowledged organization are entitled to the use of the property, whether or not they retain the original doctrines.[18]   Thus, a religious society in Texas, having decided upon a particular set of principles, be-

16. *German Evangelical Lutheran Trinity Congregation v. Deutsche Gemeinde,* 246 Ill. 328, 92 N. E. 868 (1910); *Clevenger v. McAfee,* 170 S. W. (2d) 424 (1943); *Vaughan v. Maynard,* 294 Ky. 38, 170 S. W. (2d) 897 (1943).

17. *Lutheran Trefoldighed Congregation v. St. Paul's English Evangelical Lutheran Congregation,* 159 Wisc. 56, 150 N. W. 190 (1914).

18. 54 *C. J.* 36; *Master v. Second Parish of Portland,* 124 F. (2d) 622 (C. C. A., 1941); *Purcell v. Summers,* 54 F. Supp. 279 (D. C., 1944); *Stone v. Bogue,* 181 S. W. (2d) 187 (1944).   But see *Parker v. Harper,* 295 Ky. 686, 175 S. W. (2d) 361 (1943); *Skyline Missionary Baptist Church v. Davis,* 17 So. (2d) 533 (1944).

came incorporated and obtained a church. Years later a minority of the members claimed that the majority had given up the original principles and as a result had lost their right to possession of the building. The court ruled that since there was no specific trust the original organization had a right to use the structure until outvoted by a new majority.[19] In other words, the court upheld the right of the majority to decide the issue.

When evidence points to the conclusion that a local religious society never formally conveyed its property to a superior religious organization, the civil courts will not infer that a dedication to the purposes of the superior organization has taken place.[20] For example, a suit was brought by representatives of a superior religious agency to restrain the officers of a local religious society from allegedly interfering with the duties performed by a pastor under the direction of the superior society. The local officers had installed another pastor and had diverted the property from its dedicated uses, it was alleged. The findings of fact, however, indicated that the property of the local society had never been conveyed to the superior group. Even though the ritual of the higher body was followed to a certain extent, the court refused to conclude that the local sect ever impliedly gave the property to the superior body. The suit was dismissed.[21]

Procedure.—It is important to note that the doctrine of civil non-interference usually rests upon the qualification that some formal vote be taken or that a decision be made at a meeting held in accordance with the regulations of the society.[22] At least the membership must have been accorded the opportunity

19. *First Baptist Church v. Fort,* 93 Tex. 215, 54 S. W. 892 (1900).
20. 23 *R. C. L.* 452.
21. *Malanchuk v. St. Mary's Greek Catholic Church,* 336 Pa. 385, 9 Atl. (2d) 350 (1939).
22. *Le Duc v. Normal Park Presbyterian Church,* 142 F. (2d) 105 (C. C. A., 1944); 54 *C. J.* 90; 23 *R. C. L.* 440. So held in the District of Columbia, Illinois, Missouri, New Jersey. Oklahoma, Texas, Kentucky, Pennsylvania, and Vermont.

of being represented.[23] Before an ecclesiastical decision is accepted as final, the Texas Court of Civil Appeals, for example, has pointed out that as an inherent right the evidence should be amply sufficient to warrant the conclusion that a resolution of a religious society was passed by an affirmative vote and that the meeting was a regular, legal, and authorized conference of a church society.[24]

In the congregational form the majority of those present and voting at any regular meeting can control the internal affairs of the church. Evidence that decisions pertaining to the erection of a new church and the removal of an old structure were made at regular business meetings, and that all business could be transacted at regular meetings without special notice to members, has led to judicial denial of the petition of a dissenting minority to restrain the removal of the old church.[25] In the absence of proof that the majority acted contrary to the rules and regulations, as expressed at a regular meeting, a group of complaining members was not entitled to a decree recognizing them as the church organization distinct from the former group.[26]

Because no civil law was violated, the Georgia Supreme Court once refused to act even though there was a flagrant disregard of church law. Although a rule of the church allowed every member in full communion and at least twenty-one years of age to vote, the pastor of the church demanded the payment of a fee as a condition of voting. Civil action was started to prohibit this interference with the election process. The petition stated that without judicial relief many members would be denied the franchise. The court, nevertheless, replied that the civil courts had no jurisdiction over the internal affairs of a religious society whether or not they had been previously

23. *First Baptist Church v. Ward*, 290 S. W. 828 (1927).
24. *Stogner v. Laird*, 145 S. W. 644, 647 (1912); *In re Evangelical Church of Lansford v. Lesher*, 24 A. (2d) 42 (1942).
25. *Yeary v. White*, 268 Ky. 471, 105 S. W. (2d) 609 (1937).
26. *Cooper v. Bell*, 269 Ky. 63, 106 S. W. (2d) 124 (1937).

adjudicated by the ecclesiastical courts. The petition was denied.[27]

Relation of members to society.—The legal relation of an individual member to a religious society has not yet been fully crystallized by judicial opinion. The question whether such a relationship is contractual is important because the right of a member to invoke the appellate power of a civil court is often involved. The courts of five states[28] have treated this relation as one of contract. The constitution of a Michigan sect vested power to make or repeal any rule of discipline in a general conference, subject to the restriction that no rule at any time would be passed to change the existing confession of faith. The constitution of the particular church itself could not be changed except by request of two-thirds of the whole society. One conference formulated substantial changes in the practices of the group and declared the altered articles adopted on a two-thirds vote of the members voting (but not two-thirds of the society). The legality of the change was brought before the Michigan Supreme Court. Resting its decision on the theory of contractual relationship, the court decided that the action of the conference in question was void. Title to the church property was vested in the group which complied with the original articles.[29]

A legal writer has pointed out that a major difficulty inherent in the contractual theory of membership lies in the fact that many religious societies embrace no definite method of introduction of new members.[30] Further, persons often become communicants of a church society automatically by baptism, or by mere residence. How, then, it may be asked, can a contract result?

The right of a church member to hold a pew is contractual.

27. *Gibson v. Singleton,* 149 Ga. 502, 101 S. E. 178 (1919).
28. Kentucky, Missouri, New York, Pennsylvania, and Michigan.
29. *Bear v. Heasley,* 98 Mich. 279, 57 N. W. 270 (1893).
30. Edward M. Boyne, "Religious Societies—Reinstatement of an Expelled Member" (1928) 13 *Cornell Law Quarterly* 464-469.

By a contract, the religious society may make reasonable regulations respecting the renting and sale of pews so as to exclude persons of an obnoxious character who might seek to change the practices of the society. Provisions against alienation in an effort to control membership are valid.[31] Civil courts will settle differences arising from obligations of this type. Thus a pewholder may maintain an action for trespass or ejectment, or bring suit against one who improperly disturbs him in the legitimate exercise of his legal right to use the pew during services, or against the religious society in whom title to the land rests.[32]

With these exceptions the predominant judicial viewpoint holds that a person who assumes the position of a clergyman or a member of a church organization voluntarily agrees, impliedly if not expressly, to conform to the canons and rules and to submit to the authority of the church.[33] By becoming a member an individual approves the rules provided by the government of the society and agrees to be governed by its usages and customs. He becomes a member on the condition of continuing or not, as he or his church may determine.[34] Under this conception there is no ground for appeal based on an alleged breach of contract by the religious society. The Supreme Court of Tennessee succinctly summarized the prevailing theory in the following words: "The relations of a member to his church are not contractual. No bond of contract, express or implied, connects him with his communion, or determines his rights. Church membership stands upon an altogether higher plane, and church membership is not to be compared to

31. 54 *C. J.* 83-84.
32. *French v. Old South Society in Boston,* 106 Mass. 479 (1870).
33. 54 *C. J.* 16.
34. See especially *Presbyterian Church v. Myers,* 5 Okla. 809, 50 Pac. 70 (1897); *German Evangelical Lutheran Trinity Congregation v. Deutsche Gemeinde,* 246 Ill. 328, 92 N. E. 868 (1910); *Krecker v. Shirey,* 163 Pa. 534, 30 Atl. 440 (1894); *Hayes v. Manning,* 263 Mo. 1, 172 S. W. 897 (1914); *Marsh v. Johnson,* 259 Ky. 305, 82 S. W. (2d) 345 (1935).

that resulting from connection with mere human associations for profit, pleasure, or culture."[35]

Consequently a member of a religious society may be removed by appropriate ecclesiastical procedure.[36] Where a pastor has never been tried by a tribunal for which the discipline of a religious society makes provision, the findings of a committee purporting to try the pastor have been held nugatory.[37] In one instance, the board of trustees of an incorporated religious society brought an action in the name of the society to enjoin a clergyman, whom they alleged they had removed, from preaching in the plaintiffs' church and to restrain him from exercising any other religious functions therein. The difficulty arose when the pastor began negotiations for the sale of the church structure and for the purchase of another building without authorization from the trustees. The board then called a meeting of the entire corporate membership and voted to dismiss the pastor. The pastor, when notified of the corporate action, contended that the corporate body had no power to remove corporate members or to dismiss him. The question presented was especially important because there was no statute applicable to the situation. The plaintiff contended that the pastor was removable by the corporate meeting; the defendant declared that removal was possible only in accordance with the custom of the church, as distinguished from that of the corporation. The conclusion of the trial court was that the corporation, at a meeting duly called for the purpose, possessed the legal authority to dissolve the pastoral relation.[38] The highest court in the

35. *Nance v. Busby*, 91 Tenn. 218, 233, 18 S. W. 874, 879 (1891).

36. *Petition of Hayes*, 38 N. Y. S. (2d) 66 (1942); *Jones v. Johnson*, 295 Ky. 707, 175 S. W. (2d) 370 (1943); Carl Zollman, "Powers of American Religious Corporations" (1915) 13 *Michigan Law Review* 646-666; 54 *C. J.* 18.

37. *Trustees of Delaware Annual Conference of Union American Methodist Episcopal Church v. Ennis*, 29 A. (2d) 374 (1942); *Skinner v. Holmes*, 133 N. J. Eq. 593, 33 A. (2d) 819 (1943).

38. *Walker Memorial Baptist Church v. Saunders*, 17 N. Y. S. (2d) 842, 173 Misc. 455 (1940).

state, however, overruled the trial court and held that, under the rules of the sect, the pastor was not an officer of the religious corporation; he was an officer of the religious society. Since termination of membership in the religious society had to be made by the religious body upon recommendation of a board of deacons, the church corporation was deemed to have no power to expel the pastor, a church member, from ecclesiastical membership.[39] When a clergyman has been removed by the proper ecclesiastical officials for a sectarian offense, he no longer has the right to exercise the duties of his office nor the right to further salary.[40]

Likewise, when a majority of a congregational society, or when the appropriate agency of an organization of the monarchical or presbyterian type, withdraws membership or fellowship from a member or members, the individuals so named in the ecclesiastical order lose their rights in and to church property.[41] In one case a member of a religious society strenuously objected to the election procedure used in the selection of officials of the society. Ultimately, the society suspended the objector from the membership roll. Thereupon the individual submitted to a civil court the question of whether the election of the officers in dispute should be by vote of the congregation after nomination by certain church members or whether the election should be by ballot as directed by the clergyman. The judiciary refused jurisdiction on the theory that the member, having been suspended, had no standing in court.[42]

Generally civil courts will not assume jurisdiction to determine the validity of the judgment of a church tribunal expelling

39. *Walker Memorial Baptist Church v. Saunders*, 285 N. Y. 462; 35 N. E. (2d) 42 (1941); *Presbytery of Huron v. Gordon*, 68 S. D. 228, 300 N. W. 33 (1941); *St. Mary's Greek Catholic Church v. Gaydos*, 58 Montg. Co. (Pa.) L. R. 62 (1942); *Caples v. Nazareth Church of Hopewell Association*, 245 Ala. 656, 18 So. (2d) 383 (1944).

40. *Chase v. Cheney*, 58 Ill. 509 (1871).

41. 54 C. J. 19; see also *First Baptist Church v. Ward*, 290 S. W. 828 (1927).

42. *Kompier v. Thegza*, 13 N. E. (2d) 229 (1939).

a member from further communion and fellowship in the religious society.[43]   In an instance where the congregational type of organization prevailed, with no ecclesiastical appeal from a decision on the question of excommunication, a court commented that the existence of the power of excommunication in the majority of an independent church society might be a defect in organization, but that it was not for the court to say, nor for those affected by its judgment to complain.   By voluntarily submitting themselves to the absolute power of the majority, the expelled members had tacitly promised submission to its judiciary decisions, the court declared.[44]   Thus, a civil court has no power to decide who ought to be members of a church group.[45]   The United State Supreme Court, likewise, has stated that the civil courts will not take jurisdiction to review an alleged irregularity in the action of a religious society in expelling a member where there is no question of an invasion of property rights.[46]

The communicants of a church, in one case, were forbidden by a religious society to associate religiously, socially, or financially with an expelled member.   The excommunicated individual had no right of action to have the ecclesiastical order rescinded.[47]   It has been judicially stated that if a congregation has removed officers or excluded members irregularly, the correction rests with the body of the membership of the church and not with the civil courts.[48]

In another instance the majority of those present at a regular meeting had required members to repledge their allegiance to the faith of Christ in order to retain their membership.   Failure to do so automatically resulted in a forfeiture of membership. Action by members of the society so expelled to restrain the

43. 54 *C. J.* 19.
44. *Nance v. Busby,* 91 Tenn. 218, 18 S. W. 874 (1891).
45. *Poynter v. Phelps,* 129 Ky. 381, 111 S. W. 699 (1908).
46. *Bouldin v. Alexander,* 15 Wall. 131, 21 L. Ed. 69 (1872).
47. *Kauffman v. Plank,* 214 Ill. App. 306 (1919).
48. *Sale v. First Regular Baptist Church of Mason City,* 62 Iowa 26 (1883).

corporation from interference with their attempted exercise of membership rights was dismissed. The court remarked that where no property rights were jeopardized no jurisdiction existed, even assuming the expulsion conflicted with church customs and usages.[49]

The abolition of a particular parish and the creation of a larger one from various smaller ones by the proper ecclesiastical authority will affect the status of a member of the parish. The member residing in the area will lose his membership in the first parish and become a member of the second parish. A member so affected cannot maintain an action to enforce alleged property rights in the first parish because his relation to the original parish had been dissolved.[50] Hence the members of a parish dismembered by a bishop in accordance with church law were no longer members of it and were without standing to maintain a legal action.[51]

Carried to its extreme, the doctrine of civil non-interference, in one situation, seemingly defeated the ends of justice. In Mississippi, one Mr. Dees, who had labored for years to build a church and had contributed nearly fourteen hundred dollars to complete the structure, incurred the dislike of a group of communicants. At a secret meeting he was excommunicated from the church by a vote of nine members out of a membership of fifty persons. Action was brought to nullify the sectarian excision. A judge refused jurisdiction and apologetically held: "The civil government must be free from all ecclesiastical interference, and the church of Jesus Christ, except in property rights, is not to be controlled by state authority. . . . If we had jurisdiction in matters ecclesiastical (and we thank God we have not), the order of excommunication in this painful case should be reversed and rescinded, for a more petty, unfair, and unjust

---

49. *Minton v. Leavell,* 297 S. W. 615 (1927).
50. See *Post v. Dougherty,* 326 Pa. 97, 191 Atl. 151 (1937).
51. *Canovara v. Brothers of the Order of Hermits,* 326 Pa. 76, 191 Atl. 140 (1937).

exhibition of religious tyranny can hardly be imagined."[52]   This injustice is the exception rather than the rule.

Some American jurists contend that the courts may intervene to determine whether the body which seeks to expel is constituted properly and has jurisdiction over the person excommunicated.[53]   In support of this theory it has been decided that although the civil courts will not review the exercise of discretion on the part of a superior ecclesiastical agency nor inquire to discover if the results are justified by the truth of a case, the court will inquire whether the organization's officers or tribunal had the power to act.[54]

In another case a minister who had committed a crime was suspended by a church agency.   After he believed that he had shown sufficient penitence he applied for reinstatement, which was denied.   Then he brought a suit for libel because of statements made in the finding of the agency's report.   A civil court ruled that the remarks in the report were qualifiedly privileged and that hence there was no ground for suit.   To the argument that the original order was invalid, the court replied that a secular tribunal would not undertake to determine whether the resolution of suspension was passed pursuant to church law except in so far as it was essential to do so in order to determine whether it was the proper church agency that had acted.[55]

Consequently courts have inquired to determine whether a church tribunal, which has undertaken to expel a member, has been organized in conformity with the church constitution and whether a member of such tribunal is disqualified under the rules of the church from sitting as a judge in the case.   These questions are not sectarian and within the exclusive jurisdiction

52. *Dees v. Moss Point Baptist Church,* 17 So. 1 (1895).
53. 54 *C. J.* 19, note 27; 23 *R. C. L.* 433-434.   So held in Massachusetts, Nebraska, Indiana, Washington, Kentucky, Tennessee, New York, Michigan, and in federal courts.
54. *Hendryx v. Peoples United Church,* 42 Wash. 336, 84 Pac. 1123 (1906); *S. S. & B. Live Poultry Corp. v. Kashruth Association,* 285 N. Y. S. 879, 158 Misc. 358 (1936); *Turbeville v. Morris,* 26 S. E. (2d) 821 (1943).
55. *Van Vliet v. Vander Naald,* 290 Mich. 365, 287 N. W. 564 (1939).

of the sect, despite the fact that the decisions of church courts, if properly constituted, will be binding on civil courts on all matters properly before them. Hence in a suit to enjoin an excommunicated clergyman from entering a religious structure to perform religious duties, and from hindering his successor in the performance of his duty, the evidence indicated that the ecclesiastical decree of excision was entered by a religious officer who was disqualified from acting as a judge under the rules of the sect. Because of the ecclesiastical irregularity, the plaintiff was unsuccessful in his action.[56]

The United States Supreme Court has ruled that it may inquire whether a resolution of expulsion was an act of the church or of persons who were not members of the church and who, consequently, had no right to excommunicate others. In one such excommunication case the action of a small minority of a church in the District of Columbia was designed to remove veteran trustees and a large number of church members from membership. Judicial investigation concluded that the minority action opposed the mandate of the church society and was, therefore, inoperative.[57]

If excommunication is linked with an infringement of a civil or property right,[58] the courts will intervene.[59] Even though ordinarily an excommunicated member has no such beneficial interest in the property of the organization as to entitle him to sue in relation thereto, expulsion accompanied by a fraudulent scheme to gain control of property will give secular authority jurisdiction.[60] When a fraudulent attempt was made to expel certain members, accompanied by a wrongful diversion of church property, a lower court denied the expelled members

56. *Bonacum v. Murphy*, 71 Neb. 463, 104 N. W. 180 (1904).
57. *Bouldin v. Alexander*, 15 Wall. 131, 21 L. Ed. 69 (1872).
58. 54 *C. J.* 19.
59. See, for example, *Poynter v. Phelps*, 129 Ky. 381, 111 S. W. 699 (1908).
60. *People v. German United Evangelical St. Stephens Church*, 53 N. Y. 103 (1873); *Thomas v. Lewis*, 224 Ky. 307, 6 S. W. (2d) 255 (1928).

a right to be heard. An appellate civil court reversed the lower court with the explanation of an implied obligation which existed among all members to treat each other fairly. Religious societies, the court stated, are largely based on faith in God and faith in each other. Raising the question whether a faction of a religious society may, by chicanery, deceit, and fraud, for selfish ends, divert the property of the society to a purpose foreign to the purposes of organization by the expulsion of members or in any other fraudulent manner, the court replied that neither law nor public policy will uphold the contention that such a situation is beyond the purview of the civil authority.[61]

Finality of ecclesiastical decisions involving property rights.— Recognition of the finality of ecclesiastical discretion has not been confined to cases where the exercise of discretion has been concerned with a strictly religious issue. In the absence of breach of trust, sectarian action has been upheld when it has directly or indirectly affected civil or property rights over which the civil courts have had control.[62]

The United States Supreme Court has specifically approved the doctrine of the finality of ecclesiastical jurisdiction as applied to the disposal of property in *Watson v. Jones.*[63] The case had its origin in the slavery issue. The General Assembly of the Presbyterian Church at its annual meeting in 1863 gave instructions to presbyteries that when any person from a Southern state should seek membership or apply for employment as a missionary or minister of the church, inquiry should be made as to his sentiments in regard to loyalty to the Federal Government. If

61. *Hendryx v. Peoples United Church*, 42 Wash. 336, 344, 84 Pac. 1123, 1126 (1906).
62. *Bouldin v. Alexander*, 15 Wall. 131, 21 L. Ed. 69 (1872); *Barton v. Fitzpatrick*, 187 Ala. 273, 65 So. 390 (1914); *Lutheran Trefoldighed Congregation v. St. Paul's English Evangelical Lutheran Congregation*, 159 Wisc. 56, 150 N. W. 190 (1914); *Fernstler v. Seibert*, 114 Pa. 196, 6 Atl. 165 (1886); *LeBlanc v. LeMaire*, 105 La. 539, 30 So. 135 (1900); *Tucker v. Paulk*, 148 Ga. 228, 96 S. E. 339 (1919); *Morris v. Featro*, 340 Pa. 354, 17 A. (2d) 403 (1941).
63. 13 Wall. 679, 20 L. Ed. 666 (1871).

he had aided the rebellion, or believed slavery was a divine institution, he was required to repent and forsake these sins before he could be received. This regulation was contrary to the church constitution prohibiting the intermeddling by the General Assembly into civil affairs. The Louisville presbytery split over the rule. The congregation of a particular church in the city became divided, and each asserted it was the church. Legal action with respect to the validity of the new rule and the ultimate disposal of certain church property ensued. The Kentucky Court of Appeals reversed a chancellory decision and held that whether the General Assembly had violated the constitution of the religious group was a matter on which the civil courts could properly pass. The anti-slavery resolutions of 1865 were declared void.[64]

When a subsequent phase of the litigation reached the United States Supreme Court that court took a contrary position. Speaking for the majority of the Court, Mr. Justice Miller classified the cases concerning property rights of religious societies (other than alleged breach of trust) which come before the civil courts as involving: (1) property held by an independent church society, or (2) property held by a subordinate body of a general church organization having supreme jurisdiction over the whole membership of that general organization. When the property is held by a religious congregation which, by nature of its organization, is strictly independent of other ecclesiastical associations and, so far as church government is concerned, owes no obligation to any higher authority, Mr. Justice Miller was of the opinion that "in such cases where there is a schism which leads to a separation into distinct and conflicting bodies, the rights of such bodies to the use of the property must be determined by the ordinary principles which govern voluntary associations. If the principle of government in such cases is that the majority rules, then the numerical majority of members must control the right to the use of the property. If

64. *Watson v. Avery*, 2 Bush (Ky.) 332 (1869).

there be within the congregation officers in whom are vested the powers of such control, then those who adhere to the acknowledged organism by which the body is governed are entitled to the use of the property. The minority in choosing to separate themselves into a distinct body, and refusing to recognize the authority of the governing body, can claim no rights in the property from the fact that they had once been members of the church or congregation."[65]

Where the religious congregation or ecclesiastical body holding the property is but a subordinate member of some general church organization in which there are superior ecclesiastical tribunals with ultimate power of control over the whole membership of that general organization, the Justice stated that "the rule of action which should govern the civil courts, founded in a broad and sound view of the relations of church and state under our system of laws, and supported by a preponderating weight of judicial authority is, that, whenever the questions of discipline, or of faith, or ecclesiastical rule, custom, or law have been decided by the highest of these church judicatories to which the matter has been carried, the legal tribunals must accept such decisions as final, and as binding on them, in their application to the case before them."[66]

In reality strict adherence to the doctrine expressed by Mr. Justice Miller meant that the property interest of a member of a religious society was completely under the domination of the appropriate church authority; there could be no appeal to a secular group.[67] However, the broad doctrine of the finality of sectarian discretion in the Watson case, while not technically overruled, has since been limited in practice. The origin of the judicial reasoning distinguishing Mr. Justice Miller's opinion dates from 1846. At that time, in an action to compel a trustee

65. *Watson v. Jones,* 13 Wall. 679, 725, 20 L. Ed. 666, 675 (1871).
66. *Ibid.,* p. 727.
67. Note, "Determination of Rights in Church Property" (1908) 13 *Columbia Law Review* 492-494.

to apply a fund to the purposes for which the trust was created, a New Jersey chancery court said that "the civil tribunal possesses no authority whatever to determine on ecclesiastical matters, on a question of heresy or as to what is orthodox, or unorthodox, in matters of belief. So the ecclesiastical tribunals have no authority, as recognized by law, to entertain any civil question, or in any manner effect a disposition of property by the decisions of their judicatories."[68] Here is judicial recognition of a modified theory of ecclesiastical supremacy, namely, that civil courts have jurisdiction in questions involving civil and property rights.

Two years after the Watson decision, in 1873, the Missouri Supreme Court followed the reasoning in the New Jersey chancery case and criticized the decision of the United States Supreme Court in *Watson v. Jones*. The controversy grew out of the action of the General Assembly of the Presbyterian Church in dissolving the Presbytery of St. Louis. Suit was brought for recovery of a church building, parsonage, and grounds. At the outset of the case Judge Adams of the Missouri Supreme Court noted the arguments that the judgment of ecclesiastical judicatories was final and that the civil courts had no authority except to register their decrees and carry them into execution. The judge regretted that the Supreme Court of the United States, in *Watson v. Jones*, had given prominence to these ideas by making them the chief foundation of its opinion. The theory of that decision, Judge Adams said, assumed that civil judges were not sufficiently learned in ecclesiastical law to pass on such questions, and that the ecclesiastical courts, being better qualified than the civil courts, ought to be allowed to be the exclusive judges.

The Missouri Supreme Court presumed the civil courts knew the law touching property rights; if questions of ecclesiastical law, connected with property rights, came before them, the civil

68. *Wilson v. Presby. Ch. of Johns Island,* 2 Rich. Eq. (N. J.) 192 (1846).

courts had no power to abdicate their own jurisdiction and transfer it to other tribunals. The court held that "the true ground why civil courts do not interfere with the decrees of ecclesiastical courts, where no property rights are involved, is not because such decrees are final and conclusive, but because they have no jurisdiction whatever in such matters, and cannot take cognizance of them at all, whether they have been adjudicated or not by those tribunals. This principle forms the foundation of religious liberty in Republican governments. The civil authorities have no power to pass or enforce laws abridging the freedom of the citizen in this regard, and, hence, in matters purely religious or ecclesiastical, the civil courts have no jurisdiction.

"A deposed minister or an excommunicated member of a church, cannot appeal to the civil courts for redress. They can look alone to their own judicatories for relief, and must abide the judgment of their highest courts as final and conclusive. But when property rights are concerned, the ecclesiastical courts have no power whatever to pass on them so as to bind the civil courts."[69]

In 1893 the United States Circuit Court for the Northern District of Ohio distinguished the Watson case in deciding a factional dispute. The extent to which the civil non-interference doctrine was narrowed is discernible in the words of the court: "Certainly, the effect of *Watson v. Jones* cannot be extended beyond the principle that a bona fide decision of the fundamental law of the church must be recognized as conclusive by civil courts. Clearly, it was not the intention of the court to recognize as legitimate the revolutionary action of a majority of a supreme judicatory, in fraud of the rights of a minority seeking to maintain the integrity of the original compact. This is the case stated by the bill, as I understand it, and such a case the language of Mr. Justice Miller in *Watson v. Jones* does not cover."[70]

69. *Watson v. Garvin*, 54 Mo. 353, 377 (1873).
70. *Brundage v. Deardorf*, 55 Fed. 839, 847 (C. C., 1893).

However, a District Court in 1913 relied upon the doctrine in the Watson case in deciding a controversy involving the question of property rights of religious societies having representative bodies vested with ecclesiastical control where questions of doctrine, discipline, ecclesiastical law, and church government were concerned. The court expressly rejected the Missouri opinion as inapplicable and ruled that the decision of the highest church tribunal of the organization would be accepted by the civil courts as conclusive.[71] Two years later in another case a Circuit Court of Appeals decided similarly.[72]

In a few instances decisions of the final church tribunal have been held to be persuasive on civil courts.[73] In some instances courts have expressly repudiated the doctrine that the decision of an ecclesiastical tribunal is conclusive in the disposal of property.[74] A federal court recently stated that a civil court will exercise equitable jurisdiction in a church controversy for the protection of property rights, the jurisdiction to adjudge an ecclesiastical matter resulting as a mere incident of the jurisdiction to determine the civil right.[75] The weight of judicial authority, nevertheless, holds that the decision of the religious tribunal will be accepted in matters of creed, teachings, and doctrine, and that property rights will be disposed of accordingly.[76]

Generally, then, the civil courts will not interfere with the will of religious societies, as expressed through the appropriate sectarian agency, in matters pertaining to the conduct of the temporal affairs of the society and to the disposal of its property for church purposes, unless the action is illegal or prohib-

71. *Barkley v. Hayes*, 208 Fed. 319 (D. C., 1913).

72. *Duvall v. Synod of Kansas of the Presbyterian Church*, 222 Fed. 669 (C. C. A., 1915).

73. See *Mack v. Kime*, 129 Ga. 1, 58 S. E. 184 (1906); 23 *R. C. L.* 450, note 8. So held in Georgia, Vermont, and Iowa.

74. 23 *R. C. L.* 450, note 9. So held in Indiana, Vermont, Michigan, Missouri, New Jersey, Pennsylvania, and Tennessee.

75. *First English Lutheran Church of Oklahoma City v. Evangelical Lutheran Synod of Kansas*, 135 F. (2d) 701 (C. C. A., 1943).

76. *Ibid.*, pp. 449, 450; *Gibson v. Trustees of Pencader Presbyterian Church in Pencader Hundred*, 20 A. (2d) 134 (1941).

ited by sectarian rules.[77] For example, after a church meeting at which charges against a pastor were not deemed sufficient cause for removal, a disgruntled group of twenty-two members asked that they be dismissed from church membership. Great dissention followed, and eventually one hundred and fifty complaining members met outside the church building and organized. After having been denied the use of the property belonging to the congregation, the dissenters brought a civil suit in order to be enabled to occupy the church property for a portion of the time. The court assumed jurisdiction with the statement that civil authority might protect church members against unconstitutional invasion of their civil rights whenever such invasion is attempted by a sectarian government. However, since the form of church organization here was the congregational type in which the majority rules, the court concluded that no secular appeal was permissible. The faction was not entitled to the use of the property any of the time.[78]

Members of a religious society, having a prelatical type of government in which the governing power resided in an archbishop, disagreed with the archbishop's order dismembering their parish and consolidating it with another parish. The members sought to maintain a bill in equity to obtain possession of the local church property, but a court decided they had no standing in court, since under the canons of the parent society the archbishop had the power to dismember a parish and his action was binding on the members. Though it touched directly on property rights within the jurisdiction of the secular courts, the church tribunal's decision must be accepted by the civil courts.[79]

77. See *Spenningsby v. Norwegian Lutheran Trinity Congregation*, 152 Minn. 164, 188 N. W. 217 (1922); *Petition of Presbytery of Philadelphia of Presbyterian Church in United States*, 347 Pa. 263, 32 A. (2d) 196 (1941); *Smith v. Board of Pensions of Methodist Church*, 54 F. Supp. 224 (D. C., 1944).

78. *Thomas v. Lewis*, 224 Ky. 307, 6 S. W. (2d) 255 (1928).

79. *Canovaro v. Brothers of the Order of Hermits*, 326 Pa. 76, 191 Atl. 140 (1937); *Mathia v. Holmes*, 134 N. J. Eq. 186, 34 A. (2d) 645 (1943); R. G. Connolly, "Control of Property" (1937) 4 *University of Pittsburgh Law Review* 76-80.

One of the most unique cases involving the finality of ecclesiastical rule affecting property rights arose in New York in 1936. In order to understand the case it is necessary to explain the Jewish dietary laws as they applied in this particular situation. One of the oldest Jewish laws pertains to food. Jewish dietary regulations are mandatory and are traditionally regarded as a cornerstone of the faith. The adjective "kosher" (noun, *kashruth*) denotes what may be eaten. Both the orthodox Jew and the rabbi have the duty to obey and enforce the principle of *kashruth*. Proper consideration to the selection of the proper food is prompted by hygienic principles and by mercy for humble animals. The selection, inspection and preparation of articles of food are especially scrutinized, as animals must be killed in a particular manner under rabbinic supervision. Inasmuch as the continuous attendance by any one rabbi at any one market is impossible, a delegation of certain duties to subordinate supervisors is made. The three officials, the rabbi, the supervisor, and the schochet (the person who performs the ritual slaughtering) are regarded as filling sacred offices.

In the New York case a series of meetings held in New York City at the request of fifty orthodox rabbis had been attended by rabbis, laymen, poultry men, and others for the purpose of discussing alleged abuses in the killing and the sale of poultry, the economic condition of the participants, and the need of reform. Further conferences had been conducted by a lay mediator appointed by the mayor of the city. After recommendations for an alleviation of the condition had been made by the mediator, the Rabbinical Board of Greater New York, the largest association of rabbis, issued a prohibitory decree. The decree provided (1) that a new official, the seal fixer, should be designated, (2) that the penalty for selling or buying poultry not slaughtered and sealed should be the prohibition of further participation in *schechita* (ritual slaughtering) of any kind, and (3) that non-conformists should be declared rebel sons. On the business side the decree was supported by a union of ritual slaughterers. A Jewish association was empowered by charter to enforce compliance with the state kosher laws[80] by the prosecution of offenders. A poultry corporation brought action against the association on a charge of conspiracy with the other two groups (the Rabbinical Board and the Slaughterers Union), not made parties to the suit, to interfere with the corporation's contractual rights. Specifically, the defendants had allegedly injured the corporation by obtaining religious edicts prohibiting the faithful among orthodox Jews from buying, and the plaintiff from selling, ritually killed fowl without an identification not required by Jewish law, namely, a seal. The relief sought was rescission of a contract and an injunction with incidental damages.

The defense of the association was that it was a rabbinical duty to safeguard the faith, that *schechita* had never been questioned, that since there existed the power to confiscate poultry sold in defiance of law, the price of one cent for a seal was permissible when it became necessary to provide a safeguard, and that there had been no protest at the time of the previous meetings. In answer to the allegation by the plaintiff that the defendant's actions constituted a monopoly, it was countered that one who enters the kosher business assumes certain obligations, that the association must be a monopoly in the hands of those best qualified to administer it, and that, by tradition, those individuals are the rabbis, whose decree is final.

The court ruled that unless there was shown to be a flagrant violation of Jewish law, the decision of the church judicatory was final. In instances of doubt the decisions of the church should receive great weight. The court explained that, had there been only one agency instead of two, all the acts complained of would clearly have resulted from the actions of a religious group. The fact that the enforcement and collection of the funds were carried on by a membership organization did not alter the situation. The poultry corporation depended upon

80. *New York Penal Law*, secs. 435, 435a, 435b.

the principle of *kashruth* for the success of its business. Further, it had defied the association on the theory that the latter had violated the Jewish law. The court denied the plaintiff's claim that the defendant's acts were not done in accordance with Jewish law; the plaintiff was entitled to no relief whatever. Even if the poultry corporation did not agree with the result, the court concluded, the alternative to compliance was the discontinuance of kosher sales.[81]

Temporalities not used in accordance with procedural rules of the society.—A civil court will interfere with sectarian practices to restrain a use of church property which is not in accordance with the procedural rules of the religious society.[82] Thus, according to the regulations of one sect, the election of a rector was not complete until ratified by the bishop of the diocese. When a situation arose in which this religious practice was not followed, the bishop was permitted to bring action to restrain a certain individual of a local congregation from acting in the capacity of rector.[83] The rule of another sect provided that the trustees of a local unit were bound to follow the directions of the congregation duly given in a parish meeting. When a central agency, of which the local church society was a member, attempted to adjudicate the use of a parsonage, a civil court assumed jurisdiction to decide that in a dispute between the central agency and the congregation over property the former must yield to the latter, according to the rules of the sect. The central body might intervene only on the allegation that the majority of the parish had violated the church constitution.[84]

A clergyman who continued to use a church structure to conduct services after he had been deposed was enjoined from

81. *S. S. & B. Live Poultry Corporation v. Kashruth Association,* 285 N. Y. S. 879, 158 Misc. 358 (1936); Note, "Review of Ecclesiastical Decisions by the Civil Courts" (1937) 46 *Yale Law Journal* 519-524.

82. 54 *C. J.* 70.

83. *Fiske v. Beaty,* 201 N. Y. S. 441, 206 App. Div. 349 (1923).

84. *Everett v. First Presbyterian Church,* 53 N. J. Eq. 500, 32 Atl. 747 (1895).

further use of the property because his exercise of spiritual authority in a church under the jurisdiction of a superior body contravened church rule.[85] On another occasion, a church law specified that every local parish was subordinate to a regional bishop, and that after election by the local group the officers of the parish must be confirmed by the bishop. The by-laws of a local church providing for the election of trustees and the appointment of a clergyman independent of regional approval were thus declared invalid. The court added that final decisions of the governing body of a general church organization, in so far as they pertain to religious affairs exclusively, are binding on local units.[86]

Religious activity contrary to civil law.—Regulatory legislation affecting the temporalities of a religious society may be sustained by the courts. In the case of actions of religious societies contrary to civil law, the courts have assumed jurisdiction to dispose of the property at issue.[87] Fraud committed for the purpose of obtaining possession of church buildings has furnished grounds for secular interference. For example, where certain members of a church society secretly and fraudulently changed the legal status of church property with the intention of acquiring ownership thereof, civil authority injected itself to correct the fraud thus perpetrated.[88]

Fraudulent dealings by Major J. Divine, under the banner of the Father Divine Peace Mission, caused a civil court to settle conflicting property claims. According to her affidavit, one Madame Brown became a follower of Father Divine and moved, with her husband and about twenty-five other devotees, into his Long Island "Home." She soon found herself "tingling with excitement and religious fervor and soon visioned the halo

85. *Tsenoff v. Nakoff*, 326 Pa. 549, 192 Atl. 873 (1937).
86. *Russian Serbian Holy Trinity Orthodox Church v. Kulik*, 202 Minn. 560, 279 N. W. 364 (1938).
87. 54 C. J. 91.
88. *Baptist Church v. Mt. Olive Missionary*, 92 Cal. App. 618, 268 Pac. 665 (1928).

around Father Divine, as did all the others." Ere long the Father began to question her about her money. To appease him she presented him with a bundle of sheets and a suit of clothes, which he took without comment. She was told by the Father that the sole way to eternal life was to give up everything for Father Divine, and a short time later she gave him a dining room suite, bedroom suite, and other expensive furniture and bedding. She was then informed by the Father that her sacrifices had caused her to arrive at a state of perfection, and as evidence of her promotion he permitted her to adopt a spiritual name, "Rebecca Grace." Later she gave the Father gold coins and cash, until the whole amount she had presented to him in goods and money totaled over four thousand four hundred dollars. After she realized that instead of having been deposited in his Heavenly Treasure the greater part of her money and property had been concealed and misappropriated, Madame Brown, alias "Rebecca Grace," brought proceedings to secure the appointment of a receiver for the rents and profits of the property of the Peace Mission so that she might recoup her losses.

In his affidavit the Father admitted he had received the money, but he maintained that he had not received it "as a person." The inference was that he had acted in a spiritual capacity. To that argument the court replied that a civil court operates only in the realm of a material universe and that when the Father spoke he spoke in his human form and capacity, as a person no different from any other earthly being. Whether he inspired faith and transcendent belief did not concern the court except as a factor in a description of what had occurred. Even though one witness stated that the food on the table in the "Heaven" seemed to multiply miraculously, the court said that it must ascertain only material facts in order to preserve legal rights. Inasmuch as the Peace Mission amounted to a voluntary association, it was not beyond the reach of the law. The court concluded that the activities of Father Divine constituted fraudulent action, not only because he took money by misrepresentation, but also because he used others as instruments to hold property purchased with such money. It was held that Madame Brown was entitled to recover.[89]

Failure of a religious society to comply with the requirements of a state law[90] imposing upon the trustees of a religious corporation a duty to post notice of the time and place of the annual corporate meeting has been held to be sufficient reason for vacating the election of the trustees chosen by the society. In a particular situation a religious society was incorporated in 1900. Under the articles of incorporation the management of the temporal affairs was vested in a board of six lay trustees elected by the church membership. Later a schism developed. During this latter time the business meetings were described as having been opened by prayer but "ended in such confusion and uproar that the police were often called to restore order." A new corporate certificate was taken out in 1913 vesting the management in a group of five trustees (the bishop of the diocese, the vicar-general of the diocese, the parish clergyman, and two persons elected from the congregation). The title to the property, however, remained in the 1900 corporation. From 1913 to 1932 the original corporation did not function; instead, the administrative pattern provided in the 1913 charter was followed. When internal differences developed within the church group again in 1932, an insurgent group, in opposition to the clergyman, attempted to revive the 1900 corporation, elected six trustees and claimed title to the property which had been administered by the five trustees. To complicate the situation, a second group of six trustees were elected, who favored the clergyman. A civil court was called upon to decide which group was entitled to the property. The court decided that because the notices of the meetings at which the various sets of trustees had been elected were defective, a new election must be held,

89. *Brown v. Father Divine,* 298 N. Y. S. 642, 163 Misc. 796 (1937).
90. *New York Religious Corporation Law,* sec. 194.

strictly according to law, for the election of trustees who would control the property.[91]

Summary.—The relationship of secular authority to sectarian rule is a matter of vital importance in the practical enjoyment of religious freedom. It is as necessary to permit religious societies to make and administer their religious rules as it is to allow civil government to legislate and execute laws for its constituents. The American judiciary has consistently refused to assume jurisdiction over purely religious controversies. Further, the civil courts have never questioned a decision of a church tribunal relating to doctrine, discipline, ecclesiastical law, or church government, in the absence of an interference with civil or property rights. In such matters, when the appropriate sectarian agency has spoken, its decision is beyond the reach of secular inquiry.

Depending upon the type of church organization, the courts will not permit a disgruntled minority to hamper the will of the majority or of the duly constituted membership. The doctrine of civil non-interference, however, assumes that the ecclesiastical decision has been reached by methods consonant with the regulations of the society.

Although there has been a lack of judicial agreement on the legal relation of the members of a religious society to the organization, the dominant judicial view holds that individual members voluntarily agree to conform to the regulations and authority of the society. Under this theory, a member, or even a clergyman, may be removed by proper sectarian procedure without recourse to the civil courts. Generally, the judiciary will not determine the validity of the judgment of a church tribunal expelling a member. Some jurists, however, believe that the civil courts may intervene to determine whether the church judicatory was properly constituted and had jurisdiction over the person excommunicated. When excommunication is

91. *Application of Kaminsky,* 295 N. Y. S. 989, 251 App. Div. 132 (1937).

allied with a denial of a civil or property right, the courts will intervene.

Courts have disagreed over the extent to which ecclesiastical adjudications are final where civil or property rights are involved. The United States Supreme Court in the notable case of *Watson v. Jones* decided that the property interest of a member of a religious society was completely under the domination of the appropriate church authority whenever questions of discipline, faith, or ecclesiastical rule or law were concerned. The rule of the Watson case has been both approved and repudiated since 1871. In a few instances, decisions of the church tribunal of last resort have been regarded by the civil judiciary as merely persuasive. In others, the Watson rule has been definitely rejected. Most courts, however, lean to the theory that the decisions of a church court in matters of creed, teachings, and doctrine are final and that property rights will be disposed of accordingly.

Civil courts will restrain the use of church property employed contrary to the rules of the religious society. Violations of regulatory legislation affecting the temporalities of a religious society may furnish grounds for civil jurisdiction. In case of actions of religious societies contrary to civil law, courts have assumed jurisdiction to decide title to property. The courts, however, are extremely reluctant to interfere with the decisions of religious societies which affect the property of those societies.

V

The Right of Religious Assembly

Legal status of the right of religious assembly.—A religious assembly is a meeting of people for the purpose of performing religious services or acts of adoration to the Supreme Being as an object of worship. At common law every man had a perfect right to worship God and to assemble and unite with others in the same act of worship as long as the equal rights of others were not violated. By permitting private action for damages, the common law protected the individual who was unjustly denied this right. Whenever the injury affected an indefinite number of people, the private injury was transformed into a public wrong and became an appropriate case for public prosecution. Disturbance of public worship, therefore, was an offense at common law.[1]

Even though this doctrine applied in England to the state-established church, laws were passed to protect dissenters in their worship. The theory prevailed that the assembly of the latter was otherwise illegal. In America all religious groups have been equally protected by law. Each denomination has as perfect a right to be free from disturbance in its public worship as the established church in England had at common law.[2]

1. 18 *C. J.* 1389; S. D. Chamberlain, "Disturbing Religious Meetings" (1914) 20 *Case and Comment* 518-524.
2. *State v. Wright*, 41 Ark. 410 (1883); *United States v. Brooks*, 4 Cranch 427, 24 Fed. Cas. No. 14655 (C. C., 1834).

All American states have passed statutes which protect the exercise of the right to assemble for religious purposes. The legislative regulations vary widely both in description and in application to a particular state. In size the statutes vary from a short sentence to a half page; in punishment they range in fines from seven dollars to five hundred dollars and in imprisonment from ten days to one year. Six states have no statutes which deal especially with disturbance of religious meetings.[3] In these states religious meetings are covered by statutes which protect any lawful assembly against wilful disturbance. Eleven state laws prohibit the disturbance of religious assemblies and do not expressly require that the individual actions be wilfully done as a requisite for conviction.[4] Laws of twelve states are brief and specify that whoever interrupts or disturbs an assembly of people met for religious worship shall be punished.[5] Statutes in twelve other states are comparatively lengthy.[6] They prohibit any person from wilfully disturbing, interrupting, or disquieting an assembly of people met for religious worship by profane discourse, by rude and indecent behavior, or by making a noise either within a place of worship or near it, so as to disturb the assemblage. Legislation in seven states not only includes the prohibitions contained in the laws of the preceding group of twelve states but also bans certain businesses, such as shows and racing, within one mile of a religious meeting, obstructions on any highway within a similar distance, and the injury or destruction of the property of any worshiper.[7] Upon these and similar regulations the courts have based their interpretation. Desite the degree of legislative diversity, a broad

3. Arizona, Connecticut, Louisiana, Ohio, Washington, and West Virginia.

4. Arkansas, Colorado, Georgia, Illinois, Indiana, Kansas, North Carolina, New Hampshire, New Mexico, Nebraska, and Wyoming.

5. Delaware, Florida, Kentucky, Maryland, Massachusetts, Mississippi, Pennsylvania, Rhode Island, South Carolina, Texas, Virginia, and Wisconsin.

6. Alabama, California, Indiana, Iowa, Michigan, Missouri, Montana, New Jersey, Oregon, Tennessee, Vermont, and Utah.

7. Maine, Minnesota, Nevada, New York, North Dakota, Oklahoma, and South Dakota.

interpretation of the right of religious assembly has been judicially enunciated.[8]

A fundamental attribute of the right of religious assembly is equal protection to the religious views of all sects.[9] The particular set of religious beliefs entertained by persons assembled has no legal significance. Typical of decisions of American courts is the expression of the Oklahoma Criminal Court of Appeals to the effect that "in attempting to construe our statutes with reference to disturbing religious meetings and religious worship, we must remember that the crowning glory of American freedom is absolute religious liberty; and that every American has the unquestioned and untrammeled right to worship God according to the dictates of his own conscience, without let or hindrance from any person or from any source."[10] The law attempts neither to delimit the purposes of ecclesiastical gatherings nor to define methods of procedure. The fact is that the privilege of assembling cannot be suspended by any person, with or without pretense of authority, and that "the quiet of the body public demands that the religion which the citizens profess, and which it is supposed they would profess even against the laws of human institutions, may be safely professed, and sincerely exercised in public assemblies."[11]

The theory of religious assembly rests upon the assumption that all religion is founded upon the principle of diffusive benevolence towards one's fellow creatures; that its practice implies ministerial imparting of instruction in its doctrines upon points of faith and moral precepts; that the concept of practical religion cannot be separated from that of the assemblage of the members and clergy for communion of doctrine, of charity, and of worship.

8. Carl Zollman, "Disturbance of Religious Meetings in the American Law" (1915) 49 *American Law Review* 880-893.
9. 18 *C. J.* 1389.
10. *Cline v. State*, 9 Okla. Crim. App. 40, 43, 130 Pac. 510, 512 (1913).
11. *State v. Jasper*, 15 N. C. 323, 325 (1833); *Ashworth v. Brown*, 198 So. 135 (1940).

What constitutes a disturbance.—Disturbance consists of any conduct which, contrary to the customs of the particular meeting and group of worshipers assembled, interferes with the due process of the meeting or annoys the assembly. What constitutes an interruption of a religious assembly depends on the nature and character of the meeting. "Disturbed" has been judicially paraphrased as "agitated, hindered, roused from a state of repose, molested, interrupted, perplexed, disquieted, or turned aside or diverted from the object" for which the meeting is assembled.[12]

An unincorporated religious society is protected in the exercise of its right of assembly as well as an incorporated one. A group of denominations meeting together are guaranteed the right, even if the aggregate membership has no definite name. Men of different creeds may thus meet together to unite in public worship and, when so assembled, form a congregation legally protected.[13]

Courts rely on juries to determine whether the assemblage involved was a religious meeting or whether the conduct constituted a disturbance. In reaching a verdict the jury is guided by the evidence and proper instructions from the court. Court instructions to the jurors in such cases clarify the issues and incidentally furnish grounds for possible appeal.[14]

When assembly begins and ends.—The courts have been called upon to determine the time at which freedom from disturbance begins and terminates. Unless a statute provides otherwise, the general judicial rule is that protection from disturbance commences as soon as the members have assembled and continues until the assembly has ceased and the members have dispersed.[15]

12. *Richardson v. State,* 5 Tex. App. 47 (1880); 18 C. J. 1391.
13. 18 C. J. 1389; *State v. Stuth,* 11 Wash. 423, 39 Pac. 665 (1895); *Commonwealth v. Bearse,* 132 Mass. 542 (1882); *State v. Ringer,* 6 Blackf. (Ind.) 109 (1841).
14. *Walker v. State,* 103 Ark. 336, 146 S. W. 862 (1912); *Bloodsworth v. State,* 107 So. 321 (1926); 18 C. J. 1390.
15. 18 C. J. 1391.

The South Carolina Supreme Court generalized judicial practice with respect to the protection of religious worship by stating that individuals "have the right to convene on the church ground for that purpose, to enter the church, and engage in religious worship, and, after church, to disperse without being disturbed, made afraid, or annoyed by profanity, [or by] fighting on the part of any persons, who, by their conduct willfully and maliciously interrupt or disturb the congregation assembled for religious worship, either in convening for the purpose of religious worship, or while actually engaged therein, or in dispersing from the church or grounds of the church, after the congregation is dismissed. The congregation has the right to convene, worship, and disperse without malicious or willful interruption."[16] In that case the record showed that immediately after dismissal a situation was created which caused the congregation on the grounds to flee, alarmed and frightened, in various directions. The individual who was responsible for the commotion on church property while part of the congregation was still in the churchyard was found guilty of disturbing a religious assembly.

In accordance with the general rule, a man who at the conclusion of the morning service, and a short while before time for afternoon service, cursed another on the church grounds while church members were eating, created a disturbance. The court stated: "The congregation could properly be said, under the circumstances shown, to have recessed for the purpose of eating dinner between the times for regular services."[17] In Alabama an individual who cursed and swore on church grounds after the members had been dismissed and while part of the congregation still remained on the grounds was guilty of a disturbance.[18] The judiciary has held that the protection of religious assembly extended to the congregation so long as any of

16. *State v. Matheny*, 101 S. E. 661 (1919).
17. *Ellis v. State*, 10 Ala. App. 252, 65 So. 412 (1914).
18. *Kinney v. State*, 38 Ala. 224 (1862).

them were on the grounds, either before, during, or after the service.[19]

In another instance conviction for disturbance was sustained even though the congregation had been dismissed and the remaining members had assembled around an arbor to feed their animals and prepare their own dinners.[20] One who blew a tin horn at night on a camp meeting ground after religious worship had been concluded was found guilty of a disturbance. The court held that there was nothing either in the language or intent of the law to justify a statutory construction that the disturbance contemplated might occur only during divine service.[21]

Although protection may be extended as long as any part of the congregation remains, a statute may limit the protection so as to include the group only during its religious services.[22] Thus a Missouri court dismissed a charge of interference by one who used violent language in the churchyard while people were preparing to depart after services. The court held that after a minister dismissed a congregation it ceased to be a congregation meeting for religious purposes.[23] There must be a point of time when the purpose for which the individuals assembled is concluded; that time was deemed in this case to have been when the head of the congregation dismissed it.

Two contrasting decisions on the question of whether or not the prevention of a religious meeting constitutes a disturbance indicate differences of judicial viewpoint. In Georgia a woman stood in a church door and declared that "I am the truth, the way, and the light, and no one can enter here except through me." By force and violence she kept out of the church members who had assembled for worship. The Supreme Court of the state upheld her conviction for disturbing a religious assem-

---

19. *Love v. State*, 35 Tex. Crim. 27, 29 S. W. 790 (1895).
20. *Minter v. State*, 104 Ga. 743, 30 S. E. 989 (1898).
21. *Commonwealth v. Jennings*, 44 Va. 806 (1846).
22. 18 *C. J.* 1391.
23. *State v. Jones*, 53 Mo. 486 (1873).

bly. It stated that if a number of persons have lawfully assembled for worship, the fact that they failed to enter the church structure at which they have gathered, and that they departed therefrom without attempting to hold services, will not change the criminality of the action of a person who, by threatening and boisterous behavior, prevents the çarrying out of the religious purpose for which the congregation met.[24] Thus the protection was extended to begin as soon as members have assembled at the place of holding services. In Pennsylvania two men locked the church door and thus prevented members from gaining entrance. Contrary to the previous decision the court held that there could be no conviction for disturbance because the worshippers had not "assembled" within the meaning of the word as used in the statute.[25]

Persons who assembled at a church in response to a rumor that there would be preaching were held to constitute a congregation assembled for religious worship and were protected thereby from disturbance, even though the rumor was false. The evidence showed that it had been rumored around the neighborhood that there would be preaching at the church at a particular time. The preacher contradicted the rumor before the group assembled, but those who met had not been informed by the preacher and truthfully believed religious worship would take place. Individuals who disturbed the unauthorized meeting were judged guilty of violating the law.[26]

Place of assembly.—It is not necessary to consider only a group assembled in a church edifice, chapel, or meeting house. Legislatures and courts often widen the application of protection on the theory that it is the right of conscience and worship which is protected, not merely the church structure. The right of religious assembly, free from disturbance, has been upheld when

24. *Tanner v. State*, 126 Ga. 77, 54 S. E. 914 (1906).
25. *Commonwealth v. Underkoffer*, 11 Pa. Co. 589 (1892); Public Law 392 of Pennsylvania State Legislature, enacted March 31, 1860.
26. *Laird v. State*, 69 Tex. Crim. 553, 155 S. W. 260 (1913).

individuals met at a private house for religious reasons,[27] at a Sunday school,[28] near a bush arbor two hundred yards from a church,[29] and at a camp meeting.[30] In one instance misconduct at a Christmas tree celebration resulted in a conviction for disturbing a religious group. The record indicated that the crowd had assembled to celebrate the birth of Christ and that there had been a prayer and scriptural talk by a clergyman before the disturbing conduct occurred. The court reasoned that the exercises were intended as a celebration of the birth, life, death, and resurrection of the Lord and in commemoration of the beginning of the Christian era and therefore constituted a religious meeting.[31]

However, another indictment stated that a defendant had disturbed by profane discourse a group who had met for religious purposes at a street corner and had attempted to drive a horse and wagon through the crowd. The evidence was deemed insufficient to sustain a conviction, because the religious assembly afforded protection by the statute under consideration meant a meeting within a house of worship or a camp meeting, not a public gathering. A protective regulation was here interpreted to have no such scope as to set apart the streets of the city as places of religious worship.[32] But although the public square had not been dedicated for religious worship in this case, neither had all of the areas considered as protected in the previous illustrations.

Number protected.—The mere number of individuals gathered together does not determine whether the group forms a religious assembly to be protected.[33] It has been held that so long as there are only two or three gathered together to worship

27. *State v. Swink,* 20 N. C. 492 (1839).
28. *Martin v. State,* 65 Tenn. 234 (1873); *State v. Branner,* 149 N. C. 559, 63 S. E. 169 (1908).
29. *Minter v. State,* 104 Ga. 743, 30 S. E. 989 (1898).
30. *Meyers v. Baker,* 120 Ill. 567, 12 N. E. 79 (1887).
31. *Stafford v. State,* 154 Ala. 71, 45 So. 673 (1908).
32. *State v. Schieneman,* 64 Mo. 386 (1877).
33. 18 C. J. 1389.

according to the dictates of their conscience, the law casts its mantle of security around them and protects them from all interruption. In no circumstance will religious worship "be left at the mercy or discretion of a mob, which is always worse than the laws of a tyrant."[34]

The molestation need not necessarily involve the whole group assembled.[35] The right of assembly is guaranteed to every individual separately, so that relief will be granted if even one person is disturbed.[36] Every individual worshiper may thus be protected throughout the public worship. The protection envisaged by law would amount to little benefit if the congregation might, through each of the members composing it, be disturbed. According to this principle, talking loudly in such a way as to disturb a communicant is grounds for conviction.[37]

Freedom from interruption applies to the clergyman as well as to the church membership. Such freedom has been guaranteed to a church official even though he has temporarily left a religious assembly. In Mississippi, improper language was used by an individual when a deacon was soliciting a collection from among bystanders on the grounds outside a church building while a collection was being taken up inside. Upholding a conviction for disturbance, the court noted that the taking up of a collection was a part of religious worship. The opinion admitted that every member of the congregation was not disturbed, but insisted that persons like the deacon might withdraw from a religious meeting for a temporary purpose without losing the guarantee of protection.[38]

Wilful intent.—One of the important elements which the courts frequently seek to discover in a case of alleged disturbance is the presence or lack of "wilful intent." Many actions which

34. *Commonwealth v. Sigman*, 3 Pa. L. J. 252, 264 (1844).
35. 18 *C. J.* 1391. See J. M. Jarrett and V. A. Mund, "The Right of Assembly" (1931) 9 *New York University Law Quarterly Review* 18-25.
36. *Walker v. State*, 103 Ark. 336, 146 S. W. 862 (1912).
37. *Cockreham v. State*, 26 Tenn. 11 (1846).
38. *Stovall v. State*, 163 So. 504 (1935).

otherwise would be considered illegal become unpunishable in the absence of malice.[39] The Texas Court of Appeals stated the rule as follows: "The act which causes the disturbance must be wilfully done—that is, willingly, designedly, purposely, obstinately, or stubbornly done."[40] And in Alabama, "such interruption or disturbance must be willfully made by the person or persons accused. The intent of the party or parties is of the very essence of the offense, and to be willful, it must be something more than mischievous—it must be in its character vicious and immoral."[41] Thus evidence tending to show wilfulness on the part of the defendant in the commission of the alleged disturbance is relevant.

While the conduct of the accused must have been actuated by malice, it has been decided that it is not essential that the accused have the specific intent to disturb the congregation in order to constitute an offense. If the natural tendency of an act is to disturb a meeting, and it does in fact disturb it, an intention to disturb may not be a necessary factor in the crime. The fact that the act itself was done intentionally may be sufficient to sustain conviction, since the law may presume the intention was to disturb the meeting. This presumption cannot be rebutted by proof of a secret intention not to interrupt. In other words, if a defendant's manner was calculated to insult or interrupt a congregation, and what he did was maliciously done, he is guilty whether or not he specifically intended to disturb the group.[42]

The element of wilfulness was found in a situation where bad feeling existed between a defendant and another member of the church. Evidence that the defendant had said "I am going

39. 18 *C. J.* 1394, note 94. Courts have emphasized "wilfulness" in Alabama, Iowa, Kentucky, Massachusetts, Missouri, New York, Tennessee, and Texas.

40. *Richardson v. State*, 5 Tex. App. 47, 48 (1880).

41. *Brown v. State*, 46 Ala. 175, 183 (1871).

42. 18 *C. J.* 1394, notes 86, 89. Convictions were upheld where there was no specific "intent" in Alabama, Georgia, North Carolina, South Carolina, Tennessee, Texas, and Washington.

to stay here until I get satisfaction" was held to be indicative of wilful intent.[43]

In another instance, a defendant asked and received permission to make a statement before the congregation. He then requested that his stepdaughter be excused from the baptismal ceremony to be held that evening. Receiving no satisfactory answer, he later interrupted the religious meeting without permission to state that he would hold the congregation responsible for murder if his stepdaughter died from the baptism. He further commented: "As long as you pray and go on like this, you are making your way to hell as fast as you can." At this remark some women fainted. The defendant then made motions which were interpreted by some members to mean that the defendant was looking for a club. On trial for disturbance of a religious assembly, the defendant argued that what he did was as mildly done as he could do it, that instead of allegedly looking for a club he sought his hat, and that he wanted to protect the health of his stepdaughter, who had had heart trouble three times previously. Even on appeal his conviction was upheld upon the doctrine that his manner disquieted the church.[44]

On the other hand, a taxpayer complained that a preacher on a street corner was attracting a group which obstructed the traffic on the street. The mayor personally went to the scene and suggested to the preacher either that the latter should disband the congregation or that he should take it to the courthouse yard, where such impromptu religious gatherings were customarily held. A few minutes later, upon finding the condition unchanged, the mayor took the preacher by the arm and escorted him to the courthouse yard. At the same time the mayor reminded the clergyman that although his action made him liable for a fine he would not be subjected to it. Suit was later brought by sympathizers of the preacher against the mayor for disturbing religious worship (on the street corner). The court dis-

43. *Price v. State,* 107 Ala. 161, 18 So. 130 (1895).
44. *Walker v. State,* 103 Ark. 336, 146 S. W. 862 (1912).

missed the charges on two grounds: first, that the mayor had only prevented unlawful obstruction of the streets; and, second, that the mayor's actions were not done with the intent of embarrassing the preacher.[45]

In North Carolina a member at a religious service sang in such a maner as to disquiet the assembly. His singing was described as so peculiar that it produced mirth in one part of the congregation and indignation in another. His voice was heard at the end of each verse after the rest of the congregation had ceased. When he was reprimanded by fellow church members, he stated that he would worship God as he pleased and that singing was part of his religious duty. His character was above reproach. The solicitor (state's prosecuting attorney) admitted that the man was conscientiously participating in the meeting. He was not found guilty of disturbing the religious group because it was judged that he had no intention so to disturb. The court remarked that he was a proper subject for discipline by the church but not by the courts.[46] The presence or absence of "wilful intent" in a statute does not necessarily become determinative, inasmuch as the court of its own accord may raise the issue.

Disturber need not be in church.—In the majority of instances the person who commits the disturbance is not in the church or place of worship at the time. The locality of the offender at the time he disturbs the religious group is not usually the important factor.[47] Starting a riot forty feet from a church structure,[48] engaging in a fight within a few feet of the building in which people are assembled for religious worship,[49] and cursing at the church door[50]—all have been treated as violations of the right of religious assembly, since in each case the

45. *Woodward v. State*, 173 Ark. 906, 293 S. W. 1010 (1927).
46. *State v. Linkhaw*, 69 N. C. 214 (1873).
47. 18 *C. J.* 1393.
48. *State v. Jones*, 77 S. C. 385 (1907).
49. *Goulding v. State*, 82 Ala. 48 (1886).
50. *Holmes v. State*, 39 Tex. Crim. App. 231, 45 S. W. 487 (1898).

congregation was directly disturbed. A study of the cases reveals that the seriousness of the offense is not inversely proportional to the distance of the disturbance from the religious assembly.

Convictions have been judicially upheld where one beat on a tin can during religious services;[51] where one made unpleasant noises outside a church;[52] and where one fired a shot (not in self defense) in close proximity to a church where services were being conducted, thereby causing great commotion inside.[53] A defendant who looked through a church window with his face against the glass, grinned and winked at different persons in the congregation, and carried on a converastion outside until the noise broke up the meeting, was held guilty of a disturbance.[54] The throwing of a jug at a church window sufficiently interfered with the group assembled to justify a conviction.[55] Standing outside the church in an intoxicated condition and talking in a loud voice constituted ground for conviction.[56]

Causing animals to behave in an unusual manner near a church has frequently resulted in sentences for disturbance. A person who ran a mule at a gallop up to a place of worship was convicted,[57] as well as one who unhitched a shabby horse and drove it near a religious gathering with the intention of mortifying the owner.[58] Pouring carbon disulphide on a horse standing near a church, so that the church was disturbed when the horse made efforts to escape, was sufficient to contravene the protection afforded religion.[59]

An unusual instance of canine behavior occurred in Texas.

51. *Cantrell v. State*, 29 S. W. 42 (1895).
52. *Stewart v. State*, 31 Ga. 232 (1860).
53. *Moore v. State*, 135 So. 411 (1931); *Ball v. State*, 67 Miss. 358, 7 So. 353 (1889).
54. *State v. Simpson*, 297 S. W. 993 (1927).
55. *Laird v. State*, 69 Tex. Crim. 553, 155 S. W. 260 (1913).
56. *Holt v. State*, 186 S. E. 147 (1936).
57. *Hunter v. State*, 20 Ala. App. 152, 101 So. 100 (1924).
58. *Wyath v. State*, 56 Tex. Crim. 50, 119 S. W. 1147 (1909).
59. *Pigford v. State*, 16 Okla. Crim. 304, 74 S. W. 323 (1903).

While church services were in progress some boys conceived the idea of pouring liquid known as "hot drops" on a certain dog then within the congregation. The boys had no money to purchase the "hot drops"; however, an adult (defendant in the case) permitted the boys to obtain the fluid at a nearby store on his charge account. When the boys returned to the church from the store the adult told the boys not to put the "hot drops" on the dog until the services were completed. Then the adult left the scene. The boys, however, soon afterward, while services were being conducted, poured the "hot drops" on the dog. The animal immediately ran to the interior of the church, barking, yelping, and scraping himself on the floor of the church. He annoyed the congregation. In fact, a few women and children in attendance became so frightened that they jumped over church benches to avoid the helpless animal. After the circumstances were known, the adult defendant was tried for disturbance and convicted. Upon appeal the court commented that from the circumstances of the case the jury must have concluded that at the time the defendant permitted the boys to have the fluid he must have known of their intention of having entertainment at the expense of the congregation. The fact that the liquid was sent for while the services were in progress, coupled with the assumption that the dog could not be expected to stay after the services were over, was cited as further evidence of intent. The court further stated that the evidence was such that the jury could infer that the defendant expected the event to happen as soon as the boys received the "hot drops." Conviction was consequently upheld.[60]

A nineteenth-century New York case is particularly interesting in a review of the right of religious assembly. A congregation objected to the running of interurban street cars, which blew off steam and sounded warning noises in the neighborhood of the church during Sunday worship. Action was brought against the traction company by the congregation on the ground

60. *Winnard v. State*, 30 S. W. 555 (1895).

that a nuisance had been thereby created. The verdict favored the religious group, and an award of six cents was assessed against the street car company.[61]

In a North Carolina case a person who participated in a fight within thirty-five feet of a church was tried for disturbing the congregation. The jury found in a special verdict that the religious assembly was annoyed by some one (other than the defendant) who excitedly reported that there was a fight in progress. Because the disturbance itself was not the act of the defendant, nor necessarily the result of his actions, the charge was dismissed.[62] Shooting in self defense near a congregation has been deemed justifiable and consequently not a cause for conviction.[63]

Congregation member may be disturber.—Although the majority of the cases of religious disturbance involve individuals not affiliated with the sect disturbed, those guilty of annoyances may include members of the congregation.[64] It appears that whether a single member acts to disturb his colleagues illegally depends upon the rules and customs of the particular sect.

Interruption of services by an excommunicated member may result in a conviction. Thus when an expelled member continued to speak from his seat while a congregation was about to begin services and the minister had commanded him to stop, the individual was found guilty of a disturbance.[65] Judicial attitude toward disturbances arising out of factional disputes, which often involve excommunication of a losing faction, is typified by the remark that the right of religious assembly was never intended "to be used as a means of settling, by a criminal prosecution, the respective rights of contestants for the privilege

61. *First Baptist Church in Schenectady v. Schenectady & Troy Railroad Co.*, 5 Barb. (N. Y.) 79 (1848).
62. *State v. Kirby*, 108 N. C. 772, 12 S. E. 1045 (1891).
63. *Cummings v. State*, 8 Ga. App. 534, 69 S. E. 918 (1911); see also 13 *C. J.* 1395, note 12.
64. 18 *C. J.* 1396.
65. *State v. Ramsey*, 78 N. C. 448 (1877).

of carrying on divine worship at a particular time or in a particular house of worship."[66] It is thus considered beyond the power of the courts to adjudicate the respective rights of opposing claimants by such a criminal action.

Misbehavior sufficient to sustain a conviction has been varied. When one entered a Salvation Army meeting with a cigar in his mouth, wore a hat, and conducted himself in an ungentlemanly manner, he created a legal disturbance,[67] as did one who cracked and ate nuts during church services.[68] Interrupting the Lord's Supper,[69] and groaning during a service and offering to fight when corrected,[70] have been held to be punishable actions. One who wore a false mustache and excited laughter by getting out of his seat when the preacher called for mourners was guilty of disturbance.[71] At an open air religious meeting a person who placed one hand on the ground and pointed to the heavens in mockery during a prayer was convicted.[72]

At certain Christmas tree exercises a minister was interrupted by someone in the rear of the group who threw a pecan at him and by young men who created confusion. A fight among the young men resulted, and the disturbers were tried in court. The Court of Appeals commented that it would be difficult to imagine any action more highly calculated to injure the religious sentiments of a group assembled than the behavior of which the defendants were guilty. The court held that "to sustain the contention of counsel for appellants would be to make a burlesque of both religion and the law, and to place the most sacred emotions of the human heart at the mercy of brutality, ruffianism, and rowdyism."[73] Conviction was sustained.

A church official was convicted of a violation of the right of

66. *Woodal v. State*, 4 Ga. App. 783, 62 S. E. 485 (1908).
67. *Hull v. State*, 120 Ind. 153, 22 N. E. 117 (1889).
68. *Hunt v. State*, 3 Tex. App. 116 (1877).
69. *Hicks v. State*, 60 Ga. 464 (1878).
70. *Stewart v. State*, 31 Ga. 232 (1860).
71. *Williams v. State*, 83 Ala. 68, 3 So. 790 (1887).
72. *Chisholm v. State*, 32 Tex. Crim. 512, 24 S. W. 646 (1894).
73. *Cline v. State*, 9 Okla. Crim. App. 40, 43, 130 Pac. 510, 512 (1913).

peaceful assembly because he created a disturbance by exceeding his duty. He had a duty to notify a clergyman not to preach on a particular Sunday. In addition to so notifying the clergyman he hurled challenging threats at him. He proceeded further by snatching the preacher from the pulpit and said that if the preacher attempted to preach he would give him a whipping. Commotion resulted. The harmful action of the officer thereby became individual, not representative, because he exceeded his instructions. His conviction was upheld.[74] Conviction of a sexton who quarreled and distracted the attention of a congregation was judicially approved.[75] Official position apparently does not render one immune from the charge of disturbance.

Actions of a group of members of the congregation in preventing the holding of orderly worship has resulted in judicial intervention. One bill of complaint alleged that a group of members (1) pretended to teach a religious class and "hollowed out" in a loud and boisterous manner; (2) laughed, talked and made faces at others trying to teach or listen; (3) stalked up and down the aisle of the church when services began; (4) made great noises going in and out of church; (5) wrote in song books; (6) grimaced at the minister and the congregation; (7) sardonically laughed and grinned; (8) at the close of services, blocked aisles of the church; (9) called members names; (10) shook their fists in the face of the minister; (11) when singing was going on, pitched their voices a step higher or a step lower than the tune being carried; (12) sang another verse while other members sang the regular verse chosen by the leader; (13) changed the reading from "we" to "you"; and (14) wrote on the margin of song books such expressions as "ask Johnnie (referring to the minister) if he loves you and me." The defendants refused to desist although requested to do so. An injunction was granted to prevent the interferences described.[76]

74. *Coleman v. State*, 4 Ga. App. 786, 62 S. E. 487 (1908).
75. *Dorn v. State*, 4 Tex. App. 67 (1878).
76. *Davidson v. Church of Christ of Parrish*, 245 Ala. 203, 16 So. (2d) 179 (1943).

However, a member may, if permitted by usage, in a becoming manner and with good motives interrupt a minister to correct utterances at variance with established tenets. A proper exercise of these rights, though resulting in commotion, has been held not punishable in a criminal court. In one instance, in the middle of a sermon, a clergyman said that deacons, in conducting communion services, could rightfully pass a member whom they considered unworthy. A member of the congregation arose and declared: "You have no authority for what you are saying. You have already said too much." The member then turned his back to the pulpit, asked permission to speak, and after stating that no one could judge another, he referred to scripture to substantiate his point. During the interruption, the minister remained standing. Afterwards the latter finished his sermon and dismissed the congregation. In an action for disturbing a religious assembly, the court noted that the defendant member had made no gestures, that he had been sincere, and that no objection was registered when the member asked permission to speak. The defendant no doubt reasoned that silence on his part would imply consent to a practice which would deprive his fellow members of communion on the mere belief of a deacon, the court remarked. The utterance of the clergyman was contrary to church doctrine; the interruption did not violate the law.[77]

When the character of an individual is assailed in a religious assembly, the individual so harmed is not required to submit to inferences of guilt that might result from his silence. The individual has a right to maintain his innocence without being guilty of disturbing the assembly.[78] A clergyman of one faith protested vigorously when he and his sectarian group were denounced by the leader of a prayer meeting who was of another

77. *Gaddis v. State*, 105 Neb. 303, 180 N. W. 590 (1920).
78. *Lovett v. State*, 239 Pac. 274 (1925); *West v. State*, 105 Ark. 175, 150 S. W. 695 (1912); *Brown v. State*, 14 Ga. App. 21, 80 S. E. 26 (1913); *Cummings v. State*, 8 Ga. App. 534, 69 S. E. 918 (1911).

faith. The latter, after offering prayer and reading a chapter from the Bible, instead of commenting thereon, began verbally to abuse the visiting clergyman and his followers. The action of the minister in so defending himself was upheld[79] The fact remains that one may protect himself from personal abuse.

Removal of disturber.—Removal of a disturber from the church by sectarian officials is permissible.[80] The general rule is that if a person is guilty of disturbing a religious meeting and interrupting its decorum, application of such force as may be necessary to remove him is justifiable. Vestrymen, or even members of the congregation, may assist in the removal. Where a person refused to leave his seat, the clergyman and other members who attempted to remove him were judged not liable in an action for assault.[81]

The fact that a member who creates a disturbance is a lessee of a pew is no barrier to his removal from the church, by force, if necessary.[82] It has been judicially stated that a member may not use his pew as a place from which to interrogate the clergyman, quarrel with him, or in any way interrupt religious services or impede monetary collections taken up in a congregation assembled for religious worship. Thus, in New York, the removal from a church of a person who had risen in his pew and demanded an explanation of the clergyman's remarks was upheld. In this instance, the court said that what the lessee of a pew might do lawfully, others might do also; if other members had attempted to exercise the same privileges, the assembly might then have resembled anything but a meeting for religious purposes.[83]

Secondary religious purpose.—For meetings in which the religious purpose is secondary to some other purpose, the right to be free from disturbance may not exist. For example, pro-

79. *Jackson v. State,* 21 Ga. App. 779, 95 S. E. 302 (1918).
80. 54 *C. J.* 17-19.
81. *Commonwealth v. Sigman,* 3 Pa. L. J. 252 (1844).
82. 54 *C. J.* 86-87.
83. *Wall v. Lee,* 34 N. Y. 141 (1865).

tection was denied an assemblage professing some form of religious worship which had as its main objective instruction in the rendition of sacred music.[84] A New Hampshire court refused to extend the protection to a temperance camp meeting although the meeting was opened with a prayer.[85] It is a question for the jury to decide whether the assemblage has convened primarily for religious worship.

Usually business meetings of religious societies are assemblies, in the sense of possessing freedom from interruption. The prevailing opinion is predicated upon the theory that when persons attending a lawful meeting of any description conduct themselves in a manner lawful in itself but at variance with the purpose of the gathering and inconsistent with orderly procedure, a jury may decide whether the behavior constituted, in the circumstances, a breach of the peace.[86] Since business meetings concern activities in which the religious group has a vital interest, protection has usually been extended. Thus where a person on trial for certain offenses interrupted the religious business meeting by using violent language, he was guilty of disturbance.[87]

Commercial restrictions.—The judiciary usually upholds statutes prohibiting specific kinds of business within a certain area near a religious assembly.[88] In that they prevent overanxious vendors from taking advantage of those who gather together for religious ceremonies, such laws have been considered necessary for good order.[89] Camp meetings especially, which are held in the out-of-doors for periods of days in succession and are intended to influence those who are not regular

84. *Adair v. State,* 134 Ala. 183, 32 So. 326 (1901).
85. *State v. Norris,* 59 N. H. 536 (1880).
86. 18 *C. J.* 1390, notes 35, 36. Such business meetings have not been protected in Texas. *Wood v. State,* 11 Tex. A. 318 (1882). See *State v. Mancini,* 91 Vt. 507, 101 Atl. 581 (1917).
87. *Hollingsworth v. State,* 37 Tenn. 518 (1858).
88. 18 *C. J.* 1392, note 70. So held in Georgia, Illinois, Indiana, Massachusetts, New Hampshire, New Jersey, Pennsylvania, Rhode Island, and Tennessee.
89. *State v. Scheneman,* 64 Mo. 386 (1877); *Riggs v. State,* 75 Tenn. 475 (1881); *West v. State,* 28 Tenn. 66 (1848).

worshipers, are by nature more liable to interruption than the religious services of a regular congregation.

Usually no one is required to forego his regular business pursuits because of the presence of a religious meeting in the vicinity, but persons who seek to use their property in a particular way, and secure profits thereby because of the religious occasion, may be restricted. The legal right to confine the exercise of specific trades, such as selling provisions and refreshments at particular times and places, is based upon the police power. The protection of the meeting is an objective in which the public welfare is concerned.[90]

For example, a vendor at a temporary place of business sold articles within one mile of a religious gathering without a permit[91] and was convicted of a violation of an Indiana law.[92] A New Hampshire regulation[93] forbidding the selling of goods within two miles of a sectarian assembly was judicially approved with the declaration that "it [the law] is in aid of that provision of the Bill of Rights which guarantees to all the right of religious worship unmolested. It applies only while the assembly is convened for religious worship. Its object evidently was, to prevent a temporary and unusual traffic; to prevent an assemblage convened for religious worship being made the occasion for engaging in any special and unusual business that might disturb them in the enjoyment of their rights. This is within the police power of the state."[94] Courts have thus construed the intent of legislatures not as a desire to check legitimate business carried on within a specified distance from a meeting but rather as an attempt to guarantee to a lawfully assembled sect

90. *Commonwealth v. Bearse,* 132 Mass. 542 (1882).
91. *State v. Solomon,* 33 Ind. 450 (1870).
92. *Indiana Acts of 1865,* Spec. Sess. p. 201. An act of November 30, 1865, amended the original law entitled "An act for the better protection of religious meetings, etc.," passed March 3, 1859.
93. *New Hampshire Gen. Stats.,* chap. 255, sec. 9.
94. *State v. Cate,* 58 N. H. 240 (1878).

freedom from interference by passing vendors attracted by pecuniary motives.[95]

Summary.—Every religious society has a right to conduct its religious services free from disturbance. Although the statutory provisions protecting such assemblies vary among the several states, the courts have consistently adopted a broad interpretation of the law. The result has been a widening of the area of protection to the fullest possible extent.

A disturbance consists of any conduct which interferes with the orderly processes of the meeting. Assemblies of unincorporated religious societies are protected as well as those of incorporated bodies. It is a question for a jury to decide whether a particular assemblage is a religious meeting and whether the conduct at issue constituted a disturbance.

The courts have often been called upon to determine the time at which freedom from disturbance begins and ends. Usually, the protection of the law commences as soon as the group has assembled and continues until the group has left the site or has dispersed. Religious gatherings held at places other than in church structures may be under the protecting influences of the law. The interference need not involve the whole group assembled; freedom from disturbance is guaranteed to every individual separately. Relief may be granted even if only one member has been disturbed.

The presence or lack of wilful "intent" often receives judicial consideration. In some instances it has been decided, however, that proof of specific intent to disturb is not essential to conviction. If the natural tendency of an act is to disturb a meeting and it does in fact disturb it, an intention to disturb may not be a necessary element.

The location of the offender at the time he disturbs the religious group is not usually the important factor. A congregation member may be a disturber as well as an individual not

95. *Neely v. State,* 20 Ga. App. 83, 92 S. E. 542 (1917).

on church property. Whether a single member acts in such a manner as to disturb his colleagues illegally depends upon the rules and customs of the particular sect. Removal of a disturber from the church building by sectarian officials is permissible.

The question whether a business meeting of a religious society is protected from disturbance is usually answered in the affirmative. Statutes banning specific kinds of business within a certain area near a religious assembly are upheld. In each instance, the courts have shown profound respect for religious assemblies.

VI

The Exemption of Church Property from Taxation

Development of the concept of tax exemption.—The exemption of church property from taxation in America may be traced to the fundamental relationship which existed between church and state in the colonial period. The church was an agency of the state, and for the state to tax its own instrumentalities was considered an unsound financial practice. The unwritten custom of church exemption preceded any legal formulation of the doctrine through constitutional or statutory provisions.[1]

A New Hampshire court declared that as long as towns provided for parochial affairs and levied taxes for the support of public worship, "those places of worship were exempt from taxation as public property by the nature of things, and not by the constitution or by statute."[2] When the practice of levying taxes for the support of public religious worship was discontinued, and the matter of public worship became a function of private religious societies organized for that purpose, the natural reason for exempting church property from taxation came to an end. The custom of exempting such property from any public burden continued, however, even though the houses of worship were not specifically described as tax-freed property by

1. Claude Stimson, "Exemption of Property from Taxation in the United States" (1934) 18 *Minnesota Law Review* 411-428.
2. *Franklin Street Society v. Manchester*, 60 N. H. 342, 349 (1880).

law. So long as the exemption was enjoyed, whether it was a constitutional right or a legislative privilege subject to repeal was not judicially considered in the early period. The exemption was so obviously proper and in harmony with public sentiment that it universally prevailed. One judge said that the courts probably would have approved the exemption, had the question formally arisen.[3] It is evident, therefore, that church meeting houses enjoyed a privilege not formally extended to them and that favorable public reaction enabled the right to endure, even after there had been a complete separation of church and state.

In later years courts have based justification for the exemption of church property from taxation upon the moral and social benefit which the whole community receives from churches.[4] The exemption is granted on the hypothesis that religious organizations are of benefit to society, that they promote the social and moral welfare, and that, to some extent, they are bearing burdens that would otherwise be imposed upon the public to be met by general taxation.[5] In discussing the reason for church immunity from taxation, one jurist remarked that by thus rendering homage to religion the legislatures have obeyed the almost universal, innate promptings of the human heart. Man has always made public acknowledgment of his dependence upon the Lord, he stated, and has deemed sacred the places in which he and his fellowmen seek the Lord's blessings.[6]

To the argument urged by counsel for early religious societies that the original enjoyment of the right constituted an inviolable contract, the courts answered that an exemption not founded on a grant in a constitution or on any contract in a charter or legislative act was not prescriptively established by

3. *State v. Collector*, 24 N. J. L. 108 (1853).
4. 61 C. J. 480.
5. *Young Men's Christian Association v. Douglas County*, 60 Neb. 642, 83 N. W. 924 (1900).
6. *Hornell v. Philadelphia*, 8 Phila. 280 (1870).

enjoyment, no matter how long continued.[7] "No prescription runs against the sovereign, nor does the state, by omission to use, waive or lose the right to exercise its supreme power, and the citizen can have no vested right in the continuance of any statute of general exemptions."[8] It was judicially admitted that an agreement by the state to exempt certain property rights from taxation may form a contract protected by the federal Constitution from impairment. In the instance of the non-taxability of religious institutions, however, no intention to relinquish the prerogatives of taxation was deemed to have been manifested.

The ascendancy of a judicial doctrine that property claimed to be exempt from taxation must come clearly within the provisions of a law granting such exemption threatened the continuance of the freedom of churches from taxation. Legislators and constitution writers decided to translate American custom into legal rules and therefore incorporated the right of exemption into formal documents. Such action became necessary as judicial determination in the nineteenth century made the affirmation of the right, either constitutionally or legislatively, a requisite for its enjoyment.[9]

Thirty-two of the state constitutions contain specific references to the exemption from taxation of property used for religious purposes. In fifteen of these thirty-two constitutions the exemption is mandatory. Ten of these fifteen constitutions state that property used *exclusively* for religious purposes shall be exempt from taxation.[10] The remaining five constitutions spec-

7. See cases in *Franklin Street Society v. Manchester*, 60 N. H. 342 (1880).

8. *Franklin Street Society v. Manchester*, 60 N. H. 342, 349 (1880).

9. 61 C. J. 480, note 89; 26 R. C. L. 323, note 20. This doctrine was especially emphasized in Massachusetts, New Hampshire, New York, and Pennsylvania.

10. Alabama (Art. IV, sec. 91), California (Art. XIII, sec. 1 1/2), Florida (Art. XVI, sec. 16), Kansas (Art. XI, sec. 1), North Dakota (Art. XI, sec. 176), Oklahoma (Art. X, sec. 6), South Dakota (Art. XI, sec. 6), Utah (Art. XIII, sec. 2), Virginia (Art. XIII, sec. 183), Wyoming (Art. XV, sec. 12).

ify that church property as such (without reference to exclusive use) shall be exempt.[11]

In sixteen of these thirty-two constitutions, the exemption is *optional* with the state legislatures. Nine of the sixteen constitutions give the legislators power to exempt from taxation property used for religious purposes.[12] In the remaining seven the legislatures may exempt such property if it is used exclusively for religious purposes.[13] In one state the exemption provision contains both a mandatory and an optional feature.[14]

Sixteen state constitutions have no specific reference to the exemption of property used for religious purposes.[15] In each case, however, there is legislative authorization or implied power to exempt property from taxation by general law. As an illustration the Delaware constitution provides: "All taxes shall be uniform upon the same class of subjects within the territorial limits of the authority levying the tax . . . but the General Assembly may by general laws exempt from taxation such property as in the opinion of the General Assembly will best promote the public welfare."[16] Pursuant to such provisions, the legislatures of the sixteen states have passed laws to confer the exemption under varying conditions.

An attempt was made in Iowa in 1877 to have the judiciary nullify such an exemption statute, passed without positive permissive authority, on the theory that exemption of church prop-

11. Arkansas (Art. XVI, sec. 5), Kentucky (sec. 170), Louisiana (Art. X, sec 4), Minnesota (Art. IX, sec. 1), New Mexico (Art. VIII, sec. 3).
12. Arizona (Art. IX, sec. 2), Georgia (Art. VII, sec. 2, par. 2), Indiana (Art. X, sec. 1), Nevada (Art. VIII, sec. 2), North Carolina (Art. V, sec. 5), New York (Art. XVI, sec. 1), Pennsylvania (Art IX, sec. 1a), South Carolina (Art. X, sec. 1), West Virginia (Art. X, sec. 1).
13. Illinois (Art. IX, sec. 3), Missouri (Art. X, sec. 6), Montana (Art. XII, sec. 2), Nebraska (Art. VIII, sec. 3), Ohio (Art. XII, sec. 2), Tennessee (Art. II, sec. 28), Texas (Art. VIII, sec. 2).
14. Colorado (Art. X, sec. 5).
15. Connecticut, Delaware, Idaho, Iowa, Maine, Maryland, Massachusetts, Michigan, Mississippi, New Hampshire, New Jersey, Oregon, Rhode Island, Vermont, Washington, Wisconsin.
16. Delaware (Art. VIII, sec. 1).

erty from taxation had the effect of compelling a contribution to churches, contrary to the Iowa constitution.[17] The Iowa Supreme Court decided that the constitutional prohibition nullifying compulsory support extended only to the levying of tithes, taxes, or other rates for church purposes.[18] The implication remains that the courts will uphold legislative exemption, even though there may be no constitutional provision.

In one state, Vermont, the constitution impliedly enables the legislature to exempt religious property. The provision states: "All religious societies, or bodies of men that may be united or incorporated for the advancement of religion and learning, or for other pious and charitable purposes, shall be encouraged and protected in the enjoyment of the privileges, immunities and estates which they in justice ought to enjoy, under such regulations as the General Assembly of this state shall direct."[19] Subsequently the Vermont Supreme Court, in determining the applicability of a law[20] exempting from taxation land improved for "pious and charitable" uses, gave an historical sketch of the constitutional provision cited above and even exempted certain funds of a religious society from taxation.[21]

It is significant that the exemption of religious property from taxation in each state now rests upon a constitutional or statutory basis.[22] The similarity of the exemption provisions lies in the uniformity of their application to all denominations. Judicial discretion has been circumscribed by a variety of constitutional and statutory provisions. Nevertheless certain judicial principles are ascertainable.

Strict construction.—The American judiciary favors a strict construction of the exemption privilege. The United States

17. *Constitution of Iowa*, Art. I, sec. 3, which forbids the compelling of any person to pay taxes for building or repairing places of worship.
18. *Trustees of Griswold College v. State*, 46 Iowa 275 (1877).
19. *Constitution of Vermont*, sec. 64.
20. *Vermont Statutes of 1825*, sec. 2.
21. *Congregational Society of Poultney v. Ashley*, 10 Vt. 241 (1838).
22. 26 *R. C. L.* 323.

Supreme Court has emphasized that the rule is that in claims for exemption from taxation under legislative authority the exemption must be plainly granted.[23] It cannot exist by implication. According to Judge Cooley, in questions of tax exemptions the law must not be enlarged but rather confined to the specific terms of the legal provision.[24] It was Mr. Chief Justice Marshall who stated the general rule to be that taxation must be levied equally upon all property within the state.[25] The burden devolves upon the individual or group seeking the exemption to bring themselves under the terms of the statutory or constitutional provisions. Should there be any doubt as to the property being properly exempt, the doubt is resolved in favor of the government.[26] The greater the amount of property which escapes from taxation, the heavier the burdens upon the remaining property owners to support the government. While this consideration alone should not prevent the courts from sanctioning a construction of constitutional and statutory provisions which will extend to religious groups the immunity legally guaranteed, public convenience and private justice require a careful examination of the law allegedly conferring the privilege.[27] Preference for a strict limitation of exemption rather than a broad construction is understandable, too, because otherwise the immunity may serve as a subterfuge to unscrupulous societies and corporations desiring to take unfair advantage of their status.

What exemption includes.—Once the judiciary decides that property is used for religious purposes and is therefore exempt, the exemption includes land reasonably necessary for convenient

23. *Chicago Theological Seminary v. Illinois,* 188 U. S. 662, 23 Sup. Ct. 386, 47 L. Ed. 641 (1903).

24. Thomas Cooley, *The General Principles of Constitutional Law in the United States* (3d ed.), p. 357.

25. *McCulloch v. Maryland,* 4 Wheat. 316, 4 L. Ed. 579 (1819).

26. *Trinity Methodist Episcopal Church v. San Antonio,* 201 S. W. 669 (1918).

27. *Church of the Holy Faith v. State Tax Commission,* 39 N. Mex. 403, 48 P. (2d) 777 (1935).

ingress and egress, light, air, and proper and decent ornamentation.[28] Land on which the exempt structure rests is automatically free from taxation. Land used for recreation by an adjoining seminary has also been declared exempt.[29]

In one instance a part of a church lot was used by the congregation free of charge for parking while the owners of the cars were attending church. In ruling the lot tax-free, the California District Court of Appeals remarked that the finding of the trial court that the property on which the parking space was maintained, which was immediately adjacent to the church, was necessary and required for the convenient use and operation of the building was the only conclusion the trial court could have reached.[30]

On the other hand, if land is not reasonably needed for the convenient enjoyment of exempted property, taxes may legally be levied.[31] Considering whether a portion of land adjoining a church should be taxed, since the land in question was used only as an entrance to the church, the Mississippi Supreme Court decided that the land in question was not used for religious purposes in any way except to the extent that the church maintained a plank walk on it. Because such use was too insignificant in comparison with the whole property, the disputed portion was legally taxable.[32]

In the District of Columbia a church building had been taken down and a new church with sufficient space for light and air had been built on other land within the same enclosure. Some of the land formerly used was no longer used after the new structure had been completed. The church corporation sought

28. 26 *R. C. L.* 324, note 5; 61 *C. J.* 486, note 96. So held in California, Illinois, Indiana, Iowa, Massachusetts, New Hampshire, New York, Ohio, Pennsylvania, and Texas.

29. *People v. Catholic Bishop*, 311 Ill. 11, 142 N. E. 520 (1924).

30. *Immanuel Presbyterian Church v. Payne*, 90 Cal. App. 176, 265 Pac. 547 (1928).

31. 26 *R. C. L.* 324, note 6; 61 *C. J.* 482, note 45. So held in District of Columbia, Massachusetts, and Mississippi.

32. *Enochs v. Jackson*, 144 Miss. 360, 109 So. 864 (1926).

exemption from taxation on all of the enclosed lot. Denying the privilege of tax exemption for the whole church lot, the United States Supreme Court announced that "land which is neither actually occupied for a church building, nor reasonably needed and actually used for the convenient enjoyment of the building as a church, is not exempt from taxation, whether it is used for any other purpose or not."[33] The point to be emphasized here is that the interpretation renders extraneous land taxable, even though it is not put to commercial use. The application of court discretion in limiting the extent of taxless property is significant.

When exemption begins.—When ownership is the legal test of exemption, freedom from taxation begins when title is transferred to the religious group. When constitutional or statutory provisions require occupation by a religious institution as a prerequisite to tax exemption, exemptions begin when the property is so occupied. In cases where the physical use of the property by a religious society has not yet begun, although title has passed, three elements are judicially analyzed in deciding when in point of time the exemption commences. These are the location of the property with reference to buildings in which the institution already carries on its activities, the present need of the institution for the use of the property, and the bona fide intention to make use of the property in the near future.

When a religious society has obtained a lot for the erection of a church and is prosecuting the erection of the building the plot may be tax-free.[34] Liberal interpretation holds that exemption should not be so strictly construed that a religious society, to enjoy it, must have sufficient funds on hand to proceed at once to construct all of the needed church buildings as soon as the site is obtained.

In one case, after the land was procured, an architect was

33. *Gibbons v. District of Columbia*, 116 U. S. 404, 6 Sup. Ct. 427, 29 L. Ed. 680 (1886).
34. 61 *C. J.* 483; 26 *R. C. L.* 324.

hired to draw up plans for a new structure. Construction work on the building was not actually commenced, however, until four years later. Suit was brought over the collection of taxes accruing during the four-year period of inactivity in construction. The court ruled that as the church corporation had purchased the property in good faith and intended to build a church within a reasonable time, exemption began from the time the architect was employed. The fact that a small incidental amount of money was received as rent for the use of the land before actual building operations began was immaterial.[35]

A modification of the judicial concept of when exemption begins was made in 1935 in Colorado. A religious group had purchased a $25,000 piece of property as a site for a new church. After a nineteen-room house and ten garages had been removed, as prerequisite to beginning actual construction of the religious edifice, the building program was suspended because the financial condition of the church had become impaired. The city then assessed the property and sought to collect taxes. The Colorado court took judicial notice of the economic depression, with its consequent harm to the building plans, and declared the undeveloped church property tax free. The broadness of the decision is revealed in the statement that "the church organiza-tion having no objectives other than religious, charitable, and educational, under the rule we have applied, is entitled to the benefit of the presumption that when the building is completed it will be used exclusively for religious purposes."[36]

On the other hand, exemption has been denied when actual construction had not been begun.[37] Mere plans of construction in such instances are insufficient. In Massachusetts a religious

35. *State v. Second Church of Christ, Scientist*, 185 Minn. 242, 240 N. W. 532 (1932).

36. *McGlone v. First Baptist Church of Denver*, 97 Colo. 427, 433, 50 P. (2d) 547, 549 (1935). See W. D. E., "Current Decisions" (1934) 6 *Rocky Mountain Law Review* 293-296.

37. 61 *C. J.* 485. So held in Louisiana, Massachusetts, Ohio, and Pennsylvania.

society bought a lot upon which to construct a large stone church. Plans for the new building had been prepared but, due to a lack of funds, work was not begun for two years. Meanwhile on one side of the site a small wooden church was built and used. During the two years before beginning construction on the stone church, the local assessors taxed one-half the lot, after exempting the wooden building and its surrounding land. The tax was judicially upheld on the theory that the whole lot was not needed for the small wooden church.[38]

Property acquired for indefinite future use or in anticipation of an increase in population has been held taxable. Argument of counsel for a religious sect that it was advisable for a church to have ground for improvements in the event that the city should increase in size was met by judicial declaration that nothing prevented the owner (the religious society) from abandoning the land at will. After a period during which no taxes might be levied the church society might convert the land into business property or sell it advantageously to a private purchaser. In that event the potestative dedication would inure unfairly to the religious society, the court reasoned. Because the undeveloped property had been held for ten years, the court concluded that the vague religious purpose was not any nearer fruition than at the time the land was purchased.[39]

Exemption ceases when the church building is abandoned.[40] Exemption cannot be claimed as to premises wholly vacant and unoccupied.[41] A change from the religious motive may provide adequate cause for the assessment of property. However, the mere fact that a religious society has contracted to sell its church building may not render the structure taxable.

In one instance exempt land belonging to a religious society was platted and subdivided into city lots with the intention of

38. *All Saints Parish v. Brookline*, 178 Mass. 404, 59 N. E. 1003 (1901).
39. *Enaut v. McGuire*, 36 La. Ann. 804 (1884).
40. 61 *C. J.* 485, notes 85, 86; 26 *R. C. L.* 324, note 10. So held in California, Massachusetts, Pennsylvania, and in federal courts.
41. *State v. Richardson*, 197 Wisc. 390, 222 N. W. 222 (1928).

future sale. Gravel had been placed on the streets of the subdivision and curbing and gutters laid. Meanwhile the society continued to use the land in connection with its program. An action to assess the land because of the development operations was brought on the theory that these operations transformed the religious use of the land. The religious society maintained that the lots were still used in connection with the religious work. The court upheld the exemption with the statement that it was the present use to which the land was put, not the disposition which was intended in the future, which determined the liability for taxes.[42]

Exclusive use.—In some jurisdictions, by virtue of constitutional and statutory provisions, courts specify that the religious use to which the property is put must be exclusive in order to warrant exemption from taxation.[43] In such cases dominant use cannot be substituted for exclusiveness. In one situation, although an estimated eighty-five per cent of the property was utilized for religious purposes, the owner was liable for taxes on the whole structure because the statute[44] required an exclusive religious use for exemption.[45]

An intention to use a part or all of the property in the future for direct religious purposes which would exempt it when so used is not considered a present exclusive use as contemplated by particular legal provisions. Thus, "an occupation which is to be—though here it is only which may be—is no present use. Nor is ownership evidence of use. Full possession and perfect title are consistent with total failure to use."[46] The possibility of a modification of the religious intention precludes judicial reliance upon the future.

42. *Chandler v. Executive Committee on Education, Synod of Presbyterian Church,* 165 Miss. 690, 146 So. 597 (1933).
43. 61 *C. J.* 484, note 71. So held in Illinois, Missouri, New York, Pennsylvania, Rhode Island, and Texas.
44. *Revised Statutes, Missouri* (1909), sec. 11335.
45. *State v. St. Louis Young Men's Christian Association,* 259 Mo. 233, 168 S. W. 589 (1914).
46. *Washburn College v. Commissioners,* 8 Kan. 344, 349 (1871).

There is a material difference between a building used exclusively for purely religious objectives and one used commercially in whole or in part where the proceeds are used exclusively for religious purposes. In jurisdictions upholding the exclusive use doctrine, the former situation falls under the legal exemption, while in the latter circumstance the property is taxable. Under this principle, a camp meeting association which leased a piece of ground for a private cottage lost its exemption.[47] A private dwelling donated to a religious college was not allowed to become tax-free since the house was not used exclusively for religious purposes.[48]

Property belonging to various branches of the Young Men's Christian Association has frequently been the subject of litigation in states where the exclusive doctrine prevails. The strict application of the doctrine to such buildings, a part of which are usually used for commercial purposes, results in the determination that the property is taxable. Hence a public hall owned by the Young Men's Christian Association and leased for entertainments was taxed, although the rents were applied to the activities of the organization.[49] A bowling alley in which the public could play for a fixed price and an auditorium in which occasional programs were given for a fee rendered the whole Young Men's Christian Association building taxable.[50] The general practice of the management of such a building to rent rooms to tenants for a profit was held inconsistent with the doctrine of exclusive use.[51] Judicial construction has denied exemption to barber shops, tailor shops, and other services for the general public in a building operated by the Young Men's

47. *Inhabitants of Foxcroft v. Straw*, 86 Me. 76, 29 Atl. 950 (1893).
48. *Stahl v. Kansas Educational Association*, 54 Kan. 1, 37 Pac. 135 (1894).
49. *People v. Sayles*, 53 N. Y. S. 67, 32 App. Div. 197 (1898).
50. *Young Men's Christian Association v. Paterson*, 61 N. J. L. 420, 39 Atl. 655 (1898).
51. *People v. Young Men's Christian Association*, 157 Ill. 403, 41 N. F 557 (1895).

Christian Association.[52]   In each of these instances the Association contended that profits from the commercial activities furthered the purposes of incorporation.

The operation in a building owned by the Young Men's Christian Association of a cafeteria in which the same kind of food was served and prices charged as at similar cafeterias in the neighborhood, and to which the public might go, raised the issue of the taxability of the whole property.   The defendant association not only pointed out that food was often given away to the needy but that the personnel of the association itself carried on the corporate activities in rooms in the same building. The court held that the test for tax exemption was not the number of good purposes to which the building might be put nor the amount of good derived by the general public from the carrying out of such purposes, but rather whether the property was used exclusively for educational, charitable, or religious purposes.   The building having been used for one or more commercial objectives, the association was deemed liable for taxes on the whole structure.[53]

In Texas a law was passed specifically exempting from taxation property of the Young Men's Christian Association "where property is used exclusively for furthering the interests of religious work and not for profit."[54]   A court declared the law void as contrary to the constitutional requisite of exclusiveness. The court held that the constitution did not permit exemption for furthering religious work but only for actual places of religious worship.[55]   Whether property is used exclusively for religious purposes has been held to be a question of degree, depending on the facts and circumstances of the individual case.[56]   In the

52. *Young Men's Christian Association v. Lancaster County,* 106 Neb. 1, 182 N. W. 593 (1921).

53. *State v. Gehner,* 320 Mo. 1172, 11 S. W. (2d) 30 (1928).

54. *Acts of Texas 33d Legislature,* chap. 81 (1913).

55. *City of San Antonio v. Young Men's Christian Association,* 285 S. W. 844 (1926).

56. *Congregation Gedulath Mordecai v. City of New York,* 238 N. Y. S. 525, 135 Misc. 823 (1930).

face of the allegation of city taxing officials that a certain piece of property was not used exclusively for religious purposes, but rather as a boarding house for persons who paid rentals, a court explained that the use of the corporate property for material rather than for spiritual purposes did not in and of itself deprive the corporation of its right to exemption. The use of the premises by workers and members of the corporation as a headquarters or as a resting place during the carrying out of religious work was considered by the court an inherent part of the work, necessarily following from the performance of duties incidental to the fulfillment of the corporate purposes. The nominal sum paid by the workers to defray expenses was held not to deprive the religious corporation of the right to tax exemption. The court emphasized that this was not a situation where rents and profits obtained from the use of the property for other than religious purposes were used for carrying on the religious work. If it had been, the opinion concluded, the exemption would have been lost.[57]

Property may be exclusively used for religious purposes within the legal requirements despite an incidental use of a sectarian nature.[58] The housing of a janitor has been permitted in a tax-exempt building,[59] as well as the irregular or occasional use of a church building for worldly purposes, such as for entertainment[60] or for schooling.[61] The housing of hired help in an annex to the buildings of a missionary society did not take away from the annex the exclusiveness of its user for the purposes of the religious organization. The court pointed out that no in-

57. *Syracuse Center of Jehovah's Witnesses v. City of Syracuse,* 297 N. Y. S. 587, 163 Misc., 535 (1937).

58. Note, "Tax Exemptions—Charitable Institutions" (1926) 10 *Minnesota Law Review* 358-359; 61 *C. J.* 484, note 72. So held in Connecticut, Illinois, New York, and Rhode Island.

59. *Congregation Gedulath Mordecai v. City of New York,* 238 N. Y. S. 525, 135 Misc. 823 (1930).

60. *First Unitarian Society of Hartford v. Town of Hartford,* 66 Conn. 368, 34 Atl. 89 (1896).

61. *St. Mary's Church v. Tripp,* 14 R. I. 307 (1883).

come was derived from the land or building, and that the property was thus used exclusively for the purposes of the corporation.[62]

The theory of exclusiveness, however, may render the residence of a clergyman taxable. Such a dwelling house may not be considered as used exclusively for religious purposes, whether located within the church structure itself or adjoining the church building.[63] A tax on a residence owned by a church and occupied rent-free by a teacher of the church's parochial school was upheld in Illinois, even though the house was used frequently for religious tutoring. The court added that the fact that the property was owned by a religious organization or that it yielded no income was immaterial.[64] Under legal provisions placing exemption solely upon religious use of property, it is not necessary for the property to be owned by a religious society.[65]

Primary religious use.—In some cases the general principle of judicial construction is that the primary use to which property is put determines its taxability. If the primary use is one of religious worship, the courts in such cases will exempt the property from taxation.[66] Thus an incidental secular use will not affect the exemption of church property if the doctrine of primary religious use prevails. Where land owned by a religious society and used for college purposes was partly leased and partly planted, the Colorado Supreme Court decided that an exemption was still effective.[67] Property of a corporation, organized as nonsectarian for the purpose of fostering the religious activities of students on a university campus without regard to

62. *Board of Foreign Missions v. Board of Assessors*, 244 N. Y. 42, 154 N. E. 816 (1926).

63. *Congregation Gedulath Mordecai v. City of New York*, 238 N. Y. S. 525, 135 Misc. 823 (1930).

64. *St. John's Evangelical Lutheran Church v. Board of Appeals*, 191 N. E. 282 (1934).

65. 61 *C. J.* 482, note 48. So held in Alabama, Illinois, Kentucky, Nebraska, Ohio, Pennsylvania, and Vermont.

66. 61 *C. J.* 484, notes 65-67. So held in Illinois, New Hampshire, New Jersey, New York, Rhode Island.

67. *Kemp v. Pillar of Fire*, 94 Colo. 41, 27 P. (2d) 1036 (1933).

denominational affiliation, but under the auspices of a religious denomination, was adjudged tax-free.[68]

Under the doctrine of primary use rectories and parsonages have been exempted.[69] Under this doctrine the use of these dwellings has been considered appropriate for the objectives of the church. When certain religious organizations have a system of itinerant clergy, the frequent removal of the clergyman necessitates a system of domiciles. Judicial opinion has decreed that exempting these buildings is not an incentive to build up a class of property for the purpose of rendering it exempt from taxation. Such dwellings may not be used with a view to pecuniary profit.[70]

A very broad application of the primary use doctrine was made in New Hampshire in 1934. ·Property dedicated as a residence for superannuated clergymen was held exempt. The character of the religious use was not defeated by the limitation of occupancy at any given time to one beneficiary or by his occupancy without the religious society's immediate superintendence.[71]

Primary secular use.—Conversely, when property owned by a religious group is devoted primarily to a secular purpose, especially to an economic use, such as the establishment of a business, exemption generally ceases.[72] In such cases the claim of the complete application of the income to a religious purpose will not affect the taxable status of the property.

To illustrate, church-owned land rented for the purpose of stabling horses and for the use of cottagers was judged non-exempt.[73] A rooming house owned and rented by a religious

68. *Wesley Foundation v. King County*, 185 Wash. 12, 52 P. (2d) 1247 (1936).

69. 26 R. C. L. 325, note 13; 61 C. J. 484, note 66. So held in Iowa, New Hampshire, New York, Rhode Island, and South Dakota.

70. *Trustees of Griswold College v. State*, 46 Iowa 275 (1877).

71. *Trustees of New Hampshire Conference of Methodist Episcopal Church v. Sandown*, 87 N. H. 47, 173 Atl. 805 (1934).

72. 61 C. J. 484, note 64. So held in Connecticut, Illinois, Indiana, Iowa, Maine, Massachusetts, Minnesota, New Jersey, New York, North Carolina, Pennsylvania, and federal courts.

73. *Inhabitants of Foxcroft v. Piscataquis Valley Camp-Meeting Assn.*, 86 Me. 78, 29 Atl. 951 (1894).

corporation was held taxable.[74] Exemption was revoked when a dwelling house and lot owned and used by a church was rented to a third party.[75] Business property, controlled by trustees who under the terms of a will were to sell it, was deemed taxable, although a percentage of the proceeds was to be distributed to religious and charitable institutions.[76] Even when the rentals from a building owned by a religious society were used to pay off interest and debts on certain church property, the commercial use of the property made it taxable.[77]

When a dwelling house formerly occupied by a pastor was rented, constitutionally it ceased to be "church property," just as a house of worship ceases to be such if it is abandoned for that purpose and used for business purposes.[78] The stock of a church-operated book store, the proceeds from which were constantly reinvested in new goods, was held taxable, even though the net income was spent by the religious society to further its objectives. The court significantly reasoned that if the contentions of the church were legally correct, a religious society might enter the markets of trade and commerce, tax-free, in competition with business burdened by taxes. Theoretically, the court continued, a church society could thus own the controlling stock of a railroad, for example, and operate it tax-free. Judicial approval of the church's position might attribute to the legislature a motive of encouraging churches to become commercialized.[79]

Frequently residences of the clergy have been taxed on the theory that such dwellings are used primarily for secular purposes.[80] Evidence that a rector's library was in the parsonage,

74. *State v. Church of Advent*, 208 Ala. 632, 95 So. 3 (1923).
75. *Church of the Holy Faith v. State Tax Commission*, 39 N. M. 403, 48 P. (2d) 777 (1935); Clarence Tapscott, "Taxation—Exemption of Church Property" (1936) 15 *Oregon Law Review* 152-157.
76. *Latta v. Jenkins*, 200 N. C. 255, 156 S. E. 857 (1931).
77. *Fort Worth Baptist Church v. City of Fort Worth*, 17 S. W. (2d) 130 (1929).
78. *State v. Union Congregational Church*, 173 Minn. 40, 216 N. W. 326 (1927).
79. *Gunter v. Jackson*, 130 Miss. 637, 94 So. 844 (1923).
80. 61 *C. J.* 487, note 2. So held in Georgia, Illinois, Indiana, Kansas, Kentucky, Louisiana, Massachusetts, New Jersey, New York, Ohio, Pennsylvania, Rhode Island, Texas, and Washington.

that he prepared his religious work there, and that confirmation classes and vestry meetings were held there failed to change the taxable nature of the property.[81]   The proximity of the dwelling to the church has been held immaterial,[82] despite the fact that the church lot, without a dwelling, would have been tax-free.[83]

A farm given to the trustees of a church society for the purpose of maintaining a home for the aged was not exempt where the home was not located on the farm and the farm was rented for profit. Although the proceeds were devoted exclusively to the use of the home, the court reiterated the prevalent view, namely, that "it is the primary use to which the property is put which determines the question whether it is exempt from taxation. If it is devoted primarily to the religious or charitable purposes which exempt from taxation, an incidental use for another purpose will not destroy the exemption, but an incidental use for religious or charitable purposes of property whose primary use is for another purpose will not warrant exemption."[84]

A notable exception to the preceding rule occurred in Tennessee. There the Supreme Court of the State exempted from taxation a publishing house controlled by a religious society, where the entire income from the business inured to the benefit of superannuated clergy and their immediate relatives. The court thought that it was too narrow a view to hold that the direct, physical use of the property of a religious institution was essential to the exemption. The court stated that the members of the society could not subsist upon the publications, for they were neither food, clothing, nor shelter. Only by sale of publications could these necessaries be obtained. From the charter

81. *State, The Church of the Redeemer, Prosecutor v. Axtell,* 41 N. J. L. 117 (1879).

82. *Trustees of Methodist Church v. Ellis,* 38 Ind. 3 (1871).

83. *State, The Church of the Redeemer, Prosecutor v. Axtell,* 41 N. J. L. 117 (1879).

84. *People v. Jessamine Withers Home,* 312 Ill. 136, 139, 143 N. E. 414, 415 (1924).

of the publishing house it was clear to the court that the business was to be used as an arm of the church in the publication and distribution of periodicals and in support of its preachers.[85]

Social organizations approximating in some respects religious societies frequently claim exemption from taxation because of their alleged religious purposes. Their claims are denied by the courts if their religious motives are secondary. For example, the property of a social club, having incidental religious services, has been judged taxable.[86] In forcing a building owned by a fraternal order to remain on the tax lists, a jurist reiterated that an organization whose membership was partly based on social considerations was not entitled to exemption on religious grounds. The judge further held that the conception that, to be entitled to an exemption, a building devoted to religious uses must be a place of worship was implicit in the theory of religious exemption.[87]

The articles of incorporation of a college fraternity listed the purpose of incorporation as the promotion of the general moral, social, educational, and literary welfare of its members and the acquisition of a dormitory. The fraternity claimed exemption from taxation partially on the ground that the articles of incorporation bestowed on it a religious status. But a court replied that the predominant use of the property, not the declaration in the charter, determined the question of exemption. Exemption was denied.[88]

Doctrine of divisibility.—Occasionally the doctrine of divisibility of taxability is laid down by the courts.[89] By this doctrine,

85. *Methodist Episcopal Church v. Hinton,* 92 Tenn. 188, 21 S. W. 321 (1893); *Assessors of Boston v. Lamson,* 316 Mass. 166, 55 N. E. (2d) 215 (1944).
86. 61 *C. J.* 481, note 18. So held in Connecticut, Florida, Iowa, New York, and Wisconsin. See *University Club v. Lanier,* 119 Fla. 146, 161 So. 78 (1935).
87. *Masonic Building Association v. Town of Stamford,* 119 Conn. 53, 174 Atl. 301 (1934).
88. *Theta XI Building Association of Iowa City v. Board of Review,* 217 Iowa 1181, 251 N. W. 76 (1933).
89. 26 *R. C. L.* 324, note 4; 61 *C. J.* 485, note 77. So held in New York, Pennsylvania, Texas, Maine, and New Hampshire.

when one piece of property is logically divisible, and the part that is used for religious purposes can be separated distinctly from the part devoted to secular affairs, a property tax will be levied on the value of the portion of the property utilized for secular pursuits. The legal exemption is thereupon made applicable to the remainder.

The Pennsylvania Supreme Court sustained a ruling which divided a building according to the relative rental values of the floor space rented and allotted to others and that occupied by a Board of Home Missions and Church Extension of the Methodist Episcopal Church. The portion occupied by the mission was exempt, while the former part was taxed.[90]   In another case, where different floors of a building were used for sectarian and non-sectarian ends—specifically one floor for worship and the others for living quarters—taxation on the value of the part of the structure constituting the upper floors was upheld. The first floor devoted to religious worship was exempted.[91]   Where the ground floor of one church-owned building and part of the ground floor of another were rented for commercial purposes, the rented portions were declared taxable.[92]   In Maine, a building owned by the Young Men's Christian Association was taxed as to that part of the property used for commercial purposes.[93]

The doctrine of divisibility was applied with logical precision in a case involving the taxation of a tract of property belonging to a camp meeting association. Portions of a store building, dining hall, cookhouse, and toolhouse which were rented by the association to third persons were held not exempt. Water and electric systems used partly in the conduct of religious worship and partly for the convenience of tenants in the rented property

90. *Board of Home Missions v. City of Philadelphia*, 266 Pa. 405, 109 Atl. 664 (1920).
91. *Congregation Gedulath Mordecai v. City of New York*, 238 N. Y. S. 525, 135 Misc. 823 (1930).
92. *Fort Worth Baptist Church v. City of Fort Worth*, 17 S. W. (2d) 130 (1929).
93. *Auburn v. Young Men's Christian Association*, 86 Me. 244, 29 Atl. 992 (1894).

were exempt to the extent of their use for religious purposes. The caretaker's farmhouse was fully exempt.[94] In courts accepting the divisibility doctrine it is evident that the use factor alone determines the extent of the exemption.

Ownership as test.—In a few jurisdictions ownership is the criterion for the exemption of property from taxation, regardless of its character, extent, location, or the purposes for which the property is used.[95] The use made of the property is immaterial provided it is owned by a religious group. Legislation and constitutional provisions must clearly indicate the ownership test as sufficient; inference of such intent is not enough. Hence the New Mexico Supreme Court recently remarked: "If the framers of the Constitution had intended to depart entirely from use as a test and make ownership by religious institutions and societies the sole test of whether church property was exempt, they would have used words appropriate to manifest such intention."[96]

Application of this doctrine has been made to exempt realty owned by a religious group, even where surplus farm products were sold to the public. Under such an interpretation the fact that the proceeds from the products were applied to religious use was immaterial. The constitutional clause apropos the situation excluded from taxation all property owned by religious societies, regardless of its character, extent, location, or use.[97]

Leased land.—Land leased to a religious society for religious purposes may not be exempt. In Florida a building and lot leased by a business corporation to a church organization for religious purposes was held liable for taxation. To the contention of the owning corporation that the property was used for

94. *Hedding Camp Meeting v. Epping,* 88 N. H. 321, 189 Atl. 347 (1937).
95. 61 *C. J.* 482, note 49. So held in Illinois, Massachusetts, New York, North Carolina, South Dakota, and Wisconsin. See *In re Dakota Wesleyan University,* 48 S. D. 48, 202 N. W. 284 (1925).
96. *Church of the Holy Faith v. State Tax Commission,* 39 N. M. 403, 411, 48 P. (2d) 777, 782 (1935).
97. *Dakota Wesleyan University v. Betts,* 47 S. D. 618, 201 N. W. 524 (1924).

religious purposes and was therefore tax-free, the court replied that property held for rental purposes was not used exclusively for religious purposes within the meaning of the provisions of the constitution.[98]   In Kentucky a church society contracted to remain in possession of the structure and to pay rent until a new building was erected. Upholding the tax payable by the secular owner, the court remarked that when one let his property for rent, such use could not be claimed to be a use for religious worship.[99]

Similarly, under a statute[100] exempting property used for religious purposes, church property leased to another society engaged in religious work was not exempt, even though the rent was used to carry on the religious endeavors of the former sect. The court reasoned that when an owner leases property he parts with the possession and the use for a consideration. Under such circumstances, the owner holds the property for the purpose of receiving an income therefrom and his use becomes commercial. Property leased is not wholly used for religious purposes even though the rent received is expended for the furtherance of such purposes, the court declared. "To hold otherwise would permit of religious organizations being endowed with vast holdings of real estate consisting of business blocks and other large improved properties devoted to commercial uses, all of which would be exempted from taxation by the mere using of the revenue for the support of religious work."[101]

Private worship.—Generally the property must be devoted to public worship, as contrasted with private or individual devotions, in order to claim the exemption. Property given over to

98. *Jefferson Standard Life Insurance Co. v. City of Wildwood*, 118 Fla. 771, 160 So. 208 (1935).
99. *Commonwealth v. First Christian Church of Louisville*, 169 Ky. 410, 183 S. W. 943 (1916).
100. *Rem. Rev. Stats. of Washington*, sec. 11111.
101. *Norwegian Lutheran Church v. Wooster*, 176 Wash. 581, 590, 30 P. (2d) 381, 385 (1934).

the private worship of a sectarian order has been held taxable.[102] The private chapel of an orphan asylum which only the inmates might use for religious worship was judged to be not a building for public worship within the rule of exemption from taxation. Here religious services were periodically held, but no visitors were allowed except under pressing circumstances, and then only with the consent of the superintendent.[103]

In Pennsylvania over fifty acres of land devoted to individual meditation apart from a church was taxable. The retreat was maintained solely as a place of religious worship, where at stated periods during a part of the year, people attended for worship. The court excluded from the tax roll only that portion of a house devoted to a chapel and the land on which the Stations of the Cross were erected. The opinion significantly stated that "to come within the exempting clause, it must be an actual place of religious worship—which contemplates a place consecrated to religious worship, where people statedly join together, in some form of worship, and not merely individual communion with one's Maker apart from a church, meetinghouse, or some regular place of stated worship—otherwise anybody could claim exemption as to his individual property by using it for religious meditation at stated intervals."[104]

Recently in Connecticut the existence of a chapel in a house of retreat did not render the house a place of worship within the exemption. The latter term was held applicable to churches. Since the property was used by clergymen and laymen as a place of temporary sojourn, taxes were levied on the property.[105]

Liberal exemption provisions have been interpreted as excluding from taxation a structure in which religious services are

102. 61 *C. J.* 484, note 70. So held in Connecticut, Illinois, New York, and Pennsylvania. See especially *People v. Muldoon*, 306 Ill. 234, 137 N. E. 863 (1922).

103. *Association for Benefit of Colored Orphans v. Mayor, Aldermen and Commonalty of the City of New York*, 104 N. Y. 581, 12 N. E. 279 (1887).

104. *Layman's Weekend Retreat League v. Butler*, 83 Pa. Super. 1, 6 (1924).

105. *Woodstock v. Retreat*, 125 Conn. 52, 3 A. (2d) 232 (1938).

conducted only for the benefit of a religious order. The rules of one religious order required daily religious services and the attendance of the membership of the order for prayer in the building. Believing that it was not necessary for the religious services to be open to the public to enable the structure in which they were conducted to become entitled to exemption, a New York court emphasized that the important factor was the use of the building for religious purposes.[106] A contrary narrow view would render the property taxable in which the cloistered orders are housed and in which the members perform their religious duties.

Cemetery lands.—The cemetery lands of a religious society are generally exempt.[107] The exemption includes paths, ornamentation, and land within the cemetery limits acquired but not yet used for the burial of the dead. The exemption extends to contiguous land to be used for such purposes in the near future. In fact, in one case the court commented that the church officials showed good judgment in looking forward to future expansion.[108]

Land intended for cemetery purposes will not be exempt if used strictly for commercial purposes.[109] For example, where, out of forty acres allegedly held for cemetery purposes, only one acre was actually so utilized and the remaining acres were under cultivation, the latter portion of thirty-nine acres was judged taxable. While all of the land was church property, it was not devoted to the objects of the church.[110]

Special assessments.—Special assessments are payments for special benefits received whereas taxes are burdens, charges, or imposts placed on property for general public use. Church

106. *St. Barbara's Roman Catholic Church v. City of New York,* 277 N. Y. S. 538, 243 App. Div. 371 (1935).

107. 26 *R. C. L.* 325.

108. *St. Stanislaus Church Society v. Erie County,* 275 N. Y. S. 84, 153 Misc. 511 (1934).

109. 61 *C. J.* 491, notes 62-65. So held in California, Indiana, Iowa, Kentucky, and Pennsylvania.

110. *Mulroy v. Churchman,* 52 Iowa 238, 3 N. W. 72 (1879).

property forms no exception to the uniform application of special assessments.[111]   A general religious exemption does not apply to a special assessment unless the measure levying such an assessment specifically so provides.   No exemption is created by implication.   For example, a law[112] levied a charge against abutting church property amounting to two-thirds of the cost of improving a street.   Upholding the law, the court commented that the necessary statutory construction would not relieve property not assessed for general taxation from the special tax levied.[113]   Unless so specifically provided, exemption of property of religious institutions from taxation is only from taxation imposed for the general purposes of government and does not extend to taxation for local improvements.[114]

In another instance lots abutting newly paved streets and owned by church societies were assessed a proportionate amount of the cost.[115]   Upon application for exemption a sympathetic city administration offered to pay out of the city treasury the costs assessed against the church property.   Suit was then brought by a taxpayer to enjoin the mayor and aldermen from paying the money from public funds.   The court upheld the validity of the tax and nullified aldermanic action in attempting to circumvent the taxing provision.[116]   The rule of strict construction has resulted in the payment by a church corporation of a charge arising from local sewer improvements.   For an improvement beneficial to a particular local area, it has been held that the property benefited should bear the burden.[117]

A liberal interpretation of a special assessment provision[118]

111. Carl Zollman, "Tax Exemptions of American Church Property" (1916) 14 *Michigan Law Review* 646-657.
112. *Tennessee Acts of 1923*, chap. 18.
113. *Athens v. Dodson,* 154 Tenn. 469, 290 S. W. 36 (1926).
114. *Boston Seamen's Friend Society v. City of Boston,* 116 Mass. 181 (1875).
115. *Georgia Laws of 1919,* p. 1294.
116. *Savannah v. Richter,* 160 Ga. 177, 127 S. E. 140 (1925).
117. *Lockwood v. City of St. Louis,* 24 Mo. 20 (1856).
118. *Georgia Acts of 1880,* p. 359.

acted in favor of a Georgia church. The court held that it was not the intent of the legislature to make either public property or property held exclusively for religious worship subject to the assessment. The court inferred that the state constitution permitted a legislature to encourage religious instruction by exempting from taxation for the support of the state government places of religious worship.[119] Such an interpretation is contrary to general state practice.

Legislative policy assists the judiciary in deciding the legality of a tax levied on inheritances accruing to religious societies. It has been judicially pointed out that a church cannot accept such gifts tax-free without express state permission. An inheritance tax is not a property tax, but one upon the right of succession, a right created by the state. The state has given the privilege to the owner of the property to bequeath it and has given to religious societies the right of receiving legacies under the will of a testator. Clearly the state has the power to impose an excise tax upon such right.[120]

Summary.—The exemption of church property from taxation may be traced to the fundamental relationship which existed between church and state in the colonial period. Even after the complete separation of church and state religious societies continued to enjoy their privilege of tax exemption by custom. Later, courts emphasized the moral and social benefit inuring to the community as legal justification for church exemption. Gradually the exemption was written into state constitutions and statutory laws, until today every state has some provision for the exemption from taxation of property used for religious worship.

American courts favor a strict construction of the exemption privilege. Judicial interpretation confines the exemption to the specific terms of the constitution or statute. Freedom from

119. *First Methodist Episcopal Church v. City of Atlanta,* 76 Ga. 181 (1881).

120. *Leavell's Administrator v. Arnold,* 131 Ky. 426, 115 S. W. 232 (1909); *In re Rudge,* 114 Neb. 335, 207 N. W. 520 (1926); *Barrington v. Cowan,* 55 N. C. 436 (1856); 61 *C. J.* 489.

property taxation is judicially applied not only to the church structure itself but also to land reasonably necessary for convenient ingress and egress, light and air, and proper and decent ornamentation.

Where ownership is the test of exemption, the courts hold that freedom from property taxes begins when title is transferred to the religious society. When religious use is the criterion, exemption may begin when physical occupation by the religious society takes place. Under the criterion of religious use, the courts have exempted property not yet directly used by a congregation, after a consideration of the location of the property with reference to the buildings of the institution, the need for the property, and the bona fide intention of the society.

Some jurisdictions demand as an essential of tax exemption that the religious use be exclusive. Other courts consider a primary religious use as sufficient. Usually property devoted to a primary secular use is taxable, even though the income from the secular use be devoted to religious purposes. Occasionally a court will apply the doctrine of divisibility of taxability. By this theory, when one piece of property is logically divisible, and the part that is used for religious purposes can be separated from that used for secular activities, a property tax will be levied on the value of the portion of the property utilized for secular pursuits. In a few instances religious ownership is the sole test for exemption.

Land leased to a religious society for religious purposes may not be exempt. Generally the courts hold that property must be devoted to public worship, in contrast to private worship, in order to be exempt. Cemetery lands will be exempt unless they are used for strictly commercial purposes. The courts have drawn a distinction between property taxes and other forms of levy potentially applicable to religious societies. From some levies of the latter type churches are not automatically exempt. As a result, special assessments as applied to religious property are judicially upheld.

VII

Religious Rights in Marriage and Divorce

Early procedure.—American colonists brought with them the canon and the civil law regulating marriages as administered by ecclesiastical and civil tribunals in England,[1] but the early settlers did not always introduce corresponding courts to enforce these laws.[2] Consequently colonial history reveals civil authorities regulating marriage by defining the relations of the parties, by proclaiming the procedure by which the marriage contract might be executed, by bestowing civil rights on the contracting parties, and by providing methods to nullify the marital status.[3]

Colonial regulations further provided for the performance of the ceremony by a civil magistrate after the intention to enter into the marriage had been publicized. A marriage entered into by individuals authorized to do so by statute was considered binding by the civil courts.[4] The creation of the marriage contract was facilitated by laws authorizing every justice of the peace and every settled clergyman to perform the marriage ceremony.[5] The necessity of specifying an intention to wed was emphasized through the establishment of stringent penalties against the officiating magistrate or clergyman who failed to enforce this civil regulation.

1. James Schouler, *A Treatise on the Law of Domestic Relations* (6th ed.), pp. 17-19. See also *Milford v. Worcester*, 7 Mass. 48 (1810).
2. *Town of Londonderry v. Town of Chester*, 2 N. H. 268 (1820).
3. *Harrison v. State*, 22 Md. 468 (1863); 18 R. C. L. 390.
4. *Milford v. Worcester*, 7 Mass. 48 (1810).
5. 38 C. J. 1311-1312.

Validity of marriages.—Judicial approval of the common law marriage minimizes the importance of the church in the marriage process. Such a marriage is a method of entering into the marital relationship without observing the solemnities or forms prescribed by church or state.[6] During the last century the courts of twenty-five states have upheld the validity of common law marriages.[7] Due to recent legislative amendment and judicial modification, the status of the common law marriage has changed.[8] At present there are twenty-two states in which such a union is valid.[9]

Except in the case of common law marriages, however, some kind of solemnization has always been practiced, the form and manner differing among the numerous sects. Statutes in every state except Pennsylvania define what civil or religious officials may solemnize marriages. Solemnization by either civil or religious officials is permitted in all states except three.[10] No statute requires or defines a particular form of religious ceremony.[11] Today the civil courts have jurisdiction over the legal status of the parties, while the church controls the religious practices incident to marriage. A marriage which is valid where celebrated is held valid everywhere, with two general exceptions: first, marriages deemed contrary to the laws of nature as generally recognized in Christian countries, such as polygamous

6. R. Black, "Common Law Marriage" (1928) 2 *University of Cincinnati Law Review* 113-133; E. O. C., "Common Law Marriage" (1939) 14 *Indiana Law Journal* 539-540.

7. 38 *C. J.* 1315. So held in Alabama, Colorado, Florida, Georgia, Indiana, Iowa, Kansas, Michigan, Minnesota, Mississippi, Montana, Nebraska, Nevada, New Jersey, New York, Ohio, Oklahoma, Pennsylvania, Rhode Island, South Carolina, South Dakota, Texas, Utah, Wisconsin, Wyoming.

8. Note, "Necessity of Cohabitation in Common Law Marriage" (1937) 23 *Iowa Law Review* 75-83; Note, "Common Law Marriage Abolished" (1934) 3 *Brooklyn Law Review* 155-156.

9. Alabama, Colorado, Florida, Georgia, Idaho, Indiana, Iowa, Kansas, Michigan, Minnesota, Mississippi, Montana, Nevada, New Jersey, Ohio, Oklahoma, Pennsylvania, Rhode Island, South Carolina, South Dakota, Texas, and Wyoming.

10. Maryland, Maine, and West Virginia.

11. T. Vernier, *American Family Laws*, I, 105-109; 18 *R. C. L.* 400; 38 *C. J.* 1309-1310; *State v. Walker*, 36 Kan. 297 (1887).

marriages; and, second, marriages positively forbidden by statute because contrary to local public policy.[12]

Where a marriage ceremony is performed according to the ritual of a particular religious sect, the courts will assume that the parties gave their consent and that they possessed the capacity to contract. There is a presumption that the clergyman who performed the marriage had the authority to perform it.[13] The incompetency of the administrating official does not nullify a marriage relationship entered into in good faith by the man and the woman.[14] The New Hampshire Supreme Court early stated the prevailing rule: "It is a principle, both salutary and well settled, that the official acts of a person, not duly qualified, are valid as to third persons and the public, when the want of the qualifications is punished by a mere penalty, and when the acts themselves are not in their nature void, or are not expressly made void by statute."[15]

However, a marriage which is shown not to have been solemnized before any third person acting or believed by either of the parties to be acting as a magistrate or minister may be invalid. At a particular public religious meeting no minister of the gospel was present. An individual occupied the pulpit, gave out a text of the Bible, talked about repentance, read five verses of Matthew, and then joined hands with a woman. Both individuals offered prayer; there was no other ceremony. The parties then cohabited as husband and wife under the belief that they were lawfully married. They certified to the city clerk that they had been married to each other by mutual public vows. In an action in which the validity of the marriage was brought into question, the court held that since no third

12. Schouler, *op. cit.*, pp. 31-33, 56; 38 *C. J.* 1277.
13. T. O. McCraney, "Presumption of the Legality of a Marriage and of Its Continued Existence (1938) 26 *California Law Review* 270-273; 38 *C. J.* 1310-1311. So held in California, Connecticut, Massachusetts, Minnesota, New Hampshire, North Carolina, Ohio, Maine, and Utah.
14. 38 *C. J.* 1307.
15. *Town of Londonderry v. Town of Chester*, 2 N. H. 268, 276 (1820).

person participated and no civil magistrate or minister of the gospel was present, no lawful marriage had taken place.[16] Even a clergyman authorized to solemnize marriages between other persons cannot marry himself.

A marriage ceremony may be valid although the minister who performed it did not believe he was performing a marriage ceremony. Thus an ecclesiastical marriage was performed in Maryland by a clergyman of a faith not believing in divorce. Later the married couple were granted a civil decree of divorce. After the former husband and wife had lived apart for a period of years, the pair was reunited. A wedding ceremony was performed again in full accord with church procedure by a clergyman of the original faith. At a later date the question of the marital status of the individuals arose in a civil court. The clergyman testified that in church theory the first marriage was still in force but that he had blessed their agreement to resume the relations of matrimony. The court decided that the validity of the remarriage was not open to question, even though no license had been obtained for the second ceremony. The purpose of the second marriage was to enable the parties to live together lawfully, the court held, and religious sanction had been given to the reunion. In the opinion of the court, therefore, the blessing of the reunion constituted a remarriage.[17]

The guarantee of the enjoyment of religious freedom exempts at least two religious groups, Quakers and Mormons, from the legal rule that the marriage ceremony must be performed by an ordained clergyman or judicial officer. The necessity for special solemnizing provisions for Quakers arises from the fact that their religious ceremonies do not call for intervention by a solemnizing officer. Statutes pertaining to marriages of particular sects are of three types. Twenty-one states pro-

16. *Commonwealth v. Munson,* 127 Mass. 459 (1879); see also *U. S. v. Chatwin,* 56 F. Supp. 890 (D. C., 1944), affirmed 146 F. (2d) 730 (C. C. A., 1945); reversed on other grounds, 326 U. S. 455, 66 Sup. Ct. 233, 90 L. Ed. 198 (1946).

17. *Feehley v. Feehley,* 129 Md. 565, 99 Atl. 663 (1916).

vide that marriage may be solemnized according to the customs of any religious society;[18] seventeen states specifically authorize Quaker marriages;[19] seven states permit a marriage to be solemnized by any officer of any religious society.[20] The courts have upheld the validity of such procedures.[21]

An unusual method of contracting marriage among the Mormon sect has been recognized as valid by the Supreme Court of Utah. In one instance the first wife of a deceased Mormon brought suit to obtain title to certain property on the contention that she was the lawful wife. Her claim to marriage rested upon a religious "sealing" ceremony, whereby a marital relationship was set up between her and the deceased man. The second wife maintained that the sealing ceremony whereby the first wife and the deceased man had been "sealed" meant that they agreed to be husband and wife only after death. In other words, the issue was whether the sealing ceremony was a marriage contract or a mere expression of a Mormon tenet. The ceremony consisted of certain Mormon ritual, and in this case had been performed when the first wife was ill, supposedly with only a few hours to live. The contention that the sealing ceremony was ineffective as a marriage contract rested upon the further argument that the circumstances of the particular situation indicated an intention of both parties to be joined *only* in eternity. The Utah court, however, stated that where marriage has been celebrated by a properly authorized ceremony, apparently with the assent of both parties, no secret reservation of one of the parties, unknown to the other, can avoid the mar-

18. Arkansas, California, Connecticut, Delaware, Illinois, Iowa, Kentucky, Michigan, Montana, Nebraska, New Jersey, New Mexico, New York, Ohio, Oregon, South Dakota, Virginia, Washington, West Virginia, Wisconsin, and Wyoming.

19. Alabama, Illinois, Indiana, Kansas, Maine, Maryland, Massachusetts, Michigan, Minnesota, Nevada, New Hampshire, New York, North Carolina, North Dakota, Rhode Island, Pennsylvania, Vermont.

20. Alabama, Arizona, Georgia, Mississippi, Nevada, Ohio, and Wisconsin.

21. 18 *R. C. L.* 402; see *Commonwealth v. Munson*, 127 Mass. 459 (1879).

riage. Taking judicial notice of Mormon literature, the court concluded that to be "sealed" was to be married "for time *and* eternity." When the parties were "sealed" according to the tenet, they became bound by the obligations of husband and wife. The plaintiff was adjudged the lawful widow.[22]

Polygamy.—At common law a second marriage entered into during the existence of the first was void. In America, as early as the eighteenth century, polygamy was recognized as an offense against society. Bigamous or polygamous marriages are both criminally and civilly condemned by all forty-eight states and the District of Columbia. Judicial opinion is unanimous that a person's religious belief cannot justify the practice of bigamy or polygamy.[23] In a series of four memorable decisions, the United States Supreme Court dealt a death blow to polygamy. The highest court of the land assumed jurisdiction in the situation by virtue of exclusive Congressional control over territories. The decisions themselves have been considered landmarks for later judicial treatment of cases involving the alleged religious right to practice polygamy.

In 1862 Congress made bigamy a crime in American territories. The law declared that every person having a husband or wife living, who married another, whether married or single, in a territory or other place over which the United States had exclusive jurisdiction, was guilty of bigamy. Punishment was fixed by a fine of not more than five hundred dollars and by imprisonment for a term of not more than five years.[24] One George Reynolds, who was convicted in the Supreme Court of the Territory of Utah for violation of the law, insisted that the statute violated his religious liberty, and appealed to the United States Supreme Court. He proved that at the time of his

22. *Hilton v. Roylance*, 25 Utah 129, 69 Pac. 660 (1902).
23. 38 *C. J.* 1274; 18 *R. C. L.* 381, 382; see, for example, *State v. Barlow*, 107 Utah 292, 153 P. (2d) 647 (1944); appeal dismissed 324 U. S. 829, 65 Sup. Ct. 916, 89 L. Ed. 1396 (1945); rehearing denied 324 U. S. 891, 65 Sup. Ct. 1026, 89 L. Ed. 1438 (1945).
24. Act of July 1, 1862, 12 *Stat.* 501, 48 *U. S. C.*, sec. 1480.

alleged second marriage he was a member of the Mormon
Church, and argued that it was the duty of the members of the
Mormon sect to practice polygamy. He stated that the members
of the church believed that the practice of polygamy was directly
enjoined upon the male members by Almighty God, in a revelation to Joseph Smith, the founder and prophet of said church.
He contended that the refusal by a male member to practice
polygamy, when circumstances would permit, would be punished
in the life to come.

Sustaining the prohibition as a valid exercise of Congressional
power over the territories, Mr. Chief Justice Waite ruled that
the constitutional guarantee of religious liberty was not designed
to nullify legislation pertaining to marriage. Marriage, he said,
was not only a sacred obligation by nature, but also a civil contract usually regulated by statute. If a man believed that human
sacrifice was a requisite of religious worship, could it be legally
argued that the civil government under which he lived could
not interfere with such a sacrifice? Of, if a wife believed it her
religious duty to burn herself on the funeral pyre of her dead
husband, would the civil government be powerless to prevent
her from effectuating her belief? The Chief Justice implied a
negative answer to each question. To permit a man to excuse
his illegal practices because of his religious views would let
every person become a law unto himself. Because the conviction
was sustained, no doubt remained of the authority of the government to prevent polygamy.[25]

In a later trial for bigamy, exception was taken to the practice of a federal prosecuting attorney of challenging prospective
jurors because of their bigamous inclinations. An appeal was
directed to the Supreme Court on the assumption that no right
to inquire into a juror's religious belief existed. However, it

25. *Reynolds v. United States*, 98 U. S. 145, 25 L. Ed. 244 (1878). In
analyzing the history of the adoption of the First Amendment, the court (pp.
162-163) also emphasized attempts to legislate with respect to the establishment of religion and religious doctrines, particularly in Virginia. See pages
21-22, *supra*.

was held that a jury composed of men believing in polygamy could not have been free from bias or prejudice during the trial of a person who entertained the same belief, and whose offense consisted in the act of living in polygamy. No invasion of the constitutional rights of the prospective juror called to try a party charged with bigamy occurred when an inquiry was made to discover whether the individual was living in polygamy, and whether he believed it to be in accordance with Divine Will.[26]

Each prospective voter in the territory of Utah was required to swear that he was no bigamist and that he did not and would not, publicly or privately, or in any manner whatsoever, teach, advise, counsel, or encourage any person to commit the crime of bigamy or polygamy, or any other crime defined by law, either as a religious duty or otherwise.[27] An individual who practiced polygamy registered for voting contrary to law. A charge of conspiracy to obstruct the administration of territorial laws by unlawfully seeking to be admitted to registration as an elector resulted in the conviction of the defendant in a district court of the territory. Upon appeal the United States Supreme Court said that bigamy and polygamy tended to destroy the purity of the marriage relationship and to disturb the peace of families. Few crimes, said the court, were more dangerous to the best interests of society; therefore to exempt such crimes from punishment would unnecessarily shock the moral judgment of the community. Although the free exercise of religion was deemed desirable, it was held subordinate to the criminal laws of the country, passed with reference to actions regarded as proper subjects of punitive legislation. Upholding the power of the legislature to prescribe such qualifications, the court concluded: "Whilst legislation for the establishment of a religion is forbidden, and its free exercise permitted, it does not follow that everything which may be so called can be tolerated. Crime

26. *Miles v. United States,* 103 U. S. 304, 26 L. Ed. 481 (1880).
27. Act of March 22, 1882, 22 *Stat.* 31, c. 47, 48 *U. S. C.,* sec. 1461.

is not less odious because sanctioned by what any particular sect may designate as religion."[28]

Congress passed an act[29] requiring the United States Attorney General to institute proceedings designed to nullify the charter of a defunct religious corporation known as the Church of the Latter Day Saints, and to bring about a forfeiture of its property to the United States in the absence of other legal owners. Under the statute the property was to be disposed of according to the principles applicable to property devoted to religious and charitable uses. In an action contesting the constitutionality of the law the Supreme Court declared that Congress had the power to repeal the act of incorporation, not only by virtue of its general and plenary power over the territories, but because of an express reservation in the organic act of the territory of Utah specifying the power to disapprove and to annul the acts of the territorial legislature. Since polygamy had been forbidden by law, and since the church had persistently used the funds with which the late corporation was endowed for the purpose of promoting the unlawful practice as an integral part of religious usage, the government had a right to seize the funds and to devote them to the benefit of the whole community. Further analysis was made of the alleged conflict between polygamy and the limitation of religious freedom: "One pretense for the obstinate course is, that their belief in the practice of polygamy or in the right to indulge in it, is a religious belief, and, therefore, under the protection of the constitutional guaranty of religious freedom. This is altogether a sophistical plea. No doubt the Thugs of India imagined that their belief in the right of assassination was a religious belief; but their thinking so did not make it so. . . . The offering of human sacrifices by our own ancestors in Britain was no doubt sanctioned by an equally conscientious impulse. But no one, on that

28. *Davis v. Beason*, 133 U. S. 333, 345, 10 Sup. Ct. 299, 301, 33 L. Ed. 637, 641 (1890).
29. Act of March 3, 1887, 24 *Stat.* 635, c. 397, 28 *U. S. C.*, secs. 633, 660.

account, would hesitate to brand these practices, now, as crimes against society, and obnoxious to condemnation and punishment by the civil authority."[30]

The principles of these judicial decisions have not been modified.[31]

Divorce procedure.—The marriage relation differs from the ordinary contractual relation in that when the status is once created the state becomes an interested party. Thereafter the marriage is not subject, as to its continuance or dissolution, to the mere intention and pleasure of the contracting parties.[32] During the American colonial period the English law pertaining to divorce was not the common law but the ecclesiastical law, chiefly under the jurisdiction of the ecclesiastical courts. At the time of the separation of the American colonies from England divorce from "bed and board" was sanctioned by church tribunals, while absolute divorce decrees were granted by special acts of Parliament for the benefit of a favored few. In fact, in England, divorce was controlled by the church until 1858.[33]

Since the establishment of the American State, the regulation of divorce has been a right of the various state legislatures.[34] The early statutory history of divorce in America was characterized by special acts for particular individuals. Provisions contained in early state laws were copied from the regulations of

30. *Church of Latter Day Saints v. United States*, 136 U. S. 1, 49, 10 Sup. Ct. 792, 805, 34 L. Ed. 478, 493 (1890).

31. For an analysis of attempts to amend the United States Constitution so as to prohibit polygamy in the states and to disqualify polygamists for office-holding, see *Musmanno, op. cit.*, pp. 131-135. Since 1875, fifty-three such amendments have been presented.

32. Benjamin Brewster, "Marriage and Divorce in State and Church" (1905) 3 *Michigan Law Review* 541-553; 38 *C. J.* 1275; 9 *R. C. L.* 245.

33. Schouler, *op. cit.*, pp. 1295-1299; 19 *C. J.* 19; 9 *R. C. L.* 244.

34. Jurisdiction of the federal courts over divorce has always been denied. For discussion relative to the lack of jurisdiction of federal courts over divorce, especially in instances where the parties are such that federal jurisdiction would ordinarily apply to them, as in the case of consuls, see *Ohio ex. rel. Popovici v. Aigler*, 280 U. S. 379, 50 Sup. Ct. 154, 74 L. Ed. 489 (1930); for recommendations as to constitutional change to extend federal control over divorce, see Musmanno, *op. cit.*, pp. 104-108.

the English ecclesiastical courts. Subsequently, the method of granting divorce was changed from special legislative action to a judicial process based on general divorce laws. This transfer of divorce jurisdiction to the courts was generally effected through state constitutional amendments. The restriction placed upon legislative action is typified by the North Carolina constitution of 1835 which provided, in Art. 1, Section 4, that "the General Assembly shall have power to pass general laws, regulating divorce and alimony, but shall not have power to grant a divorce or secure alimony in any individual case." In defining the rights and liabilities of the affected parties, the courts in this country have frequently employed the same rules of construction and procedure that the ecclesiastical courts formulated, unless such methods were found by the courts to be unadaptable to conditions in this country, or in conflict with constitutional or statutory regulations.[35] Therefore, English ecclesiastical principles have become a guide for the American judiciary.

In the opinion of certain religious groups, the interests of society are served best by making marriage an indissoluble contract. Other religious sects believe the rule of permanency is too severe. But under legislative regulation every state except South Carolina provides for the granting of an absolute divorce. The regulations differ widely according to views of expediency. In the instances which will be described in this chapter requirements of the law allegedly conflicted with the exercise of religious freedom. In such cases judicial decision has been determinative.

It is unanimously held that a decree of divorce can be granted only in accordance with provisions of civil law.[36] Consequently the civil courts are not bound to recognize the validity

35. *Brinkley v. Brinkley,* 48 N. Y. 184 (1872); 9 R. C. L. 244, note 16. So held in Arkansas, Georgia, Maryland, Massachusetts, New York, and Texas.

36. 9 R. C. L. 252; K. N. Llewellyn, "Behind the Law of Divorce" (1932) 32 *Columbia Law Review* 1281-1308.

of an ecclesiastical divorce. A Mormon divorce, granted by the church, by means of which the parties agree to dissolve their marital relations, is consistently declared illegal.[37] The Utah Supreme Court ruled that the rights and liabilities of marriage were so sacred and binding between the parties that they could not be terminated by mutual consent. Although the parties to a Mormon divorce considered it valid, and one of them later remarried, the divorce decree was nonetheless ineffectual.[38] The decision of the Utah court pertaining to the illegality of a Mormon divorce was cited with approval in a subsequent decision of the Supreme Court of Idaho.[39]

An attempted dissolution of a marriage by a rabbi has no legal effect in either federal or New York state courts. A District Court in New York considered as a bigamous act a second marriage performed after procurement of a divorce according to the Jewish ritual. Whether or not the rabbinical divorce was valid according to sectarian ritual was held to be beside the question, as such alleged divorces were not recognized in the state.[40] In another instance the Court of Appeals of New York ruled that the transactions purporting to grant a rabbinical divorce were performed contrary to the rule providing that no divorce should be granted other than by judicial proceedings. The purported divorce was wholly ineffectual.[41]

In Indiana an individual was accused of bigamy. He defended himself with the assertion that only because he believed the spirit of his first wife had vanished and that the departed spirit ordered him to remarry (although her body was still alive) did he enter into the second marriage. He allegedly obeyed a supernatural power. Conviction of the defendant was upheld on the ground that the law of the land was superior to any religious beliefs. Criminal intent was judged unnecessary

37. 9 R. C. L. 251, note 5.
38. *Tufts v. Tufts,* 8 Utah 142, 30 Pac. 309 (1892).
39. *Hilton v. Stewart,* 15 Idaho 150, 96 Pac. 579 (1908).
40. *Petition of Horowitz,* 48 F. (2d) 652 (D. C. 1931).
41. *In re Goldman's Estate,* 282 N. Y. S. 787, 156 Misc. 817 (1935).

for the successful prosecution of a case where the defendant deliberately contracted a second marriage although guided by his religious belief.[42]

A divorce granted in accordance with a custom of the Mohammedan religion in Turkey, however, was recognized in Massachusetts. When the wife of a Christian renounced Christianity and became a Mohammedan, such action, in Turkish theory, nullified a previous marriage to a living husband. The Massachusetts court permitted the man, who lived in the United States, to remarry. In this case, however, it should be noted that the national law of Turkey and the religious tenet coincided. The general principle applied was that every sovereign has the right to determine the domestic and social status of those residing within its territory.[43]

Divorce for religious oppression.—The divorce law of no state specifically mentions religious oppression as a ground for dissolution of the marriage contract. Nevertheless, a few divorce suits have raised the issue of religious differences between husband and wife. Civil courts sometimes deny divorces sought on the ground of alleged religious oppression or because of a mere difference of religious opinion. It has been stated that since the fundamental law of the land guarantees the right to worship according to the dictates of one's conscience, defendants in such cases have a legal right to pursue their creeds free from court denial of such right or adverse criticism by the courts of the proper exercise of that right.[44]

In New York, after a husband had refused to permit his wife to attend a particular church, suit was brought by the wife for judicial separation. During an investigation into the financial obligation of the husband to the wife, pending final settlement of the suit, the court remarked that an act of great unkindness and of unreasonableness had been committed by the husband

42. *Long v. State*, 192 Ind. 524, 137 N. E. 49 (1922).
43. *Kapigian v. Der Minassian*, 212 Mass. 412, 99 N. E. 264 (1912).
44. *Krauss v. Krauss*, 163 La. 218, 111 So. 683 (1927).

by his use of his marital status to separate his wife from the church of which she was a member, and in which she preferred to worship. However, the court stated that she had mistaken her marital duty in not submitting to her husband's demand if she could not obtain his consent by kindness.[45] In Texas a divorce decree was denied in the face of the charge that, among other acts, the husband had ridiculed the wife's religious creed and its teachings. The fact that he had told her before marriage that he was a member of the same church was deemed immaterial.[46]

Nevertheless, a decree of divorce may be given where the complaint describes harmful circumstances resulting from religious beliefs. When a charge of religious persecution was made in a divorce action in Idaho, it was shown that one of the parties had persistently attempted to convert the other. The defendant husband had reviled his wife's religion and had compelled her to perform the particular religious practices of his church. The Supreme Court of the state decided that the right of each individual to hold any religious beliefs existed after marriage as well as before. Granting the decree, the court held that "where one of the spouses abuses such right by exacting from the other spouse compliance with the religion of the other, where it is against the belief of the one from whom the demand is made, and such demand causes worry and pain and suffering on the part of the spouse from whom the same is demanded, such action will be taken to be a violation of the obligation and vows of their marriage contract."[47]

A suit for divorce in Iowa was based upon charges of cruel treatment caused by divergent religious beliefs. Since the evidence showed that the defendant, in undertaking to enforce his religious beliefs, had been guilty of inhumane treatment, a decree of divorce was given.[48] In Louisiana a husband abandoned

45. *Lawrence v. Lawrence,* 3 Paige (N. Y.) 266 (1832).
46. *Ryan v. Ryan,* 114 S. W. 464 (1908).
47. *DeCloedt v. DeCloedt,* 24 Idaho 277, 286, 133 Pac. 664, 667 (1913).
48. *Edwards v. Edwards,* 193 Iowa 87, 185 N. W. 2 (1921).

his original faith and devoted a large part of his time to the religious work of another sect. He left his wife for months at a time in order to attend a religious school, and he forbade her to leave his house or to take part in the temporal affairs to which she had been accustomed. In a successful divorce action the court ruled that although the defendant had a legal right to pursue his own religious faith, no law, divine or human, could justify his practicing his faith in such a way as to neglect his wife and children.[49] A New Hampshire wife became a Christian Science healer in the belief that this calling was her duty. Her husband, who regarded Christian Science as a fanaticism, did not object to her belief in the doctrine, but opposed her practicing as a healer. He sought a divorce decree on the ground of conduct seriously injurious to his health and reason. The court decided that the wife's actions had injured his health, and a decree was awarded.[50]

Refusal to cohabit.—Whether the refusal of one party to the marriage contract to cohabit with the other for religious reasons is grounds for divorce is an unsettled question. In some states the courts have denied that refusal to cohabit is legal cruelty.[51] Thus, where a wife joined a religious society professing as one of its tenets that its members were married to Christ and could not be married to anyone else, her refusal to cohabit did not justify a divorce. The Supreme Court of Florida declared that the mere refusal of a wife to accord to the husband marital privileges lawful only to him was not of itself such a desertion of the husband as to authorize him to obtain a divorce.[52] Refusal of a wife to cohabit until the Lord notified her of her conversion did not constitute "an intolerable condition" for which relief could be given.[53]

49. *Krauss v. Krauss,* 163 La. 218, 111 So. 683 (1927).
50. *Robinson v. Robinson,* 66 N. H. 600, 23 Atl. 362 (1891).
51. 19 *C. J.* 56, notes 38, 40. So held in Florida, Georgia, Maine, Massachusetts, New Jersey, Ohio, Pennsylvania, Texas, West Virginia, and Wisconsin.
52. *Prall v. Prall,* 58 Fla. 496, 50 So. 867 (1909).
53. *Johnson v. Johnson,* 31 Pa. Super. 53 (1906).

A few jurisdictions have regarded the refusal of one party to cohabit with the other as a cause for divorce, regardless of the reason.[54] An early New Hampshire law provided that living for a continuous period of three years with a religious sect which believed that the relation between husband and wife was unlawful was a legal basis for divorce.[55] A husband joined the Shakers, a sect believing that the relation between husband and wife was unlawful. During his period of membership of more than three years in the Shaker organization he refused to cohabit with his wife. There was no question of his making comfortable provision for her financial support. An action for a divorce decree brought by the wife was successful.[56] At present two states, New Hampshire and Kentucky, have legislation on the subject of non-cohabitation. The law of New Hampshire specifies as a ground for divorce six months' membership in a religious sect disbelieving in the cohabitation of husband and wife.[57] Kentucky makes membership for five years in a religious sect opposed to cohabitation a legal basis for a divorce action.[58] Both statutes are apparently constitutional.[59]

Alienation of affections.—An action for damages against a religious society for alienation of affections arose in Oregon in 1924. At marriage a wife promised her husband that she would refrain from attending the meetings of a mission known as the "Apostolic Faith." Later, after visits by members of this sect, she associated with the group. Her husband charged the society with meddling with his family affairs, and accordingly brought suit for damages. The Supreme Court of Oregon ruled that the plaintiff would have to prove that the acts of the defendants were maliciously committed with the intent of alien-

54. 19 *C. J.* 56, note 39. So held in California, Michigan, New Hampshire, Oregon, and Washington.
55. New Hampshire law of December 21, 1821.
56. *Dyer v. Dyer*, 5 N. H. 271 (1830).
57. *New Hampshire Laws of 1926*, chap. 287.
58. *Kentucky Statutes of 1922*, sec. 2117.
59. Vernier, *op. cit.*, II, 67-68.

ating the affections of the wife, and that said acts produced the results described before he would be entitled to recover. The court pointed out that members of a religious sect were under no obligation to co-operate with a man in preventing his wife from attending services at their place of worship. The members of the defendant society, in fact, had a right to take part in religious services with her. The action for damages was fruitless.[60]

Summary.—Until the middle of the eighteenth century English ecclesiastical courts had exclusive jurisdiction over marriages. American colonists brought with them the canon and civil law regulating marriages, but the early settlers did not always introduce the corresponding English courts to interpret these laws. Civil authorities regulated marriage contracts. The creation of the civil contract was facilitated by laws authorizing every justice of the peace and every settled clergyman to perform the marriage ceremony.

Common law marriages are recognized in many states. Except in the case of such marriages, some kind of solemnization has always been practiced. The civil courts now have jurisdiction over the legal status of the parties, while the church controls the religious practices incident to marriage. Where a marriage ceremony is performed according to the ritual of a particular sect, the courts assume that the parties gave their consent and that they possessed the capacity to contract. There is a presumption that a clergyman who performs a marriage ceremony has the authority to perform it. Guarantees of religious freedom have exempted at least two religious groups from the legal rule that the marriage ceremony must be performed by an ordained clergyman or a judicial official. On the other hand, judicial opinion unanimously holds that one's religious beliefs cannot justify bigamy or polygamy.

In contrast to ordinary contractual relations, the marriage

60. *Hughes v. Holman,* 110 Ore. 415, 223 Pac. 730 (1924).

contract is not subject, as to its continuance or dissolution, solely to the intention and pleasure of the contracting parties. The regulation of divorce, consequently, is a matter for the state legislatures. In defining the rights and obligations of the affected parties, the courts play an essential role. In instances where requirements of the law have allegedly conflicted with the exercise of religious freedom, judicial opinion has been determinative.

The judiciary permits the granting of a divorce only in accordance with the provisions of the civil law. Civil courts are not bound to recognize the validity of ecclesiastical divorces. Sometimes the judiciary has denied divorce decrees sought on the ground of alleged religious oppression. Nevertheless, a divorce decree has infrequently been given where the complaint described harmful circumstances resulting from the religious beliefs of one spouse. The judicial attitude toward the refusal of one party to the marriage contract to cohabit with the other for religious reasons has been varied.

An analysis of judicial doctrine indicates that the courts have sought to consider carefully the interests of both society and the aggrieved parties before arriving at any conclusion in the sphere of marital relations.

VIII

Religious Rights in Parental Conflicts over Child Control

Historical background.—Parents—both natural and foster— have sometimes disagreed between themselves in the matter of the religious training of their children. By the death of one parent, by the action of relatives, and by the existence of ante-nuptial agreements, for example, the judicatory facilities of the government have been called upon to analyze parental conflicts in which religious beliefs have played a vital part. Those cases in domestic relations where the religious training of children has been magnified through parental conflict serve as basic material for this chapter.

Because of our inheritance of the common law, a brief reference to English principles is illuminating. In the sixteenth and seventeenth centuries the English government suppressed all religious education except that afforded by the Church of England. During that time the chancery courts exercised much control over the religious training of minors.[1] Following a period of persecution, however, a more rational attitude became characteristic of judicial thought, in that the common law rights of the father became judicially recognized.[2]

Under the common law the married couple was considered

1. Schouler, *op. cit.*, p. 848.
2. Lee M. Friedman, "The Parental Right to Control the Religious Education of a Child" (1916) 29 *Harvard Law Review* 485-500.

a unit, the right to determine the religious training of the children being a prerogative of the father.[3] The first statutory modification of the common law was the Parliamentary Act of 1839,[4] which granted to the Chancellor the power to determine custody of infants under seven years of age. This authority was changed in 1886 to include infants of any age.[5] Nevertheless, in the absence of paternal declaration, English courts frequently assumed that the father desired his surviving minors to be brought up in his religion.[6] By virtue of judicial treatment, the father's reasonable convictions prevailed over the mother's religious beliefs. From a practical viewpoint it was impossible to prove unfitness against the father or to obtain a decision against his wishes. Paternal supremacy over the child has existed in England, in a modified form, up to the present.[7]

In early American statutes and decisions the father's right to control the child was sharply emphasized. This rule of paternal supremacy was often prompted by the fact that the father was originally the sole property owner and wage earner, with the duty of providing for the family. Unless disqualified in some way, the father usually had the primary right to control the person and residence of the child. Even where a child might previously have been awarded to the mother, the right to custody of a child was held to revert to the father upon the mother's death.[8]

Changing laws reflecting changing conditions of society have modified the principle of paternal supremacy. Just as common law developed from ancient customs, so the law of domestic relations has evolved from the changing customs of the people. In America the legal rights and duties involved in the relationship

3. Schouler, *op. cit.*, p. 847; see *Ex parte Flynn*, 87 N. J. Eq. 413, 100 Atl. 861 (1917).
4. Talfourd's Act, *2 and 3 Vict.*, c. 54 (1839).
5. Guardianship of Infants Act, *49 and 50 Vict.*, c. 27 (1886).
6. Schouler, *op. cit.*, p. 847, note 14.
7. See *Stegall v. Stegall*, 151 Miss. 875, 119 So. 802 (1928).
8. *Pinney v. Sulzen*, 91 Kan. 407, 137 Pac. 987 (1914); Vernier, *op cit.*, IV, 17.

of parent and child are defined by the legislatures of the several states. The fundamental idea behind their regulations is the natural and legal incapacity of the child to care for himself. The laws of four states still give the father preference in the custody of children.[9] In two states the statutes do not specify whether the mother or the father is entitled to the custody of the children.[10] In the remaining forty-two states the rights of both parents are made equal by law.[11] The strict view of paternal right which the early English and American legislatures and courts followed is not generally accepted today. Against such an historical background assertions of religious liberty have been projected. In response, the American judiciary has formulated rules of behavior consistent with the legal guarantees of religious freedom.

Doctrine of co-equality.—In determining the custody of children where the question of religious beliefs is involved, the courts, following legislative declaration, emphasize the co-equality of both mother and father when both are living, or the exclusive right of the survivor, assuming the welfare of the children is not at stake.[12] The co-equality doctrine is well illustrated by a New York case. A parental disagreement over the education and religious training of five small children resulted in the father's placing the children in a religious academy fifty miles from home without the mother's consent. In an action by the mother to secure custody of the children, the existence of the mother's co-equal right over the children was judicially recognized. The attempt of the father to transmit custody of the children to the academy without his wife's consent was nullified.[13]

The exclusive right of the survivor is demonstrated in cases in Florida and New York. Upon the granting of a decree of

9. Georgia, Louisiana, Oklahoma, and Texas.
10. Alabama and North Carolina.   11. Vernier, *op. cit.*, IV, 24-52.
12. R. C. Brown, "The Custody of Children" (1927) 2 *Indiana Law Journal* 325-330; 46 *C. J.* 1221.
13. *People v. Mt. Joseph's Academy,* 189 N. Y. S. 775, 198 App. Div. 75 (1921).

divorce in Florida, a mother was awarded custody of her children. Later the mother died and left the custody of her children by will to certain relatives. The father, however, put the children in a religious home of his choice, contrary to the wishes of a maternal aunt. Disregarding the mother's will, the Supreme Court of Florida stated that "he, as their father, has the legal right to their custody and control, and to have them educated in any religious faith he sees proper, whose tenets do not inculcate violation of the laws of the land."[14] In New York, a mother, who was separated from her two children, was an inmate of a tuberculosis sanatorium. The children lived with a paternal aunt while the father was living. At the death of the father, the children were sought by the mother, who desired their custody in order that she might place them in her sister's home. Religious friction was accentuated by the fact that the paternal aunt had instructed the children in one religious faith, while the maternal aunt desired to bring them up in a different faith. The court held that the mother, the surviving parent, was the sole guardian of the children and, as such, had the right to determine how they were to be reared.[15]

Parental conflict over the religious training of a child resulted in an unusual ruling in New York State in 1936. A father who believed in a religious sect called "Megiddo" occasionally took his ten-year-old daughter to "Megiddo" meetings over one hundred miles away from home, without the mother's consent. As part of his religious belief the father caused the child to be dressed in "unfashionable wearing apparel," and to be taught religious lessons which allegedly produced queerness and fanaticism. In an action to prevent her daughter from attending such meetings, the mother contended that the father unduly deprived her of custody of the child and hampered the mother's right to participate in the education of her child. A special term of a lower court ordered complete release of the

14. *Hernandez v. Thomas*, 50 Fla. 522, 536, 39 So. 641, 645 (1905).
15. *People v. Woolston*, 239 N. Y. S. 185, 135 Misc. 320 (1930).

child from the control of the father, and awarded exclusive custody to the mother on the theory that such an atmosphere as that into which the father was accustomed to taking her was not conducive to the child's best interests.[16] An appeal to the Appellate Division of the New York Supreme Court brought about a modification of the order: the father and the mother were given joint guardianship; the mother's consent was declared necessary if the father desired to accompany the child out of town; and the child could not be taken to a distance greater than that which could be traveled in two hours. Prolonged absences of the child were deemed injurious to both mother and child.[17] Further appeal to the Court of Appeals was made by both parties. Commenting that the health and welfare of the child was not in danger, and that judges should not try to instruct parents in the techniques of training their children, the highest court of the State of New York reversed both the order of the Appellate Division and that of the special term. The religious conflict was thus thrust back into the home, whence it originated. The dictum that the court could not regulate the internal affairs of the home was an important feature of the final decision. As a result, the parents were denied the assistance of the courts in harmonizing their discordant religious tenets.[18]

Limitation of the doctrine of co-equality.—The co-equality of the parents when both are living, or the exclusive right of the survivor, does not prevail when the welfare of the child is in jeopardy.[19] In awarding custody of the child, American courts give primary consideration to the welfare of the child. In determining the child's welfare "the court will consider the ties of nature and of association; the character and feelings of the parties contending for the custody; the age, health, and sex

16. *People v. Sisson*, 281 N. Y. S. 559, 156 Misc. 236 (1936).
17. *People v. Sisson*, 246 App. Div. 151, 285 N. Y. S. 41 (1936).
18. *People v. Sisson*, 271 N. Y. 285, 2 N. E. (2d) 660 (1936); S. S., "Parent and Child-Custody" (1936) 11 *St. John's Law Review* 126-129.
19. 20 *R. C. L.* 598-599.

of the child; the moral or immoral surroundings of its life; benefits of education and development; and the pecuniary prospects."[20] Parental attitude toward religious training becomes secondary to the mental and physical advantages of the minor. It has been judicially stated that if the permanent welfare of the child is best served by awarding it to one or the other of the parents, the fact that the child had been baptized in a particular faith will not be determinative.[21] Thus, in awarding a child to foster parents instead of to its mother, a Massachusetts court held that "the wishes of the parent as to the religious education and surroundings of the child are entitled to weight; if there is nothing to put in the balance against them, ordinarily they will be decisive. If, however, those wishes cannot be carried into effect without sacrificing what the court sees to be for the welfare of the child, they must so far be disregarded. The court will not itself prefer one church to another, but will act without bias for the welfare of the child under the circumstances of each case."[22]

The Pennsylvania Superior Court in 1935 allowed the foster parents of a child to retain custody, in preference to the natural father, although the effect was to defeat the carrying out of the father's ideas on religious education.[23]

An interesting attempt to blend religious creed and temporal welfare was made by the Domestic Relations Court of New York City. A woman belonging to a Christian faith and a man professing Mohammedanism had been married by a clergyman of a sect different from that of either spouse. The parents vehemently disagreed between themselves over the religious education of their four children. The court at first sent the four to a sectarian institution of the same creed as the mother's faith, with the stipulation that only the oldest was to receive religious

20. Joseph Madden, *Persons and Domestic Relations*, p. 376.
21. *Commonwealth v. Kelley*, 83 Pa. Super. 17 (1924).
22. *Purinton v. Jamrock*, 195 Mass. 187, 199, 200, 80 N. E. 802, 805 (1907).
23. *Commonwealth v. Wilcox*, 118 Pa. Super. 363, 179 Atl. 808 (1935).

training. Later disagreements prompted the court to shift the three youngest to a "neutral" sectarian child institution. Continued dissatisfaction of all four children was so clear that both sectarian institutions sought to be relieved of the children because of the problems created by the parental conflict over religious education. When the case came before the court for the third time the children were asked privately by the court to express their religious preferences. The result of judicial inquiry placed the oldest child in the custody of a paternal uncle; the three youngest were sent to a neutral home with the proviso that no religious instruction was to be given. Father and mother were each permitted to take one of the three youngest to a church of the father's or the mother's choice.[24] The decision is significant in that it illustrates the breadth of the religious problem which the American judiciary has been called upon to settle.

Supremacy of the father in matters of religious belief.—Subject to the primary consideration of the welfare of the child, the father sometimes has the first right to prescribe the child's religious education.[25] The religious convictions of a father usually do not constitute a cause for awarding the custody of the child to another.[26] In fact, the father generally may educate his children according to his religious tenets, unless the latter violate the law.[27] Thus a father, rather than a relative, was entitled to the custody of his child, in spite of conflicting parental religious beliefs, where there was no evidence to show that although he believed in divine healing, he would not procure adequate medical attention if the child should need it.[28]

In another case a mother was an inmate of an institution. A maternal aunt was appointed guardian of the child after a

24. *In re Vardinakis*, 289 N. Y. S. 355, 160 Misc. 13 (1936).
25. Madden, *op. cit.*, p. 371. See also *Verser v. Ford*, 37 Ark. 27 (1878).
26. 46 *C. J.* 1247, notes 54-55. So held in Arkansas, Kansas, Missouri, and New York.
27. *Hernandez v. Thomas*, 50 Fla. 522, 39 So. 641 (1905); 46 *C. J.* 1222, notes 47-48. So held in Florida, Missouri, and New Jersey.
28. *Johnson v. Borders*, 155 Ark. 218, 244 S. W. 30 (1922).

petition for such appointment stated that the whereabouts of the father was unknown. Later the father, who had never left the city, instituted proceedings to revoke the appointment, which had been made without his consent or knowledge. The father sought his own appointment as guardian of the child so that he might educate him in his own religion. The court revoked the original appointment with the comment: "In the absence of statutory regulations and manifest unfitness, the father, as between himself and his wife, is entitled to the custody of his infant children."[29] In Missouri, when custody of a child was given to adherents of the father's faith instead of to a family of a different creed who had previously aided the child, a Missouri judge held: "Few men would be willing to assume the burdens of a legal paternity, if they supposed that their children could, against their will, be taken from them to be educated in religious systems which they believed to be false, and to be taught thus to despise their father for his superstition, or for his infidelity, as the case might be. . . . I can conceive no more poignant anguish than that of the true father who sees his child, against his will, brought up before his eyes in a religious system which he abhors, as being, according to his belief, injurious to the spiritual interests of his child."[30]

However, if a father professes a belief in a sect obnoxious to society, he may be deprived of the custody of his child.[31] For example, where a father wanted to place his children in a Shaker colony, the court awarded custody to a maternal relative on the ground that, in a communistic community such as the Shaker colony, the natural affection a father should have for his children would be absent. The court pointed out that the Shaker faith did not recognize the normal relation of parent

29. *In re Jacquet*, 82 N. Y. S. 986, 987, 40 Misc. 575, 576 (1903).
30. *In re Doyle*, 16 Mo. App. 159, 167 (1884).
31. 46 *C. J.* 1222, note 48; 46 *C. J.* 1247, note 56. So held in Florida and Ohio.

and child, but, instead, embraced the concept that all children should be reared by the community.[32]

Non-interference with state custody.—The surrender of a child by a parent to the state's care has prevented the parent from prescribing the religious education of the child. A child of one sect in Connecticut was placed by the state in a respectable family of a different sect. One year after commitment a clergyman of the sect to which the child belonged applied for the child, in the name of the mother, and offered to place the child in a sectarian orphan asylum and carefully provide for it. The clergyman's petition was fruitless when the court, upholding the refusal of the state-supervised board of management, held that the action of the state should not be set aside upon the mere demand of a parent.[33]

Non-interference at age of discretion.—A father generally has no right to interfere with the freedom of conscience of a minor child who has reached the age of discretion.[34] However, in two instances the reverse was true. In Pennsylvania it was held that a father could lawfully prevent a child who had reached the age of discretion from violating the latter's own religious pledges. The father could not force his child to become a member of a specific religious denomination; but, after the child had become a member of a particular denomination, the father was permitted to restrain him from severing his connection with that denomination and joining another.[35] A girl of seventeen years entered a convent with the purpose of becoming a nun, although she had no right to do so without her mother's consent. A Louisiana court issued a writ of habeas corpus releasing her from the convent and restoring her to the custody of her mother.[36]

32. *State v. Hand,* 1 Ohio Dec. 238 (1848).
33. *Whalen v. Olmstead,* 61 Conn. 263, 23 Atl. 964 (1891).
34. 46 C. J. 1222.
35. *Commonwealth v. Armstrong,* 1 Pa. Law J. 393 (1842).
36. *Prieto v. St. Alphonsus Convent of Mercy,* 52 La. Ann. 631, 27 So. 153 (1900).

Guardians as public officers.—In determining the custody of children as between individuals other than parents, the judiciary usually considers temporal welfare superior to religious doctrine. Nevertheless, the child generally is given to the custody of persons of the same faith as that of the father if the temporal welfare will be as well taken care of by such persons as by those of another faith.[37]

The fact that guardians of minors are regarded as holding offices of "profit or trust" under state constitutions usually renders such individuals immune from removal because of religious beliefs or disbeliefs.[38] The Supreme Judicial Court of Massachusetts, for example, dismissed a petition seeking the removal of the guardian of a child on account of her alleged religious beliefs. The court held that the guardian should not be removed merely because the child's surviving father desired her to be reared in his religion. It seemed reasonably certain to the court that the child's welfare did not require the proposed change of control.[39] In reply to a charge that a testamentary guardian was not a proper person because he was an infidel, the Superior Court of Georgia held that constitutional guarantees prevented discrimination on account of one's religious opinions. Over such opinions, the court stated, it had no jurisdiction.[40]

The futility of the attempt to revoke the appointment of a guardian upon the showing that her religious views differed from those of the child's parents was emphasized by the Supreme Court of Missouri. No religious test could be applied in appointing a person to a position of profit or trust, even though a law[41] stated that a minor should not be committed to the custody of a person adhering to a religion different from that of the child's parents, the prevailing opinion held. The practice of appointing guardians having the same religion as

37. 46 *C. J.* 1247, 1222.
38. Schouler, *op. cit.*, p. 519; 16 *C. J. S.* 605.
39. *Harding v. Brown*, 227 Mass. 77, 117 N. E. 638 (1917).
40. *Maxey v. Bell*, 41 Ga. 183 (1870).
41. *Missouri Rev. Stats. of 1909*, sec. 420.

minors was judged to be a good custom, limited, however, by the social, moral, and financial welfare of the minor.[42]

Inasmuch as the individual having custody of the child is in a strategic position to impress his religious beliefs upon the minor, it is easy to see that the appointment of the guardian by the court may raise religious issues. The conflicting rights of parents or near relatives to inculcate religious teachings in children does not often become a matter for judicial investigation, but those instances which have arisen have been responsible for an important body of judicial doctrine.

Antenuptial agreements.—At common law a father could not divest himself of the custody of his children, even by contract with his wife, either before or after his marriage.[43] An antenuptial agreement that children should be educated in a certain religious sect or set of beliefs was consequently held void in England as early as 1873 by the Court of Appeals in Chancery. At that time the court declared that a father could not bind himself conclusively by contract to exercise, in a special manner, the rights which the law gave him for the benefit of his children and not for his own benefit. In 1878 an agreement by a husband for a similar purpose was held not enforceable in England.[44] American courts have refused to enforce antenuptial agreements relating to the religious education of future children.[45] James Schouler states that public policy is against the permanent transfer of the natural rights of a parent.[46]

Thus, after a mother's death, a suit was instituted by the maternal grandfather to direct the defendant father to permit an infant to be baptized in a religious sect and to allow a four-year-old child to attend church services and be instructed in his mother's religious beliefs, pursuant to an antenuptial agreement.

42. *State v. Bird,* 253 Mo. 569, 162 S. W. 119 (1913).
43. 46 C. J. 1231-1232.
44. *American Law Reports,* XII, 1153.
45. 46 C. J. 1222, note 45. So held in Kansas, Missouri, and Pennsylvania. See especially *Weir v. Marley,* 99 Mo. 484, 12 S. W. 798 (1889).
46. Schouler, *op. cit.,* pp. 490-502.

The grandfather alleged that the father had, by the agreement, divested himself of the usual privilege of a surviving parent in this respect. The Court of Appeals of Missouri reasoned that courts of equity cannot decree the specific performance of a moral duty, nor determine the welfare of an infant on considerations of religion. The right to decide in matters of secular and religious education was judged reserved to the father in this instance. The contract stipulating that the children were to be educated in the fundamentals of a particular religion was declared non-enforceable.[47]

An antenuptial agreement may, however, be persuasive on the judiciary. One such agreement provided that a child should be reared in the mother's faith. Upon the death of the mother, the father's right to educate the child in whatever religious creed he desired was judicially established. The previous agreement was considered merely persuasive. Apart from teachings subversive to morality, the Supreme Court of Kansas said the courts have no control over that part of a child's training which pertains to religious discipline. Religious views were deemed no basis for depriving a parent of custody if he is otherwise qualified.[48]

In Pennsylvania, however, a written agreement was signed by a mother and a father providing for the education of the children of the union in the mother's faith. In 1918 both parents died leaving three children as survivors. The maternal grandaunt opposed the petition of the paternal grandfather to be appointed guardian because the latter was not a member of the mother's religious group. The question raised was whether the antenuptial agreement compelled the court to appoint a guardian of the mother's faith, in view of the law[49] stipulating that persons of the same religious creed as the parents of minors were preferable. The court decided that the welfare of the

47. *Brewer v. Cary*, 148 Mo. App. 193, 127 S. W. 685 (1910).
48. *Denton v. James*, 107 Kan. 729, 193 Pac. 307 (1920).
49. *Pennsylvania Laws of 1917*, Public Law 447.

child was the primary consideration. Although it appeared that
the paternal grandfather did not believe in "too intensive religious training," he testified that he would bring up the children
in the mother's religion until they were able to choose for
themselves. In other words, the guardian would train the children in religious matters as the agreement stated, but his personal persuasion was not the same as that of the mother's.
Under the circumstances the court made him guardian.[50]

The issue as to the validity of one antenuptial agreement
was disposed of on the ground of tardiness. Two children attended a church of their father's choice for many years while
he lived, although the father had promised, in an antenuptial
agreement, to educate the children in the mother's faith. The
mother had been confined in an insane asylum. Prior to the
death of the father, and for approximately three years thereafter, custody was given to the paternal grandmother having the
same religious faith as the father. Subsequently the children
were placed in a private family also having the father's religious
faith. For a total period of seven years the children were
reared in the father's religion. Then a maternal aunt sought
to enforce the anteuptial agreement. The court, however, refused to be drawn into the controversy, and commented that
the request was too tardy for judicial consideration.[51]

Apparently the only statement tending to favor such contracts was made *obiter* in an Ohio decision. After the death of
a mother, a prior agreement between the parents to educate the
children in a specific faith was not observed by the father, who
later died before the case went to trial. In an action for custody, the court, in its regard for the children's welfare, preferred the father's relative to any other person. Nevertheless,
the judge added that, had the controversy been between the
mother and the father instead of the respective relatives of
each, the court would have been bound to treat the agreement

50. *Butchers Estate*, 266 Pa. 479, 109 Atl. 683 (1920).
51. *Commonwealth v. McClelland*, 70 Pa. Super. 273 (1918).

as estoppel of the father's prerogative to change the religion of the children.[52]

Although an antenuptial agreement may possibly give a hint to the judiciary in determining the custody of a child, it remains true that such an agreement is unenforceable per se, confers no legal rights, and will not be upheld by the courts.

Neglect of medical care.—The question whether a parent who believes in divine healing is guilty of homicide for neglecting to obtain a physician for his sick minor child has been posed before the courts. In England in 1868 it was declared that if from conscientious religious conviction that God would heal the sick, and not from any intention to avoid the performance of their duty, the parents of a sick child refused to call in medical assistance, though well able to do so, and the child consequently died, it was not culpable homicide.[53] In the same year the first English act[54] on the subject made it a criminal offense to neglect medical assistance for minors when a life was in danger. On the strength of this statute, convictions for manslaughter were sustained in 1875[55] and in 1899,[56] in the latter case a member of a sect known as "Peculiar People" being found guilty.

By the law of every American state parents are bound to protect the lives of their children. Generally American courts have accepted the English reasoning as to guilt for neglect of performance, and have upheld the punitive action thus prescribed. The practice of refusing to call a physican on the belief that prayer for divine aid is a proper remedy is inconsistent with the peace and safety of the state. Provisions for peace and safety include protection of the lives and health of children, as well as obedience to the laws.[57]

The technical charges themselves have varied. A Pennsyl-

52. *In re Luck*, 10 Ohio Sup. & C. P. Dec. 1 (1899).
53. *Reg. v. Wagstaffe*, 10 Cox. C. C. 530 (1868).
54. *31 and 32 Vict.*, chap. 122 (1868).
55. *Reg. v. Downes*, 13 Cox. C. C. 111 (1875).
56. *Reg. v. Senior*, 1 Q. B. 283 (1899).
57. 16 C. J. S. 603.

vania County Court judgment emphasized criminal negligence. Belief in divine healing as taught by the Christian Science Church, and the subsequent inviting of elders of that sect to a home for the purpose of anointing a sick daughter according to the precepts of the faith, constituted an illegal excuse for the failure to provide medical aid in such circumstances. The court further suggested that if the omission to call a physician, as the ordinary prudent man would have done for the care of his child, caused death, the omission would amount to criminal negligence, religious scruples to the contrary notwithstanding.[58] The State of Indiana prosecuted for manslaughter a father who permitted his child to die without medical attention. The defendant swore that, believing in divine healing, he had procured an elder of his faith to anoint his child with oil and pray for its restoration. The Indiana Supreme Court upheld the conviction for manslaughter.[59] In Oklahoma a conviction on a charge of committing a misdemeanor by similar neglect was sustained.[60]

An exception to the rule of parental responsibility occurred in Maine. The head of a religious community was prosecuted for manslaughter for failure to provide proper medical attendance. The trial court instructed the jury to the effect that when death was hastened by the omission to call a doctor, not because of criminal indifference but because of conscientious disbelief in physicians, it was not criminal negligence if religious methods deemed appropriate by the believers were applied as a cure. The instruction, however, was given in such a way that conviction or acquittal depended upon the belief of individual members of the jury in the efficacy of prayer as a means of caring for the sick. Considering the defense counsel's exception to this instruction by the trial judge, the appellate court pointed out that the guilt or innocence of any person accused of crime, whatever

58. *Commonwealth v. Hoffman*, 29 Pa. Co. Ct. 65 (1901).
59. *State v. Chenewith*, 163 Ind. 94, 71 N. E. 197 (1904). See also *People v. Pearson*, 176 N. Y. 201, 68 N. E. 243 (1903).
60. *Owens v. State*, 6 Okla. Crim. Rep. 110, 116 Pac. 345 (1911).

his religious belief might be, should not depend upon the beliefs of the members of the jury. To permit this would lead to government of men, not government of laws, the court asserted. The exception of defense counsel was sustained.[61]

Summary.—Parents have sometimes disagreed between themselves in the matter of the religious training of their children. By the death of one parent, by the action of relatives, and by the existence of antenuptial agreements, for example, the judicatory facilities of the government have been called upon to analyze parental conflicts in which religious beliefs have played a vital part.

Under the common law the married couple was considered a unit; the right of the father to determine the religious training of his children was paramount. In early American statutes and decisions the father's right to control his child was emphasized. Changing laws, however, have modified the principle of paternal supremacy. As a result of later state laws the American courts, in cases of custody, now give primary consideration to the welfare of the child.

In determining the custody of children where the question of religious beliefs is involved, most courts emphasize the co-equality of both mother and father when both are living, or the exclusive right of the survivor, assuming the welfare of the children is not at stake. The co-equality of the parents when both are living, or the exclusive right of the survivor, does not prevail when the welfare of the children is in jeopardy. In such instances the parental attitude toward religious training becomes secondary to the mental and physical advantages of the minor.

Subject to the primary consideration of the welfare of the child, the father sometimes is awarded the right to prescribe the child's religious education. The religious convictions of a father usually do not constitute an excuse for the court's award-

61. *State v. Sandford*, 99 Me. 441, 59 Atl. 597 (1905).

ing the custody of the child to another. However, if a father professes belief in a sect obnoxious to society, he may be deprived of the custody of his child. A father may have no right to interfere with the freedom of conscience of a minor child who has reached the age of discretion.

In determining the custody of children as between individuals other than parents, the judiciary usually considers temporal welfare superior to religious doctrine. Nevertheless, the custody of the child is generally given to persons of the same faith as that of the father, if the temporal welfare of the child will be as well taken care of by such persons as by those of another faith.

American courts have refused to enforce antenuptial agreements relating to the religious education of children. Such agreements, however, may be persuasive on the courts in their determination of the custody of children. The question whether a parent who believes in divine healing is guilty of a crime in neglecting to obtain a physician for his sick minor child is generally answered affirmatively by the American judiciary. Such a parental practice contravenes the protection which the state, in the exercise of its police power, has extended to its young citizens.

IX

Educational Practices Involving the Right of
Religious Freedom

Non-sectarianism in public education.—For over three hundred years, individuals representative of cosmopolitan Europe
and embracing a host of religious creeds have established themselves upon American shores. The great diversity of their
religious practices has been a matter of historical record. As
the forefathers had frequently expressed their determination to
establish a land of religious freedom, they were not content
merely to write into their early state constitutions guarantees
of freedom of conscience and worship. Recognition of a solemn
obligation to retain religious liberty for future generations
prompted pioneer American statesmen to incorporate into their
legal documents specific provisions assuring an educational system of free common schools in which their children were to be
educated on an equal plane and where sectarian instruction and
intolerance should never enter.[1]

In this respect "sectarian" has meant "denominational"; that
is, devoted to, peculiar to, or promotive of the interest of a sect.
A sectarian institution has been defined as "an institution affiliated with a particular religious sect or denomination, or under
the control or governing influence of such sect or denomination;
one whose purpose, as expressed in its charter, and whose acts,

1. B. Brown, "Religious Liberty and the Schools" (1939) 18 *Oregon Law
Review* 122-128. See A. W. Johnson, *The Legal Status of Church-State
Relationships in the United States.*

done pursuant to powers conferred, are promotive of tenets or interests of a denomination or sect."[2] Such institutions remain outside the sphere of political control.

Cognizant of the necessity of a complete divorce of the public school from any partisan influence, states have become imbued with the concept that all state constitutions should definitely provide for the isolation of public education from sectarianism; thus no person may rightfully expect that the state will use the facilities of its educational system to further the religious interests of any specific sect within its boundaries. However, the general principle of nonsectarianism in public education has sometimes become clouded in particular situations. Consequently the courts have been called upon to analyze educational practices assertedly a denial of religious freedom.

Public aid.—Public aid for schools of a sectarian nature, either in the form of a grant of money or the use of public property, is prohibited either directly or indirectly by every state constitution.[3] Indicative of the financial cleavage between denominational and public schools is the history of the pertinent rules in the State of New York.

In 1805 the New York state legislature declared[4] that public money for the establishment of free schools in the City of New York could be expended only in those instances where the students were not controlled by a religious group. The revised state constitution of 1821 provided for a common school fund for the exclusive use of non-sectarian schools throughout the state.[5] The Appropriation Act of 1842[6] specifically prevented schools which taught any religious doctrine from receiving state money. The Educational Law of 1844[7] stated that no school

2. 56 *C. J.* 1272-1273.

3. 59 *C. J.* 211; see also doctrine of "public purpose," 61 *C. J.* 88-96; for declaration of policy making no appropriation for education in any sectarian school see *Quick Bear v. Leupp*, 210 U. S. 50, 28 Sup. Ct. 690, 52 L. Ed. 954 (1907).

4. *New York Laws of 1805*, chap. 108.

5. Art. VII, sec. 10.   6. *New York Laws of 1842*, chap. 150.

7. *New York Laws of 1844*, chap. 320.

would be entitled to a portion of the school appropriation in which a religious sectarian doctrine or tenet of any particular Christian or other religious sect was taught or practiced. No financial aid would be extended to any school in which any book was used containing compositions favorable or prejudicial to the particular doctrine or tenets of any Christian sect.

The rule of the Constitution of 1821 was reaffirmed by Article IX of the Constitution of 1846. In 1853, despite the urgence of a religious group that the state set up and finance schools in which religion might be taught, the legislature reasserted the general policy of separation of church and state. It has been reported that the legislature at this time believed that a reversal of this policy would ruin the common schools and initiate controversies among various sects.[8] In the constitutional convention of 1894, after a reconsideration of the whole problem, Article IX of the constitution of 1846 was restated as follows: "Neither the State nor any subdivision thereof, shall use its property or credit or any public money, or authorize or permit either to be used, directly or indirectly, in aid or maintenance, other than for examination or inspection, of any school or institution of learning wholly or in part under the control or direction of any religious denomination, or in which any denominational tenet or doctrine is taught."[9] With a desire to continue the state's traditional policy, the Home Rule Amendment for Cities, which was adopted in 1923, included the proviso that "nothing in this article contained shall apply to or affect the maintenance, support, or administration of the public school systems in the several cities of the State, as required or provided by article nine of the constitution."[10] The New York State Constitutional Convention of 1938 incorporated Article IX in the revised constitution of 1938. This section[11] became effective on January 1, 1939.

8. See *Judd v. Board of Education*, 278 N. Y. 200, 15 N. E. (2d) 576 (1938).

9. Art. IX, sec. 3.   10. Art. XII, sec. 7.   11. Art. XI, sec. 4.

Thus the attitude of the New York state legislature, expressed early in the nineteenth century, that the state should remain aloof from financial support for sectarian educational institutions, has become crystallized into the fundamental law as expressed by the state constitution. This legislative background, paralleled in other states, has constituted the basis for judicial thought on the subject. As Justice Rippey of New York wrote in 1938, "Any contribution directly or indirectly made in aid of the maintenance and support of any private or sectarian school out of public funds would be a violation of the concept of complete separation of Church and State in civil affairs and of the spirit and mandate of our fundamental law."[12]

The illegality of proposals to extend state aid directly is thus foreshadowed. Flagrant attempts to appropriate public money for specific sectarian educational activities are basically unconstitutional. However, for an evaluation of legislation of a less obvious nature, the power of the judiciary has been invoked to determine whether the constitutional limitations upon public financial assistance have been transgressed.

Judicial decree will enjoin the payment of a share of the public school fund to a sectarian orphan asylum conducting a school in which its wards are receiving instruction similar to common school education. A special appropriation law[13] which assisted the sectarian institution was illegal.[14] The issue has been raised whether a mandamus should be issued to require a state superintendent of public instruction to apportion part of the interest and income from the state common school trust fund to an allegedly non-sectarian school. A court in 1932 noted that a particular building and its surroundings created an atmosphere reflecting the essence of sectarianism and decided in the negative. The opinion declared that the inculcation of a particular religion was part of the school work. To make the

12. *Judd v. Board of Education,* 278 N. Y. 200, 211, 15 N. E. (2d) 576, 582 (1938).
13. *New York Laws of 1848,* chap. 76.
14. *People v. Board of Education,* 13 Barb. (N. Y.) 400 (1851).

resulting apportionment would have amounted to an illegal diversion of public funds. The exercise of discretion by the administrative officer in denying the apportionment was upheld.[15]

In spite of allegations to the contrary, the fact that teachers in a public school system contribute a large part of their earnings to a religious order does not constitute an appropriation of public money for sectarian purposes, within the meaning of state constitutions. An action in Pennsylvania questioned the legality of the payment of public money as salary to denominationally trained teachers employed by a public school district. A court dismissed the action. On the issue of the use of the salary so paid, a judge held that "it is none of our business, nor that of these appellants, to inquire into this matter. American men and women, of sound mind and twenty-one years of age, can make such disposition of their surplus earnings as suits their own notions."[16]

Similarly the North Dakota Supreme Court concluded that a person employed by the state or any of its subdivisions was not prevented from contributing money, earned by service so performed, for the support of a religious body of which he or she might be a member. To deny the right to make such a contribution would have in itself constituted a denial of that right of religious liberty which the constitution guaranteed, the court stated. The employment of duly qualified nuns as teachers in the public schools was upheld.[17]

Prior to 1947, in the absence of constitutional authorization, the free transportation of pupils at the expense of the school district to other than public schools had been nullified by court action, on the theory that such service was paid for by public money contrary to fundamental law. The decision by the New York Court of Appeals in 1938 to restrain a local school board,

15. *State v. Taylor*, 122 Neb. 454, 240 N. W. 573 (1932).
16. *Hysong v. School District*, 164 Pa. 629, 656, 30 Atl. 482, 484 (1894).
17. *Gerhardt v. Heid*, 66 N. D. 444, 267 N. W. 127 (1936).

acting under state law, from furnishing transportation for pupils attending a private school, and to cancel an assessment of $3,350 on the property of the district for bus hire, was characteristic of judicial reasoning where no constitutional approval existed.

In that instance the court stated that in so far as public funds were authorized to pay for pupil transportation to religious schools, such authorization contravened the state constitution.[18]   In other words, all public money for educational purposes must be used exclusively for the public schools. The court further explained that any contribution made not directly but nevertheless beneficially to a sectarian institution was indirect aid and illegal. Since free transportation of pupils promoted attendance at school, the interests of the school, too, were promoted. The opinion dismissed as illogical the argument that offering transportation was not an aid to the school.[19]   Similar decisions in Wisconsin[20] and Delaware[21] preceded the New York interpretation.

The New York decision was made by a four-to-three vote. From a legal point of view, at least, a review of the minority opinion is interesting. The judge writing the dissent reasoned that having made attendance at school compulsory, and having approved attendance at certain schools other than public, the state legislature merely permitted the district to provide transportation to a school which the students might legally attend. The statute was not intended to aid institutions, insisted the minority, but simply to assist children of the district in reaching school. The dissent observed that "there is no benefit to the schools except, perhaps, as one may conceive an accidental benefit in the sense that some parents might place their children in religious schools when they anticipate transportation provision, although they might hesitate to do so if the children were com-

18. Art. IX, sec. 4.
19. *Judd v. Board of Education,* 278 N. Y. 200, 15 N. E. (2d) 576 (1938).
20. *State v. Milquet,* 180 Wisc. 109, 192 N. W. 392 (1923).
21. *State v. Brown,* 36 Del. 181 (1938).

pelled to make their own way. The constitutional provision is not designed to discourage or thwart the school where religious instruction is imparted."[22] Approving the minority viewpoint, the New York State Constitutional Convention of 1938 amended the basic education law by permitting the legislature to provide for the transportation of children to and from any school.[23] On the strength of this amendment the transportation of children to other than public schools in New York State at the expense of the school district is legal.

In Maryland free transportation of children to sectarian schools was upheld. A state statute provided that children attending Baltimore County schools not receiving state aid were entitled to transportation on school buses on the same terms as public school children.[24] The highest court of the state ruled that the law did not authorize an unconstitutional use of public funds for private purposes, since attendance at private or parochial schools constituted compliance with the law making school attendance compulsory. The fact that private schools, including parochial schools, received a benefit from the use of public funds did not prevent what was deemed to be the legislature's performance of a public function.[25]

A landmark decision involving the free transportation of sectarian school pupils was rendered in 1947. A New Jersey statute permitted local school districts to contract for the transportation of children to and from public and private schools (except those operated for profit). A local board of education, acting pursuant to the statute, authorized the reimbursement of parents for money they had expended for the transportation of their children on regular busses operated by the public transportation system. Part of this money was payment for the transportation of some children to sectarian schools. A taxpayer

22. *Judd v. Board of Education*, 278 N. Y. 200, 221, 15 N. E. (2d) 576, 586 (1938).
23. Art. XI, sec. 4.
24. *Maryland Acts, 1937*, c. 185.
25. *Board of Education v. Wheat*, 174 Md. 314, 199 Atl. 628 (1938).

challenged the right of the board to reimburse parents of sectarian school students, allegedly because the law and the resolution violated both the state and federal constitutions. After the New Jersey Court of Errors and Appeals had upheld the law and the resolution, the case was appealed to the United States Supreme Court.

The Supreme Court, by a five-to-four vote, sustained the state's action.[25a] To the argument that the law and the resolution authorized the state to take private property by taxation and bestow it upon others, for the latter's private purposes, contrary to the due process clause of the Fourteenth Amendment, the Court answered that the state legislature had decided that a public purpose would be served by using tax-raised funds to pay the bus fares of all school children, including those who attended sectarian schools. It is much too late to argue, Mr. Justice Black commented in the majority opinion, that legislation intended to facilitate the opportunity of children to obtain a secular education serves no public purpose. To the contention that the law and the resolution forced individuals to pay taxes to help support sectarian schools, contrary to the First Amendment (which the Fourteenth Amendment made applicable to the states), the Court stated that it could not say that the First Amendment prohibited the state from spending tax-raised funds to pay the bus fares of sectarian school pupils as a part of a general program under which it pays the fares of pupils attending public and other schools.

Two vigorous dissenting opinions highlighted the Court's determination in the foregoing case. Mr. Justice Jackson accused the majority of sustaining the legislation by making two deviations from the facts of the case: first, by assuming a state of facts not supported by the record; and second, by refusing to consider

25a. *Everson v. Board of Education of the Township of Ewing*, 330 U. S. 1, 67 Sup. Ct. 504, 91 L. Ed. 472 (1947); rehearing denied 330 U. S. 855 (1947); J. E. Cosgrove and E. J. Flattery, "Transportation of Parochial School Pupils" (1947) 22 *Notre Dame Lawyer* 192-200.

facts which were inescapable on the record. Mr. Justice Rutledge, holding that the state's action furnished support for religion by use of the taxing power, concluded that the prohibition of the First Amendment forbids a state to give to religion, financially or otherwise, support in any guise or form.

The use of public funds to furnish textbooks to students in other than public schools has resulted in two conflicting judicial conclusions. Analysis of decisions in New York and Louisiana reveal sharp inconsistencies.

The New York state legislature passed an act[26] permitting local school boards to provide textbooks or other supplies to all the children attending the schools of cities in which free textbooks or other supplies were lawfully provided. In 1922 an action was brought by a taxpayer to restrain a board of education from procuring with public funds and delivering free textbooks and ordinary school supplies for the use of pupils in schools other than public. The action was sustained by the Appellate Division of the New York Supreme Court. The Appellate Division indicated that the law pertained only to those schools which were under the management of a local board of education. Discounting the assertion that the texts and supplies were given to the students themselves and not to the private religious school, the court commented: "The scholars do not use textbooks and ordinary school supplies apart from their studies in the school. They want them for the sole purpose of their work there. There is no question but that the text-books and ordinary supplies are furnished direct to the public schools; there is no thought that they are furnished to the scholars as distinct from the schools; neither can there be such a thought in the case of the parochial schools."[27] The benefit of the books to the student was here held inseparable from the benefit of the books to the school.

26. *New York Education Law*, sec. 868.
27. *Smith v. Donahue*, 195 N. Y. S. 715, 719, 202 App. Div. 656, 661 (1922).

The Louisiana legislature in 1928 provided for the furnishing of school books free to all of the children of the state, regardless of whether they attended a public school.[28] The Louisiana Supreme Court by a four-to-three decision declared that the act was a legal exercise of legislative power. Although the Louisiana constitution, similar to that of New York, prohibited the expenditure of public money for the aid of any church or sect, the court held that the sectarian institutions were not the beneficiaries. Rather, the school children and the state alone were assisted. The interpretation given the statute is revealed in a statement of the prevailing opinion: "It is . . . true that the sectarian schools, which some of the children attend, instruct their pupils in religion, and books are used for that purpose, but one may search diligently the acts, though without result, in an effort to find anything to the effect that it is the purpose of the state to furnish religious books for the use of such children."[29]

On the other hand the minority opinion of the Louisiana State Court was similar to the majority decision of the Appellate Division of the New York Supreme Court. Observing that the maintenance of private or sectarian schools was not a public purpose so as to justify the expenditure of public money in support of such schools, the Louisiana dissenting opinion declared that school books were as essential to school instruction as were school houses and teachers. The court minority denied the ability of the legislature to separate benefits to the individual student from benefits to the sect and repudiated the theory that public money could be used for the purpose of furnishing students in private and sectarian schools with necessary educational facilities. Consequently, the appropriation of the public funds for the purchase of books for all the children of the state was deemed an attempt to do indirectly that which could not be done directly.

28. *Louisiana Acts of 1928*, nos. 100, 143.
29. *Borden v. Louisiana State Board of Education*, 168 La. 1005, 1020, 123 So. 655, 661 (1929).

A similar opinion of the majority of the Louisiana Supreme Court in a subsequent case[30] was reviewed by the United States Supreme Court with respect to the federal question whether taxation for the purpose of providing such school books constituted a taking of private property for a private purpose. The United States Supreme Court said that, in view of the determination by the State court that only the use of the books was granted to the children, the taxing power of the State was exerted for a public purpose.[31]

The Louisiana doctrine was followed in Mississippi. A law of Mississippi empowered a state board to purchase and distribute free textbooks by loaning them to the pupils through the first eight grades in all qualified elementary schools located in the State.[32] An appropriation of $1,250,000 was made during the same year to pay the expenses of the board and to purchase free textbooks. Suit was brought alleging that the distribution or loan of these books to pupils in other than free public schools constituted an appropriation of funds for the support of sectarian schools.

The Mississippi Supreme Court reasoned that, in enacting the law, the Mississippi legislature had had in mind its constitutional duty to encourage the promotion of intellectual improvement and the need of furnishing aid to children of school age in order to have uniform textbooks available for their use. The appropriation was deemed not a use or diversion of educational funds as prohibited by the State constitution. It was considered that the books belonged to, and were controlled by, the State; they were merely loaned to the individual pupil. The request for an injunction against the loaning of such books to pupils in private sectarian schools was denied.[33]

30. *Cochran v. Louisiana State Board of Education,* 168 La. 1030, 123 So. 664 (1929).
31. *Cochran v. Louisiana State Board of Education,* 281 U. S. 370, 50 Sup. Ct. 335, 74 L. Ed. 913 (1930).
32. Laws of 1940, chap. 202.
33. *Chance v. Mississippi State Textbook R. & P. Board,* 190 Miss. 453,

However, the courts will prohibit the use of public money for the payment of the tuition fees of students in sectarian schools. The argument that such tuition fees are for the benefit of the students exclusively has been held of no avail.[34]

Reading the Bible in public schools.—Much litigation arising over alleged sectarianism in the public schools has revolved about the question of whether reading the Bible, in whole or in part, without comment, in the classroom, infringes upon the American concept of religious freedom. The basis of the conflict lies in the differences in the King James and Douay versions of the Bible, followed, respectively, by the Protestants and Catholics. Judicial decisions have been sharply divided over the question whether presentations of biblical excerpts constitute religious exercises contrary to constitutional provisions.[35]

The general view of those courts upholding Bible reading by the classroom teacher, without comment, is that the schoolhouse is not transformed into a place of worship thereby, and that the object of constitutional inhibitions is to prevent the collection of taxes for a place distinctly used as a place of worship, rather than to prohibit the casual rendition of biblical passages.[36]

Judicial comment in cases approving biblical reading in the public schools has varied. Holding the Bible to be a nonsectarian book, the Maine Supreme Court once said that although the common schools are not established for the purpose of instruction in the theological doctrines of any religion or of any

---

200 So. 706 (1941); see also Sylvan M. Cohen, "Relation of Freedom of Religion to Loan of Textbooks to Private Schools" (1941) 1 *Bill of Rights Review* 307-310.

34. *Otken v. Lamkin*, 56 Miss. 758 (1879); *People v. Board of Education*, 13 Barb. (N. Y.) 400 (1851).

35. L. A. Stith, "Bible Reading in the Public Schools" (1929) 32 *Law Notes* 225-228; T. V. K., "Reading the Bible in Public Schools" (1930) 28 *Michigan Law Review* 430-436.

36. 16 *C. J. S.* 604, notes 87-89. So held in Pennsylvania, Maine, Colorado, California, Minnesota, Massachusetts, Kentucky, New York, Iowa, Michigan, Georgia, and Texas.

sect, "reading the Bible is no more an interference with religious belief, than would reading the mythology of Greece or Rome be regarded as interfering with religious belief or an affirmance of the pagan creeds."[37] It was stated in Massachusetts that no more appropriate method could be adopted for keeping in the minds of both teachers and scholars the fact that one of the chief objects of education is to impress on the minds of children the principles of piety and justice, and a sacred regard for the truth.[38]

In a suit seeking to prevent certain Kentucky school trustees from allowing the reading of a particular version of the Bible, the court was careful to remind the parties at bar that the meetings of the State legislature were opened by prayer. Concerning the nature of the Book itself, the court remarked: "That the Bible, or any particular edition, has been adopted by one or more denominations as authentic, or by them asserted to be inspired, cannot make it a sectarian book. The book itself, to be sectarian, must show that it teaches the peculiar dogmas of a sect as such, and not alone that it is so comprehensive as to include them by the partial interpretation of its adherents. Nor is a book sectarian merely because it was edited or compiled by those of a particular sect."[39]

A Pennsylvania school board once set aside a school room for the convenient and exclusive use of children who did not desire to participate in opening Bible exercises. An action challenging the validity of the board's decision alleged that discrimination against those who did not desire to participate violated the constitutional guarantees of religious freedom. The court decided, however, that no infringement of their constitutional rights resulted.[40] Reading the Bible, repeating the Lord's Prayer, and singing religious songs in the public schools were

37. *Donahue v. Richards,* 38 Me. 379, 399 (1854).
38. *Spiller v. Inhabitants of Woburn,* 94 Mass. 127 (1866).
39. *Hackett v. Brooksville,* 120 Ky. 608, 617, 87 S. W. 792, 794 (1905).
40. *Hart v. School District,* 2 Lanc. Law Rev. 346 (1885).

upheld in Iowa.[41]   The charter of the City of New York prohibits the Board of Education from excluding the holy Scriptures from any of the local schools.[42] A taxpayer's suit to restrain
readings of the Bible in the public schools of New York City
through an attack on the constitutionality of the charter provision was not sustained.   In no sense was the practice of reading from Scriptures considered destructive of the proper division
between church and state.[43]

In reply to the argument that the reading of the Bible in a
public school violated the guarantee that no person should be
required to attend a place of worship, the Supreme Court of
Colorado pointed out that a schoolhouse was not such a place,
even if the Bible was read there.   To the argument over the
differences in the versions of the Bible, it was stated that pro-
scription could not make that sectarian which was not actually
so.   If it could, the court held, the atheist could proscribe the
Star Spangled Banner.   The court maintained that the sectarianism of a book could not be determined by the way various
sects might regard it.[44]

Compulsory attendance in a public school in which the Ten
Commandments were taught did not constitute compulsory attendance at a place of religious worship in Michigan.[45]   A city
ordinance requiring the reading of a specific version of the
Bible and the saying of a prayer daily in the schools was not
illegal in Georgia.[46]   Morning exercises in a public school in
Texas consisted of the reading of the Bible by the teacher and
the singing of appropriate songs in which the students were
invited but not required to join.   Such practices were held not
to render the school a place of worship, which was defined as

41. *Moore v. Monroe*, 64 Iowa 367, 20 N. W. 475 (1884).
42. *City of New York Charter*, sec. 1151.
43. *Lewis v. Board of Education*, 285 N. Y. S. 164, 157 Misc. 520
(1935); D. L. Q., "Constitutional Law—Religion in the Public Schools"
(1936) 34 *Michigan Law Review* 1237-1239.
44. *People v. Stanley*, 81 Colo. 276, 255 Pac. 610 (1927).
45. *Pfeiffer v. Board of Education*, 118 Mich. 560, 77 N. W. 250 (1898).
46. *Wilkerson v. City of Rome*, 152 Ga. 762, 110 S. E. 895 (1921).

a place where a number of persons meet for the purpose of worshiping God.[47]

Placing copies of a particular version of the Bible in a public school library was not prohibited by a California law[48] requiring school authorities to exclude all sectarian books and papers from the schools and school libraries. The mere act of purchasing a book to be added to the school library was held not to carry with it any implication of the adoption of the theory or dogma contained therein.[49] An action was brought to prevent alleged waste of city money through the purchase of biblical readings to be used in the public schools of the city of New York. The chief argument of the prosecution was that the purchasing of such books from public funds intended for secular education constituted an illegal act by the board of education. The suit was dismissed.[50]

On the other hand, the use of the Bible as a text or as selected reading has been held to inculcate sectarian principles in the public educational system.[51] The use of the Bible has been deemed to constitute a preference of Christians over Jews. Excusing children from attendance at classrooms in which the Bible is to be read has been said to place a religious stigma on the children so excused.[52]

A leading decision refusing to countenance the use of the Bible in the public schools was handed down by the Illinois Supreme Court in 1911. The facts in the case were typical: some of the teachers in the public schools commenced the school day by causing their pupils to rise in their seats, fold their hands, and bow their heads while the teachers read from the

47. *Church v. Bullock*, 104 Tex. 1, 109 S. W. 115 (1908).
48. *California Revised Statutes*, sec. 2307.
49. *Evans v. Selma Union High School Board*, 193 Cal. 54, 222 Pac. 801 (1924).
50. *Lewis v. Board of Education*, 258 N. Y. 117, 179 N. E. 315 (1932).
51. 16 C. J. S. 604, note 92. So held in Illinois, Louisiana, Wisconsin, Ohio, Washington, and Nebraska.
52. *Herold v. Parish Board of School Directors*, 136 La. 1034, 68 So. 116 (1915).

King James version of the Bible and while the teachers and pupils recited together the King James version of the Lord's Prayer. Occasionally the pupils were asked the meaning of the passages read. Five residents of a school district applied for a writ of mandamus directed to the board of education commanding the board to require the teachers to desist from such practices. The constitution of the state prohibited the appropriation of any public fund in aid of any church or sectarian school or other sectarian institution.[53] The chief argument of the residents was that the practices of the teachers rendered the schools sectarian institutions. The Illinois Supreme Court held that the reading of the Bible in the public schools was equivalent to giving sectarian instruction within the meaning of the constitution. The court went on to explain that religion should be taught in religious schools and meetings and at home instead of in the common schools. The parts of the Scripture forming the basis of sectarian differences could not be intelligently read without making an impression, favorable or unfavorable, in reference to the ideas derived therefrom, the court concluded.[54]

Refusing to sanction the reading of the Bible in the public schools in Wisconsin, the State Supreme Court ruled: "When, as in this case, a small minority of the pupils in the public school is excluded, for any cause, from a stated school exercise, particularly when such cause is apparent hostility to the Bible, which a majority of the pupils have been taught to revere, from that moment the excluded pupil loses caste with his fellows, and is liable to be regarded with aversion, and subjected to reproach and insult."[55]

A public school teacher in Nebraska conducted exercises during school hours which consisted of reading biblical passages,

53. Art. VIII, sec. 3.
54. *People v. Board of Education*, 245 Ill. 334, 92 N. E. 251 (1910); Henry Schofield, "Religious Liberty and Bible Reading in Illinois Public Schools" (1911) 6 *Illinois Law Review* 17-32.
55. *State v. District Board*, 76 Wisc. 177, 199, 44 N. W. 967, 975 (1890).

singing songs and hymns, and offering prayer to the Deity in accordance with the doctrine, beliefs, and customs of a sectarian organization. In a taxpayer's application for mandamus to stop such practices, the Supreme Court of the state suggested that the reading of the Bible in public schools constituted both compulsory religious worship and sectarian instruction. Issuing the writ, the court said: "If the system of compulsory education is persevered in, and religious worship or sectarian instruction in the public schools is at the same time permitted, parents will be compelled to expose their children to what they deem spiritual contamination, or else, while bearing their share of the burden for the support of public education, provide the means from their own pockets for the training of their offspring elsewhere."[56] In Washington, the provision for an optional course of Bible study in public high schools, with the work to be prepared outside of school, contravened a constitutional policy against the use of public money for religious exercises.[57]   A resolution of a school board prohibiting the reading of the Bible in public schools was attacked in Ohio. The question was whether a constitutional provision,[58] imposing a duty to protect every religious denomination, required religious instruction in the public schools. Stating that the constitution of the state did not require religious instruction and that the court had no authority to dictate to a board of education what instruction should be given or what books should be read in the public schools, the court upheld the resolution.[59]

Compulsory flag salute.—Prior to 1943 an increasing number of localities adopted statutes or regulations requiring all public school students to salute and pledge allegiance to the American flag. The legality of such regulations has been questioned by religious minorities, particularly members of a sect

56. *State v. Scheve*, 65 Neb. 853, 872, 91 N. W. 846, 847 (1902).
57. *State v. Frazier*, 102 Wash. 369, 173 Pac. 35 (1918).
58. Art. I, sec. 7.
59. *Board of Education v. Minor*, 23 Ohio St. 211 (1872).

known as Jehovah's Witnesses, who conscientiously believe that the ritual of the flag salute is forbidden by scripture. The Bible as the Word of God is the supreme authority to members of this sect. Great stress is placed on verses four and five of chapter twenty of the Book of Exodus which read: "(4) Thou shall not make unto thee any graven image, or any likeness of any thing that is in heaven above, or that is in the earth beneath, or that is in the water under the earth: (5) Thou shalt not bow down thyself to them, nor serve them: . . ." Does requiring children of Jehovah's Witnesses to participate in a flag salute ceremony in the public schools violate their religious liberties?

Until 1940 court opinion on the problem was divided.[60] One group of cases questioning the constitutionality of regulations requiring the salute of the flag in the public schools resulted in judicial approval of such regulations. In 1937 in New Jersey,[61] Massachusetts,[62] and Georgia[63] it was declared that saluting the flag had no religious significance; a pledge to the American flag violated no religious right.

In the same year, however, the contrary rule was adopted in connection with a regulation of the Minersville, Pennsylvania, School Board. The defendant school board had adopted a rule requiring all teachers and pupils to salute the flag as part of the daily school exercises. According to the regulation, refusal to salute was to be considered an act of insubordination. After two minor children of the plaintiff, both Jehovah's Witnesses, had been expelled by the superintendent for refusal to salute the flag, the parents, financially unable to provide private education for their children, sought an injunction to restrain enforcement of the board's rule.

60. E. M. Million, "Validity of Compulsory Flag Salutes in Public Schools" (1940) 28 *Kentucky Law Journal* 306-320; Note, "Compulsory Flag Salutes and Religious Freedom" (1938) 51 *Harvard Law Review* 1418-1424.
    61. *Hering v. State Board of Education*, 117 N. J. Law 455, 189 Atl. 629 (1937).
    62. *Nicholls v. Mayor of Lynn*, 7 N. E. (2d) 577 (1937).
    63. *Leoles v. Landers*, 184 Ga. 580, 192 S. E. 218 (1937).

A United States District Court declared that the minors in question had a right to attend public schools, and further that they had a duty to do so if they were unable to secure an equivalent education privately. It seemed to the court that the refusal of the children to salute the flag in school exercises could not in any way prejudice or imperil the public safety, health, or morals or the property or personal rights of their fellow citizens. The court held that no one, school board member, superintendent, or judge, could set the bounds to the areas of human conduct in which religious convictions should be permitted to have control, unless the public necessity compelled the exercise of the police power. Requiring a flag salute as a condition of exercising the right or performing the duty of attending school was thus held to contravene the Pennsylvania constitution and the Fourteenth Amendment to the Federal Constitution. The pertinent part of the court's decision reasoned: "If an individual sincerely bases his acts or refusals to act on religious grounds they must be accepted as such and may only be interfered with if it becomes necessary to do so in connection with the exercise of the police power, that is, if it appears that the public safety, health or morals or property or personal rights will be prejudiced by them. To permit public officers to determine whether the views of individuals sincerely held and their acts sincerely undertaken on religious grounds are in fact based on convictions religious in character would be to sound the death knell of religious liberty. To such a pernicious and alien doctrine this court cannot subscribe."[64]

Incidentally, this decision ran counter to per curiam decisions of the United States Supreme Court. In two instances the United States Supreme Court had dismissed, on the ground of want of a substantial federal question, appeals from the judgments of state courts upholding the validity of regulations re-

64. *Gobitis v. Minersville School District*, 21 F. Supp. 581, 584 (D. C., 1939); see also F. W. Grinnel, "Children, the Bill of Rights and the American Flag" (1939) 24 *Massachusetts Law Quarterly* 1-7.

quiring the pledge of allegiance and salute to the flag as applied to public school pupils objecting on religious grounds.[65]

In 1938 the expulsion from public school of a minor who refused because of religious convictions to pledge allegiance and salute the flag raised the issue of religious liberty in the Supreme Court of California. The child had been willing to stand quietly and respectfully during the ceremony, but would not participate in the exercises. The state court decided that, in view of the refusal of the United States Supreme Court to entertain appeals from state court judgments affirming the legality of such requirements, evidently no federal rights were involved. By analogy no state constitutional rights were held to be infringed, and the expulsion was upheld.[66] In the same year the Court of Civil Appeals of Texas was asked to enjoin the enforcement of an order suspending two children from a local school because of their refusal to salute the flag at certain school exercises. Because the school year, and hence the period of suspension, had ended before the appellees had filed their motion, the question was deemed to be moot, and the attitude of the Texas Civil Court of Appeals was thus not expressed.[67]

In 1939 the question of compelling a salute to the flag in alleged violation of religious freedom was raised in the state courts of two states, New York and Florida, and in a federal district court in Massachusetts. In each instance the court upheld the requirement, refusing to follow the decision in the Minersville case. Each regulation requiring pupils to salute the American flag and recite a pledge of allegiance was held not to interfere with religious freedom.

In the Massachusetts case a United States District Court

65. *Leoles v. Landers,* 302 U. S. 656, 58 Sup. Ct. 364, 82 L. Ed. 507 (1937); *Hering v. State Board of Education,* 303 U. S. 624, 58 Sup. Ct. 742, 82 L. Ed. 1086 (1938).

66. *Gabrielli v. Knickerbocker,* 82 P. (2d) 391 (1938); W. Bonaparte, "Expulsion from School for Refusal to Salute the Flag" (1940) 13 *Southern California Law Review* 222-227.

67. *Shinn v. Barrow,* 121 S. W. (2d) 450 (1938).

held that the constitutional right of children to attend the public schools was not an absolute right, but was subject to such reasonable conditions as the state might desire to impose.[68] In the New York case the conviction of parents for failing to require their thirteen-year-old daughter to attend school because of their religious convictions against saluting the flag was sustained. The court commented: "To enjoy the benefits of freedom and the privileges offered in these United States correspondingly demands of its citizens that they support, defend, and obey its laws. Where better to start than to salute its flag, the symbol of government? . . . The religious zealot, if his liberties were to be thus extended, might refuse to contribute taxes in furtherance of a school system that compelled students to salute the flag."[69]

The Florida Supreme Court upheld the expulsion of children of Jehovah's Witnesses with the remark that saluting the flag was merely a symbolical expression of loyalty, or, in effect, patriotism in action, having no reference to religious faith. The court explained that saluting the flag connoted a love and patriotic devotion to one's country while religious practice connoted a way of life, the brand of one's theology, or his relation to God. A county board of public instruction did not violate the legal guarantees of religious freedom by requiring that all students show such respect to the flag.[70]

Thus by the end of 1939 the overwhelming majority of decisions sustained the requirement that children in the public schools should salute the flag, including the children of persons who might believe that saluting the flag contravened the law of God. But the prominence of the Minersville decision and the fact that it was affirmed by a Federal Circuit Court of Appeals left the issue unsettled until the Supreme Court overruled

68. *Johnson v. Deerfield*, 25 F. Supp. 918 (D. C., 1939).
69. *People v. Sandstrom*, 3 N. Y. S. (2d) 1006, 1008-1009, 167 Misc. 436 (1938); P. S., "Compulsory Salute to the Flag and the Guaranty of Religious Freedom" (1938) 13 *St. John's Law Review* 144-147.
70. *State v. Board of Public Instruction*, 139 Fla. 43, 190 So. 815 (1939).

the decisions of the lower federal courts in the Minersville case.[71]

Although the Supreme Court admitted that the case was not concerned with an exercise of power to promote a specific need of society, as is the case in the usual exertion of the police power, every specific activity of government was thought to presuppose the existence of a cohesive political society. In other words, national unity as symbolized by the flag was deemed fundamental to the exercise of the police power. Viewed in this light, the issue for the court to determine was whether the state legislatures had the power to decide the appropriateness of various techniques designed to induce a unifying sentiment, without which no religious liberty could exist. The end being legitimate, the court refused to substitute its judgment for that of the legislature. The court admitted that the wisdom of training children in patriotic impulses by those compulsions which necessarily pervaded much of the educational process was not a matter for its exclusive judgment. "But the court-room is not the arena for debating issues of educational policy."[72]

The opinion went on to explain that "what the school authorities are really asserting is the right to awaken in the child's mind considerations as to the significance of the flag contrary to those implanted by the parent. In such an attempt the state is normally at a disadvanage in competing with the parent's authority, so long—and this is the vital aspect of religious toleration—as parents are unmolested in their right to counteract by their own persuasiveness the wisdom and rightness of those loyalties which the state's educational system is seeking to promote. Except where the transgression of constitutional liberty is too plain for argument, personal freedom is best maintained—so long as the remedial channels of the democratic proc-

71. *Minersville School District v. Gobitis*, 310 U. S. 586, 60 Sup. Ct. 1010, 84 L. Ed. 1375 (1940). See also 16 C. J. S. 603; H. G. Balter, "Freedom of Religion Interpreted in Two Supreme Court Decisions" (1940) 15 *California State Bar Journal* 161-165.
72. *Ibid.*, p. 598.

ess remain open and unobstructed—when it is ingrained in a people's habits and not enforced against popular policy by the coercion of adjudicated law. That the flag-salute is an allowable portion of a school program for those who do not invoke conscientious scruples is surely not debatable. But for us to insist that, though the ceremony may be required, exceptional immunity must be given to dissidents, is to maintain that there is no basis for a legislative judgment that such an exemption might introduce elements of difficulty into the school discipline, might cast doubts in the minds of other children which would themselves weaken the effect of the exercise."[73]

The heart of the judicial reasoning appeared in the declaration that a society dedicated to preserve the values of civilization might use its educational system to teach national loyalty, so long as the rights to believe, to win others to one's belief, and to assemble for devotional ceremonies were fully respected. In upholding the legality of the compulsory flag salute, the Supreme Court thus overruled the Pennsylvania District Court and the Circuit Court of Appeals.

The U. S. Supreme Court reversed itself, however, in a significant case in 1943. Adopting a resolution containing phraseology taken largely from the Minersville opinion, the State Board of Education of West Virginia ordered that the salute to the flag become a regular part of the program of activities in the public schools and that all teachers and pupils be required to participate in the salute honoring the nation represented by the flag. Under the order, failure to conform to the prescribed behavior was regarded as insubordination, to be punished by expulsion from school. During a period of expulsion the expelled child was deemed unlawfully absent. Readmission was denied until compliance with the order was forthcoming; parents of children so expelled were held liable for prosecution for the absence of such children from school.

Certain public school children in West Virginia who be-

73. *Ibid.*, pp. 599-600.

longed to the sect, Jehovah's Witnesses, refused to salute the flag. In consequence thereof, the children were expelled from school and their parents were prosecuted for causing delinquency. After a federal district court had restrained the enforcement of the order of the West Virginia State Board of Education, the question of the validity of the order was presented on appeal to the United States Supreme Court.[74]

The majority opinion of the court reasoned that the compulsory flag salute and pledge required affirmation of a belief and of an attitude of mind. "To sustain the compulsory flag salute," Mr. Justice Jackson stated, "we are required to say that a Bill of Rights which guards the individual's right to speak his own mind, left it open to public authorities to compel him to utter what is not in his mind."[75] The court stated that national unity as an end was not in question; the problem was whether under our constitution compulsion as here employed was a permissible means for its achievement.

Stating that those who began coercive elimination of dissent soon found themselves exterminating dissenters, the court pointedly remarked, "If there is any fixed star in our constitutional constellation, it is that no official, high or petty, can prescribe what shall be orthodox in politics, nationalism, religion, or other matters of opinion or force citizens to confess by word or act their faith therein."[76] Specifically overruling the decision in the Minersville case, the Supreme Court held that the action of the authorities in compelling the flag salute transcended constitutional limitations on their power to invade the sphere of intellect and spirit which the First Amendment reserved from all official control.[77]

74. *West Virginia State Board of Education v. Barnette*, 319 U. S. 624, 63 Sup. Ct. 1178, 87 L. Ed. 1628 (1943).
75. *Ibid.*, p. 634.
76. *Ibid.*, p. 642.
77. Madalin K. Remmlein, "Constitutional Implications of Compulsory Flag Salute Statutes" (1943) 12 *George Washington Law Review* 70-80; Thomas A. Rover, "Constitutional Law—Resolution of State Board of Education Compelling Salute to Flag Held Unconstitutional" (1943) 32 *Georgetown Law*

Compulsory dancing lessons.—One decision indicates that compulsory dancing courses in the public schools are illegal as a violation of religious freedom. A local board of education included in the course of study of a school under its jurisdiction compulsory dancing exercises, based upon a state requirement of physical training. Certain pupils sought an excuse from the class on the ground that their conscientious scruples and religious beliefs opposed such practices. When the excuse from the exercises was not granted, resort was taken to the courts by the parents of the children.

Posing the question whether children of persons religiously opposed to dancing in any form might be compelled, on pain of expulsion from school, to participate in such dancing exercises, the California court reasoned that a person might have religious views or principles of his own, different, perhaps, on doctrinal matters, from those of any church organization or any other person. There could be no logical ground for holding that in thus worshipping his Maker he was not equally entitled with every other person or church society to the protection of his religious beliefs, assuming, of course, that his mode of worshiping was not offensive or detrimental to the peace and safety of

Journal 93-99; Tom B. Slade, "Constitutional Law—Guaranty of Liberty—State Law Requiring Public School Pupils to Salute the Flag Held Unconstitutional" (1944) 6 *Georgia Bar Journal* 249-250; Edward F. Waite, "The Debt of Constitutional Law to Jehovah's Witnesses" (1944) 28 *Minnesota Law Review* 209-46; Alfred W. Wilke, "Civil Liberties—Jehovah's Witnesses Define Religious Freedom" (1943) 7 *University of Detroit Law Journal* 11-17; for broadening of Barnette doctrine, see page 73; F. W. Grinnel, "Children, the Bill of Rights and the American Flag" (1939) 24 *Massachusetts Law Quarterly* 1-7; William Fennell, "The 'Reconstructed Court' and Religious Freedom: The Gobitis Case in Retrospect" (1941) 19 *N. Y. U. L. Q. Rev.* 31-48; Thomas H. Skemp, "Freedom of Religious Worship" (1940) 25 *Marquette Law Review* 19-22; see *Morgan v. Civil Service Commission,* 131 N. J. L. 410, 36 A (2d) 898 (1944), in which the New Jersey State Supreme Court held that a government agency cannot deny an individual his statutory right to appointment to a government position on the ground that he entertains religious scruples against saluting the flag; see also G. C. Hasson, "Jehovah's Witnesses" (1946) *Notre Dame Lawyer* 82-94; H. B. Howerton, "Jehovah's Witnesses and the Federal Constitution" (1946) 17 *Mississippi Law Journal* 347-371.

society. To hold that any such overreaching power as was claimed existed in the state or any of its agencies was considered distinctly revolutionary. The court pointed out that, instead of dancing, calisthenics and other athletics including different types of physical exercises to which no reasonable religious grounds could be urged could have been chosen by the board. No right existed to expel the children from the school for their refusal, in obedience to their parents' desires, to dance.[78]

Admission.—Inasmuch as public schools are supported wholly by public funds contributed by all the people, an applicant having the usual qualifications but transferring from a private religious school must ordinarily be admitted into the public schools.

Attempted discrimination against students attending a sectarian school who sought admission into a public-financed manual training school was denounced by a Pennsylvania District Court in 1912. The decision insisted that all pupils should be entered upon the same terms and qualifications.[79] Admission requirements for public schools must be free from bias for or against any faith, creed, church, or established religion.

Wearing distinctive garb.—Whether fredom of public educational institutions from sectarian control is infringed because a teacher who is a member of a religious order wears a distinctive garb has been considered by American courts. Allegations have been made that the presence of teachers dressed in such fashion renders such a school sectarian. Legislative declaration may greatly influence judicial judgment.

Some courts uphold the right of an individual to wear a particular garb.[80] In such instances specific dress characteristic of certain Quaker, Amish, Dunkard, and Catholic religious orders, as well as of many clergymen, has been considered commonplace. In Pennsylvania, in 1894, where no legislative in-

78. *Hartwick v. Board of School Trustees,* 54 Cal. App. 696, 205 Pac. 49 (1921).

79. *Commonwealth v. Plummer,* 21 Pa. Dist. 182 (1912).

80. 16 C. J. S. 604, note 93. So held in Pennsylvania and North Dakota.

tent had been stated, a court agreed that such manner of dress imparted to pupils the idea of membership in a sect. However, the court pointed out that the religious belief of such teachers was well known to the neighborhood and to the pupils, even without their wearing a special type of dress. The court suggested that the legislature might, by statute, force all teachers in the public schools to wear a particular style of dress and to prohibit all others. At the same time doubt was expressed that this method would suppress knowledge of the fact of adherence to a specific creed. The right of such teachers to be employed in the public schools was upheld.[81]

Following the suggestion of the court, however, the Pennsylvania lawmaking body in 1895 passed an act[82] to prevent the wearing by any teacher in the public schools of any dress, insignia, marks, or emblems indicating the fact that such teacher was an adherent or member of any religious order, sect, or denomination. In a subsequent decision the act was judged valid, the court commenting that the prohibition was directed against the actions, not the beliefs, of a teacher while in the performance of his or her duties.[83]

In New York, in 1906, the action of the State Superintendent of Public Instruction, based upon state law,[84] in ordering that distinctive religious garb be prohibited in the public schools, was contested. A teacher who wore the garb of a religious order brought suit to recover for services rendered in a public school. Specifying its intention of strengthening the public policy of the state as opposed to sectarian influences, the court declared the regulation to be a reasonable and valid exercise of power conferred upon the State Superintendent to establish regulations with respect to the management of public

81. *Hysong v. Gallitzen Borough School District*, 164 Pa. 629, 30 Atl. 482 (1894).
82. *Pennsylvania Acts of 1895*, Public Law No. 395.
83. *Commonwealth v. Herr*, 229 Pa. 132, 78 Atl. 68 (1910).
84. *New York Laws of 1894*, chap. 556.

schools.[85] The court further declared that the effect of the costume worn was to inspire respect and sympathy for the religious denomination to which the wearer belonged. To this extent the influence was judged to be sectarian.

In a recent case in North Dakota, where no previous legislative policy on the subject existed, the right of one to wear religious garb was upheld by the Supreme Court of the state. The action of four qualified teachers in a consolidated school to secure approval of their wearing the particular dress of a religious order was sustained. The court noted that "we are all agreed that the wearing of the religious habit described in the evidence here does not convert the school into a sectarian school, or create sectarian control within the purview of the Constitution. . . . The laws of the state do not prescribe the fashion of dress of the teachers in our schools. Whether it is wise or unwise to regulate the style of dress to be worn by teachers in our public schools, or to inhibit the wearing of dress or insignia indicating religious belief is not a matter for the courts to determine. The limit of our inquiry is to determine whether what has been done infringes upon and violates the provisions of the Constitution."[86]

The right of an individual to clothe himself in whatever garb his religious belief may dictate appears to be no more absolute than his right to give utterances to his religious sentiments. The legislatures apparently enjoy a wide range of discretion in this question.

Use of school for religious purposes.—The courts of some states hold that a public school building may not be used for sectarian purposes outside of regular school hours.[87] The reasoning of these cases is to the effect that since such buildings have been erected and maintained for the education of the

85. *O'Connor v. Hendrick*, 184 N. Y. 421, 77 N. E. 612 (1906).
86. *Gerhardt v. Heid*, 66 N. D. 444, 459, 267 N. W. 127, 135 (1936).
87. 56 C. J. 472, notes 72-76. So held in Arkansas, Connecticut, Kansas, Missouri, Michigan, Indiana, and Pennsylvania.

youth of the community out of tax funds, there is no inherent right in any citizen or in any religious group to use the structures for any purposes other than those of public nondenominational instruction. If school facilities are made available during the school term for meetings of religious organizations, to some extent the interests of the educational program might be jeopardized.

Upon the theory that a schoolhouse is occupied for school purposes from the time a school term opens until the term is completed, the Appellate Court of Indiana permitted a sectarian group to use a school building only between terms, that is, from June until September.[88] In Michigan the inhabitants of a school district were upheld in voting to refuse permission to a religious group to use a school structure after regular school hours.[89] The use of a school building for Sunday school during the year was prohibited in Connecticut. The court held that a Sunday school under the supervision of the religious teachers of an ecclesiastical society was an institution entirely different from our statutory common schools. "If it can be sanctioned in one district," the court went on, "it obviously can in any and all of them, where a vote can be obtained for the purpose; and if it can thus be established, then it follows that it can be done in favor of any denomination of christians who apply for it and are able to obtain a majority of the legal voters of the district in their favor."[90] Controversy once thus introduced into school districts might easily hinder both religion and education.

In a few cases permission to use public schools for religious purposes after school hours has been judicially approved.[91] In Nebraska the religious use of schools when no other classes were in session was held to be so infrequent as not to turn the

88. *Baggerly v. Lee*, 37 Ind. App. 139, 73 N. E. 921 (1905).
89. *Eckhardt v. Darby*, 118 Mich. 199, 76 N. W. 761 (1898).
90. *Scofield v. Eighth School District*, 27 Conn. 499, 505 (1858).
91. 56 *C. J.* 472-473, notes 78-81. So held in Illinois, Indiana, Iowa, Nebraska, and New York.

building into a place of worship.[92] A statute[93] in Illinois permitting school directors to grant occasional use of the school buildings to religious societies has been upheld.[94] Electors of a school district were declared to possess the requisite discretion to permit the use of a schoolhouse for religious services in Iowa.[95]

In New York in 1936 a taxpayer's suit to restrain the New York City Board of Education from permitting school buildings to be used as assembly places for religious groups was dismissed. Examining into the sectarianism of those seeking to use the public school buildings would be violative of liberty of conscience, the New York Supreme Court reiterated. Instead of being harmful to the educational policy of the state, the court deemed it wholesome to have the school structures used for religious purposes.[96] Statutes vesting in appropriate school officials discretion to permit Sunday school services in public school buildings may be upheld.[97]

There seems to be no settled judicial principle with regard to the use of school structures for religious purposes.

Use of religious property for public school.—The use of church-owned property for public educational purposes is valid where there has been no intent to support sectarian education by public funds thereby. The Court of Appeals of Kentucky in 1928 aptly stated the prevailing view: "It was never intended . . . to withhold the right to teach public schools in buildings rented, or their use otherwise acquired, from others, if the circumstances justified it, although the building may be owned by

92. *State v. Dilley,* 95 Neb. 527, 145 N. W. 999 (1914).
93. *Illinois Rev. Stat. of 1874,* sec. 39.
94. *Nichols v. School Directors,* 93 Ill. 61 (1879).
95. *Davis v. Boget,* 50 Iowa 11 (1878).
96. *Lewis v. Board of Education,* 285 N. Y. S. 164, 157 Misc. 520 (1935).
97. *School Directors v. Toll,* 149 Ill. App. 541 (1909); *Baggerly v. Lee,* 37 Ind. App. 139, 73 N. E. 921 (1905); *Nichols v. School Directors,* 93 Ill. 61 (1879).

a particular religious denomination."[98]   The condition sought
to be prevented by constitutional provisions is the teaching of
religious sectarianism in schools maintained by public money.
Thus the Wisconsin Supreme Court decided that there was no
policy of law which prevented a school district in meeting
assembled, or a school board itself, from renting a building or
part of a building in which to maintain public education, even
though the building had been dedicated to parochial instruction.[99]

The use of a church for graduating exercises does not constitute compulsory attendance at a place of worship for the parents
of the graduates.   The act of holding the exercises in a church
is not giving sectarian instruction at a place of worship.   One
court held that although a man might feel constrained to enter
a place of worship of a sect different from his, he was not forced
to worship contrary to his conscience at such exercises if sectarian services were not offered.   What was done, not the name
of the place where it was done, was the determining factor.[100]

Freedom of choice in the selection of school property was
overstepped in a case where trustees of a public school district
leased a sectarian school building, employed two former sectarian teachers, and practically turned the management of the
school over to a church.   The arrangement treated a sectarian
school as a county high school.   Graded school graduates were
allowed to attend it for a stipulated fee paid by the board of
education.   In fact, the action of the trustees amounted to an
abdication of their duties.   Public support was consequently
denied.   The court stated: "To authorize the validity of this
arrangement here in question would be to encourage the creation
of other like arrangements between other graded and common
schools and other sectarian institutions, and presently we would
have the common schools here and there throughout the state

98. *Crain v. Walker*, 222 Ky. 828, 839, 2 S. W. (2d) 654, 659 (1928).
99. *Dorner v. Luxemburg School District*, 137 Wisc. 147, 118 N. W. 353
(1908).
100. *State v. District Board*, 162 Wisc. 482, 156 N. W. 477 (1916).

operated in connection with that denominational school that happened to have the largest influence and membership in the particular community where the union was made."[101]

An arrangement in Iowa whereby public school students were transferred to a room in a sectarian school and taught by a former sectarian teacher was nullified. The students in the two rooms were organized like a single school of two departments; the younger children were taught in the lower room and the older ones in the upper. The net effect of the board's change was a practical elimination of the public school as such and a transfer of its revenue and name to the upper section of a parochial school, the court held. The use of the religious property amounted to an illegal exercise of the discretion which the law gave to the board to rent a schoolroom when the conditions made that action necessary.[102]

In instances of the use of religious property for public school purposes, the judiciary has scrutinized the arrangements very carefully to discover possible abuses of administrative or legislative discretion.

Excusing students for religious instruction.—Permitting students to leave school during regular school hours for the purpose of attending religious instruction in a church of their parents' choice has led to protest before the judiciary. Allegations have been made that such action on the part of a school board or school commissioner violates constitutional provisions respecting the status of religion. Prior to 1948, it was held, however, that church and state were still separated, even though a cooperative sectarian-secular plan of religious instruction existed.[103]

Judicial interpretation in New York has indicated the scope of administrative discretion in the matter of excusing students for religious instruction. The Education Law[104] required that

101. *Williams v. Board of Trustees,* 173 Ky. 708, 726, 191 S. W. 507, 514 (1917).
102. *Knowlton v. Baumhover,* 183 Iowa 691, 166 N. W. 202 (1918).
103. See *People v. Graves,* 245 N. Y. 195, 156 N. E. 663 (1927).
104. *New York Education Law,* sec. 621, as amended by Laws of 1921, chap. 386.

every child within particular ages and in good physical and mental conditions must regularly attend instruction for the entire time during which schools were in session. Judicial construction of state statutory and constitutional law at first denied the validity of any such co-operative arrangement as providing for the release of students during regular school hours for attendance at religious instruction. A plan whereby pupils were excused from school for forty-five minutes each week to attend religious instruction in the churches to which their parents desired them to be sent was invalidated in 1925. The court stated that because the state prescribed the curriculum for the public schools, to substitute religious instruction in school in place of the required instruction would be illegal; excusing students from school for religious lessons at a church was judged in effect to be a substitution of religious instruction for the instruction required by law. Although the court asserted that educational officials should have the right to excuse students from attendance occasionally for good reasons (and that church attendance might be among such good reasons), the adoption of an arrangement for periodically shortening of school hours was thought a violation of the state constitution providing for no public aid for any religious denomination.[105] Pointing out that the presses and property of the city had been used in the preparation of the cards on which the parents were to express their religious preference, the court held immaterial the fact that no particular denomination was favored. In conclusion the court said that religious instruction belonged to the parents of the children and to the churches and religious organizations of the country. As such it should have been given outside of the public schools and outside of school hours.[106]

Subsequently an order of a lower court denied to a taxpayer a mandamus to compel the State Commissioner of Education to order the board of education of a city to discontinue school

105. Art. IX, sec. 4.
106. *Stein v. Brown*, 211 N. Y. S. 822, 125 Misc. 692 (1925).

regulations whereby public school children, at the request of their parents, were excused one-half hour each week before the termination of the regular school period in order that they might attend religious instruction in church schools. The taxpayer thereupon carried his case to the Appellate Division of the State Supreme Court which held that the rule of the local board of education did not violate the Education Law nor the state constitution.[107] The court specified that all the petitioner could claim in regard to public expense was the time spent by the teacher during school hours in issuing cards for parents' signatures, excusing children, and ascertaining whether the parents' directions had been obeyed. This was merely ordinary school routine and discipline, the court reasoned. It was stated that parents have as much right to have their children receive religious instruction as music instruction during some portion of the school week.

Appeal from the decision of the Appellate Division was made to the State Court of Appeals, which stated that, although the Education Law specified regular attendance, the practical administration of public education required a degree of elasticity in this respect. Discretion was thus vested in school officials; otherwise, the court said, the phrase "regularly attend" would be superfluous. Regular attendance was held not to imply actual attendance for the entire time school was in session. If an improper exercise of discretion should take place, such as the formulation of a plan of weekday religious instruction which unduly interfered with regular school work, the commissioner was deemed to have the power to make the proper regulations to restrict local officials.

Applying this reasoning, the Court of Appeals ruled as constitutional the arrangement whereby children between the ages of seven and fourteen years, on written request of the parents, were excused for one-half hour of the school session each week. The court was clear in pointing out that in the case at bar no

107. *People v. Graves*, 219 N. Y. S. 189, 219 App. Div. 233 (1927).

school recitations were missed and no credit for work taken in the church school was given. Application for a mandamus to compel the State Commissioner of Education to direct local school authorities to discontinue the regulations was therefore denied.[108]

Although the practice of excusing children to participate in church or religious festivals and to attend confirmation classes and other religious instructions, at the request of parents, has been considered valid, the legality of co-operative sectarian-secular plans for religious instruction is now open to question in view of a significant decision of the United States Supreme Court[108a] in which the Court nullified as unconstitutional an arrangement of a local board of education which permitted religious teachers employed by private religious groups to come weekly into the school buildings during regular school hours and substitute their religious teaching for secular education.

The question of periodical irregularity of individual attendance due to alleged religious beliefs was presented in an unusual case in Pennsylvania in 1944. A Moslem refused to permit his children to attend public schools on Fridays, with the contention that such attendance violated his religious beliefs as taught in the Koran. Dismissing an appeal from a conviction of a state statute requiring children to be educated, the court stated that to send Moslem children to school on Friday in no way violates the principles of the Moslem faith.[109]

Teaching of evolution.—A Tennessee law[110] forbidding the teaching of the evolutionary theory as applied to man in the state public schools was upheld in the famous Scopes case of 1927. Conviction of the defendant, who had been fined one hundred dollars for teaching, was sustained by the Supreme Court of Tennessee. The court professed its inability to understand how the prohibition of the teaching of the theory that

108. *People v. Graves*, 245 N. Y. 195, 156 N. E. 663 (1927).
108a. *People ex rel. McCollum v. Board of Education*, —— U. S. ——, 68 Sup. Ct. 461, —— L. Ed. ——, decided March 8, 1948.
109. *Commonwealth v. Bey*, 92 Pittsburgh Legal Journal 84 (1944).
110. *Tennessee Acts of 1925*, chap. 27.

man has descended from a lower order of animals gave preference to any religion contrary to the state constitution.[111]
There was no organized body of religion that had in its creed
any section denying or affirming such a theory. Belief or unbelief in the theory of evolution was held no more characteristic
of any religious establishment or mode of worship than was
belief or unbelief in the wisdom of the prohibition laws. The
court further stated that in making rules for its own employees
doing its own work, the state was not limited by the religious
provisions of the United States or Tennessee constitutions. The
conviction was upheld, but, for a technical reason, the fine itself
was stricken out.[112]

Teachers' views as to war.—A Quakeress school teacher in
a public school was dismissed solely because she declared before
her superiors that she would not help the country resist invasion
by an enemy nation nor assist the United States in carrying on
war. She appealed her case on the ground that there had been
discrimination against her on account of her religious beliefs and
an attempted restraint upon her observance of the Quaker faith.
The action of the board of education was upheld by the Supreme
Court of the State of New York on the theory that she had been
dismissed, not on account of her religion, but because the board
thought her views prevented her from properly discharging her
duties.[113] Where a person makes an agreement to perform a
public duty, the claim that his religious tenets forbid its fulfillment does not excuse nonperformance.

Vaccination.—In a few cases parents have expressed their
reluctance to comply with compulsory vaccination requirements
for their school-attending children on the ground that such
medical practice contravened their religious beliefs. But the
courts have unanimously denied to the parents relief for this

111. Art. I, sec. 3.
112. *Scopes v. State*, 154 Tenn. 105, 289 S. W. 363 (1927); see Johnson,
op. cit., chap. 15.
113. *McDowell v. Board of Education*, 172 N. Y. S. 590, 104 Misc. 564
(1918).

reason, unless the law contained an express exemption.[114] The prevailing judicial attitude is that individual religious ideas, allegedly a defense to compulsory vaccination, are merely opinions, and that if such individual opinions are equivalent to rights, law might be replaced by anarchy.[115]

One complaint alleged that a resolution of the City of Indianapolis requiring vaccination "is in violation of Article 1 of Amendments of the Constitution of the United States, and of Article 1 of Section 243 of Bill of Rights of the State of Indiana . . . in that it abridges religious and civil liberties and matters relating to conscience of many of the citizens of said city." The Indiana State Supreme Court refuted the claim with the comment: "Neither in brief nor in argument is it pointed out how the constitutional rights mentioned are infringed."[116] Hence, a suit to restrain the enforcement of an order of a city board of health preventing children who had not been vaccinated from attending school was dismissed in spite of religious objections. In another case a defendant's sole defense to a charge of neglecting to send his children to school was that because of his religious belief and conscientious scruples concerning vaccination he should not be held to have violated the law.[117] The Supreme Judicial Court of Massachusetts declared that the defendant could not affect the validity of the law nor seek exemptions by reason of his religious views.[118]

A suit attacking the validity of an ordinance[119] providing that no one could attend a public or private school within the city without a physician's certificate to the person's vaccination within six years was predicated on the assumption of an abridgement of religious liberty. It was held that such a health pre-

114. 16 *C. J. S.* 603, note 77. So held in Indiana, New Hampshire, Texas, and Massachusetts.
115. See *State v. Drews*, 192 Atl. 629 (1937).
116. *Vonnegut v. Baun*, 206 Ind. 172, 179, 188 N. E. 677, 680 (1934).
117. *Massachusetts General Laws*, c. 76, as amended by St. 1921, c. 463.
118. *Commonwealth v. Green*, 168 N. E. 101 (1929).
119. *New Braunfels, Texas, Ordinance* of Sept. 18, 1916.

caution did not interfere with any rights of conscience of a
Christian Scientist, since the Bill of Rights of the Texas constitution excused no one from obeying reasonable health rules
passed by virtue of the police power. The court stated that the
ordinance did not in any way undertake to control or interfere
with any rights of conscience in matters of religion.[120]

Language restriction.—The authority of a state to restrict
the teaching of modern languages other than English to students
in sectarian schools has been challenged as a violation of the
liberty protected by the Fourteenth Amendment. In four cases
the Supreme Court of the United States has sustained objections
to restrictions of this kind. The cases are important in an
analysis of educational practices involving the right of religious
freedom, because they determine the validity of certain governmental restrictions as applied to sectarian schools.

A Nebraska law[121] forbidding the teaching of any modern
language other than English to a student in any elementary
denominational or public school invaded the liberty of the
Fourteenth Amendment and thereby exceeded the power of the
state, according to the Supreme Court in the famous Meyer
case.[122] The conviction in a state court of a sectarian instructor
who taught German to a ten-year-old child had been based upon
the police power to promote safety by inhibiting training in
foreign tongues. The liberty in the Federal Constitution included the right of the individual to worship as his conscience
dictated, the court asserted. The legislature of Nebraska was
judged guilty of attempting to hamper the opportunities of
students to acquire knowledge and the prerogative of parents to
control the education of their children. The alleged use of the
police power was nullified because no emergency had arisen to

120. *City of New Braunfels v. Waldschmidt,* 109 Tex. 302, 207 S. W.
303 (1918).
121. *Nebraska Laws of 1919,* chap. 249.
122. *Meyer v. Nebraska,* 262 U. S. 390, 43 Sup. Ct. 625, 67 L. Ed. 1042
(1923).

render a pupil's knowledge of an inhibited language harmful so as to legalize the curtailment.

On the basis of the Meyer decision, three other judgments sustaining convictions on similar charges in Iowa,[123] Ohio,[124] and Nebraska[125] were reversed by the Supreme Court. The forcefulness of judicial analysis in each instance indicates finality of judicial thought in this respect.

Legality of sectarian schools.—An Oregon Compulsory School Law[126] requiring every parent of children between the ages of eight and sixteen years to send his children to the public school in the district for the duration of the public school year was adopted by the people of the state at a referendum in 1922, to become effective in 1926. The act exempted non-normal students and those who had completed the eighth year of school, and provided that every violation was a misdemeanor.

Two Oregon educational corporations, one sectarian and the other military in nature, each owning and conducting private schools in the state, obtained preliminary court orders restraining state officials from attempting to carry out the terms of the act. The state appealed to the United States Supreme Court for a reversal of the lower court decree. The issue specifically involved was the reasonableness or unreasonableness of interference with the liberty of parents to educate their children in a private school, denominational or otherwise. Obviously the upholding of the law would have been a serious blow to a type of religious-secular education offered by various religious groups throughout the country.

The Supreme Court declared the state law an illegal restriction upon the liberty protected by the Fourteenth Amend-

123. *Bartels v. State*, 262 U. S. 404, 43 Sup. Ct. 628, 67 L. Ed. 1047 (1923).
124. *Bohning v. State*, 262 U. S. 404, 43 Sup. Ct. 628, 67 L. Ed. 1047 (1923).
125. *Nebraska District of Evangelical Lutheran Synod v. McKelvie*, 262 U. S. 404, 43 Sup. Ct. 628, 67 L. Ed. 1047 (1923).
126. *Oregon Laws*, sec. 5259.

ment. The court indicated that the inevitable result of the act would be the destruction of parochial schools. A conclusion forcibly drawn was that the fundamental theory of liberty inherent in all state governments excluded any general power of the state to standardize its children by forcing them to accept instruction from public school teachers only.[127] The right of parents to choose schools where children will receive appropriate religious and mental training is apparently secure.

Validity of private school regulations.—Particular regulations of private schools and of public institutions of higher learning have been attacked as violative of the American concept of religious freedom. Although such cases are rare, they are significant because they represent the efforts of individuals who voluntarily seek special educational opportunities but who at the same time endeavor to be excused from reciprocal activity accompanying the extension of those opportunities.

An order of the Regents of the University of California required every able-bodied male student to complete a course in military science. The parents of two minors contested the validity of the order on the ground that compulsory military training imposed on religious objectors violated their religious freedom. The fathers of the two boys were ministers; the two boys were not only conscientious members of their fathers' church but also affiliated with supplementary youth organizations of the same sect. All believed that participation in war was a denial of their supreme allegiance to the Lord, a statement of faith previously drawn up by their ecclesiastical superiors. The Regents suspended the minors because they declined to take the course. The parents contended that the minors were unable financially to obtain higher education elsewhere than at the state-supported institution, and applied for a writ of mandamus to compel their admittance to the university.

The Supreme Court decided that the state had authority to

127. *Pierce v. Society of the Sisters,* 268 U. S. 510, 45 Sup. Ct. 571, 69 L. Ed. 1070 (1925).

train its male citizens and was the exclusive judge of both the means to be used and the amount of training necessary. The fact that the minors could not pay elsewhere was not important. To the contention that the due process clause of the Fourteenth Amendment conferred the right upon one to be a student at the university without compulsory military training, the court replied that every citizen owed the reciprocal duty, according to his capacity, to support and defend his government against all enemies. The order of the Regents was upheld.[128]

Whether the University of Maryland had a right to suspend a student because of his refusal, based on sincere religious convictions, to take a regular university course in military training arose in the Supreme Court of that state in 1933. The court ruled against the student when it reasoned: "A great majority of people of this country are opposed to war, but unlike those of whom we have been speaking, they recognize the necessity of being prepared for war when it comes upon us. In preparing for defense, a military training for those who may be called upon to take arms in defense of their country is a necessary incident thereto, and any effort on the part of any of the people to hinder or defeat the government in doing so should not be countenanced by the courts so long as the government acts in the lawful exercise of such power."[129]

A rule of the trustees of the University of Illinois which stipulated that all students must attend nonsectarian religious services in the university chapel was challenged as contrary to a provision of the state constitution providing that no person could be compelled to attend a place of worship against his consent.[130] The state court held, however, that attendance at chapel did not constitute compulsory attendance or support of any place of worship, as prohibited by the fundamental law. The con-

128. *Hamilton v. Regents*, 293 U. S. 245, 55 Sup. Ct. 197, 79 L. Ed. 343 (1934).
129. *University of Maryland v. Coale*, 165 Md. 224, 239, 167 Atl. 54, 60 (1933).
130. Art. V, sec. 3.

clusion seemed inevitable to the court that the student was only using the constitutional clause as a shield for insubordination. The trustees' rule was upheld.[131]

The legality of a regulation of a private military school requiring the attendance of the entire cadet corps at Sunday services of various Christian churches in the village but outside of the school grounds was the chief issue in a suit for damages for breach of contract in 1926. A non-Christian youth who refused to attend particular Christian church services because the ritual was contrary to his religious instruction and faith, was expelled. He offered to attend a church of his own faith in the village, but there was none available. He declined the permission of the school authorities to attend at his own expense a church of his own faith fourteen miles away. The school officials brought action to collect the full amount of the tution for the school term, as provided by the contract between the father and the institution.

The court decided that Sunday attendance at Christian churches was not part of the school curriculum as provided by the contract; but even if it were, such a regulation would be unreasonable and invalid as applied to a non-Christian student. Attendance in opposition to one's religious faith was a violation of constitutional rights. The institution was not permitted to collect the unpaid tuition.[132]

Summary.—State constitutions provide for the separation of public education from the influences of sectarianism. Public aid for sectarian schools, either in the form of a grant of money or the use of public property, is prohibited, either directly or indirectly, by every state constitution. The history of the State of New York typifies the financial cleavage between denominational and public schools. Judicial decree has consistently enjoined the payment of public money to sectarian institutions.

131. *North v. Board of Trustees*, 27 N. E. 54 (1891).
132. *Miami Military Institute v. Leff*, 220 N. Y. S. 799, 129 Misc. 481 (1926).

A landmark decision in 1947 by the United States Supreme Court has upheld a statute of the State of New Jersey authorizing school districts to contract for the transportation of children to and from public and private schools, including sectarian schools. The Supreme Courts of New York and Louisiana have sharply disagreed over the legality of the use of public funds to furnish textbooks to pupils attending sectarian schools.

Much litigation arising over alleged sectarianism in the public schools has revolved about the question of whether the reading of the Bible, in whole or in part, without comment, in the classroom infringes the American concept of religious freedom. The general view of those courts which uphold Bible reading by the classroom teacher is that the schoolhouse has not been transformed into a place of worship thereby. On the other hand, the use of the Bible as a text or as selected reading has been held to inculcate sectarian principles contrary to constitutional inhibitions.

The courts have been called upon to decide the constitutionality of public school regulations providing for the compulsory saluting of the American flag. Members of Jehovah's Witnesses, who place the Bible above the law of the state, contend that participation by their children in the flag salute ceremony violates religious liberty. After conflicting court decisions on the question, the United States Supreme Court in 1943 held void the requirement of saluting the flag.

A board of education may not make dancing lessons compulsory for students who object on grounds of conscientious scruples and religious beliefs. Furthermore, students who transfer to a public school from a denominational school may not be discriminated against. However, where there is legislative authorization, the courts may sanction the withholding of the salary from public school teachers who wear distinctive religious garb.

It has often been held that a public school building may

not be used for sectarian purposes outside of regular school hours, although in a few cases such permission has been judicially approved. The use of church-owned property for public educational purposes is valid where there has been no intent to support sectarian education. An arrangement which permits religious teachers employed by private religious groups to come into public school buildings during regular school hours and substitute their religious teaching for secular education is illegal.

Where parents have refused to comply with requirements making vaccination for their school-attending children compulsory on the ground that such medical practice contravened their religious beliefs, the courts have unanimously denied the parents' defense, unless the law contained an express exemption.

The United States Supreme Court has sustained objections to the attempt of various states to restrict administrative discretion in the conduct of sectarian schools by limiting the teaching of modern languages other than English. A state plan to compel children between the ages of eight and sixteen to attend public schools was judicially nullified in the belief that religious liberty was unduly infringed. Nevertheless, the courts have usually upheld collegiate regulations providing for compulsory military training or chapel attendance in spite of allegations of a denial of religious liberty.

X

Religious Rights in Court Trials

Competency of witnesses.—An oath may be defined as an outward pledge given by the person taking it that his attestation or promise is made under an immediate sense of his responsibility to God. In taking an oath a witness generally raises his hand and signifies that the testimony he is about to give will be truthful. A reference to God's help usually follows. In order to take an oath and testify, a witness at common law had to profess a belief in a Supreme Being and in a present or future punishment for evil. The common law requirement of an oath from every witness and the existence of a religious belief as a condition of taking the oath is based upon the theory that the veracity of a witness is largely insured by an oath, the effectiveness of which results from fear of certain divine retribution if a falsehood is uttered.[1] Lord Coke wrote that a Jew could not be sworn as a witness, but Lord Hale subsequently stated that a Jew was competent to be a witness and might be sworn on the Old Testament.[2] Not until the Statute of 1869[3] did Parliament remove the disqualification for nonbelievers. By

1. Frank Swancara, "Judicial Disregard of the Equal Protection Clause as It Affects the Non-Religious" (1934) 68 *United States Law Review* 309-316; John H. Wigmore, *Evidence in Trials at Common Law* (3d ed.), VI, 284-295.

2. J. C. Biggs, "Religious Belief as Qualification of a Witness" (1929) 8 *North Carolina Law Review* 31-43.

3. *32 and 33 Vict.*, chap. 68.

that act, if a presiding judge was satisfied that the taking of an oath would have no binding effect on a person's conscience, that person was nevertheless permitted to make a declaration.

In early American decisions lack of belief in a God or in ultimate punishment disqualified a prospective witness.[4] Atheists were rendered incompetent because the necessity that witnesses be sworn required an invocation of God's help. Fear of civil punishment could not be substituted for moral sanction.[5] An understanding that the truth must be told for the benefit of society was insufficient in Pennsylvania.[6] The Louisiana Supreme Court observed that "if the witness has no knowledge of God or belief in his existence, and shows no sense of accountability to him for false testimony, there is no guaranty of the truth of his testimony."[7]

Gradually the common law disqualification for nonbelievers has been modified.[8] Forty American jurisdictions have made atheists competent witnesses by court decision or by constitutional or statutory enactments.[9] In substance these laws declare that no person shall be rendered incompetent as a witness in consequence of his opinions on matters of religion. A cloak of privacy is thus thrown about the religious creed of a prospec-

4. D. G., "Witnesses—Competency—Religious Belief" (1933) 7 *Tulane Law Review* 457-458; 70 C. J. 97, note 71. So held in Alabama, Connecticut, Delaware, Illinois, Kansas, Louisiana, Massachusetts, Minnesota, New Hampshire, New York, North Carolina, Ohio, Pennsylvania, South Carolina, Tennessee, and Vermont.

5. *Central Military Tract Railroad Co. v. Rockafellow*, 17 Ill. 541 (1856).

6. *Commonwealth v. Winnemore*, 2 Brewst. (Pa.) 378 (1867).

7. *State v. Washington*, 49 La. Ann. 1602, 1603, 22 So. 841, 842 (1897).

8. Scott Rowley, "The Competency of Witnesses" (1939) 24 *Iowa Law Review* 482-497; Note, "Evidence—Witnesses—Religious Belief as a Prerequisite to Competency" (1933) 33 *Columbia Law Review* 539.

9. Alabama, Arizona, California, Colorado, Connecticut, Florida, Georgia, Idaho, Illinois, Indiana, Iowa, Kansas, Kentucky, Louisiana, Maine, Massachusetts, Michigan, Minnesota, Mississippi, Missouri, Montana, Nebraska, Nevada, New Mexico, New York, North Dakota, Ohio, Oklahoma, Oregon, Rhode Island, South Dakota, Tennessee, Texas, Utah, Vermont, Virginia, Washington, West Virginia, Wisconsin, and Wyoming. See Biggs, "Religious Beliefs as Qualifications of a Witness," *loc. cit.*, p. 31.

tive witness.[10] The competency of a witness is a question to be decided by the trial judge.[11] Under modern constitutions and statutes courts have not disqualified a prospective witness because he refused to believe in future rewards[12] or because he did not believe in God.[13] Objections to questions involving the religious training of a prospective witness[14] and to inquiries designed to test an Indian woman's belief in God[15] have been properly sustained. However, in eight states a witness must believe in Divine punishment or in the existence of a Supreme Being in order to be competent to testify.[16] Even though there may be no specific prohibition against an atheist serving as a witness, it is generally agreed in these states that the witness must believe that some form of religious or moral sanction accompanies the temporal sanction in the event of false testimony. The inability of a person to obtain testimony from an unbeliever in religion is not the denial of the equal protection of the laws nor of any other civil right. That inability rests equally on a person who is a believer and on one who is not.[17]

There is a presumption in favor of a person's having a competent belief. Thus in Nebraska a defendant objected to the competency of a witness who was a Japanese citizen. The witness could not speak English and needed an interpreter to assist him in his statements. The objection was based on the allegation that since Japan was a heathen nation there was presumptive evidence, which the state had not removed, that the witness was not qualified to take an oath. Further argument suggested that

10. Burr Jones, *The Law of Evidence* (3d ed.), pp. 1090-1091.
11. 70 *C. J.* 191.
12. *Hunter v. State*, 137 Miss. 276, 102 So. 282 (1924).
13. *Mueller v. Coffman*, 132 Ark. 45, 200 S. W. 136 (1918).
14. *Hanley v. Chicago City Railway Co.*, 180 Ill. App. 397 (1913).
15. *Fernandez v. State*, 16 Ariz. 269, 144 Pac. 640 (1914).
16. Arkansas, Delaware, Maryland, New Hampshire, New Jersey, North Carolina, Pennsylvania, and South Carolina. See Biggs, "Religious Beliefs as Qualification of a Witness," *loc. cit.*, pp. 39-40.
17. *State v. Levine*, 109 N. J. L. 503, 162 Atl. 909 (1932). See Frank Swancara, "A Religious Fiction of the Common Law" (1923) 23 *Journal of Criminal Law and Criminology* 614-619.

the witness was an idolator who would not be bound by an appeal to the invisible God of Christianity. The court ruled that in a Christian land the burden of proof as to incompetency rested upon the objecting party. Since the defense had not shown that the oath administered was not in a form to bind his conscience, the Japanese witness was judged competent.[18]

Simon Greenleaf notes that the status of a person's religious belief at the time he is a prospective witness is a fact to be shown by evidence of declarations made by him to others previously. Lack of such religious belief must be established by means other than the examination of the witness upon the stand. He may not be questioned as to his religious belief, nor required to divulge his opinion upon that subject, in answer to questions put to him while under examination.[19]   The Supreme Judicial Court of Massachusetts typically held that a lack of belief in the existence of a God might render a witness incompetent, but that such lack must be established by means other than an examination of a witness upon the stand. Counsel for the defense in a trial had inquired of one of the prosecution's witnesses: "Do you believe in the existence of God?" Disapproving this line of attack, the appellate court stated that if a witness was incompetent the fact must be demonstrated by other witnesses and by evidence of previous statements voluntarily given to others.[20]

Casual remarks which may have been made at some time previous to a trial and which may have indicated a peculiarity of an individual's belief may not be taken seriously by the court. No slight or casual sayings can be given in evidence for the purpose of rendering individuals incompetent.[21]   A former unbeliever who changed his views was held a competent witness in

18. *Pumphrey v. State*, 84 Neb. 636, 122 N. W. 19 (1909).
19. Simon Greenleaf, *A Treatise on the Law of Evidence* (16th ed.), I, 508.
20. *Commonwealth v. Smith*, 68 Mass. 516 (1854).
21. *State v. Cooper*, 2 Tenn. 96 (1807).

a state where religious faith was a legal requisite.[22] An objection that a witness was an atheist, since he had been quoted to that effect previously, was not sustained. A pamphlet was introduced in the trial court to show that the witness did believe in God.[23]

The problem of accepting as witnesses individuals who have religious scruples against taking an oath arose in England in the seventeenth century. Various sects pointed to the Bible, Matthew V, which states: "But I say unto you, Swear not at all; neither by heaven; for it is God's throne: Nor by the earth; for it is his footstool: neither by Jerusalem; for it is the city of the great King. Neither shalt thou swear by thy head, because thou canst not make one hair white or black. But let your communication be, Yea, yea; nay, nay: for whatsoever is more than these cometh of evil."

In 1696 Parliament permitted members of the Society of Friends (Quakers) to testify by declaration. But, as they objected to the making of a declaration because in their opinion a declaration contained an impious reference to the Deity, Parliament in 1721 authorized the Quakers to affirm instead of to declare. The substance of the affirmation is that the witness solemnly and sincerely states the truth of whatever statements follow his action of affirming. The words "So help me God," appended to an oath, are omitted. Later the English statute was extended to Moravians and Separatists, and still later to all persons of any sect who maintained that they had conscientious convictions against swearing.[24]

American legislatures have reflected the English experience. Typical of the trend was an early judicial statement that "the legislature, with becoming respect and deference, to the religious sentiments and opinions of a numerous, and highly respectable portion of the community, has provided a substitute for the *sacramental*, or *corporal* oath, for such as are *conscientiously*

22. *Scott v. Hooper*, 14 Vt. 535 (1842).
23. *Farrell v. State*, 111 Ark. 180, 163 S. W. 768 (1914).
24. See *State v. Levine*, 109 N. J. L. 503, 162 Atl. 909 (1932).

scrupulous of submitting to that ceremony."[25] Later judicial comment justified the change from the common law for the reason that those with conscientious scruples should not be excluded from court participation when they were willing to take the manner of oath most binding on their consciences.[26]

A prospective witness who has religious scruples against taking an oath is usually permitted to affirm.[27] Equal credit is afforded the testimony of a witness whether he swears or affirms. The penalty for swearing falsely in either event is identical. A person does not have a choice between taking an oath or an affirmation; the latter ordinarily can be taken only because of bona fide objections to the first method. Inquiry into one's reasons for desiring to affirm is permissible.[28] When a person objects by reason of conscientious scruples, it is the duty of the trial judge to permit an affirmation. For example, a trial judge asked an individual about to testify: "Do you believe in God?" Receiving an affirmative answer, the person was ordered to take the customary oath. He replied that the law of his church would not permit him to take an oath. The judge was asked to permit the person to affirm, but the judge refused. An appellate court ruled that the trial court had erred by denying the individual the right to affirm.[29]

Permission for a witness who has conscientious scruples against taking an oath to make an affirmation may be applicable only to a witness whose scruples are conscientiously founded on religious beliefs.[30] In New Jersey a prospective defense witness declined to take an oath because he did not believe in the Bible. On cross-examination by the prosecution the individual admitted that he did not believe in God and had no religious belief. The

25. *Williamson v. Carroll*, 16 N. J. L. 217, 218 (1837).
26. *Riddles v. State*, 46 S. W. 1058 (1898).
27. Greenleaf, *op. cit.*, p. 509; Wigmore, *op. cit.*, VI, 317.
28. 70 *C. J.* 484.
29. *State v. Dudicoff*, 109 Conn. 711, 145 Atl. 655 (1929).
30. 70 *C. J.* 484; L. L. B., Jr., "Evidence—Witness Having Conscientious Scruples Against Taking Oath" (1932) 10 *Tennessee Law Review* 232-234.

trial judge sustained the position of the prosecution that, since the objection of the witness to taking an oath was based on non-belief, he should not be permitted to affirm. The appellate court agreed with the trial judge that the privilege of making an affirmation was for the benefit of those who had conscientious scruples based on religious beliefs. Because the scruples of the prospective witness were based on disbelief in religion and in God, he did not have the privilege.[31]

Credibility of testimony.—Once a witness is placed on the stand and is judged *competent* to present his views, may the *credibility* of his testimony be attacked on religious grounds? Provisions insuring the competency of a witness, regardless of the presence or absence of religious beliefs, usually are applicable to the credibility of his testimony. Where no person is incompetent to testify on account of religious belief and no control of or interference with the rights of conscience is permitted, not only is an individual *competent* to testify without regard to religious belief or disbelief, but any inquiry into that belief for the purpose of affecting his *credibility* is prevented.[32] Seven states through statutory law or constitutional provision expressly forbid the questioning of any witness about his religious beliefs for the purpose of affecting the weight of his testimony.[33] The general situation was summarized by the Missouri Supreme Court in 1934, when it noted that the weight of authority was that "the question of a witness' personal belief, even as to there being a God or Supreme Being, cannot be inquired into, especially of the witness himself, for the purpose of affecting his credibility."[34]

In that case one witness had been asked on cross-examination

31. *State v. Levine,* 109 N. J. 503, 162 Atl. 909 (1932).

32. Frank Swancara, "Non-Religious Witnesses" (1932) 8 *Wisconsin Law Review* 49-66; 70 *C. J.* 861; 40 *Cyclopedia of Law and Procedure* 2613.

33. Arizona, Colorado, Michigan, Oregon, Pennsylvania, Vermont, and Washington. See Frank Swancara, "Non-Religious Witnesses," *loc. cit.,* p. 61.

34. *McClellan v. Owens,* 335 Mo. 884, 898, 74 S. W. (2d) 570, 577 (1934).

if he believed in Jesus Christ. The trial judge refused to require the witness to reply to the query. In an attempt to overrule the trial court's decision, the appellant contended that a section of the constitution providing that a person should not be disqualified from testifying on account of his religious belief did not prevent the showing of his disbelief in God for the purpose of affecting the credibility of his statements. The Missouri Supreme Court approved the action of the trial judge with the remark that even though the jury, as sole judge of the credibility of a witness, should have been presented with all pertinent facts which would have permitted it to estimate properly the degree of credit to be imputed to every witness, information which merely tended to prejudice the jury had been properly excluded. "No question should . . . be allowed and its answer compelled for the purpose of discrediting the witness unless the fact which the question seeks to elicit has an inherent or obvious tendency by general consensus of opinion among civilized people to make the witness, in the eyes of honest and right-thinking men, less likely to tell the truth. The mere nonbelief in God does not measure up to this standard."[35]

Likewise it was once judged improper in Iowa to show that a witness did not believe in a future state of rewards or punishments.[36] A witness in California was not impeachable by showing him to be an atheist.[37] Previous references to matters of faith wherein a witness had expressed doubts many years previously about a Supreme Being did not affect the credibility of a witness who testified that he believed in a Supreme Being at the time of the trial.[38] Belief in spiritualism was ruled not to affect a witness' credibility.[39]

Questions to test a witness' belief in God or a Great Spirit have consequently been ruled out as improper. The Supreme

35. *Ibid.*, p. 899.
36. *Searcy v. Miller*, 57 Iowa 613, 10 N. W. 912 (1881).
37. *People v. Copsey*, 71 Cal. 548, 12 Pac. 721 (1887).
38. *Winter v. Winter*, 102 Pa. Super. 300, 156 Atl. 603 (1931).
39. *Blaisdell v. Raymond*, 9 Abb. Pr. (N. Y.) 178 (1859).

Court of Arizona declared that permission given to a lawyer by a trial court to inquire of witnesses whether they were members of the Seventh Day Adventist Church was illegal.[40] The court denied the contention that an inquiry into a witness' membership in a particular church was not questioning him concerning his religious belief. "The fact that a man belongs to a certain church is certainly presumptive evidence that he believes in the fundamental principles of that church. When, therefore, a witness is asked in regard to his membership in a particular church, he is, in effect, being questioned in regard to his religious belief."[41]

In 1939, in Oregon, a witness for the defendant was cross-examined by a district attorney with reference to doctrines of the Christian Science Church, with the intent of affecting her testimony. The Supreme Court of that state ruled that the questions asked were directed to matters of the witness' religious scruples. The trial court had erred in permitting the district attorney to pursue that line of questioning.[42]

On the other hand, delving into the faith of a witness on the stand to influence the credibility of his testimony is permissible in a few instances. Ten states have laws which directly or indirectly preserve or grant permission to show disbelief in a personal, judging Deity for the purpose of affecting the credibility of a witness.[43] Judicial approval of the practice rests upon the theory that to discover what religious opinions a witness entertains will enable the jury, as far as indications will allow, to understand his manner of thinking.[44]

Thus an inquiry into the religious creed of a witness was permitted in a court trial in North Carolina. The appellate

40. *Fernandez v. State*, 16 Ariz. 269, 144 Pac. 640 (1914).
41. *Tucker v. Reil*, 51 Ariz. 357, 363, 77 P. (2d) 203, 206 (1938).
42. *State v. Estabrook*, 162 Ore. 476, 91 P. (2d) 838 (1939).
43. Connecticut, Georgia, Indiana, Iowa, Maine, Massachusetts, Montana, Nebraska, New Mexico, and Tennessee. See Frank Swancara, "Non-Religious Witnesses," *loc. cit.* p. 61.
44. 40 *Cyc.* 2613. So held in Indiana, Iowa, Massachusetts, New York, and Pennsylvania.

court minimized the importance of the unusual procedure of the trial court. In the light of the answers obtained it was held that no appreciable harm had resulted to the defendants through the efforts to impeach the credibility of the witness.[45] Emphasizing the desirability of the presence of a moral sanction, the Mississippi Supreme Court concluded that it was proper to show that an individual had no sense of the binding force of his oath because he did not believe in a Supreme Being.[46]

Irrespective of what attitude a court may take in the matter of competency, the religious faith of a witness is not considered a proper subject for argument or proof where the intention is to discriminate between religious creeds. Although on cross-examination a witness may be asked questions to test his veracity or to shake his credit by injuring his character, it is inappropriate in modern practice to permit inquiry into the peculiarities of a man's religious faith. This is so, not to shield him from possible disgrace, but to prevent scrutiny into the state of his faith contrary to the spirit of American law. Thus ordinarily no tribunal will allow inquiry to ascertain whether a witness is Protestant, Catholic, Shaker, Mormon, Jew, Spiritualist, or Materialist. Defect of religious faith is not presumed.

An attorney in his summation of a case stated that all of the witnesses for the defense belonged to the same church as the defendant pastor and that not one of the witnesses would testify differently from the clergyman. The trial judge stopped this method of attack. Counsel objected and took exception to the ruling. On appeal the Supreme Court of the state held that the trial court did not abuse its discretion. The action of the lower court was sustained.[47]

Witnesses in the federal courts.—The federal judiciary has indicated in a series of decisions handed down by the United State Supreme Court the rules with respect to competency of

45. *State v. Beal*, 199 N. C. 278, 154 S. E. 604 (1930).
46. *Gambrell v. State*, 92 Miss. 728, 46 So. 138 (1908).
47. *Rudolph v. Landwerlen*, 92 Ind. 34 (1883).

witnesses in federal courts. Inasmuch as the disqualification of a witness because of certain religious beliefs or lack of them is characteristic of the common law, and inasmuch as the common law is involved in each of these cases, an appreciation of the present qualifications of federal witnesses is predicated upon an understanding of these decisions. It is pertinent to mention that, by the Judiciary Act of 1789,[48] the laws of the several states, except where federal laws provided otherwise, were to be regarded as the rules of decision in trials at common law in the federal courts in cases where they applied.

In early American decisions the application by federal courts of the common law rule disqualifying a witness because of the presence or absence of certain religious beliefs is observable. For example, in one case the testimony of an atheist was rejected.[49] In a district court in New York, too, a belief in rewards and punishments in the next life was held necessary for the competency of a witness.[50]

At common law a codefendant in a trial could not testify as a witness for the other defendant. In 1851, after the question whether a codefendant could testify had arisen in a federal district court, the United States Supreme Court, deciding in the negative, ruled that the competency of witnesses in criminal trials in the federal courts had to be determined by the rules of evidence operating in the respective states when the Judiciary Act of 1789 was passed. The Judiciary Act itself was held applicable only to civil cases. The reasoning of the court in this case was based upon the declaration of Congressional policy in the Judiciary Act itself.[51]

In 1891, in answer to an inquiry whether a witness was disqualified in a federal case arising in Texas because of a previous conviction and subsequent pardon, the Supreme Court declared

48. Act of September 24, 1789, 1 *Stat.* 73, c. 20.
49. *Wakefield v. Ross*, 28 Fed. Cas. 1346 (C. C., 1827).
50. *United States v. Kennedy*, 26 Fed. Cas. 761 (D. C., 1843); see also *United States v. Lee*, 26 Fed. Cas. 908 (C. C., 1824).
51. *United States v. Reid*, 12 How. 361, 13 L. Ed. 1023 (1851).

that the competency of witnesses in criminal trials in the federal courts was governed, except as Congress otherwise made provision, by the common law which prevailed in Texas when Texas was admitted to the Union. In any state other than the original thirteen, therefore, the competency of a witness in a criminal case was to be ascertained by the law in effect in that state at the time of its admission to the Union.[52]

In 1892, in deciding that a codefendant who was not himself on trial at the time could testify, the Supreme Court said that the tendency of jurisprudence was to enlarge the domain of the competency of a witness and to submit to the consideration of the jury the issue of credibility in regard to matters which previously had been deemed sufficient to justify the exclusion of the witness. This liberal trend was judicially attributed partly to legislation and partly to court construction. A tendency to widen the scope of competency for federal witnesses was thus discernible.[53]

In 1918 the Supreme Court approved the rulings of a district court in two separate cases in permitting individuals who had been convicted of crime to testify. The court held that the federal courts are not conclusively bound, with respect to the competency of witnesses, by the rules of the common law which prevailed in 1789 or at the date of the admission of a state to the Union. The court stated that "the disposition of courts and of legislative bodies to remove disabilities from witnesses has continued . . . under dominance of the conviction of our time that the truth is more likely to be arrived at by hearing the testimony of all persons of competent understanding who may seem to have knowledge of the facts involved in a case, leaving the credit and weight of such testimony to be determined by the jury or by the court."[54]

52. *Logan v. United States*, 144 U. S. 263, 12 Sup. Ct. 617, 36 L. Ed. 429 (1891).

53. *Benson v. United States*, 146 U. S. 325, 13 Sup. Ct. 60, 36 L. Ed. 991 (1892).

54. *Rosen v. United States*, 245 U. S. 467, 471, 38 Sup. Ct. 148, 150, 62 L. Ed. 406, 409 (1918).

On the same day on which the last-mentioned decision was announced, a federal circuit court of appeals reiterated the previous doctrine that the rules of a state as to the competency of witnesses, in force when the federal courts sitting within the borders of that state were created, control. In the specific instance, regulations of the State of Washington at the time the first federal court was established in that state declared that no person should be incompetent as a witness in consequence of his opinion in matters of religion. The trial judge had excluded the testimony of a non-believer. This ruling was held to be erroneous, and a non-believer was declared competent to testify in a federal trial, since atheists were not barred from participation in a trial under the state regulations.[55]

In 1920, a federal circuit court of appeals held that although a witness in a particular trial had stated he did not understand the nature of an oath, the trial court had apparently concluded that his answer indicated an inability to define the term "oath" technically, rather than an ignorance of its obligation. The circuit court concluded that, since the witness had realized that after swearing he must tell the truth, the trial court had made no error in admitting his testimony.[56]

In 1933, the United States Supreme Court enunciated the principle that one spouse might testify in behalf of another, contrary to the common law. The court again declared that the rules governing the competency of witnesses in criminal trials in the federal courts are not necessarily restricted to the local rules in effect at the time of the admission into the Union of the particular state where the trial takes place; instead, the rules are to be applied by the federal courts in the light of reason and experience.[57]

55. *Louie Ding v. United States*, 247 Fed. 12 (C. C. A., 1918); for further discussion, see also *Rendleman v. United States*, 18 F. (2d) 27 (C. C. A., 1927).
56. *Oliver v. United States*, 267 Fed. 544 (C. C. A., 1920).
57. *Funk v. United States*, 290 U. S. 371, 54 Sup. Ct. 212, 78 L. Ed. 369 (1933); see also *Wolfe v. United States*, 291 U. S. 7, 54 Sup. Ct. 279, 78 L. Ed. 617 (1934).

In summary it may be stated[58] that the competency of witnesses in criminal cases is now governed, except where the acts of Congress or federal rules otherwise provide, by the principles of common law as they may be interpreted by the federal courts in the light of reason and experience.

With respect to the competency of witnesses in civil cases, Congress in 1934 empowered[59] the United States Supreme Court to prescribe for the federal district courts, by general rules, practices and procedure in civil actions. Pursuant to this law, the Supreme Court in 1938 issued a series of rules to cover civil procedure, one[60] of which provides in part, with respect to the form and admissibility of evidence, that "all evidence shall be admitted which is admissible under the statutes of the United States, or under the rules of evidence heretofore applied in the courts of the United States on the hearing of suits in equity, or under the rules of evidence applied in the courts of general jurisdiction of the State in which the United States court is held. In any case, the statute or rule which favors the reception of the evidence governs and the evidence shall be presented according to the most convenient method prescribed in any of the statutes or rules to which reference is herein made. The competency of a witness to testify shall be determined in like manner." This rule, presently in effect, appears to have supplanted previous federal acts and judicial decisions, although the terminology of the rule is not believed to be too conclusive.[61]

It may be further pointed out that the rules of evidence for criminal cases are now predicated upon the idea of uniformity, whereas the rules of evidence for civil cases contemplate partial conformity to state regulation. Since federal jurisdiction in civil actions may be based on diversity of citizenship, the citizen of a particular state should not run the risk of losing civil rights

58. Wigmore, *op. cit.*, I, 170-205.
59. Act of June 19, 1934, 48 *Stat.* 1064, c. 651, 28 *U. S. C.* 723b, 723c.
60. Rule 43(a), Federal Rules of Civil Procedure.
61. Wigmore, *op. cit.*, pp. 200-201.

by being unable to adduce in federal courts evidence admissible under state law. In such instances, uniformity of rules of evidence among the federal courts is not deemed essential. However, since criminal cases involve violations of Congressional acts, uniformity of rule becomes necessary. The lack of uniformity of rules of evidence in criminal cases would inevitably result in the application by the various district courts of conflicting rules in cases of identical violations of federal laws.

The liberalization indicated in the more recent court decisions and in current federal rules of civil and criminal procedure tends to minimize discrimination against witnesses on religious grounds. Because only comparatively few cases involving allegedly religious rights of witnesses have been litigated in the federal courts, the full extent of the liberalizing tendency cannot yet be fully determined.

An unusual case involving the religious obligations of a witness occurred in New Jersey in 1932. A federal district court denied a motion for a continuance based upon the absence of an alleged material witness. The absence of the witness in question, the defendant's wife, was attributed to her exercise of a religious right to remain at home for seven days after the burial of her brother. The defendant maintained that the trial court had violated flagrantly the constitutional guarantees of religious worship and appealed the ruling. The appellate court held, however, that since the religious custom was a right of the witness, not of the defendant, no religious guarantee of the latter was abridged. The court pointed out that the only conceivable right which might have been denied the defendant was that of a continuance because of the absence of a material witness. Evidence did not demonstrate, however, that the absent witness was necessary to the case. Therefore the refusal of a continuance by the district court was not considered an abuse of discretion.[62]

Children as witnesses.—At common law as it prevailed in early America, a child under fourteen years of age was pre-

62. *Savitt v. United States,* 59 F. (2d) 541 (C. C. A., 1932).

sumptively incompetent to testify as a witness. Unless the competency of the child could be shown to the satisfaction of the trial judge, the child was not permitted to testify. Through legislative and judicial modification, the age factor itself has little bearing upon the competency of witnesses today. Generally, the admissibility of children as witnesses depends upon their possessing an understanding, frequently gained through religious instruction, of the nature and consequences of an oath. The trial judge determines the presence or absence of the proper degree of understanding.[63]

Cases well illustrate the application of the rule. In Illinois four witnesses, aged seven, eight, ten, and twelve years of age, who were grammar school students in grades in which children of average intelligence of their ages were found, were permitted to testify because the trial judge concluded that they knew what it meant to take an oath to tell the truth.[64] The Supreme Court of Iowa approved the acceptance as a competent witness of a seven-year-old boy who had shown the trial court that he understood the meaning of an oath and realized that he was to be honest in his testimony.[65] The Texas Court of Criminal Appeals noted that although there was no arbitrary age of competency, a child of tender age ought to be admitted with caution by the trial judge.[66] A six-year-old girl in Texas was qualified when she indicated a reasonable degree of knowledge relative to the sanctity of an oath.[67]

A nine-year-old girl told a Georgia trial judge that she did not know right from wrong but that she did know what it was to tell the truth and that she knew she would be punished for telling a lie. The trial court refused to exclude her testimony. The Supreme Court of the state upheld the trial court's ruling

63. S. W. C., '"Evidence—Witnesses—Competency of Children of Tender Years" (1929) 18 *California Law Review* 85-88; 70 *C. J.* 92-94.
64. *People v. Schladweiler*, 315 Ill. 553, 146 N. E. 525 (1925).
65. *State v. Hall*, 225 Iowa 1316, 283 N. W. 414 (1939).
66. *Flannery v. State*, 117 S. W. (2d) 1111 (1938).
67. *Lacey v. State*, 127 S. W. (2d) 890 (1939).

that the girl understood the seriousness of the occasion sufficiently to testify.[68] Permitting a child who knew nothing about religion to testify was valid in Florida because the court held that the child realized the necessity of telling the truth.[69]

Even though a child may not have understood the nature of an oath at the time he witnessed a crime, a judge may permit the child to be properly instructed in the obligations of an oath by a clergyman or others and subsequently allow the child to testify. Where an eight-year-old girl had had religious instruction enabling her to comprehend the seriousness of an oath, she was permitted to testify when she asserted that she would be punished for false testimony by the Supreme Being.[70]

A child is properly excluded as a witness when it is evident to the trial judge that he fails to understand the serious nature of offering testimony. One seven-year-old child testified she had no knowledge of an oath and that she "never heard of the devil or the bad man or what would become of her if she told a lie." After she had been permitted to give testimony which helped lead to a conviction, the appellate court noted that it was the solemn appeal of the witness to the Supreme Being that imparted the sanction on the basis of which the witness' statements on the stand were accepted. Since the sentence for crime should have rested upon a firmer basis than was indicated in the case, the final decision held that the girl should have been excluded from the witness stand.[71]

A nine-year-old girl who said that she did not know what would happen to her if she did not tell the truth was deemed incompetent to testify, although she stated that she learned in Sunday school that "little girls go to torment if they tell a lie." She did not understand the consequences of an oath, the Court of Appeals of Alabama concluded.[72] Likewise a trial judge was

68. *Gordon v. State*, 186 Ga. 615, 198 S. E. 678 (1938).
69. *Cross v. State*, 89 Fla. 212, 103 So. 636 (1925).
70. *Hall v. State*, 19 Ala. App. 229, 96 So. 644 (1923).
71. *State v. Washington*, 49 La. Ann. 1602, 22 So. 841 (1897).
72. *Morse v. State*, 173 So. 875 (1937).

held to have erred in admitting the testimony of a child who had received no religious training and had never heard of future rewards or punishments.[73]   In one instance, a judge refused to examine or permit a lawyer to examine a child of twelve years as to her knowledge of and belief in the sanctity of an oath.   Her testimony had an important bearing on the outcome of the trial. Upon appeal her testimony was ordered stricken out on the ground that, as far as the record disclosed, she might have been "as ignorant as a Hottentot" upon the subject of oaths.[74]

It is evident that the presence or absence of a religious opinion in itself is not a test in determining the competency of a minor.   Religious training is a weighty influence.   But the chief criterion in the admissibility of the testimony of children is the existence or lack of existence of a moral or religious sanction which will insure veracity on the part of the child.   The exercise of discretion by the trial court in determining its existence is final except in cases of abuse.

Aspersions on religion of parties.—Casting aspersions on the religion of one or more parties involved in a case for the purpose of arousing prejudices may be ground for a new trial or for the reversal of a decision.   Where there are such aspersions, reason is likely to yield to religious emotions which might prevent a jury from acting deliberately and fairly upon the issues under consideration.

A remark that a person was a "Jew—a Christ Killer" was improper.   An Illinois appellate court commented that it was inconceivable that such an epithet should be uttered in a trial. Because of this remark and for other reasons the judgment of the lower court was reversed.[75]   In Texas a judge did not approve of the reference by counsel in his argument to the fact that the plaintiff had graduated from a sectarian school and

73. *Carter v. State,* 63 Ala. 52 (1879).
74. *Young v. State,* 122 Ga. 725, 50 S. E. 996 (1905).
75. *Freeman v. Dempsey,* 41 Ill. App. 554 (1891).

would not be able to attend church services because of her injuries. Counsel's statements were held objectionable.[76]

In another summation an attorney for the prosecution stated in his closing argument that "the only purpose of the defense in this case has been to assassinate the character of a high minded preacher who is engaged in doing a great work, to make this earth the same kind of a place we want it to be in heaven." Defendant's lawyer objected to this statement but was overruled in the trial court. Upon conviction of the offense charged, the defendant appealed from the lower court judgment. The appellate court decided that the action of the trial judge in overruling the objection of defense counsel constituted reversible error.[77]

A district attorney said to a jury: "I am sure that this jury will not be influenced by the testimony of this congregation of negro witnesses that Ben Howard, a big Mason and church member, has been able to procure to prove the innocence of his son." It was held that the comment did not involve an appeal to the jury to base its findings on prejudice and therefore was permissible.[78] Likewise the narration of biblical stories did not constitute an appeal to prejudice. Because the biblical narratives were not calculated to arouse either racial or religious prejudice, they were permissible in the trial court.[79] Generally, however, anything savoring of an appeal to religious bias will not be tolerated.

Competency of jurors.—The religious beliefs of a prospective

76. *Morgan v. Maunders*, 37 S. W. (2d) 791 (1930).
77. *City of Chicago v. Porter*, 194 Ill. App. 590 (1915).
78. *State v. Howard*, 120 La. 311, 45 So. 260 (1908); see also *United States v. Carruthers*, 152 F. (2d) 512 (C. C. A., 1945); certiorari denied 327 U. S. 787, 66 Sup. Ct. 805, 90 L. Ed. 1014 (1946); rehearing denied 327 U. S. 817, 66 Sup. Ct. 816, 90 L. Ed. 1041 (1946), a case involving prosecution for mail fraud, wherein an instruction by the trial judge forbidding the jury to question the truth or falsity of representations relating to subjects of breathing, silence, and position of persons during sleep, if the jury believed that such were matters within the field of religion as taught by the defendant, was construed not to violate the First Amendment.
79. *Hewitt v. Buchanan*, 4 S. W. (2d) 169 (1927).

juror usually do not render him incompetent. The competency of a juror is left to the discretion of the trial judge. Appellate courts are reluctant to reverse the trial judge unless a clear abuse of discretion is apparent. Under modern constitutions and laws, any person otherwise competent may take an oath and act as a juror, whatever his religious belief, provided the oath is administered in such a way that he considers it binding upon his conscience.[80]

However, there are a minority of cases to the contrary. For instance, challenge for cause on the basis of lack of religious belief has been allowed. Thus one judge held that a prospective juror who declared that he had tried to acquit certain individuals previously, and that he would be as satisfied to swear on a spelling book as on a Bible, could be barred.[81] An atheist was presumed insensible to the obligations of an oath.[82] In another instance, objection was raised after a trial was concluded that a juror was an atheist. The appellate court disallowed the challenge on the ground of tardiness, implying a degree of justification for the objection had the challenge been made earlier.[83] These illustrations, however, are not typical of present practice.

A prospective juror is permitted to affirm instead of taking an oath if he is conscientiously opposed to the latter. The sanction of belief in a Supreme Being and in future rewards and punishments formerly was necessary, but now denial of the existence of God usually does not disqualify a juror.[84] Thus one juror answered that he had no personal fear of future punishment and did not believe in either the Old or the New Testament. He was nevertheless properly admitted to jury duty.[85]

80. Note, "Jury—Competency of Jury" (1929) 14 *Iowa Law Review* 486-487; 35 *C. J.* 248; the refusal of a Jehovah's Witness to serve as a juror because of his religious belief has been upheld as justified by the First Amendment in *United States v. Hillyard*, 52 F. Supp. 612 (D. C., 1943).
81. *McFadden v. Commonwealth*, 23 Pa. 12 (1853).
82. *State v. Levy*, 187 N. C. 581, 122 S. E. 386 (1924).
83. *State v. Davis*, 80 N. C. 412 (1879).   84. 35 *C. J.* 423.
85. *State v. Jackson*, 156 Iowa 588, 137 N. W. 1034 (1912).

If the oath is taken without protest, it will be assumed that the juror regards it as binding, in the absence of proof to the contrary.[86]

The charge of religious discrimination by officials drawing up the lists of potential jurors arose in Georgia. Allegations that the jury list had been arbitrarily made, to the exclusion of members of a particular religious sect, were rejected by the court. It was only a coincidence that one denomination was given a preference over others in the matter of numbers, the court concluded. The inference of religious discrimination was denied.[87] But in Massachusetts, in a trial involving the property rights of a bishop, two members of his faith were excluded from the panel on the ground that they had an interest in the case. The trial judge made an order excluding all prospective jurors of the defendant's faith, without reference to their residence within or without the defendant's parish. Overruling the action, the appellate court said that holding the same religious belief as one of the parties or association with him in the same church did not disqualify a person from sitting as a juror. The court order rejecting these men gave the opposing attorney an additional power of choice and made his right of peremptory challenge relatively more valuable. A new trial was ordered.[88]

An appeal to the Supreme Court of California was based upon the contention that the lower court had erred in refusing to grant a new trial because of the alleged misconduct of a juror who had failed to disclose that she was a Christian Scientist. The claim that the juror was incompetent rested upon the theory that her state of mind, as a result of her religious belief, was such that she did not recognize the existence of disease or mental incompetency. The Supreme Court held that ordinarily the religious belief of a prospective juror was immaterial, and that

86. 35 *C. J.* 244.
87. *Davis v. Arthur*, 139 Ga. 74, 76 S. E. 676 (1912).
88. *Searle v. Roman Catholic Bishop*, 203 Mass. 493, 89 N. E. 809 (1909).

there was no duty upon her to volunteer information on that subject. The court said that it had not been shown that the juror did not recognize the existence of disease and mental incompetency; the asserted state of mind was merely implied from her religious affiliation. Thus the juror was qualified and not guilty of any misconduct for failure to volunteer an explanation of her religious beliefs.[89]

A federal statute[90] stating that no polygamist could hold an office of honor or trust was judged in 1884 not to apply to jury service. Under this decision Mormons otherwise competent were eligible for the jury.[91] However, specific statutes may disqualify a bigamist or polygamist from jury service. An Idaho law[92] requiring jurors to be electors, and forbidding polygamists to be electors, had the effect of excluding Mormons from jury service. Upholding the statute, the Idaho Supreme Court believed itself justified in supposing the lawmakers took notice of the generally admitted fact that the members of the Mormon church were more obedient to the teachings of that church, which were antagonistic to the laws of the land, than to the laws themselves.[93] A presidential pardon rendered a prospective juror, previously convicted of polygamy, eligible to serve.[94]

It is erroneous to inquire of prospective jurors whether they would give more weight to the testimony of a witness of a particular sect than to that of a witness of any other sect. Questions which have the effect of raising or implying the existence of prejudices during the selection of a jury are properly excluded in trial courts. But religious inquiries to permit counsel to exercise his peremptory challenges intelligently are upheld. One lawyer asked jurors whether they were or had been members of

89. *In re Malvasi's Estate*, 96 Cal. App. 204, 273 Pac. 1097 (1929).
90. Act of March 22, 1883, 22 *Stat.* 47, 28 *U. S. C. A.*, sec. 426.
91. *People v. Hopt*, 3 Utah 396, 4 Pac. 250 (1884).
92. *Idaho Rev. Stats.*, secs. 3941, 3942.
93. *Territory v. Evans*, 2 Idaho 651, 23 Pac. 232 (1890).
94. *United States v. Bassett*, 5 Utah 131, 13 Pac. 237 (1887).

any church. Denying the impropriety of the practice of asking such questions, the Criminal Court of Appeals of Oklahoma stated: "It is true that church membership does not determine the qualifications of a juror, but a prospective juror, within reasonable bounds and limited by a fair discretion of the court, may be examined as to his membership in any organization which might give counsel information and enable him to properly exercise his peremptory challenges."[95] Likewise it was held proper for counsel to ask a juror whether he entertained any prejudice against people of the Jewish faith. However, the question: "Would the testimony of witnesses who professed that faith receive as much credit as members of any other?" was deemed properly ruled out.[96]

Laws disqualifying as jurors in criminal cases involving capital punishment persons whose opinions would preclude them from finding any defendant guilty of an offense punishable with death do not violate constitutional provisions guaranteeing religious freedom and providing that religious opinion shall not make any person incompetent as a juror. A juror who has scruples against capital punishment is prevented from weighing evidence between the government and the accused impartially and is thus not an impartial juror.[97] Such laws, disqualifying disbelievers in capital punishment from jury service, have been upheld further on the ground that they do not concern competency of jurors but rather ability.[98]

Dying declarations.—A dying declaration is a statement made by a person under a sense of impending death. At common law a dying declaration was not admissible if its maker did not believe in a God who would punish false statements. Such a declaration derives its sanction as testimony from the fact that

95. *Young v. State*, 271 Pac. 426, 429 (1928).

96. *Horst v. Silverman*, 20 Wash. 233, 55 Pac. 52 (1898).

97. *Logan v. United States*, 144 U. S. 263, 12 Sup. Ct. 617, 36 L. Ed. 949 (1938).

98. *People v. Rollins*, 179 Cal. 818, 179 Pac. 209 (1919); *State v. Leuch*, 198 Wash. 331, 88 P. (2d) 440 (1939).

it is made under the apprehension and expectation of death. Such solemn conditions are considered to create a sanction equally impressive with that of an oath.[99]

The common law disqualification has been modified by American statutory law and judicial decision. The declaration is now admissible provided the deceased would have been competent to testify to the matters contained in the declaration had he lived and been offered as a witness in the case. Whether or not a dying declaration is admissible in a trial is a problem for the determination of the court. After its admission, its weight and credibility remain to be considered by the jury. The state of mind of the declarant must be shown before the declaration is entitled to be received by the court.[100]

Francis Wharton's conclusion that the fact that a declarant was a disbeliever in a future state of rewards and punishments may be used to discredit his testimony is a generalization of court opinion.[101] As illustration, the Mississippi Supreme Court ruled that a lower court had erred by excluding testimony offered by a defendant that the religious belief of the deceased was such as to detract from the value of his dying declaration. The testimony purported to show that the deceased had often said that "there was no hell or hereafter, and all the punishment a man got was in this world."[102] A Missouri trial court erred in excluding testimony tending to show that the declarant had been an infidel. The defendant had a right to assail the credibility of the declarant.[103] Evidence to discredit a dying declaration was held admissible, even where there was a constitutional provision abrogating the common law disqualification of disbelievers.[104]

99. Frank Swancara, "Religion in the Law of Dying Declarations" (1932) 66 *United States Law Review* 192-202; 30 C. J. 278; 1 R. C. L. 532.
100. 30 C. J. 268-269; see *State v. Phillips*, 277 N. W. 609 (1938).
101. Francis Wharton, *Criminal Law* (12th ed.), I, 14.
102. *Hill v. State*, 64 Miss. 431, 1 So. 494 (1886).
103. *State v. Rozell*, 225 S. W. 931 (1920).
104. *Marshall v. State*, 219 Ala. 83, 121 So. 72 (1897).

The United States Supreme Court declared that dying declarations might be contradicted in the same manner as other testimony, even to the extent of showing that the character of the deceased was possibly infamous. Evidence of contradictory statements made by the declarant before death should be received.[105] Proof of disbelief may extend retroactively in the life of the deceased: one opinion held that it was admissible on the part of the defense to show that a disbelieving state of mind had existed at any time during the life of the deceased.[106]

In 1931 the Court of Appeals of Alabama reversed its own conclusion concerning the validity of a dying declaration made by a nonbeliever. In the first hearing of a case the court ruled that since only persons who believe in a Supreme Being controlling rewards and punishments were competent to testify, the declaration of an atheist was worthless. Such a declaration should have been excluded. But on a rehearing a short time later, two of the three judges shifted to the position that section three of the Alabama Constitution, which stated that the rights of a citizen should not be affected by his religious principles, abrogated the common law rule rendering incompetent the dying declaration of an atheist. The remarks of Judge Rice on the rehearing are interesting as indicative of the current trend: "I do not subscribe to the view that there is no place in our whole government structure for a belief which ties men to the rocks and clods and places him on a level with the beasts of the field."[107] He believed instead that "ours is 'the land of the free, and the home of the brave'; and that though to say 'there is no God,' both in Scripture and in common knowledge, proves one a fool, and may, for all I know, tie him 'to the rocks and clods,' yet it does not, and should not, deprive that one of his heritage as a citizen, nor of his standing as one of the 'free' and one of the 'brave.' "[108]

105. *Carver v. United States*, 164 U. S. 694, 17 Sup. Ct. 228, 41 L. Ed. 602 (1897).
106. *Gambrell v. State*, 92 Miss. 738, 46 So. 138 (1908); 1 R. C. L. 549.
107. *Wright v. State*, 135 So. 636, 637 (1931).
108. *Ibid.*, pp. 736-738.

The presumption favors the competency of the declarant unless the contrary is proved.[109] Where no evidence had been given during a trial to indicate whether a Chinese believed in a hereafter or future punishment, a district court of appeals in California held that it should not be presumed that he did not believe in a future life merely because he might have been a member of a heathenish religion. A statement made by him in the face of impending death presumably was attended by the same degree of solemnity as that which would attend a statement made under like circumstances by one having religious convictions of a more civilized order.[110]

The fact that the declarant does not die immediately does not affect the validity of the declaration if made under the solemn conviction of approaching death.[111] Thus, evidence that a person undergoing a surgical operation received the last rites of her church and told her clergyman that she "had to die now" was sufficient to permit the admission of her testimony, although she lived a month after making her statements.[112]

Privileged communications.—At common law no one could refuse to testify in a court trial to facts within his knowledge. State legislatures and courts have modified the common law doctrine in order to make certain communications privileged, as, for example, knowledge gained by a clergyman in the performance of his religious duties.[113] State laws on the subject are of two types: one which renders the clergyman receiving the communication incompetent to testify; the other extending to the clergyman the privilege of refusing to testify if he desires. The theory that such communications are privileged is based upon the idea that the human being sometimes has need of spiritual consolation. The privilege is applicable to all denominations.[114]

109. 1 *R. C. L.* 547.   110. *People v. Lum Foon*, 155 Pac. 477 (1915).
111. 30 *C. J.* 254-255; 1 *R. C. L.* 538.
112. *Schlesak v. State*, 232 Wisc. 510, 287 N. W. 703 (1939).
113. Note, "Evidence—Privileged Communications" (1931) 16 *Minnesota Law Review* 105-106.
114. Clarence Martin, "The American Judiciary and Religious Liberty" (1928) 62 *American Law Review* 658-688; 70 *C. J.* 452; *Dehler v. State*, 22 Ind. App. 383, 53 N. E. 850 (1900).

Usually the statutes require that the communication be made to the clergyman while in the performance of his duty. Thus, one individual confessed his guilt of a crime to church elders. Later in a civil trial there was an attempt to place the elders' evidence before the jury. The trial court, however, considered the elders to be ministers of the gospel; the confession was a privileged communication. The Iowa Supreme Court upheld the trial court and said: "Where any person enters that secret chamber, this statute [defining privileged communications] closes the door upon him, and civil authority turns away its ear."[115]

An Indiana court required the person claiming the privilege to prove he was in a repentent mood at the time of the confession.[116] The Supreme Court of Arkansas ruled that a person claiming that evidence should be excluded on the ground that the communication was privileged must have been a member of the sect with which the clergyman in question was connected.[117] Inherent in the idea of a privileged communication is the express or implied understanding that what was said should not be made known to anyone.[118]

If the statement is made to the clergyman other than in his professional capacity, no privileged status is held to exist.[119] The mere fact that the person to whom a communication is made is a clergyman does not of itself make the communication privileged. Information gained by a deacon seeking evidence against a church member was admissible.[120] A clergyman was permitted to testify to information he learned while acting as an interpreter in a nonreligious capacity.[121] Information a clergyman obtained

115. *Reutkemeier v. Nolte*, 179 Iowa 342, 161 N. W. 290 (1917).
116. *Knight v. Lee*, 80 Ind. 201 (1881).
117. *Alford v. Johnson*, 103 Ark. 236, 146 S. W. 516 (1901).
118. *Hills v. State*, 61 Neb. 589, 85 N. W. 836 (1901).
119. 70 *C. J.* 451, note 13. So held in Arkansas, California, Colorado, Indiana, Iowa, Minnesota, Missouri, Nebraska, New York, and Wisconsin.
120. *Knight v. Lee*, 80 Ind. 201 (1881).
121. *Blossi v. C. & N. W. Railway Co.*, 144 Iowa 697, 123 N. W. 360 (1909).

while performing the duties of a notary was not considered a privileged communication.[122]   A confession made to a Salvation Army major was declared admissible.[123]   An individual requested a minister to intercede with the former's first wife. Statements made to the minister at that time were appropriately admitted into evidence in a later trial for bigamy, because there had been no privileged status.[124]   Where an accused had volunteered information to a clergyman, without seeking his advice or assistance, it was proper to admit such statements into the record of a later trial.[125]   The fact that the exemption does not apply to non-religious, non-professional relations is obvious.

Summary.—Judicial opinion has frequently been sought to define the religious rights of individuals in civil and criminal trials. Early American decisions followed the English common law and disqualified a prospective witness who did not believe in a God or in ultimate punishment. Almost a century ago the common law disqualification for nonbelievers was modified by many state legislatures and judiciaries. In forty states a person may now testify, even though he does not believe in a Supreme Being. In eight states, however, belief in Divine punishment or in the existence of a Supreme Being is essential to the competency of a witness. In any event, the status of a person's religious belief is a fact to be established by means other than by examination of the individual upon the stand.

Frequently an individual who alleges he has conscientious scruples against taking an oath is permitted to make an affirmation. A person usually does not have a choice between an oath or an affirmation. Courts ordinarily permit the latter only because of bona fide objections to the former based on religious grounds. Equal credit is afforded the testimony of a witness whether he swears or affirms.

122. *Partridge v. Partridge,* 220 Mo. 321, 119 S. W. 415 (1909).
123. *State v. Morehouse,* 117 Atl. 296 (1922).
124. *Hills v. State,* 61 Neb. 589, 85 N. W. 836 (1901).
125. *State v. Brown,* 95 Iowa 381, 64 N. W. 277 (1895).

Provisions pertaining to the competency of a witness, regardless of the presence or absence of religious beliefs, likewise are usually applicable to the credibility of his testimony. Thus, in some jurisdictions the religious belief of a witness, or his lack of any such belief, is deemed to constitute an area out of the reach of legal questioning for the purpose of affecting his credibility. On the other hand, delving into the faith of a witness on the stand is qualifiedly approved by certain courts.

The United States Supreme Court has liberalized the rigidity of the common law disqualification. As a result of a series of cases heard before the court, discrimination against a witness on religious grounds has been greatly reduced.

At common law a child under the age of fourteen years was presumptively incompetent to testify as a witness. Legal and judicial modifications have reduced the importance of the age factor. The chief criterion in the admissibility of the testimony of children is the existence or lack of existence of a moral or religious sanction which will insure veracity on the part of the child. The exercise of discretion by the trial court in determining the existence of this sanction is final except in cases of abuse.

Aspersions cast on the religion of one or more parties involved in a case for the purpose of arousing prejudice have been grounds for a new trial or the reversal of a decision. In such instances the courts hold that the jury is prevented from acting fairly upon the questions before it.

The religious beliefs of a prospective juror do not usually render him incompetent. Under modern constitutions and laws, any person otherwise competent may take an oath and act as a juror, whatever his religious belief, provided the oath is administered in such a way that he considers it binding upon his conscience.

Applying the common law, American courts in our early history would not permit the admission of a dying declaration if its maker did not believe in a God who would provide punishment for false statements. Later the common law disqualification was modified by statutory law and judicial decision. Where an irreligious person is a competent witness, his dying declarations are now admissible.

At common law no one could refuse to testify in a court trial to facts within his knowledge. American legislatures and courts have modified the common law doctrine in order to make certain communications privileged, such as knowledge gained by a clergyman in the performance of his religious duties. The theory of privileged communications indicates a marked respect for the practices of religious groups. The judiciary approves the status of the privileged communication. Judicial respect for religious rights during court trials has become more of a reality.

XI

Devises and Bequests for Religious Purposes

Character of grants for religious purposes.—Gifts and grants in trust for the support of religious activities are classified as charitable trusts. Mr. Justice Gray of Massachusetts once defined a charity, in the legal sense, as a gift, to be applied consistently with existing laws, for the benefit of an indefinite number of persons, either by bringing their minds or hearts under the influence of education or religion, by relieving their bodies from disease, suffering or constraint, by assisting them to establish themselves in life, or by erecting or maintaining public buildings or works or otherwise lessening the burdens of government.[1] His definition has frequently been cited with approval by the American judiciary.[2] If a gift indicates that it is charitable in nature, even without the use of the term, it will be considered a charitable trust.

Charitable trusts were recognized in England as early as the time of Elizabeth, with courts of equity assuming jurisdiction for their execution. Judicial interpretation of such trusts was frequently detrimental to charitable interests as individual actions, subversive to the established English church, were outlawed. In America, courts of equity have exercised inherent original jurisdiction over charitable trusts and have favored

1. *Jackson v. Phillips*, 96 Mass. 539, 556 (1867).
2. Jairus Perry, *A Treatise on the Law of Trusts and Trustees* (7th ed.), II, 1183, note 35.

them unless prohibited by law.[3]   The federal courts follow the rules and decisions of the respective state courts with respect to charitable trusts.   According to the usual doctrine of the federal courts, the validity of charitable devises, as against the claims of the heirs at law, depends upon the law of the state in which the property is situated.   The validity of charitable bequests, as against the next of kin, depends upon the law of the state in which the testator had his domicile.[4]

Liberal construction favored.—Generally, American courts have favored a liberal interpretation of charitable trusts.   Speaking of charitable trusts Jairus Perry says that "the courts look with favor upon all such donations, and endeavor to carry them into effect, if it can be done consistently with the rules of law."[5] Typical is the judicial declaration that the law "favors them [charitable and philanthropic trusts], and construes them with the utmost liberality, in order to carry out the charitable purpose of the donor."[6]

The intention of the donor is held to control the whole bequest.[7]   If the intention of the testator was to apply funds for a charitable purpose, the gift will be upheld, even though a stricter construction might hold it a gift for private purposes. The United States Supreme Court holds that if the testator describes the general nature of a charitable trust, the details of its administration may be settled by the trustees.[8]

Indefiniteness of beneficiaries.—One of the features distinguishing a charitable trust from other trusts is the indefinite-

3. *Ibid.*, pp. 1170-1179.
4. *Jones v. Habersham*, 107 U. S. 174, 2 Sup. Ct. 336, 27 L. Ed. 401 (1882); *Harvard College v. Jewett*, 11 F. (2d) 119 (C. C. A., 1925).
5. Perry, *op. cit.*, p. 1200.
6. *First Congregational Society v. Bridgeport*, 99 Conn. 22, 121 Atl. 77 (1923).
7. *Estate of Mary A. Horner*, 38 Lanc. (Pa.) Law Rev. 305 (1942); *King v. Richardson*, 136 F. (2d) 849 (C. C. A., 1943); *Sands v. Church of Ascension and Prince of Peace*, 181 Md. 536, 30 A. (2d) 771 (1943); 11 C. J. 331; William L. Crow, "Why Charitable Trusts Fail" (1940) 24 *Marquette Law Review* 126-138.
8. *Russell v. Allen*, 107 U. S. 163, 2 Sup. Ct. 327, 27 L. Ed. 397 (1882).

ness of the beneficiaries. Persons to be benefited should be uncertain until they are selected to be the particular beneficiaries of the trust. In fact, indefiniteness and uncertainty as to the individuals and members to be benefited are often determining elements of a valid charitable trust.[9]

Some states insist that the instrument creating the charity specify with reasonable certainty the class to be benefited, or else confer the power of selection on the trustees.[10] In these jurisdictions uncertainty as to the class of beneficiaries of a charitable trust may be fatal. In all states, when the phraseology employed in creating a public charitable trust is so indefinite and general that the court cannot ascertain what class of persons are entitled to the benefit sought to be conferred, or what benefit will actually accrue, the trust may be held void.

Thus a trust for the society known as the Quakers has been held void because the society's membership was deemed so indefinite and unascertainable as to make it impossible to administer the trust in a court of equity.[11] One testatrix directed that after the death of her sister "the estate go to some Catholic institution." A New Jersey court of equity declared the clause was void because the beneficiaries of the trust were so indefinite that no person could demand any part of the estate or maintain an action to compel compliance.[12] A trust "to be invested in Bibles, to be distributed in home and foreign lands in such quantities and in such places as may to my said executors seem best" was held void by a California District Court of Appeals. The court explained that the trustees could limit

9. *Shrader v. Erickson's Ex'r*, 284 Ky. 449, 145 S. W. (2d) 63 (1940); Perry, *op. cit.*, p. 1202; Anthony Curreri, "Charitable Trusts—Definitions and History" (1934) 9 *St. John's Law Review* 114-121.

10. 11 *C. J.* 341. So held in Alabama, Connecticut, Illinois, Indiana, Iowa, Louisiana, Maryland, Minnesota, Nebraska, New Jersey, New York, North Carolina, South Carolina, Virginia, and West Virginia.

11. *Mayfield v. Safe Deposit Co.*, 132 Atl. 595 (1926).

12. *Chelsea v. Our Lady Star of the Sea*, 105 N. J. Eq. 236, 147 Atl. 470 (1929). This clause was also defective because there was no testamentary designation of a person to select the objects of the benefaction.

the distribution to private schools and libraries, conducted entirely for profit, "without a qualm of conscience occasioned by any limitation put upon their actions by the terms of the will. There is not one word to indicate an object of the distribution, which would serve as a guide and check on its character; nor a hint as to the class of beneficiaries, which would serve to limit the distribution to persons or institutions serving a charitable purpose."[13]

Another testator bequeathed her property "unto charity connected with the Methodist Episcopal Church of the United States." A federal court explained that there were many charities connected with that particular church. Because the wording was such that it did not specify the class of persons to be benefited, the clause was considered too vague to create a trust.[14] A New York court commented that when there were no guideposts in the will to give direction in the distribution of the proceeds the religious views of an attorney-general who might represent the indefinite beneficiaries or of a presiding judge who might appoint the trustee could affect the carrying out of the trust. The distribution of benefits under such circumstances from time to time might thus be partisan and contradictory in purpose.[15] Lack of such guideposts may be an index of invalidity.

A testator may incorrectly refer to the beneficiaries of his gift. In such instances, the courts will ascertain the beneficiaries, if possible, with the assistance of such aid as the circumstances of the case may offer.[16] One will devised property to the "First Lutheran Church of Battle Lake, Minnesota" instead of using the correct corporate name, "First Evangelical Lutheran Church of Battle Lake, Minnesota." The court ruled that the

13. *In re Vance's Estate*, 118 Cal. App. 163, 164, 4 P. (2d) 977, 978 (1931).
14. *Methodist Episcopal Church v. Walters*, 50 F. (2d) 416 (D. C., 1928).
15. *Matter of Shattuck*, 193 N. Y. 446, 86 N. E. 455 (1908).
16. 11 C. J. 331.

church was commonly known by the former title, and upheld the devise.[17]

A will left the residue of an estate "to the Authorized Agents of the Home and Foreign Missionary Societies." Although there were no societies of that specific title, the court deemed the bequest valid because the testator seemed to have had two definite societies in mind at the time he made the will. The court here laid down a rule often applicable to cases of this type: extrinsic evidence of the facts known to the testator when he executed the will, proof of the names by which he called the societies or by which they were commonly known in the religious sect with which he worshipped, and indications of his own personal interest in religious societies and of any past contributions he might have made are admissible to help the court identify the societies intended in a will.[18] In an extreme situation the church specified in a trust instrument existed only in contemplation and not in actuality at the time the instrument was executed. The evidence indicated that a church similar to the one specified had existed at one time but subsequently had become inactive. Expressing the theory that the trust did not necessarily fail because the church had become inoperative, the Georgia Supreme Court upheld the conveyance with the comment that a dormant congregation is not beyond the possibility of being awakened to ecclesiastical activity.[19]

Purposes of trusts.—In their liberal interpretation of charitable trusts, the courts uphold bequests for six types of religious activity:[20]

1. Aid to the clergy in the form of gifts for the maintenance of rectories and ministerial residences. Wills setting aside property for the benefit of ministers and their widows have

17. *Lundquist v. First Evangelical Lutheran Church,* 193 Minn. 474, 259 N. W. 9 (1935).
18. *Hinckley v. Thatcher,* 139 Mass. 477, 1 N. E. 840 (1885).
19. *Huger v. Protestant Episcopal Church,* 137 Ga. 205, 73 S. E. 385 (1911).
20. 14 *C. J. S.* 451; 5 *R. C. L.* 326-327.

been sustained as valid charitable trusts.[21]   A grant for the salary of a rector has been upheld.[22]

2. Bequests for special religious services or sermons. Gifts for the support of churches, or for an offering for saying masses, or for payment of expenses for the preaching of a particular sectarian doctrine have been considered as gifts for charity.[23]   A gift for the support of a course of sermons was approved.[24]

3. Gifts for the erection, maintenance, and repair of churches. Courts have approved gifts for the erection or repair of parts of church structures such as a spire,[25] a pulpit,[26] a grotto,[27] and a memorial chapel.[28]

4. Gifts for the promotion of missionary activities. Home missions have been assisted[29] as well as foreign missions.[30]   A trust "for the diffusion of Christian principles as taught and practiced by Christian Evangelical denominations" was judicially approved.[31]

5. Gifts for Sunday school purposes. Such schools have been considered an aid to the religious society.[32]   One court has upheld a gift for a Sunday school library.[33]

6. Bequests for the circulation and distribution of religious

21. *Rogers v. Baldridge*, 18 Tenn. App. 300, 76 S. W. (2d) 655 (1934); *In re Edge's Estate*, 288 N. Y. S. 437, 159 Misc. 505 (1936); *Hood v. Dorer*, 107 Wisc. 149, 82 N. W. 546 (1900).

22. *In re Winburn's Will*, 247 N. Y. S. 584, 139 Misc. 5 (1931).

23. *Alden v. St. Peter's Parish*, 158 Ill. 631, 42 N. E. 392 (1895).

24. *McAlister v. Burgess*, 161 Mass. 269, 37 N. E. 173 (1894); see *Hoeffer v. Clogan*, 171 Ill. 462, 49 N. E. 527 (1898).

25. *Kelley v. Welborn*, 110 Ga. 540, 35 S. E. 636 (1900).

26. *Jones v. Habersham*, 107 U. S. 174, 2 Sup. Ct. 336, 27 L. Ed. 401 (1882).

27. *Sisters of Mercy v. Lightner*, 274 N. W. 86 (1937).

28. *In re Atkinson's Will*, 197 N. Y. S. 831, 120 Misc. 186 (1923).

29. *Prime v. Harmon*, 120 Me. 299, 113 Atl. 738 (1921); *King v. Richardson*, 136 F. (2d) 849 (C. C. A., 1943).

30. *Beckwith v. St. Philip's Parish*, 69 Ga. 564 (1882); *Andrews v. Andrews*, 110 Ill. 223 (1884).

31. *Morville v. Fowle*, 144 Mass. 109, 10 N. E. 766 (1887).

32. *Eutaw Place Baptist Church v. Shively*, 67 Md. 493, 10 Atl. 244 (1887); *Andrews v. Andrews*, 110 Ill. 223 (1884).

33. *Fairbanks v. Lamson*, 99 Mass. 553 (1868).

literature. A grant to the Christian Science Church for the benefit of the *Christian Science Monitor* was valid.[34]

Trusts contrary to public policy.—A trust must be for a legal purpose; there can be no donations contrary to public policy. Courts of equity refuse to enforce a trust the object of which is the propagation of atheism. Judicial comment indicates that a man may do many things while he is living which the law will not do for him after he is dead, among these being a denial of the existence of God and the dedication of his money to disseminate infidel views. If a person leaves his fortune in trust for such purposes, the trust will be invalidated as contrary to the public good.[35]

For example, one testator left the residue of his estate to the Infidel Society in Philadelphia for the purpose of building a hall for the free discussion of religion. In an action contesting the legality of the devise, a Pennsylvania court held that a society to propagate a denial of the doctrines and obligations of revealed religion could not be legally organized in the state. Nothing could so insult the religion of the Bible to the annoyance of the great mass of believers, it was held, as a hall under the administration of infidels dedicated in perpetuity to the free discussion of religion. The devise was held void.[36] Another will set aside a building for a library and provided for the publishing of certain books of the testator for use in the library. The will was attacked by the heirs at law on the theory that the works which the deceased had specified for publication contained atheistic teachings, that said works denied the truths of Christian religion, that the effect of executing the will would be to propagate atheistic doctrines contrary to public morals, and that in a land where religion and sound morals were fundamental, no trust could exist for the protection of that which

34. *In re Smith's Estate,* 144 Ore. 561, 25 P. (2d) 924 (1933).
35. Perry, *op. cit.,* pp. 1218-1220; H. H. P., "The Promotion of a Cause as the Subject Matter of a Charitable Trust" (1937) 23 *Virginia Law Review* 439-445.
36. *Zeisweiss v. James,* 63 Pa. 465 (1870).

harmed the state. The court agreed that if the primary object of the trust was to disseminate infidel views, the trust would be against public policy and hence void. The court held, however, that the clause providing for the publication of the books in question was not a condition precedent to carrying out what the court considered to be the main objective of the will, namely, the establishment of a library.[37]

A will disposing of the great bulk of an estate valued at over $2,000,000 to the Christian Science Church was contested by a son of the deceased on the ground that the beliefs of such a sect led to irreligion and tended to a breach of the peace. The New Hampshire Supreme Court, upholding the trust, reasoned that the testatrix had the constitutional right to entertain such religious opinions as she wished, to ·make a religion out of them, and to teach others. As her legal right to teach did not terminate with her death, she was judged able to dispose of her property by a gift in public charity for any use not illegal. The court felt itself incompetent to decide whether her religious opinions were theoretically true, but pointed out that no person could be convicted of a crime upon an indictment charging the practice of Christian Science healing, because no law forbade it. The court concluded that since neither her belief, nor the acts under it, were necessarily illegal, the trust to promote the principles she attempted to inculcate was valid.[38]

Effect of incorporation.—Frequently in our early history a gift to an unincorporated religious society was held void because the individuals constituting its membership were a fluctuating body, not responsible to the courts, and incapable of accepting a gift for the purposes which the laws considered charitable, and because of the lack of a person to take legal title.[39] Gradually equity courts evolved a rule that a charitable trust, otherwise valid, must not fail for want of a competent trustee. The usual

37. *Manners v. Philadelphia Library Co.*, 93 Pa. 165 (1880).
38. *Glover v. Baker*, 76 N. H. 393, 83 Atl. 916 (1912).
39. 11 C. J. 337, notes 25-26. So held in Connecticut, Indiana, Maryland, New York, Tennessee, West Virginia, and federal courts.

practice now is for the court to appoint a trustee who in turn will apply the gift to the benefit of the society.[40] Thus a bequest to an unincorporated association organized to carry on religious activities connected with a particular religion was held sustainable as a charitable trust to be carried out through a trustee appointed by the court.[41]

Under a charter with enumerated powers, an incorporated religious group may be permitted to accept a legacy conditioned on the payment of an annuity to an individual named in the grant, although the power to pay annuities is not delegated in the charter. Courts reason that such payments arise only incidentally, and that through the legacy itself the general purposes of the society are promoted.[42] One will directed an executor to pay to an incorporated religious society ten thousand dollars upon condition that the society should pay to the testator's wife four hundred dollars per year as long as she lived. Although the society had no power to pay annuities, the provision of the will was judged valid.[43] In return for the deed to a house, another incorporated religious society adopted a resolution agreeing to pay annually to the former owner a fixed amount during the remainder of her lifetime. In a suit to contest the validity of the transaction the trial court held that the society had no power to enter into such an agreement. The appellate court upheld the arrangement and ruled that performing incidental functions which related to the accomplishment of the substantial purposes of its incorporation did not make the donee a dealer in annuities contrary to law.[44]

40. Philip A. Hart, "Charities—Capacity of an Unincorporated Association to Act as Trustee of a Charitable Trust" (1937) 35 *Michigan Law Review* 656-659; 54 *C. J.* 47; see *In re Clendenin's Estate*, 9 N. Y. S. (2d) 875 (1939).

41. *In re Winburn's Will*, 247 N. Y. S. 584, 139 Misc. 5 (1931).

42. See *Association v. Moore*, 183 U. S. 642, 22 Sup. Ct. 240, 46 L. Ed. 366 (1902).

43. *Sherman v. American Congregational Association*, 113 Fed. 609 (C. C. A., 1902).

44. *Barger v. French*, 122 Kan. 607, 253 Pac. 230 (1927).

Diversion of a trust.—Property given to a religious society is often impressed with an implied or express charitable trust to promote a particular faith or manner of worship. In such instances the society must use the gift in such a manner as to further the particular purposes of the trust. Where there has been no appreciable change from the original intention, the majority of a democratic society, or the appropriate agent of a hierarchical type of society, will be permitted to retain control of the trust in the face of legal action to prevent its continued use.[45] When, however, there is a diversion of a trust from the purpose to which it is dedicated, the intent of the testator may be enforced by the courts. As long as there are persons qualified within the meaning of the original dedication who desire to perpetuate the principles specified in the trust, and as long as such persons have a standing in court, the courts will prevent a diversion of the trust to other purposes. If a religious society acquires property for a specific purpose, any member may resist a diversion to other uses. Exclusive control may be awarded to the minority who adheres to the original intent of the testator.[46]

In one case the fact that there were more than three male members in a religious society who retained the name of the original congregation and continued to recognize its church government, acted to bar the majority from transferring the trust property to another religious group.[47] In another instance the majority members of a religious corporation holding property under a trust renounced their original faith and excluded the faithful minority from corporate meetings. Minority rights were upheld when the action of the majority was declared

45. *Marvel v. Sadtler,* 18 A. (2d) 231 (1941). Edward F. Grogan, Jr., "Creation of an Implied Trust for a Religious Charitable Purpose" (1940) 15 *Notre Dame Lawyer* 224-229; M. H. R., "Donations and Wills" (1939) 13 *Tulane Law Review* 630-632.

46. 23 *R. C. L.* 451-452; see *Kerler v. Evangelical Emanuel's Church,* 282 N. W. 32 (1938).

47. *Geiss v. Trinity Lutheran Church,* 119 Neb. 745, 230 N. W. 658 (1930).

void.[48] After the suspension of the pastor by a supreme church judicatory, the majority members of one local congregation adopted resolutions purporting to effect a withdrawal of the local society from the denomination and to retain the suspended pastor. A civil court declared that members of the congregation who remained faithful to the denomination were entitled to enjoin any diversion of the property to uses not approved by the denomination.[49]

A religious society which is connected with a superior organization cannot, by action of the local congregation or of the majority, secede from the denomination, declare itself independent, and assume title to property held as a trust for the use of the superior organization.[50] Members of the national organization whose properties are involved have a right to enjoin such use, regardless of the rights of the members of local congregations.[51] On one such occasion when a parent organization sued for possession of religious property held by a recalcitrant local group, the defendants claimed that the parent religious organization had changed the original tenets of the society. The court rejected the claim and awarded the property to the parent organization.[52]

On another occasion, the secretary-treasurer of a Sunday school union, a publishing agency of a religious society, was guilty of mismanagement of union property in which the society owned a beneficial interest. Upon the failure of the board of directors of the union to confer upon the society the right to control the union, the governing body of the society was held justified in appointing a board of directors as successors in trust to the union.[53]

48. *St. Michael's Ukranian Greek Catholic Church v. Bohachewsky*, 60 R. I. 1, 196 Atl. 796 (1938).
49. *Kelly v. McIntire*, 123 N. J. Eq. 351, 197 Atl. 736 (1938).
50. 23 *R. C. L.* 454.
51. *Gibson v. Trustees*, 10 A. (2d) 332 (1939).
52. *Bouchelle v. Trustees of the Presbyterian Congregation*, 194 Atl. 100 (1937).
53. *Sunday School Union of African Methodist Episcopal Church v. Walden*, 121 F. (2d) 719 (C. C. A., 1941).

Bequests for the saying of Masses.—In eighteenth-century England bequests for the celebration of Masses were usually considered superstitious and invalid. Bequests for religious practices other than those of the established church were also contrary to public policy. In America the doctrine of superstitious uses, under which devises for the celebration of Masses were held void in England, has not been accepted, although the validity of such bequests has been questioned on other grounds. Here, no religious observances are deemed legally superstitious. Since all religious denominations and doctrines are protected equally, a bequest for the general advancement of any specific religion may be upheld as a bequest for a valid charitable purpose.

Courts have demonstrated a high degree of inconsistency in deciding the validity of a bequest for Masses. John Curran[54] lists four different grounds upon which such a bequest has been upheld: (1) as a valid charitable trust; (2) as a valid private trust, not a charitable trust; (3) as a valid gift, not a trust; and (4) as neither a charitable nor a private trust but a valid funeral expense. The same writer notes seven different grounds on which such a bequest has been declared illegal: (1) as an invalid private trust; (2) as neither a valid gift nor a trust; (3) as an attempted private trust that failed on account of the absence of a living beneficiary; (4) as a private trust that failed because it violated the rule against perpetuities; (5) as an attempted charitable trust that failed because Masses for the soul were not for the common good; (6) as an attempted trust that failed because it was for a superstitious use; and (7) as a religious but not charitable trust, void if made within a certain period before death.

Within the last forty years, however, there has been a judicial trend toward a settled rule. Bequests for Masses are now upheld on one of three theories. A few courts uphold the

54. John Curran, "Trusts for Masses" (1931) 7 *Notre Dame Lawyer* 42-56.

bequests as *private trusts*, on the theory that they possess the essential elements of such trusts, just as if the purpose were for the erection of a monument or for the doing of other acts to perpetuate the memory of the testator.[55] A few other courts uphold bequests for Masses as *direct gifts* to clergymen for their own use.[56] However, Masses are generally considered to be religious ceremonials or observances of the church of which a testator had been a member and to come within the religious uses upheld as public charities. Predominant judicial opinion points out that such bequests have the effect of merely adding particular remembrances to religious ceremonies at which the public is admitted. Under this theory, such bequests are *charitable trusts*.[57]

Court opinion denying the validity of such legacies has ruled bequests for Masses not direct gifts because they are in the nature of trusts; not charitable trusts because they are for the benefit alone of the testator's soul; and not private trusts because there is no living beneficiary.[58] This opinion represents the exception rather than the usual judicial rule. "Practically all decisions in the United States within the last twenty years have been in favor of the validity of the bequest . . . [for Masses]."[59]

Restraints on religious practices.—The validity of a condition in a will that the enjoyment of a benefit shall depend upon future training in, or adherence to, a particular belief or custom is generally recognized. Usual judicial reasoning denies that such conditions interfere with any right of conscience, impose a reli-

55. *Coleman v. O'Leary*, 114 Ky. 388, 70 S. W. 1068 (1897); *Moran v. Moran*, 104 Iowa 216, 73 N. W. 617 (1898).

56. *Harrison v. Brophy*, 59 Kan. 1, 51 Pac. 883 (1898); *Sherman v. Baker*, 20 R. I. 446, 40 Atl. 11 (1898); *Estate of Lennon*, 152 Cal. 327, 92 Pac. 870 (1907). See also *In re Kavanaugh's Will*, 143 Wisc. 90, 126 N. W. 672 (1910).

57. Perry, *op. cit.*, p. 1219; 5 R. C. L. 327-328; 14 C. J. S. 450; Curran, "Trusts for Masses," *loc. cit.*, p. 53.

58. *McHugh v. McCole*, 97 Wisc. 166, 72 N. W. 631 (1897); *Festorazzi v. St. Joseph's Catholic Church*, 104 Ala. 327, 18 So. 394 (1894).

59. Curran, "Trusts for Masses," *loc. cit.*, p. 53.

gious test, or contravene public policy. The right to give includes the right to insert such conditions. However, the number of such conditions in testamentary dispositions has declined because of an increase in religious tolerance and a decline in the dogmatic certainty that one's own religion is irrefutable.[60]

A will bequeathing a sum of money to a son to be paid in fifteen yearly installments on condition that he attend regularly the church meetings of a certain church was valid. In its desire to uphold the bequest the court added that if the question of a definition of the religious obligations included in the will should ever arise, judicial determination of the issue would be made.[61] Another testator set aside a sum of money, and a portion of the residue of his estate, to be paid on their respective twenty-first birthdays to each of his grandchildren who had been given a "normal, Jewish, liberal education, including an abiltiy to read Hebrew," and who had visited the testator's grave at least once a year. If these conditions were not met, the legacy was to be applied to a Jewish philanthropic society. Upholding the validity of the provision, a court ruled that strict adherence to religion by the children during their formative years could not reasonably be considered other than beneficial to the individuals themselves and to the state.[62]

A testator bequeathed a fund to trustees who were to use the income to provide maintenance and education for his granddaughter, provided she was raised in a particular faith. Rejecting a claim of illegality, the court queried: "Can it be properly said to be against the spirit of the constitution, for a member of one of these religious denominations, so protected, to endeavor by peaceful and legal means to extend his faith and to influence his children and grandchildren to adhere to the church of their fathers?"[63] Restraints on religious practices, set up in wills,

60. J. E. B., "Religious Conditions in Wills" (1935) 83 *University of Pennsylvania Law Review* 670-676.
61. *Paulson's Will*, 127 Wisc. 612, 107 N. W. 484 (1906).
62. *In re Lesser's Estate*, 287 N. Y. S. 209, 158 Misc. 895 (1936).
63. *Magee v. O'Neill*, 19 S. C. 170, 187 (1882).

have included the requirement not only to participate in specific religious activities but also to refrain from particular religious practices. Thus, bequests whose enjoyment depended upon an individual's withdrawing from a sisterhood[64] or from the clergy were upheld.[65]

One court rejected a will conditioned on a particular religious observance because the legatee had no volition, owing to his infancy, to reject or comply with the terms. The legacy in question, payable when the legatee became twenty-one years of age, provided that he should be educated in a particular religion. The legatee was nine years old at the time of the testator's death. Beginning at the age of twelve he was, for four years, taken by his mother to a church of a different sect. After he became sixteen, he attended the original church, but only infrequently. The court held that the legatee had been placed at the whim of a person or persons who, by chance, had the sole control over his religious training. Such circumstances were not permitted to result in a denial of his property rights.[66]

Although conditions in general restraint of marriage are regarded as opposed to public policy at common law, restraints on marriage applicable to a certain class of individuals are constitutional.[67] A provision of a will declaring that any child of the testator who marries any person not of a specific faith shall be incompetent under the will is usually upheld. One court remarked that while a general restraint of marriage was inoperative, such a special restriction was ordinarily valid.[68]

However, one condition that a legatee remain a member of a specific sect in order to hold bequeathed property was judged illegal, partly because of the specific facts and circumstances surrounding the case. There were only six unmarried male mem-

---

64. *Mitchell v. Mitchell,* 18 Md. 405 (1862).
65. *Barnum v. Mayor of Baltimore,* 62 Md. 275 (1884).
66. *In re Kempf's Estate,* 289 N. Y. S. 74, 159 Misc. 298 (1936).
67. C. J. M., "Contracts—Restraint of Marriage" (1934) 22 *Georgetown Law Journal* 361-362; see *In Matter of Seaman,* 218 N. Y. 77, 112 N. E. 576 (1916).
68. *In re Solomon's Estate,* 281 N. Y. S. 827, 156 Misc. 445 (1935).

bers of a particular religious society living in the neighborhood where the legatee resided at the time she reached a marriageable age. As a result of the shortage of men of her sect, the woman married a man not a member of her sect. She thereby forfeited her membership in the society, and allegedly her claim under the will. Deciding that the condition of the will was a restraint of marriage contrary to public policy, the court emphasized that all unjust restrictions upon marriage should be removed, and all undue influences affecting the choice of the parties should be suppressed.[69]

An interesting situation arose in Pennsylvania. A testator sought to induce relatives to retain membership in his faith by making the enjoyment of land dependent upon specific adherence to the sect. If any legatee abandoned the testator's religion, the land was to be given to the remaining legatees who were faithful to that religion. The will did not provide for the disposition of the land if all the legatees departed from the religion, which was the situation in the instant case. The court favored the relatives by enunciating a policy of keeping the alienation of land free from embarrassing impediments. The judge pointed out that the penalty of loss of property was in the nature of punishment and that, while not as severe, physically, as the stocks and whipping posts and other forms of chastisement of another century, it would have a more lasting result. The condition was held contrary to public policy.[70]

Peculiar religious beliefs of the testator as grounds for avoiding a will.—The legality of a will has occasionally been attacked on the ground that abnormal religious beliefs or spiritualistic inclinations rendered a testator incompetent to make a will. The courts usually give the testator the benefit of the doubt. Mere religious fervor, regardless of the character of the religion, is no evidence of mental incapacity.[71]

69. *Maddox v. Maddox,* 52 Va. 418 (1854).
70. *Drace v. Klinedinst,* 275 Pa. 266, 118 Atl. 907 (1922).
71. 11 *C. J.* 343.

Evidence that a testator had believed that he could heal physical ailments by laying his hands on the sick was not accepted as proof of a weak mind.[72] That a testatrix professed to be able to communicate with her deceased parents was held not to prove her incompetency.[73] One jurist stated that there were many persons whose soundness of mind no one could doubt who believed in the possibility of communicating with the dead and who received advice from such sources with reference to their behavior. Such a person was still capable of making a will which could not be set aside as a product of an insane delusion, or as having been executed under undue influence.[74] Beliefs as to the spiritual and the supernatural, which might seem unusual to people of other religious views, were not deemed evidence of insanity sufficient to avoid a will.[75]

In an extreme case, evidence that a testator believed he was being directed by spirits in the making of his will nullified it. The testator had believed that a spirit brought him a new five dollar bill, and that a spirit once tried to take his life with a butcher knife. Evidence also indicated that many of the communications had been transmitted to the testator through mediums who "happened" to be beneficiaries in the will. The court remarked that although there could be no inquiry into the soundness of one's religious faith, one might have such a strong faith in spiritualism as to destroy one's ability to reason. The will made in consequence of such monomania was void.[76] But this illustration does not render invalid the statement of the general doctrine that mere belief in spiritualism does not destroy one's testamentary capacity.

Summary.—Gifts and grants in trust for the support of religious purposes are classified as charitable trusts. In America

72. *Spencer v. Spencer,* 221 S. W. 58 (1920).
73. *McCrocklin's Adm'r. v. Lee,* 247 Ky. 31, 56 S. W. (2d) 564 (1933); *Orchardson v. Cofield,* 171 Ill. 14, 49 N. E. 197 (1898).
74. *Henderson v. Jackson,* 138 Iowa 326, 111 N. W. 821 (1907).
75. *Donovan v. Sullivan,* 4 N. E. (2d) 1004 (1937).
76. *O'Dell v. Goff,* 149 Mich. 152, 112 N. W. 736 (1907).

courts of equity have exercised an inherent original jurisdiction over charitable trusts, and have favored them unless they are prohibited by law. Generally courts have favored a liberal interpretation of charitable trusts. The intention of the donor is held to control the whole bequest. Persons to be benefited should be uncertain until they are selected to be the particular beneficiaries of the trust.

In their liberal interpretation of charitable trusts, the courts uphold bequests for six types of religious activity: (1) aid to the clergy in the form of gifts for the maintenance of rectories and ministerial residences; (2) bequests for special religious services or sermons; (3) gifts for the erection, maintenance, and repair of churches; (4) gifts for the promotion of missionary activities; (5) gifts for Sunday school purposes; and (6) bequests for the circulation and distribution of religious literature.

Trusts contrary to public policy are void. Bequests to unincorporated religious societies formerly were void because the individuals constituting the membership were fluctuating bodies, not responsible to the courts, and because of the lack of a person to take legal title. The usual practice now in such instances is for the court to appoint a trustee who, in turn, will apply the gift to the benefit of the society. Property given to a religious society often constitutes an implied or express charitable trust to promote a particular faith or manner of worship. Where there is a diversion of a trust from the purposes to which it is dedicated, the intent of the testator may be enforced by the courts.

Bequests for the saying of Masses are upheld as private trusts or as valid gifts to clergymen in some states. However, predominant judicial opinion holds that such bequests have the effect of merely adding particular remembrances to religious ceremonies at which the public is admitted and hence considers such bequests to be charitable trusts.

The validity of a condition in a will that the enjoyment of

a benefit shall depend upon future training in, or adherence to, a particular belief or custom is generally recognized. Usual judicial reasoning denies that such a condition interferes with any right of conscience, imposes a religious test, or contravenes public policy. The right to give includes the right to insert such a condition. A provision of a will declaring that any child of a testator who marries any person not of a specific faith shall be incompetent under the will is usually upheld. Peculiar religious beliefs of a testator are generally not a ground for avoiding a will.

XII

Conclusions and Suggestions

American democracy has made great strides in the establishment of a working concept of religious freedom. However, in the opinion of the author, a reappraisal and a re-emphasis of certain factors in the present relationship between the independent church and the democratic state would result in an even more practical enjoyment of religious freedom. As a result of this study, the following conclusions and suggestions are made:

(1) In many states a voluntary association may sue or be sued in its association name, while in others a certifying officer is still liable in an individual capacity for the debts of an unincorporated religious society. A continuation of the common law theory that a voluntary non-profit association cannot be sued penalizes unfairly the church official who, through no fault of his own, finds himself in the position that the religious society will not pay. To that extent, the present situation discourages individual participation in church organization and church activity. The common law disqualification should be completely removed.

(2) The constitutions of two states prohibit the creation of religious corporations. Inasmuch as incorporation is from the practical standpoint a prerequisite for the administration of the business of a modern religious society of any appreciable size, the constitutional handicaps in these states should be removed.

(3) Some states hold that a religious society has a right to incorporate and carry on purely secular activities in connection with the fulfillment of one or more of its religious purposes. Final limits to such activities have not yet been drawn. However, such secular activities of a religious society conceivably obtain an unfair advantage over purely private business in that the former do not share the legal burdens and responsibilities of the latter. Activities of a purely secular type only generally connected with the fulfillment of one or more of its religious purposes and carried on by a religious society in competition with private business should be declared *ultra vires*.

(4) The legal relation of an individual member to a religious society has not yet been fully crystallized by judicial opinion. In five states, where the relation is considered contractual, a member may invoke the power of a civil court. Control over membership is a sectarian problem. The civil courts should consistently disclaim jurisdiction to determine sectarian membership unless, of course, property rights are involved.

(5) There is judicial disagreement over the extent to which a decision of a final church tribunal should be conclusive upon the civil courts. The predominant view, that the decision of the religious tribunal will be accepted in matters of discipline, excision, faith, and practice, and that property rights will be disposed of accordingly, ought to be unanimously adopted. It is a prerogative of every religious group to settle its internal affairs according to the rules of the society.

(6) At present the right of religious assembly free from disturbance is primarily statutory. The importance of the right of religious assembly to the practical concept of democracy suggests that the right of assembly for religious purposes free from disturbance be written into the fundamental document of every state.

(7) Many jurisdictions require proof of "wilfulness" as a necessary element in the crime of disturbing a religious assem-

bly. It should not be essential that the accused have the specific intent to disturb in order to be guilty of the offense. If the natural tendency of an act is to disturb a religious meeting, and it does in fact disturb it, proof of an intention to disturb should not be necessary for a conviction.

(8) In a few states ownership is the test for the exemption of property of religious societies from taxation. As a general rule, exemption from taxation should be discouraged in a democracy. To the degree that property is exempt, a heavier financial burden falls on non-exempt property. If religious use were substituted for ownership as the test for exemption, bona fide religious uses would still be protected, but the exemption base would be reduced.

(9) The inestimable benefits, duly recognized in innumerable court opinions, which religious societies confer upon a community strongly emphasize the need for a continuance of the practice of tax exemption for property devoted to religious purposes. However, where religious use is the criterion for tax exemption, courts have differed with respect to the point of time when exemption commences. Legislative action in many states should crystallize definite standards for judicial application.

(10) If property is used primarily, but not exclusively, for religious purposes, there is judicial disagreement whether the whole property will be exempt from taxation. The doctrine of divisibility of taxability of property partially used for religious purposes is applied in only a few states. Extension of the application of the doctrine appears to be consistent with the constitutional provisions of other states. Such extension would benefit many religious societies which presently receive no exemption under the exclusive use doctrine.

(11) There is a lack of uniformity among the several states on the question of the legality of the special marriage ceremonies of particular sects such as the Quakers. Less than half of the

states have statutes which allow marriages to be celebrated according to the customs of any religious society. If religious freedom is to be a reality, civil approval must be extended to religious ceremonial marriages of all sects, assuming that the resultant marriages do not in themselves contravene public policy.

(12) In determining the custody of children as between individuals other than parents, the judiciary usually considers temporal welfare superior to religious doctrine. Nevertheless, under usual court practice a child is given to the custody of persons of the same faith as that of the parents or of the father, if its temporal welfare will be as well taken care of by such persons as by those of another faith. A more basic guarantee of religious freedom would result if this practice became incorporated into the law of every state. Judicial discretion in unusual situations could be preserved, but the crystallization of current common practice into statutory law would minimize any tendency to disregard parental religious preference. The fact that guardians, as public officers, cannot be removed because of their religious beliefs or disbeliefs makes such a proposal especially important.

(13) Court interpretation has approved the reading of the Bible by many classroom teachers in the public schools. To the extent that Catholics must attend where the King James version of the Bible is read and that Protestants must attend where the Douay version is rendered, religious freedom is limited. The solution to the problem of biblical reading would seem to be the elimination of the reading of either version in the public schools.

(14) Arrangements whereby children, on the written request of their parents, are excused from regular school sessions to attend religious instruction have been judicially approved. The result of such arrangements is possible unconscious religious discrimination between the students of different sects, and a denial of equal privileges to the student whose religious society does

not provide local training at the same time as the other sects. Complete divorce of sectarianism from the public schools would suggest the abolition of such arrangements.

(15) In eight states a witness must believe in divine punishment, or in the existence of a Supreme Being, in order to be competent to testify. Statutory amendment, or judicial determination, or both, could remove the common law disqualification completely. A prospective witness who is an atheist would then be permitted to affirm, just as one does who has religious scruples against taking an oath.

(16) Delving into the faith of a witness on the stand to influence the credit given to his testimony is permissible in a few instances. Ten states have laws which directly or indirectly grant permission to show disbelief in a Deity for the purpose of affecting credibility. If forty-one states should follow an original group of seven states which have already passed constitutional or statutory provisions expressly forbidding the questioning of any witness about his religious beliefs for the purpose of affecting the weight of his testimony, the impairment of credibility which some witnesses now suffer would be eliminated.

(17) A dying declaration is now admissible, provided the deceased would have been competent to testify to the matters contained in the declaration if he had lived and been offered as a witness in the case. Complete removal of this qualification of the common law doctrine of admissibility would mean that no dying declaration would be automatically barred because of the religious disbelief of the declarant.

(18) The validity of a condition in a will that the enjoyment of a benefit shall depend upon future training in, or adherence to, a particular religious belief or custom is generally recognized by the courts. Nevertheless, it would seem that there is a strong public policy for invalidating such a condition when it threatens the free exercise of religious worship. It does not necessarily effectuate the real intent of a testator, because it

may secure only nominal compliance with his wishes. The state does not benefit, since the resultant religious practices may be hypocritical. By encouraging religious hypocrisy, religious conditions in wills are destructive of any true system of worship.

In the realm of religious faith sharp differences of opinion arise. The tenets of one man may seem preposterous to his neighbor. Nevertheless, the American judiciary holds that, regardless of the probability of abuse, religious liberty is essential to an enlightened citizenry. In a democracy many different types of life and opinion can develop unmolested. Such a situation is nowhere more necessary than in America, with her many races, nationalities, and creeds. A few individuals may violate civil laws under the guise of exercising religious freedom. Nevertheless, the judicial doctrines of religious rights give a very practical guarantee to freedom of religious thought, speech, and action limited only by basic considerations of the public welfare.

Bibliography

BOOKS

Adams, J. T. *Dictionary of American History*. New York. Charles Scribner's Sons. 1940.

American Law Reports. Rochester, N. Y. The Lawyers Cooperative Publishing Co. 1925. Vol. XII.

Ames, H. V. *The Proposed Amendments to the Constitution of the United States*. New York. American Historical Association. 1896. Vol. II.

Besson, M. M. *Histoire des colonies françaises*. Paris. The Bowin Co. 1931.

Black, H. C. *Handbook of American Constitutional Law*. 4th ed. St. Paul. West Publishing Co. 1910.

Bowers, Claude G. *Jefferson and Hamilton: The Struggle for Democracy in America*. Boston. Houghton Mifflin Co. 1925.

Brockunier, S. H. *The Irrepressible Democrat*. New York. The Ronald Press. 1940.

Carey, L. *American Museum*. Philadelphia. 1787. Vol. II, No. 5.

Cobb, S. H. *The Rise of Religious Liberty in America*. New York. The Macmillan Co. 1902.

Cooley, Thomas M. *The General Principles of Constitutional Law in the United States*. 3d ed. Boston. Little, Brown & Co. 1898.

Cooley, Thomas M. *A Treatise on the Constitutional Limitations*. 8th ed. Boston. Little, Brown & Co. 1927.

Corpus Juris. Brooklyn. The American Law Book Co. 1932. Vols. V, XI, XIII, XVIII, XIX, XXIII, XXX, XXXV, XXXVIII, XLVI, LIV, LVI, LIX, LX, LXI, LXX.

Corpus Juris Secundum. Brooklyn. The American Law Book Co. 1939. Vols. XI, XIV, XVI.

Cyclopedia of Law and Procedure. New York. The American Law Book Co. 1912. Vol. XL.

Elliot, Jonathan, ed. *The Debates in the Several State Conventions on the Adoption of the Federal Constitution.* 2nd ed. Philadelphia. J. B. Lippincott Co. 1876. Vols. I-V.

Encinas, Diego de. *Provisiones, Cédulas, Capitulos de Orden Anzas.* Madrid. 1596. Vol. I.

Felt, J. B. *Ecclesiastical History of New England.* Cambridge, Mass. Bolles & Houghton Co. 1850.

Forman, S. E. *The Life and Writings of Thomas Jefferson.* Indianapolis. The Bobbs-Merrill Co. 1905.

Gales, J. *Annals of Congress.* Washington, D. C. 1834. Vol. I.

Greenleaf, Simon. *A Treatise on the Law of Evidence.* 16th ed. Boston. Little, Brown & Co. 1899. Vol. I.

Hening, W. W. *Collection of Laws of Virginia.* Richmond. 1823. Vol. XII.

Hernaez, F. J. *Colección de bulas breves v otros documentos relativos a la iglesia de América y Filipinas.* Brussels. 1879. Vol. I.

Hirst, F. W. *Life and Letters of Thomas Jefferson.* New York. The Macmillan Co. 1926.

Humphrey, E. F. *Nationalism and Religion in America.* Boston. The Chipman Co. 1924.

Hutchison, David. *The Foundations of the Constitution.* New York. The Grafton Press. 1928.

Icazbalceta, J. G. *Biografía de don Fr. Juan de Zumarraga.* Mexico. 1881.

Jaray, G. L. *L'Empire français d'Amérique.* Paris. The Colon Co. 1938.

Jefferson, Thomas. *The Writings of.* P. L. Ford, ed. New York. G. P. Putnam's Sons. 1892-1899.

Johnson, A. W. *The Legal Status of Church-State Relationships in the United States.* Minneapolis. The University of Minnesota Press. 1934.

Jones, Burr. *The Law of Evidence.* 3rd ed. San Francisco. Bancroft-Whitney Co. 1934. Pp. 1090-1091.

Madden, Joseph. *Persons and Domestic Relations.* St. Paul. West Publishing Co. 1931.

Morton, R. K. *God in the Constitution.* Nashville. The Cokesbury Press. 1933.

Musmanno, M. A. *Proposed Amendments to the Constitution.* House Document 551. 70th Congress. 2nd Session. 1929.

Osgood, H. L. *The American Colonies in the 17th Century.* New York. The Macmillan Co. 1904.

Perry, Jairus. *A Treatise on the Law of Trusts and Trustees.* 7th ed. Boston. Little, Brown & Co. 1929. Vol. II.

Porter, K. H. *A History of Suffrage in the United States.* Chicago. University of Chicago Press. 1918.

Priestly, H. I., ed. *The Luna Papers.* Deland. Florida State Historical Society. 1928.

Recopilación de leyes de los reynos de las Indias. 2nd ed. Madrid. 1756. Vol. I.

Ruling Case Law. Northport, N. Y. Edward Thompson Co., 1929. Vols. I, V, IX, XVIII, XX, XXIII, XXV, XXVI.

Sarsfield, D. V. *Relaciones del estado con la iglesia en la antigua América española.* Buenos Aires. 1889.

Schouler, James. *A Treatise on the Law of Domestic Relations.* 6th ed. Albany. Matthew Bender & Co. 1921.

Schouler, James. *Thomas Jefferson.* New York. Dodd, Mead & Co. 1919.

Schroeder, T. A. *Constitutional Free Speech.* New York. Free Speech League. 1919.

Smyth, C. *Roger Williams and the Fight for Religious Freedom.* New York. Funk & Wagnalls Co. 1931.

Solorzano, J. *Política indiana.* Madrid. 1776. Vol. IV. Nos. 26-28.

Statutes of all states.

Story, Joseph. *Commentaries on the Constitution of the United States.* Boston. Little, Brown & Co. 1883.

Strickland, A. B. *Roger Williams, Pioneer and Prophet of Soul-Liberty.* Boston. The Judson Press. 1919.

Thorpe, F. N. *American Charters, Constitutions and Organic Laws, 1492-1908.* Government Printing Office. 1909. Vols. I-VII.

Trumbell, M. W. *Thomas Jefferson, Father of American Democracy.* Chicago. G. Schilling. 1890.

Vernier, T. *American Family Laws.* Stanford University. Stanford University Press. 1931.

Ward, P. W. *A Short History of Political Thinking.* Chapel Hill. The University of North Carolina Press. 1939.

Wharton, Francis. *Criminal Law.* 12th ed. Rochester. The Lawyers Co-operative Publishing Co. 1932. Vol. I.

Whipple, Leon. *The Story of Civil Liberty in the United States.* New York. The Vanguard Press. 1927.

Wigmore, John H. *A Treatise on the Anglo-American System of Evidence in Trials at Common Law.* 3rd ed. Boston. Little, Brown & Co. 1940. Vol. VI.

Williams, Roger. *Letters and Papers of.* Boston. Boston Historical Society. 1924.

Zamora, M. G. *Regio patronato español e indiano.* Madrid. 1879.

Zollman, Carl. *American Civil Church Law.* New York. Columbia University Press. 1917.

PERIODICALS

Aulgur, W. E. "Right of Jehovah's Witnesses to Distribute Religious Literature upon Street of Company Town." *Missouri Law Review.* 1947. Vol. XII, pp. 61-65.

B., J. E. "Religious Conditions in Wills." *University of Pennsylvania Law Review.* 1935. Vol. LXXXIII, pp. 670-676.

B., L. L., Jr. "Evidence—Witness having Conscientious Scruples against taking Oath." *Tennessee Law Review.* 1932. Vol. X, pp. 232-234.

Balter, H. G. "Freedom of Religion Interpreted in Two Supreme Court Decisions." *California State Bar Journal.* 1940. Vol. XV, pp. 161-165.

Biggs, J. C. "Religious Belief as a Qualification of a Witness." *North Carolina Law Review.* 1929. Vol. VIII, pp. 31-43.

Black, R. "Common Law Marriage." *University of Cincinnati Law Review.* 1928. Vol. II, pp. 113-133.

Bonaparte, W. "Expulsion from School for Refusal to Salute the Flag." *Southern California Law Review.* 1940. Vol. XIII, pp. 222-227.

Boudin, Louis B. "Freedom of Thought and Religious Liberty Under the Constitution." *Lawyers Guild Review.* 1944. Vol. IV, pp. 9-24.

Boyne, Edward M. "Religious Societies—Reinstatement of an expelled Member." *Cornell Law Quarterly.* 1928. Vol. XIII, pp. 464-469.

Brewster, Benjamin. "Marriage and Divorce in State and Church." *Michigan Law Review.* 1905. Vol. III, pp. 541-553.

Brown, B. "Religious Liberty and the Schools." *Oregon Law Review.* 1939. Vol. XVIII, pp. 122-128.

Brown, R. C. "The Custody of Children." *Indiana Law Journal.* 1927. Vol. II, pp. 325-330.

C., E. O. "Common Law Marriage." *Indiana Law Journal.* 1939. Vol. XIV, pp. 539-540.

C., S. W. "Evidence—Witnesses—Competency of Children of Tender Years." *California Law Review.* 1929. Vol. XVIII, pp. 85-88.

Chamberlain, S. C. "Disturbing Religious Meetings." *Case and Comment.* 1914. Vol. XX, pp. 518-524.

Cohen, Sylvan M. "Relation of Freedom of Religion to Loan of Textbooks to Private Schools." *Bill of Rights Review.* 1941. Vol. I, pp. 307-310.

Connolly, R. G. "Control of Property." *University of Pittsburgh Law Review.* 1937. Vol. IV, pp. 76-80.

Cosgrove, J. E., and Flattery, E. J. "Transportation of Parochial School Pupils." *Notre Dame Lawyer.* 1947. Vol. XXII, pp. 192-200.

Crow, William L. "Why Charitable Trusts Fail." *Marquette Law Review.* 1940. Vol. XXIV, pp. 126-138.

Curran, John. "Trusts for Masses." *Notre Dame Lawyer.* 1931. Vol. VII, pp. 42-56.

Curreri, Anthony. "Charitable Trusts—Definitions and History." *St. John's Law Review.* 1934. Vol. IX, pp. 114-121.

Dodd, E. M., Jr. "Dogma and Practice in the Law of Associations." *Harvard Law Review.* 1929. Vol. XLII, pp. 977-1014.

E., W. D. "Current Decisions." *Rocky Mountain Law Review.* 1934. Vol. VI, pp. 293-296.

Ernest, G. D. "Right of Jehovah's Witnesses to Distribute and Sell Their Literature Upon the Streets of an Unincorporated Privately-Owned Community." *Louisiana Law Review.* 1946. Vol. VI, pp. 707-711.

Fennell, William. "The 'Reconstructed Court' and Religious Freedom: The Gobitis Case in Retrospect." *New York University Law Quarterly Review.* 1941. Vol. XIX, pp. 31-48.

Friedman, Lee M. "The Parental Right to Control the Religious Education of a Child." *Harvard Law Review.* 1916. Vol. XXIX, pp. 485-500.

G., D. "Witnesses—Competency—Religious Belief." *Tulane Law Review.* 1933. Vol. VII, pp. 457-458.

Graham, F. J. "Negligence: Religious Societies, Charities." *Marquette Law Review.* 1930. Vol. XV, pp. 54-55.

Grinnell, F. W. "Children, the Bill of Rights and the American Flag." *Massachusetts Law Quarterly.* 1939. Vol. XXIV, pp. 1-7.

Grogan, Edward F., Jr. "Creation of an Implied Trust for a Religious Charitable Purpose." *Notre Dame Lawyer.* 1940. Vol. XV, pp. 224-229.

Hart, Philip A. "Charities—Capacity of an Unincorporated Association to Act as Trustee of a Charitable Trust." *Michigan Law Review.* 1937. Vol. XXXV, pp. 656-659.

Hartogenesis, B. H. "Denial of Equal Rights to Religious Minorities and Non-believers." *Yale Law Journal.* 1930. Vol. XXXIV, pp. 676-677.

Hasson, G. C. "Jehovah's Witnesses." *Notre Dame Lawyer.* 1946. Vol. XXII, pp. 82-94.

Howerton, H. B. "Jehovah's Witnesses and the Federal Constitution." *Mississippi Law Journal.* 1946. Vol. XVII, pp. 347-371.

Jarrard, J. O. "Freedom of Speech, Press and Religion—Conflict with Property Rights." *University of Kansas City Law Review.* 1946. Vol. XIV, pp. 112-116.

Jarrett, J. M. and Mund, V. A. "The Right of Assembly." *New York University Law Quarterly Review.* 1931. Vol. IX, pp. 18-25.

Johnson, Alvin W. "Sunday Legislation." *Kentucky Law Journal.* 1934. Vol. XXIII, pp. 131-166.

K., T. V. "Reading the Bible in Public Schools." *Michigan Law Review.* 1930. Vol. XXVIII, pp. 430-436.

Llewellyn, K. N. "Behind the Law of Divorce." *Columbia Law Review.* 1932. Vol. XXXII, pp. 1281-1308.

M., C. J. "Contracts—Restraint of Marriage." *Georgetown Law Journal.* 1934. Vol. XXII, pp. 361-362.

Martin, Clarence. "The American Judiciary and Religious Liberty." *American Law Review.* 1928. Vol. LXII, pp. 658-688.

McCraney, T. O. "Presumption of the Legality of a Marriage and of Its Continued Existence." *California Law Review.* 1938 Vol. XXVI, pp. 270-273.

Million, E. M. "Validity of Compulsory Flag Salutes in Public Schools." *Kentucky Law Journal.* 1940. Vol. XXVIiI, pp. 306-320.

Miner, Julius H. "Religion and the Law." *Chicago-Kent Law Review.* 1943. Vol. XXI, pp. 156-180.

Note. "Associations—Liability of Member of Religious Society on Note Signed as Trustee." *Harvard Law Review.* 1935. Vol. XLVIII, pp. 674-675.

Note. "Common Law Marriage Abolished." *Brooklyn Law Review.* 1934. Vol. III, pp. 155-156.

Note. "Compulsory Flag Salutes and Religious Freedom." *Harvard Law Review.* 1938. Vol. LI, pp. 1418-1424.

Note. "Constitutional Law—Fourteenth Amendment—Religious Liberty." *Columbia Law Review.* 1940. Vol. XL, pp. 1067-1071.

Note. "Constitutional Law—Freedom of Religion—Exemption of Conscientious Objectors from Military Service." *Columbia Law Review.* 1943. Vol. XLIII, pp. 112-114.

Note. "Determination of Rights in Church Property." *Columbia Law Review.* 1908. Vol. VIII, pp. 492-494.

Note. "Evidence—Privileged Communications." *Minnesota Law Review.* 1931. Vol. XVI, pp. 105-106.

Note. "Evidence—Witnesses—Religious Belief as a Prerequisite to Competency." *Columbia Law Review.* 1933. Vol. XXXIII, p. 539.

Note. "Freedom of Religion—Regulation of Solicitation of Charitable Funds by Religious Organization." *Fordham Law Review.* 1946. Vol. XV, pp. 113-117.

Note. "Jury—Competency of Jury." *Iowa Law Review.* 1929. Vol. XIV, pp. 486-487.

Note. "Necessity of Cohabitation in Common Law Marriage." *Iowa Law Review.* 1937. Vol. XXIII, pp. 75-83.

Note. "Religious Societies—Liability of Board of Stewards." *Virginia Law Review.* 1928. Vol. XV, pp. 98-99.

Note. "Review of Ecclesiastical Decisions by the Civil Courts." *Yale Law Journal.* 1937. Vol. XLVI, pp. 519-524.

Note. "Tax Exemptions—Charitable Institutions." *Minnesota Law Review.* 1915. Vol. X, pp. 358-359.

P., H. H. "The Promotion of a Cause as the Subject Matter of a Charitable Trust." *Virginia Law Review.* 1937. Vol. XXIII, pp. 439-445.

Patton, John W. "The Civil Courts and the Churches." *American Law Register.* 1906. Vol. LIV, pp. 391-423.

Q., D. L. "Constitutional Law—Religion in the Public Schools." *Michigan Law Review.* 1936. Vol. XXXIV, pp. 1237-1239.

R., M. H. "Donations and Wills." *Tulane Law Review.* 1939. Vol. XIII, pp. 630-632.

Remmlein, Madaline K. "Constitutional Implications of Compulsory Flag Salute Statutes." *George Washington Law Review.* 1943. Vol. XII, pp. 70-80.

Rotrem, Victor W., and Folsom, F. G. "Recent Restrictions Upon Religious Liberty." *American Political Science Review.* 1942. Vol. XXXVI, pp. 1053-68.

Rover, Thomas A. "Constitutional Law—Resolution of State Board of Education Compelling Salute to Flag Held Unconstitutional." *Georgetown Law Journal.* 1943. Vol. XXXII, pp. 93-99.

Rowley, Scott. "The Competency of Witnesses." *Iowa Law Review.* 1939. Vol. XXIV, pp. 482-497.

S., J. R. "Constitutional Law—Freedom of Press—Distribution of Handbills." *Washington University Law Quarterly.* 1940. Vol. XXV, pp. 611-614.

S., P. "Compulsory Salute to the Flag and the Guaranty of Religious Freedom." *St. John's Law Review.* 1938. Vol. XIII, pp. 144-147.

S., S. "Parent and Child—Custody." *St. John's Law Review.* 1936. Vol. XI, pp. 126-129.

Schaff, Philip. "Church and State in the United States." *American Historical Association Papers.* 1887. Vol. II, No. 4, pp. 440-447.

Schofield, Henry. "Religious Liberty and Bible Reading in Illinois Public Schools." *Illinois Law Review.* 1911. Vol. VI, pp. 17-32.

Skemp, Thomas H. "Freedom of Religious Worship." *Marquette Law Review.* 1940. Vol. XXV, pp. 19-22.

Slade, Tom B. "Constitutional Law—Guaranty of Liberty—State Law Requiring Public School Pupils to Salute the Flag Held Unconstitutional." *Georgia Bar Journal.* 1944. Vol. VI, pp. 249-250.

Solie, A. R. "Freedom of Speech and Religion Versus Property Rights—Jehovah's Witnesses in Company Town." *Wisconsin Law Review.* 1947. Pp. 121-125.

Stamps, Normal L. "Constitutional Law—Freedom of Speech and Religion—City License as a Prerequisite to Distribution of Religious Literature." *University of Kansas City Law Review.* 1943. Vol. XI, pp. 230-233.

Stimson, Claude. "Exemption of property from Taxation in the United States." *Minnesota Law Review.* 1934. Vol. XVIII, pp. 411-428.

Stith, L. A. "Bible Reading in the Public Schools." *Law Notes.* 1929. Vol. XXXII, pp. 225-228.

Stodola, Joseph. "Religious Societies." *Notre Dame Lawyer.* 1931. Vol. VI, pp. 387-388.

Sturges, W. A. "Unincorporated Associations as Parties to Actions." *Yale Law Review.* 1923. Vol. XXXIII, pp. 383-405.

Swancara, Frank. "A Religious Fiction of the Common Law." *Journal of Law and Criminology.* 1923. Vol. XXIII, pp. 614-619.

Swancara, Frank. "Judicial Disregard of the Equal Protection

Clause as it Affects the Non-Religious." *United States Law Review.* 1934. Vol. LXVIII, pp. 309-316.

Swancara, Frank. "Non-Religious Witnesses." *Wisconsin Law Review.* 1932. Vol. VIII, pp. 49-66.

Swancara, Frank. "Religion in the Law of Dying Declarations." *United States Law Review.* 1932. Vol. LXVI, pp. 192-202.

Tapscott, Clarence. "Taxation—Exemption of Church Property." *Oregon Law Review.* 1936. Vol. XV, pp. 152-157.

Waite, Edward F. "The Debt of Constitutional Law to Jehovah's Witnesses." *Minnesota Law Review.* 1944. Vol. XXVIII, pp. 209-246.

Wilke, Alfred W. "Civil Liberties—Jehovah's Witnesses Define Religious Freedom." *University of Detroit Law Journal.* 1943. Vol. VII, pp. 11-17.

Zollman, Carl. "Disturbance of Religious Meetings in the American Law." *American Law Review.* 1915. Vol. XLIX, pp. 880-893.

Zollman, Carl. "Classes of American Religious Corporations." *Michigan Law Review.* 1915. Vol. XIII, p. 566.

Zollman, Carl. "Powers of American Religious Corporations." *Michigan Law Review.* 1915. Vol. XIII, pp. 646-666.

Zollman, Carl. "Tax Exemptions of American Church Property." *Michigan Law Review.* 1916. Vol. XIV, pp. 646-657.

CASES

Adair v. State, 134 Ala. 183, 32 So. 326 (1901).

Agoodash Achim of Ithaca v. Temple Beth El, 263 N. Y. S. 81, 147 Misc. 405 (1933).

Alden v. St. Peter's Parish, 158 Ill. 631, 42 N. E. 392 (1895).

Alford v. Johnson, 103 Ark. 236, 146 S. W. 516 (1901).

Allen v. North Des Moines Methodist Episcopal Church, 127 Iowa 96, 102 N. W. 808 (1905).

All Saints Parish v. Brookline, 178 Mass. 404, 59 N. E. 1003 (1901).

Anderson v. Christ Church of Bay Ridge, 287 N. Y. S. 403, 248 App. Div. 584 (1936).

Andrews v. Andrews, 110 Ill. 223 (1884).

Application of Kaminsky, 295 N. Y. S. 989, 251 App. Div. 132 (1937).
Ashworth v. Brown, 198 So. 135 (1940).
Assessors of Boston v. Lamson, 316 Mass. 166, 55 N. E. (2d) 215 (1944).
Association v. Moore, 183 U. S. 642, 22 Sup. Ct. 240, 46 L. Ed. 366 (1902).
Association for Benefit of Colored Orphans v. Mayor, Aldermen and Commonalty of the City of New York, 104 N. Y. 581, 12 N. E. 279 (1887).
Athens v. Dodson, 154 Tenn. 469, 290 S. W. 36 (1926).
Attorney General v. Geerlings, 55 Mich. 562, 22 N. W. 89 (1885).
Auburn v. Young Men's Christian Association, 86 Me. 244, 29 Atl. 992 (1894).
Baggerly v. Lee, 37 Ind. App. 139, 73 N. E. 921 (1905).
Bahr v. Evangelical Lutheran St. John's Society of Poynette, 236 Wisc. 490, 295 N. W. 700 (1941).
Bailey v. Washington, 236 Ala. 541, 185 So. 172 (1938).
Ball v. State, 67 Miss. 358, 7 So. 353 (1889).
Baltimore Railroad Co. v. Washington Fifth Baptist Church, 137 U. S. 568, 11 Sup. Ct. 185, 39 L. Ed. 784 (1891).
Baptist Church v. Mt. Olive Missionary, 92 Cal. App. 618, 268 Pac. 665 (1928).
Baptist Church v. Witherell, 3 Paige (N. Y.) 296 (1832).
Barger v. French, 122 Kan. 607, 253 Pac. 230 (1927).
Barkley v. Hayes, 208 Fed. 319 (D. C., 1913).
Barnum v. Mayor of Baltimore, 62 Md. 275 (1884).
Barrington v. Cowan, 55 N. C. 436 (1856).
Bartels v. State, 262 U. S. 404, 43 Sup. Ct. 628, 67 L. Ed. 1047 (1923).
Barton v. Fitzpatrick, 187 Ala. 273, 65 So. 390 (1914).
Bear v. Heasley, 98 Mich. 279, 57 N. W. 270 (1893).
Beckwith v. St. Philip's Parish, 69 Ga. 564 (1882).
Bennett v. LaGrange, 153 Ga. 428, 112 S. E. 482 (1922).
Bennett v. St. Paul's Evangelical Lutheran Church, 137 Md. 341, 112 Atl. 619 (1921).

Benson v. United States, 146 U. S. 325, 13 Sup. Ct. 60, 36 L. Ed. 991 (1892).

Blaisdell v. Raymond, 9 Abb. Pr. (N. Y.) 178 (1859).

Bloodsworth v. State, 107 So. 321 (1926).

Blossi v. C. & N. W. Railway Co., 144 Iowa 697, 123 N. W. 360 (1909).

Board of Education v. Minor, 23 Ohio St. 211 (1872).

Board of Education v. Wheat, 174 Md. 314, 199 Atl. 628 (1938).

Board of Foreign Missions v. Board of Assessors, 244 N. Y. 42, 154 N. E. 816 (1926).

Board of Home Missions v. City of Philadelphia, 266 Pa. 405, 109 Atl. 664 (1920).

Boardman v. Hitchcock, 120 N. Y. S. 1039, 136 App. Div. 253 (1910).

Bohning v. State, 262 U. S. 404, 43 Sup. Ct. 628, 67 L. Ed. 1047 (1923).

Bonscum v. Murphy, 71 Neb. 463, 104 N. W. 180 (1904).

Borden v. Louisiana State Board of Education, 168 La. 1005, 123 So. 655 (1929).

Boston Seamen's Friend Society v. City of Boston, 116 Mass. 181 (1875).

Bouchelle v. Trustees of the Presbyterian Congregation, 194 Atl. 100 (1937).

Bouldin v. Alexander, 15 Wall. 131, 21 L. Ed. 69 (1872).

Bradfield v. Roberts, 175 U. S. 291, 20 Sup. Ct. 121, 44 L. Ed. 168 (1899).

Brewer v. Cary, 148 Mo. App. 193, 127 S. W. 685 (1910).

Brinkley v. Brinkley, 48 N. Y. 184 (1872).

Brown v. Father Divine, 298 N. Y. S. 642, 163 Misc. 796 (1937).

Brown v. State, 46 Ala. 175 (1871).

Brown v. State, 14 Ga. App. 21, 80 S. E. 26 (1913).

Brundage v. Deardorf, 55 Fed. 839 (C. C., 1893).

Burgie v. Muench, 65 Ohio App. 176, 29 N. E. (2d) 439 (1940).

Burke v. Roper, 79 Ala. 138 (1885).

Burkwaggoner Association v. Hopkins, 269 U. S. 110, 46 Sup. Ct. 48, 70 L. Ed. 183 (1925).

Burton v. Grand Rapids School Furniture Co., 10 Tex. Civ. App. 270, 31 S. W. 91 (1895).

Busey v. District of Columbia, 138 F. (2d) 592 (D. C., 1943), 78 App. D. C. 189, conforming to mandate 319 U. S. 579, 63 Sup. Ct. 1277, 87 L. Ed. 1598 (1943), after certiorari granted 319 U. S. 735, 63 Sup. Ct. 1154, 87 L. Ed. 1695 (1943).

Butchera Estate, 266 Pa. 479, 109 Atl. 683 (1920).

Buttecali v. United States, 130 F. (2d) 172 (C. C. A., 1942).

Cahill v. Bigger, 47 Ky. 211 (1848).

Cain v. Rea, 159 Va. 446, 166 S. E. 478 (1929).

Canovaro v. Brothers of the Order of the Hermits, 326 Pa. 76, 191 Atl. 140 (1937).

Cantrell v. State, 29 S. W. 42 (1895).

Cantwell v. Connecticut, 310 U. S. 296, 60 Sup. Ct. 900, 84 L. Ed. 1213 (1940).

Caples v. Nazareth Church of Hopewell Association, 245 Ala. 656, 18 So. (2d) 383 (1944).

Carter v. State, 63 Ala. 52 (1879).

Carver v. United States, 164 U. S. 694, 17 Sup. Ct. 228, 41 L. Ed. 602 (1897).

Central Military Tract Railroad Co. v. Rockafellow, 17 Ill. 541 (1856).

Chance v. Mississippi State Textbook R. & P. Board, 190 Miss. 453, 200 So. 706 (1941).

Chandler v. Executive Committee on Education, Synod of Presbyterian Church, 165 Miss. 690, 146 So. 597 (1933).

Chaplinski v. New Hampshire, 315 U. S. 568, 62 Sup. Ct. 766, 86 L. Ed. 1031 (1942).

Chase v. Cheney, 58 Ill. 509 (1871).

Checinski v. United States, 129 F. (2d) 461 (C. C. A., 1942).

Chelsea v. Our Lady Star of the Sea, 105 N. J. Eq. 236, 147 Atl. 470 (1929).

Chester Housing Authority v. Ritter, 344 Pa. 653, 25 A. (2d) 72 (1942).

Chevra Bnai Israel v. Chevra Bikur Cholim, 52 N. Y. S. 712, 24 Misc. 189 (1898).

Chicago Theological Seminary v. Illinois, 188 U. S. 662, 23 Sup. Ct. 386, 47 L. Ed. 641 (1903).

Child v. Christian Society, 144 Mass. 473, 11 N. E. 664 (1887).

Chisholm v. State, 32 Tex. Crim. 512, 24 S. W. 646 (1894).

Christian Church v. Crystal, 78 Cal. App. 1, 247 Pac. 605 (1926).

Church v. Bullock, 104 Tex. 1, 109 S. W. 115 (1908).

Church of the Holy Faith v. State Tax Commission, 39 N. M. 403, 48 P. (2d) 777 (1935).

Church of the Holy Trinity v. United States, 143 U. S. 457, 12 Sup. Ct. 511, 36 L. Ed. 226 (1892).

Church of the Latter Day Saints v. United States, 136 U. S. 1, 10 Sup. Ct. 792, 34 L. Ed. 478 (1890).

City of Chicago v. Porter, 194 Ill. App. 590 (1915).

City of Louisiana v. Bottoms, 300 S. W. 316 (1927).

City of New Braunfels v. Waldschmidt, 109 Tex. 302, 207 S. W. 303 (1918).

City of Pineville v. Marshall, 222 Ky. 4, 299 S. W. 1072 (1927).

City of Pittsburgh v. Ruffner, 132 Pa. Super. 192, 4 A. (2d) 224 (1939).

City of Portland v. Thornton, 149 P. (2d) 972 (1944).

City of St. Louis v. Hellscher, 295 Mo. 293, 242 S. W. 652 (1922).

City of San Antonio v. Young Men's Christian Association, 285 S. W. 844 (1926).

Clarke v. O'Rourke, 111 Mich. 108, 69 N. W. 147 (1896).

Clevenger v. McAfee, 170 S. W. (2d) 424 (1943).

Cline v. State, 9 Okla. Crim. App. 40, 130 Pac. 510 (1913).

Cochran v. Louisiana State Board of Education, 168 La. 1030, 123 So. 664 (1929).

Cochran v. Louisiana State Board of Education, 281 U. S. 370, 50 Sup. Ct. 335, 74 L. Ed. 913 (1930).

Cockreham v. State, 26 Tenn. 11 (1846).

Colden v. Bradford, 8 Cowen (N. Y.) 456 (1826).

Coleman v. City of Griffin, 55 Ga. App. 123, 189 S. E. 427 (1936).

Coleman v. City of Griffin, 302 U. S. 636, 58 Sup. Ct. 23, 82 L. Ed. 495 (1937).

Coleman v. O'Leary, 114 Ky. 388, 70 S. W. 1068 (1897).

Coleman v. State, 4 Ga. App. 786, 62 S. E. 487 (1908).

Collins v. Kephart, 271 Pa. 428, 117 Atl. 440 (1921).

Collins v. Martin, 290 Pa. 388, 139 Atl. 122 (1927).

Commonwealth v. Anderson, 272 Mass. 100, 172 N. E. 114 (1930).
Commonwealth v. Armstrong, 1 Pa. Law J. 393 (1842).
Commonwealth v. Bearse, 132 Mass. 542 (1882).
Commonwealth v. Bey, 92 Pittsburgh Legal Journal 84 (1944).
Commonwealth v. First Christian Church of Louisville, 169 Ky. 410, 183 S. W. 943 (1916).
Commonwealth v. Green, 168 N. E. 101 (1929).
Commonwealth v. Herr, 229 Pa. 132, 78 Atl. 68 (1910).
Commonwealth v. Hoffman, 29 Pa. Co. Ct. 65 (1901).
Commonwealth v. Jennings, 44 Va. 806 (1846).
Commonwealth v. Kelley, 83 Pa. Super. 17 (1924).
Commonwealth v. Kneeland, 20 Pick. (Mass.) 206 (1838).
Commonwealth v. McClelland, 70 Pa. Super. 273 (1918).
Commonwealth v. Munson, 127 Mass. 459 (1879).
Commonwealth v. Plaisted, 148 Mass. 375, 19 N. E. 224 (1889).
Commonwealth v. Plummer, 21 Pa. Dist. 182 (1912).
Commonwealth v. Sigman, 3 Pa. L. J. 252 (1844).
Commonwealth v. Smith, 68 Mass. 516 (1854).
Commonwealth v. Underkoffer, 11 Pa. Co. 589 (1892).
Commonwealth v. Wilcox, 118 Pa. Super. 363, 179 Atl. 808 (1935).
Commonwealth v. Winnemore, 2 Brewst. (Pa.) 378 (1867).
Congregational Gedulath Mordecai v. City of New York, 238 N. Y. S. 525, 135 Misc. 823 (1930).
Congregation of the Roman Catholic Church v. Martin, 4 Rob. (La.) 62 (1843).
Congregation of St. Augustine R. C. Church v. Metropolitan Bank of Lima, 32 N. E. (2d) 518 (1936).
Congregational Society of Poultney v. Ashley, 10 Vt. 241 (1838).
Cook v. Harrison, 180 Ark. 546, 21 S. W. (2d) 966 (1929).
Cooper v. Bell, 269 Ky. 63, 106 S. W. (2d) 124 (1937).
Corbin Young Men's Christian Association v. Commonwealth, 181 Ky. 384, 205 S. W. 388 (1918).
Cox v. United States, — U. S. —, — Sup. Ct. —, —L. Ed. —, decided November 24, 1947.
Crain v. Walker, 222 Ky. 828, 2 S. W. (2d) 654 (1928).
Cross v. State, 89 Fla. 212, 103 So. 636 (1925).

Cummings v. State, 8 Ga. App. 534, 69 S. E. 918 (1911).

Curtis v. Maryland Baptist Union Association, 5 A. (2d) 836 (1939).

Dakota Wesleyan University v. Betts, 47 S. D. 618, 201 N. W. 524 (1924).

Davidson v. Church of Christ Parrish, 245 Ala. 203, 16 So. (2d) 179 (1943).

Davis v. Arthur, 139 Ga. 74, 76 S. E. 676 (1912).

Davis v. Beason, 133 U. S. 333, 10 Sup. Ct. 299, 33 L. Ed. 637 (1890).

Davis v. Boget, 50 Iowa 11 (1878).

Decloedt v. Decloedt, 24 Idaho 277, 133 Pac. 664 (1913).

Dees v. Moss Point Baptist Church, 17 So. 1 (1895).

Dehler v. State, 22 Ind. App. 383, 53 N. E. 850 (1900).

Delk v. Commissioner, 166 Ky. 39, 178 S. W. 1129 (1915).

Denton v. James, 107 Kans. 729, 193 Pac. 307 (1920).

District of Columbia v. Robinson, 30 App. D. C. 283 (1908).

Donahue v. Richards, 38 Me. 379 (1854).

Donovan v. Sullivan, 4 N. E. (2d) 1004 (1937).

Dorn v. State, 4 Tex. App. 67 (1878).

Dorner v. Luxemburg School District, 137 Wisc. 147, 118 N. W. 353 (1908).

Drace v. Klinedinst, 275 Pa. 266, 118 Atl. 907 (1922).

Drozda v. Bassos, 23 N. Y. S. (2d) 544, 260 App. Div. 408 (1940).

Duessel v. Proch, 78 Conn. 343, 62 Atl. 152 (1905).

Duvall v. Synod of Kansas of the Presbyterian Church, 222 Fed. 669 (C. C. A., 1915).

Dyer v. Dyer, 5 N. H. 271 (1830).

Eagles v. United States ex rel. Horowitz, 329 U. S. 317, 67 Sup. Ct. 320, 91 L. Ed. 260 (1946).

Eagles v. United States ex rel. Samuels, 329 U. S. 304, 67 Sup. Ct. 313, 91 L. Ed. 252 (1946).

Easterbrooks v. Tillinghast, 71 Mass. 17 (1855).

East Norway Lake Lutheran Church v. Froislie, 37 Minn. 447, 35 N. W. 260 (1887).

Eckhardt v. Darby, 118 Mich. 199, 76 N. W. 761 (1898).

Edwards v. Edwards, 193 Iowa 87, 185 N. W. 2 (1921).

Elden v. People, 161 Ill. 296, 43 N. E. 1108 (1896).

Elliott v. State, 29 Ariz. 389, 242 Pac. 340 (1926).

Ellis v. State, 10 Ala. App. 252, 65 So. 412 (1914).

Enaut v. McGuire, 36 La. Ann. 804 (1884).

Enochs v. Jackson, 144 Miss. 360, 109 So. 864 (1926).

Estate of Lennon, 152 Cal. 327, 92 Pac. 870 (1907).

Estate of Mary A. Horner, 38 Lanc. (Pa.) Law Rev. 305 (1942).

Eutaw Place Baptist Church v. Shively, 67 Md. 493, 10 Atl. 244 (1887).

Evangelische Lutherische St. Thomas Gemeinde v. Congregation of the German Evangelical Lutherische St. Matthews Church of Milwaukee, 191 Wisc. 340, 210 N. W. 942 (1926).

Evans v. Selma Union High School Board, 193 Cal. 54, 222 Pac. 801 (1924).

Everett v. First Presbyterian Church, 53 N. J. Eq. 500, 32 Atl. 747 (1895).

Everson v. Board of Education of the Township of Ewing, 330 U. S. 1, 67 Sup. Ct. 504, 91 L. Ed. 472 (1947); rehearing denied 330 U. S. 855 (1947).

Ex parte Ferguson, 70 P. (2d) 1094 (1937).

Ex parte Flynn, 87 N. J. Eq. 413, 100 Atl. 861 (1917).

Ex parte Newman, 9 Cal. 502 (1858).

Ex parte Stewart, 47 F. Supp. 415 (D. C., 1942).

Fairbanks v. Lamson, 99 Mass. 553 (1868).

Farrell v. State, 111 Ark. 180, 163 S. W. 768 (1914).

Fealy v. City of Birmingham, 73 So. 296 (1916).

Federal Savings and Loan Insurance Corporation v. Strangers Rest Baptist Church, 156 Kans. 205, 131 P. (2d) 654 (1942).

Feehley v. Feehley, 129 Md. 565, 99 Atl. 663 (1916).

Fernandez v. State, 16 Ariz. 269, 144 Pac. 640 (1914).

Fernstler v. Seibert, 114 Pa. 196, 6 Atl. 165 (1886).

Ferraria v. Vasconcelles, 23 Ill. 403 (1860).

Ferraria v. Vasconcelles, 31 Ill. 25 (1863).

Festorazzi v. St. Joseph's Catholic Church, 104 Ala. 327, 18 So. 394 (1894).

First Baptist Church v. Fort, 93 Tex. 215, 54 S. W. 892 (1900).

First Baptist Church v. Ward, 290 S. W. 828 (1927).

First Baptist Church in Schenectady v. Schenectady & Troy Railroad Co., 5 Darb. (N. Y.) 79 (1848).

First Congregational Society v. Bridgeport, 99 Conn. 22, 121 Atl. 77 (1923).

First English Lutheran Church of Oklahoma City v. Evangelical Lutheran Synod of Kansas, 135 F. (2d) 701 (C. C. A., 1943).

First Methodist Episcopal Church v. City of Atlanta, 76 Ga. 181 (1881).

First Methodist Episcopal Church v. Dixon, 178 Ill. 260, 52 N. E. 887 (1889).

First Presbyterian Church v. Dennis, 178 Iowa 1352, 161 N. W. 183 (1917).

First Presbyterian Church v. First Cumberland Presbyterian Church, 245 Ill. 74, 91 N. E. 761 (1910).

First Society in Irving v. Brownell, 5 Hun. (N. Y.) 464 (1875).

First Unitarian Society of Hartford v. Town of Hartford, 66 Conn. 368, 34 Atl. 89 (1896).

Fiske v. Beaty, 201 N. Y. S. 441, 206 App. Div. 349 (1923).

Flannery v. State, 117 S. W. (2d) 1111 (1938).

Follett v. Town of McCormick, 321 U. S. 573, 64 Sup. Ct. 717, 88 L. Ed. 938 (1944).

Forsberg v. Zehm, 150 Va. 756, 143 S. E. 284 (1928).

Fort Worth Baptist Church v. City of Fort Worth, 17 S. W. (2d) 130 (1929).

Franke v. Mann, 106 Wisc. 118, 81 N. W. 1014 (1900).

Franklin Street Society v. Manchester, 60 N. H. 342 (1880).

Franta v. Bohemian A. C. C. Union, 164 Mo. 304, 63 S. W. 1100 (1901).

Freeman v. Dempsey, 41 Ill. App. 554 (1891).

French v. Old South Society in Boston, 106 Mass. 479 (1870).

Funk v. United States, 290 U. S. 371, 54 Sup. Ct. 212, 78 L. Ed. 369 (1933).

Gabrielli v. Knickerbocker, 82 P. (2d) 391 (1938).

Gaddis v. State, 105 Neb. 303, 180 N. W. 590 (1920).

Gambrell v. State, 92 Miss. 728, 46 So. 138 (1908).

Geiss v. Trinity Lutheran Church, 119 Neb. 745, 230 N. W. 658 (1930).

General Assembly of the Presbyterian Church v. Guthrie, 86 Va. 125, 10 S. E. 318 (1889).

Gerhardt v. Heid, 66 N. D. 444, 267 N. W. 127 (1936).

German Evangelical Lutheran Trinity Congregation v. Deutsche Gemeinde, 246 Ill. 328, 92 N. E. 868 (1910).

Gibbons v. District of Columbia, 116 U. S. 404, 6 Sup. Ct. 427, 29 L. Ed. 680 (1886).

Gibson v. Singleton, 149 Ga. 502, 101 S. E. 178 (1919).

Gibson v. Trustees, 10 A. (2d) 332 (1939).

Gibson v. Trustees of Pencader Presbyterian Church in Pencader Hundred, 20 A. (2d) 134 (1941).

Gilmer v. Stone, 120 U. S. 586, 7 Sup. Ct. 689, 30 L. Ed. 734 (1887).

Globe Furniture Co. v. Trustees of Jerusalem Baptist Church, 103 Va. 559, 49 S. E. 657 (1905).

Glover v. Baker, 76 N. H. 393, 83 Atl. 916 (1912).

Gobitis v. Minersville School District, 21 F. Supp. 581 (D. C., 1939).

Goesele v. Bimeler, 55 U. S. 589, 14 L. Ed. 554 (1852).

Goldberg v. Agudath B'Nai Israel Congregation, 66 Ohio App. 379, 34 N. E. (2d) 73 (1940).

Goodhope Colored Presbyterian Church v. Lee, 241 Ala. 195, 1 So. (2d) 911 (1941).

Goodwin v. Rowe, 49 F. Supp. 703 (D. C., 1943).

Gordon v. State, 186 Ga. 615, 198 S. E. 678 (1938).

Gospel Army v. City of Los Angeles, 27 Cal. (2d) 232, 163 P. (2d) 704 (1945).

Goulding v. State, 82 Ala. 48 (1886).

Grantham v. Humphries, 185 Miss. 496, 188 So. 313 (1939).

Green v. Church of Immaculate Conception, 288 N. Y. S. 769, 248 App. Div. 757 (1936).

Gullet v. First Christian Church of Meridian, 154 Miss. 516, 122 So. 732 (1929).

Gunter v. Jackson, 130 Miss. 637, 94 So. 844 (1923).

Haas v. Missionary Society of the Most Holy Redeemer Church, 26 N. Y. S. 868, 6 Misc. 281 (1893).

Hackett v. Brooksville, 120 Ky. 608, 87 S. W. 792 (1905).

Haight v. First Baptist Church of Camillus, 42 F. Supp. 925 (D. C., 1942).

Hale v. Everett, 53 N. H. 9 (1868).

Hall v. State, 19 Ala. App. 229, 96 So. 644 (1923).

Halperin v. Public Service Commission, 81 Pa. Super. 591 (1923).

Hamilton v. Regents of the University of California, 293 U. S. 245, 55 Sup. Ct. 197, 79 L. Ed. 343 (1923).

Hamilton v. Regents, 293 U. S. 245, 55 Sup. Ct. 197, 79 L. Ed. 343 (1934).

Hammer v. State, 173 Ind. 199, 89 N. E. 850 (1909).

Hamsher v. Hamsher, 132 Ill. 273, 23 N. E. 1123 (1890).

Hanley v. Chicago City Railway Co., 180 Ill. App. 397 (1913).

Harding v. Brown, 227 Mass. 77, 117 N. E. 638 (1917).

Harriman v. First Bryan Baptist Church, 63 Ga. 186 (1879).

Harrison v. Brophy, 59 Kan. 1, 51 Pac. 883 (1898).

Harrison v. State, 22 Md. 468 (1863).

Hart v. School District, 2 Lanc. Law Rev. 346 (1885).

Hartwick v. Board of School Trustees, 54 Cal. App. 696, 205 Pac. 49 (1921).

Harvard College v. Jewett, 11 F. (2d) 119 (C. C. A., 1929).

Hawthorne v. Austin Organ Co., 71 F. (2d) 945 (C. C. A., 1934).

Hayes v. Manning, 263 Mo. 1, 172 S. W. 897 (1914).

Hedding Camp Meeting v. Epping, 88 N. H. 321, 189 Atl. 347 (1937).

Hempkill v. Orloff, 277 U. S. 537, 48 Sup. Ct. 577, 72 L. Ed. 978 (1928).

Henderson v. Jackson, 138 Iowa 326, 111 N. W. 821 (1907).

Hendryx v. Peoples United Church, 42 Wash. 336, 84 Pac. 1123 (1906).

Hennington v. State, 90 Ga. 396, 17 S. E. 1009 (1892).

Hennington v. Georgia, 163 U. S. 299, 16 Sup. Ct. 1086, 41 L. Ed. 166 (1896).

Hering v. State Board of Education, 117 N. J. Law 455, 189 Atl. 629 (1937).

Hering v. State Board of Education, 303 U. S. 624, 58 Sup. Ct. 742, 82 L. Ed. 1086 (1938).

Hernandez v. Thomas, 50 Fla. 522, 39 So. 641 (1905).

Herold v. Parish Board of School Directors, 136 La. 1034, 68 So. 116 (1915).

Hewitt v. Buchanan, 4 S. W. (2d) 169 (1927).

Hicks v. State, 60 Ga. 464 (1878).

Hill v. State, 64 Miss. 431, 1 So. 494 (1886).

Hiller v. State, 124 Md. 385, 92 Atl. 842 (1914).

Hills v. State, 61 Neb. 589, 85 N. W. 836 (1901).

Hilton v. Roylance, 25 Utah 129, 69 Pac. 660 (1902).

Hilton v. Stewart, 15 Idaho 150, 96 Pac. 579 (1908).

Hinckley v. Thatcher, 139 Mass. 477, 1 N. E. 840 (1885).

Hoeffer v. Clogan, 171 Ill. 462, 49 N. E. 527 (1898).

Hollingsworth v. State, 37 Tenn. 518 (1858).

Holmes v. State, 39 Tex. Crim. App. 231, 45 S. W. 487 (1898).

Holt v. State, 186 S. E. 147 (1936).

Hood v. Dorer, 107 Wisc. 149, 82 N. W. 546 (1900).

Hornell v. Philadelphia, 8 Phila. 280 (1870).

Horst v. Silverman, 20 Wash. 233, 55 Pac. 52 (1898).

Housing Authority of New Orleans v. Merritt, 196 La. 955, 200 So. 311 (1941).

Huber v. German Congregation, 16 Ohio St. 371 (1865).

Huger v. Protestant Episcopal Church, 137 Ga. 205, 73 S. E. 385 (1911).

Hughes v. Holman, 110 Ore. 415, 223 Pac. 730 (1924).

Hull v. State, 120 Ind. 153, 22 N. E. 117 (1889).

Hunt v. State, 3 Tex. App. 116 (1877).

Hunter v. State, 20 Ala. App. 152, 101 So. 100 (1924).

Hunter v. State, 137 Miss. 276, 102 So. 282 (1924).

Hysong v. School District, 164 Pa. 629, 30 Atl. 482 (1894).

Immanuel Presbyterian Church v. Payne, 90 Cal. App. 176, 265 Pac. 547 (1928).

Inhabitants of Foxcroft v. Piscataquis Valley Camp-Meeting Ass'n, 86 Me. 78, 29 Atl. 951 (1894).

Inhabitants of Foxcroft v. Straw, 86 Me. 76, 29 Atl. 950 (1893).

In Matter of Andrew Frazee, 63 Mich. 396, 30 N. W. 72 (1886).

In Matter of Seaman, 218 N. Y. 77, 112 N. E. 576 (1916).

In re Application for Charter, 55 York (Pa.) L. R. 186 (1942).

In re Atkinson's Will, 197 N. Y. S. 831, 120 Misc. 186 (1923).

In re Church of God World Headquarters, Inc., 46 N. Y. S. (2d) 545 (1944).

In re Clendenin's Estate, 9 N. Y. S. (2d) 875 (1939).

In re Dakota Wesleyan University, 48 S. D. 84, 202 N. W. 284 (1925).

In re Douglass' Estate, 94 Neb. 280, 143 N. W. 299 (1913).

In re Doyle, 16 Mo. App. 159 (1884).

In re Edge's Estate, 288 N. Y. S. 437, 159 Misc. 505 (1936).

In re Evangelical Church of Lansford v. Lesher, 24 A. (2d) 42 (1942).

In re First Church of Christ Scientist, 205 Pa. 543, 55 Atl. 536 (1903).

In re German Lutheran & Reformed Wyomissing Church, 9 Pa. Co. Ct. 12 (1871).

In re Goldman's Estate, 292 N. Y. S. 787, 156 Misc. 817 (1935).

In re Jacquet, 82 N. Y. S. 986, 40 Misc. 575 (1903).

In re Kavanaugh's Will, 143 Wisc. 90, 126 N. W. 672 (1910).

In re Kempf's Estate, 289 N. Y. S. 74, 159 Misc. 298 (1936).

In re Lesser's Estate, 287 N. Y. S. 209, 158 Misc. 895 (1936).

In re Long Island Church of Aphrodite, 14 N. Y. S. 763, 171 Misc. 1032 (1939).

In re Luck, 10 Ohio Sup. & C. P. Dec. 1 (1899).

In re Maguire's Estate, 13 Phila. 244 (1887).

In re Malvasi's Estate, 96 Cal. App. 204, 273 Pac. 1097 (1929).

In re McCanna's Estate, 230 Wisc. 561, 284 N. W. 502 (1939).

In re Rogers, 47 F. Supp. 265 (D. C., 1942).

In re Rudge, 114 Neb. 335, 207 N. W. 520 (1926).

In re Smith's Estate, 144 Ore. 561, 25 P. (2d) 924 (1933).

In re Solomon's Estate, 281 N. Y. S. 827, 156 Misc. 445 (1935).

In re Vance's Estate, 118 Cal. App. 163, 4 P. (2d) 977 (1931).

In re Vardinakis, 289 N. Y. S. 355, 160 Misc. 13 (1936).

In re Winburn's Will, 247 N. Y. S. 584, 139 Misc. 5 (1931).

Jackson v. Phillips, 96 Mass. 539 (1867).

Jackson v. State, 21 Ga. App. 779, 95 S. E. 302 (1918).

Jefferson Standard Life Insurance Co. v. City of Wildwood, 118 Fla. 771, 160 So. 208 (1935).

Jepperson v. Advent Christian Publication Society, 83 N. H. 387, 142 Atl. 686 (1928).

Johnson v. Borders, 155 Ark. 218, 244 S. W. 30 (1922).
Johnson v. Deefield, 25 F. Supp. 918 (D. C., 1939).
Johnson v. Johnson, 31 Pa. Super. 53 (1906).
Jones v. Habersham, 107 U. S. 174, 2 Sup. Ct. 336, 27 L. Ed. 401 (1882).
Jones v. Johnson, 295 Ky. 707, 175 S. W. (2d) 370 (1943).
Jones v. Opelika, 316 U. S. 584, 62 Sup. Ct. 1231, 86 L. Ed. 1691 (1942).
Jones v. Opelika, 319 U. S. 103, 63 Sup. Ct. 890, 87 L. Ed. 1290 (1943).
Jones v. State, 28 Neb. 495, 44 N. W. 658 (1890).
Jones v. Watson, 63 Ga. 680 (1879).
Jordan's Administrator v. Richmond Home for Ladies, 106 Va. 710, 56 S. E. 730 (1907).
Judd v. Board of Education, 278 N. Y. 200, 15 N. E. (2d) 576 (1938).
Kapigian v. Der Minassian, 212 Mass. 412, 99 N. E. 264 (1912).
Kauffman v. Plank, 214 Ill. App. 306 (1919).
Kelly v. McIntire, 123 N. J. Eq. 351, 197 Atl. 736 (1938).
Kelly v. Welborn, 110 Ga. 540, 35 S. E. 636 (1900).
Kemp v. Pillar of Fire, 94 Colo. 41, 27 P. (2d) 1036 (1933).
Kerler v. Evangelical Emanuel's Church, 282 N. W. 32 (1938).
King v. Richardson, 136 F. (2d) 849 (C. C. A., 1943).
Kinney v. State, 38 Ala. 224 (1862).
Knight v. Lee, 80 Ind. 201 (1881).
Knowles v. United States, 170 Fed. 409 (D. C., 1909).
Knowlton v. Baumhover, 182 Iowa 691, 166 N. W. 202 (1918).
Komen v. City of St. Louis, 316 Mo. 9, 289 S. W. 838 (1926).
Kompier v. Thegza, 13 N. E. (2d) 229 (1939).
Krauss v. Krauss, 163 La. 218, 111 So. 683 (1927).
Krecker v. Shirey, 163 Pa. 534, 30 Atl. 440 (1894).
Lacey v. State, 127 S. W. (2d) 890 (1939).
Laird v. State, 69 Tex. Crim. 553, 155 S. W. 260 (1913).
Latta v. Jenkins, 200 N. C. 255, 156 S. E. 857 (1931).
Lawrence v. Lawrence, 3 Paige (N. Y.) 266 (1832).
Lawson v. Kolbenson, 61 Ill. 405 (1871).
Lawson's Estate, 264 Pa. 77, 107 Atl. 376 (1919).

Layman's Weekend Retreat League v. Butler, 83 Pa. Super 1 (1924).

Leavell's Administrator v. Arnold, 131 Ky. 426, 115 S. W. 232 (1909).

LeBlanc v. LeMaire, 105 La. 539, 30 So. 135 (1900).

Le Duc v. Normal Park Presbyterian Church, 142 F. (2d) 105 (C. C. A., 1944).

Lee v. Methodist Episcopal Church, 193 Mass. 47, 78 N. E. 646 (1906).

Lenoux v. Annual Alabama Conference of Methodist Episcopal Church, South, 236 Ala. 529, 183 So. 672 (1938).

Leoles v. Landers, 302 U. S. 656, 58 Sup. Ct. 364, 82 L. Ed. 507 (1937).

Leoles v. Landers, 184 Ga. 580, 192 S. E. 218 (1937).

Lewis v. Board of Education, 258 N. Y. 117, 179 N. E. 315 (1932).

Lewis v. Board of Education, 285 N. Y. S. 164, 157 Misc. 520 (1935).

Lindenmuller v. People, 33 Barb. (N. Y.) 548 (1861).

Lockwood v. City of St. Louis, 24 Mo. 20 (1856).

Logan v. United States, 144 U. S. 263, 12 Sup. Ct. 617, 36 L. Ed. 429 (1891).

Long v. State, 192 Ind. 524, 137 N. E. 49 (1922).

Louie Ding v. United States, 247 Fed. 12 (C. C. A., 1918).

Love v. State, 35 Tex. Crim. 27, 29 S. W. 790 (1895).

Lovell v. City of Griffin, 55 Ga. App. 609 (1939).

Lovell v. City of Griffin, 303 U. S. 444, 58 Sup. Ct. 666, 82 L. Ed. 949 (1938).

Lovett v. State, 239 Pac. 274 (1925).

Lundquist v. First Evangelical Lutheran Church, 193 Minn. 474, 259 N. W. 9 (1935).

Lutheran Trefoldighed Congregation v. St. Paul's English Evangelical Lutheran Congregation, 159 Wisc. 56, 150 N. W. 190 (1914).

Mabel First Lutheran Church v. Cadwallader, 172 Minn. 471, 215 N. W. 845 (1927).

Macintosh v. United States, 42 F. (2d) 845 (C. C. A., 1930).

Mack v. Kime, 129 Ga. 1, 58 S. E. 184 (1906).

MacLaury v. Hart, 121 N. Y. 636, 24 N. E. 1013 (1890).
Maddox v. Maddox, 52 Va. 418 (1854).
Magee v. O'Neill, 19 S. C. 170 (1882).
Malanchuk v. St. Mary's Greek Catholic Church, 336 Pa. 385, 9 A. (2d) 350 (1939).
Manners v. Philadelphia Library Co., 93 Pa. 165 (1880).
Maplewood v. Albright, 176 Atl. 194 (1934).
Marsh v. Alabama, 326 U. S. 501, 66 Sup Ct. 276, 90 L. Ed. 265 (1946).
Marsh v. Johnson, 259 Ky. 305, 82 S. W. (2d) 345 (1935).
Marshall v. State, 219 Ala. 83, 121 So. 72 (1897).
Marshburn v. City of Bloomington, 32 Ill. App. 243 (1889).
Martin v. City of Struthers, 319 U. S. 141, 63 Sup. Ct. 862, 87 L. Ed. 1313 (1943).
Martin v. State, 65 Tenn. 234 (1873).
Marvel v. Sadtler, 18 A. (2d) 231 (1941).
Masonic Building Association v. Town of Stamford, 119 Conn. 53, 174 Atl. 301 (1934).
Master v. Second Parish of Portland, 124 F. (2d) 622 (C. C. A., 1941).
Mathis v. Holmes, 134 N. J. Eq. 186, 34 A. (2d) 645 (1943).
Matter of Shattuck, 193 N. Y. 446, 86 N. E. 455 (1908).
Maxey v. Bell, 41 Ga. 183 (1870).
Mayfield v. Safe Deposit Co., 132 Atl. 595 (1926).
McAlister v. Burgess, 161 Mass. 269, 37 N. E. 173 (1894).
McCall v. Capers, 105 S. W. (2d) 323 (1937).
McClellan v. Owens, 335 Mo. 884, 74 S. W. (2d) 570 (1934).
McConkey v. City of Fredericksburg, 179 Va. 556, 19 S. E. (2d) 682 (1942).
McCrocklin's Adm'r v. Lee, 247 Ky. 31, 56 S. W. (2d) 564 (1933).
McCulloch v. Maryland, 4 Wheat. 316, 4 L. Ed. 579 (1819).
McDowell v. Board of Education, 172 N. Y. S. 590, 104 Misc. 564 (1918).
McFadden v. Commonwealth, 23 Pa. 12 (1853).
McGinnis v. Watson, 41 Pa. 9 (1861).
McGlone v. First Baptist Church of Denver, 97 Colo. 427, 50 P. (2d) 547 (1935).

McHugh v. McCole, 97 Wisc. 166, 72 N. W. 631 (1897).

McIntire v. William Penn Broadcasting Company of Philadelphia, 151 F. (2d) 597 (C. C. A., 1945); certiorari denied 327 U. S. 779, 16 Sup. Ct. 530, 90 L. Ed. 1007 (1946).

McMasters v. State, 21 Okla. Crim. 318 (1922).

McNeilly v. First Presbyterian Church of Brookline, 243 Mass. 331, 137 N. E. 691 (1923).

Mercantile Commerce Bank and Trust Company v. Howe, 113 F. (2d) 893 (C. C. A., 1940).

Merrick v. Lewis, 40 Pa. Co. 290 (1911).

Methodist Episcopal Church v. Hinton, 92 Tenn. 188, 21 S. W. 321 (1893).

Methodist Episcopal Church v. Walters, 50 F. (2d) 416 (D. C., 1928).

Meyer v. Nebraska, 262 U. S. 390, 43 Sup. Ct. 625, 67 L. Ed. 1042 (1923).

Meyers v. Baker, 120 Ill. 567, 12 N. E. 79 (1887).

Miami Military Institute v. Leff, 220 N. Y. S. 799, 129 Misc. 481 (1926).

Miles v. United States, 103 U. S. 304, 26 L. Ed. 481 (1880).

Milford v. Worcester, 7 Mass. 48 (1810).

Minersville School District v. Gobitis, 310 U. S. 586, 60 Sup. Ct. 1010, 84 L. Ed. 1375 (1940).

Minter v. State, 104 Ga. 743, 30 S. E. 989 (1898).

Minton v. Leavell, 297 S. W. 615 (1927).

Mitchell v. Mitchell, 18 Md. 405 (1862).

Mitterhausen v. So. Wisconsin Conference Association of Seventh Day Adventists, 245 Wisc. 353, 14 N. W. (2d) 19 (1944).

Mood v. Methodist Episcopal Church South, 289 S. W. 461 (1926).

Moore v. Monroe, 64 Iowa 367, 20 N. W. 475 (1884).

Moore v. State, 135 So. 411 (1931).

Moran v. Moran, 104 Iowa 216, 73 N. W. 617 (1898).

Morgan v. Civil Service Commission, 131 N. J. L. 410, 36 A. (2d) 898 (1944).

Morgan v. Leslie, 1 Wright (Ohio) 144 (1832).

Morgan v. Maunders, 37 S. W. (2d) 791 (1930).

Moritz v. United Brethren Church of Staten Island, 278 N. Y. S. 342, 244 App. Div. 121 (1935).

Morris v. Featro, 340 Pa. 354, 17 A. (2d) 403 (1941).

Morse v. State, 173 So. 875 (1937).

Morville v. Fowle, 144 Mass. 109, 10 N. E. 726 (1887).

Mueller v. Coffman, 132 Ark. 45, 200 S. W. 136 (1918).

Mulroy v. Churchman, 52 Iowa 238, 3 N. W. 72 (1879).

Murdock v. State, 319 U. S. 105, 63 Sup. Ct. 870, 87 L. Ed. 1292 (1943).

Nance v. Busby, 91 Tenn. 218, 18 S. W. 874 (1891).

Nebraska District of Evangelical Lutheran Synod v. McKelvie, 262 U. S. 404, 43 Sup. Ct. 628, 67 L. Ed. 1047 (1923).

Neely v. State, 20 Ga. App. 83, 92 S. E. 542 (1917).

New v. United States, 245 Fed. 710 (C. C. A., 1917).

Nicholls v. Mayor of Lynn, 7 N. E. (2d) 577 (1937).

Nichols v. School Directors, 93 Ill. 61 (1879).

North v. Board of Trustees, 27 N. E. 54 (1891).

Northwestern University v. Wesley Memorial Hospital, 125 N. E. 13 (1919).

Norwegian Lutheran Church v. Wooster, 176 Wash. 581, 30 P. (2d) 381 (1934).

O'Connor v. Hendrick, 184 N. Y. 421, 77 N. E. 612 (1906).

O'Dell v. Goff, 149 Mich. 152, 112 N. W. 736 (1907).

Ohio ex rel. Popovici v. Aigler, 280 U. S. 379, 50 Sup. Ct. 154, 74 L. Ed. 489 (1930).

Oliver v. United States, 267 Fed. 544 (C. C. A., 1920).

Orchardson v. Cofield, 171 Ill. 14, 49 N. E. 197 (1898).

Organ Meeting House v. Seaford, 16 N. C. 453 (1830).

Otken v. Lakin, 56 Miss. 758 (1879).

Owens v. State, 6 Okla. Crim. Rep. 110, 116 Pac. 345 (1911).

Parish of Immaculate Conception v. Murphy, 89 Neb. 524, 131 N. W. 946 (1911).

Parker v. Harper, 295 Ky. 686, 175 S. W. (2d) 361 (1943).

Partridge v. Partridge, 220 Mo. 321, 119 S. W. 415 (1909).

Paulson's Will, 127 Wisc. 612, 107 N. W. 484 (1906).

Pearson v. First Congregational Church of Joplin, 106 S. W. (2d) 941 (1937).

Pelter v. Sacred Heart Catholic Church, 186 Okla. 45, 96 P. (2d) 24 (1939).

People v. Ashley, 172 N. Y. S. 282, 184 App. Div. 520 (1918).

People ex rel. McCollum v. Board of Education, —— U. S. ——, 68 Sup. Ct. 461, —— L. Ed. ——, decided March 8, 1948.

People v. Board of Education, 13 Barb. (N. Y.) 400 (1851).

People v. Board of Education, 245 Ill. 334, 92 N. E. 251 (1910).

People v. Catholic Bishop, 311 Ill. 11, 142 N. E. 520 (1924).

People v. Copsey, 71 Cal. 548, 12 Pac. 721 (1887).

People v. German United Evangelical St. Stephens Church, 53 N. Y. 103 (1873).

People v. Goldberger, 163 N. Y. S. 663 (1916).

People v. Graves, 245 N. Y. 195, 156 N. E. 663 (1927).

People v. Graves, 219 N. Y. S. 189, 210 App. Div. 233 (1927).

People v. Hopt, 3 Utah 396, 4 Pac. 250 (1884).

People v. Jessamine Withers Home, 312 Ill. 136, 143 N. E. 414 (1924).

People v. Lum Foon, 155 Pac. 477 (1915).

People v. Marquis, 291 Ill. 121, 125 N. E. 757 (1919).

People v. Muldoon, 306 Ill. 234, 137 N. E. 863 (1922).

People v. Mt. Joseph's Academy, 189 N. Y. S. 775, 198 App. Div. 75 (1921).

People v. Pearson, 176 N. Y. 201, 68 N. E. 243 (1903).

People v. Peck, 11 Wend. (N. Y.) 604 (1834).

People v. Rollins, 179 Cal. 818, 179 Pac. 209 (1919).

People v. Ruggles, 8 Johns. (N. Y.) 290 (1811).

People v. Sandstrom, 3 N. Y. S. (2d) 1006, 167 Misc. 436 (1938).

People v. Sayles, 53 N. Y. S. 67, 32 App. Div. 197 (1898).

People v. Schladweiler, 315 Ill. 553, 146 N. E. 525 (1925).

People v. Sisson, 271 N. Y. 285, 2 N. E. (2d) 660 (1936).

People v. Sisson, 285 N. Y. S. 41, 246 App. Div. 151 (1936).

People v. Sisson, 281 N. Y. S. 559, 156 Misc. 236 (1936).

People v. Stanley, 81 Colo. 276, 255 Pac. 610 (1927).

People v. Vogelgesang, 221 N. Y. 290, 116 N. E. 977 (1917).

People v. Volunteer Rescue Army, 28 N. Y. S. (2d) 994, 262 App. Div. 237 (1941).

People v. Woolston, 239 N. Y. S. 185, 135 Misc. 320 (1930).

People v. Young Men's Christian Association, 157 Ill. 403, 41 N. E. 557 (1895).

Permoli v. First Municipality, 3 How. 589, 11 L. Ed. 739 (1845).

Peterson v. Widulo, 157 Wisc. 641, 147 N. W. 966 (1914).

Petition of Hayes, 38 N. Y. S. (2d) 66 (1942).

Petition of Horowitz, 48 F. (2d) 652 (D. C., 1931).

Petition of Presbytery of Philadelphia of Presbyterian Church in United States, 347 Pa. 263, 32 A. (2d) 196 (1942).

Pfeiffer v. Board of Education, 118 Mich. 560, 77 N. W. 250 (1898).

Phoenix Insurance Co. v. Burkett, 72 Mo. App. 1 (1897).

Pierce v. Society of the Sisters, 268 U. S. 510, 45 Sup. Ct. 571, 69 L. Ed. 1070 (1925).

Pigford v. State, 16 Okla. Crim. 304, 74 S. W. 323 (1903).

Pinney v. Sulzen, 91 Kans. 407, 137 Pac. 987 (1914).

Pirkey v. Commonwealth, 134 Va. 713, 114 S. E. 764 (1922).

Pocono Pines Assembly v. Miller, 229 Pa. 33, 77 Atl. 1094 (1910).

Post v. Dougherty, 326 Pa. 97, 191 Atl. 151 (1937).

Poynter v. Phelps, 129 Ky. 381, 111 S. W. 699 (1908).

Prall v. Prall, 58 Fla. 496, 50 So. 867 (1909).

Presbyterian Church v. Myers, 5 Okla. 809, 50 Pac. 70 (1897).

Presbytery of Huron v. Gordon, 68 S. D. 228, 300 N. W. 33 (1941).

Price v. State, 107 Ala. 161, 18 So. 130 (1893).

Prieto v. St. Alphonsus Convent of Mercy, 52 La. Ann. 631, 27 So. 153 (1900).

Prime v. Harmon, 120 Me. 299, 113 Atl. 738 (1921).

Prince v. Massachusetts, 321 U. S. 158, 64 Sup. Ct. 438, 88 L. Ed. 645 (1944).

Pumphrey v. State, 84 Neb. 636, 122 N. W. 19 (1909).

Purcell v. Summers, 34 F. Supp. 421 (D. C., 1940).

Purcell v. Summers, 54 F. Supp. 279 (D. C., 1944).

Purcell v. Summers, 145 F. (2d) 979 (C. C. A., 1944).

Purinton v. Jamrock, 195 Mass. 187, 80 N. E. 802 (1907).

Quick Bear v. Leupp, 210 U. S. 50, 28 Sup. Ct. 690, 52 L. Ed. 954 (1907).

Ramsey v. Hicks, 174 Ind. 428, 91 N. E. 344 (1910).

Rase v. United States, 129 F. (2d) 204 (C. C. A., 1942).

Reichert v. Sarembi, 115 Neb. 404, 213 N. W. 584 (1927).

Reichwald v. Catholic Bishop, 258 Ill. 44, 101 N. E. 266 (1913).

Rendleman v. United States, 18 F. (2d) 27 (C. C. A., 1927).

Reutkemeier v. Nolte, 179 Iowa 342, 161 N. W. 290 (1917).

Reynolds v. United States, 98 U. S. 145, 25 L. Ed. 244 (1878).

Richardson v. State, 5 Tex. App. 47 (1880).

Richter v. Savannah, 160 Ga. 178, 127 S. E. 739 (1925).

Riddles v. State, 46 S. W. 1058 (1898).

Riggs v. State, 75 Tenn. 475 (1881).

Robertson v. Bullions, 11 N. Y. 243 (1854).

Robinson v. Robinson, 66 N. H. 600, 23 Atl. 362 (1891).

Rogers v. Baldridge, 18 Tenn. App. 300, 76 S. W. (2d) 655.

Roodenko v. United States, 147 F. (2d) 752 (C. C. A., 1945);
certiorari denied 324 U. S. 860, 65 Sup. Ct. 867, 89 L. Ed.
1418 (1945); rehearing denied 324 U. S. 891, 65 Sup. Ct.
1022, 89 L. Ed. 1438 (1945).

Rosen v. United States, 245 U. S. 467, 38 Sup. Ct. 148, 62 L. Ed.
406 (1918).

Rosenbaum v. State, 131 Ark. 251, 199 S. W. 388 (1917).

Rudolph v. Landwerlen, 92 Ind. 34 (1883).

Russell v. Allen, 107 U. S. 163, 2 Sup. Ct. 327, 27 L. Ed. 397
(1882).

Russian Serbian Holy Trinity Orthodox Church v. Kulik, 202 Minn.
560, 279 N. W. 364 (1938).

Ryan v. Ryan, 114 S. W. 464 (1908).

St. Barbara's Roman Catholic Church v. City of New York, 277
N. Y. S. 538, 243 App. Div. 371 (1935).

St. John the Baptist Greek Catholic Church v. Gengor, 121 N. J.
349, 189 Atl. 113 (1937).

St. John's Evangelical Lutheran Church v. Board of Appeals, 191
N. E. 282 (1934).

St. Louis Colonization Association v. Hennessy, 11 Mo. App. 555
(1882).

St. Mary's Church v. Tripp, 14 R. I. 307 (1883).

St. Mary's Greek Catholic Church v. Gaydos, 58 Montg. Co. (Pa.)
L. R. 62 (1942).

St. Michael's Ukranian Greek Catholic Church v. Bohachewsky, 60
R. I. 1, 196 Atl. 796 (1938).

St. Stanislaus Church Society v. Erie County, 275 N. Y. S. 84, 153
Misc. 511 (1934).

Sale v. First Regular Baptist Church of Mason City, 62 Iowa 26
(1883).

Sanchez v. Grace Methodist Episcopal Church, 114 Cal. 295, 46
Pac. 2 (1896).

Sanders v. Baggerly, 96 Ark. 117, 131 S. W. 49 (1910).
Sands v. Church of Ascension and Prince of Peace, 181 Md. 536, 30 A. (2d) 771 (1943).
Sarahass v. Armstrong, 16 Kans. 192 (1876).
Savannah v. Richter, 160 Ga. 177, 127 S. E. 140 (1925).
Savitt v. United States, 59 F. (2d) 541 (C. C. A., 1932).
Schlesak v. State, 232 Wisc. 510, 287 N. W. 703 (1939).
Schneider v. State, 308 U. S. 147, 60 Sup. Ct. 146, 84 L. Ed. 115 (1939).
Schofield v. Eighth School District, 27 Conn. 499 (1858).
School Directors v. Toll, 149 Ill. App. 541 (1909).
Scopes v. State, 154 Tenn. 105, 289 S. W. 363 (1927).
Scott v. Curle, 48 Ky. 17 (1848).
Scott v. Hooper, 14 Vt. 535 (1842).
Searcy v. Miller, 57 Iowa 613, 10 N. W. 912 (1881).
Searle v. Roman Catholic Bishop of Springfield, 203 Mass. 493, 89 N. E. 809 (1909).
Selective Draft Cases, 245 U. S. 366, 38 Sup. Ct. 159, 62 L. Ed. 349 (1918).
Selkir v. Klein, 100 N. Y. S. 449, 50 Misc. 194 (1906).
Shaeffer v. Klee, 100 Md. 264, 59 Atl. 850 (1905).
Sheehy v. Blake, 77 Wisc. 394, 46 N. W. 537 (1890).
Sherman v. American Congregation Association, 113 Fed. 609 (C. C. A., 1902).
Sherman v. Baker, 20 R. I. 446, 40 Atl. 11 (1898).
Shinn v. Barrow, 121 S. W. (2d) 450 (1938).
Shrader v. Erickson's Ex'r, 284 Ky. 449, 145 S. W. (2d) 63 (1940).
Shradi v. Dirnfield, 52 Minn. 465, 55 N. W. 49 (1893).
Sisters of Mercy v. Lightner, 274 N. W. 86 (1937).
Skinner v. Holmes, 133 N. J. Eq. 593, 33 A. (2d) 819 (1943).
Skyline Missionary Baptist Church v. Davis, 17 So. (2d) 533 (1944).
Slaughter v. Land, 194 Ga. 156, 21 S. E. (2d) 72 (1942).
Smith v. Board of Pensions of the Methodist Church, 54 F. Supp. 224 (D. C., 1944).
Smith v. Bonhoof, 2 Mich. 115 (1851).
Smith v. Donahue, 195 N. Y. S. 715, 202 App. Div. 656 (1922).

Smith v. People, 51 Colo. 270, 117 Pac. 612 (1911).

Sosna v. Fishman, 154 S. W. (2d) 398 (1941).

Specht v. Commonwealth, 8 Pa. 312 (1848).

Spencer v. Spencer, 221 S. W. 58 (1920).

Spenningsby v. Norwegian Lutheran Trinity Congregation, 152 Minn. 164, 188 N. W. 217 (1922).

Spiller v. Inhabitants of Woburn, 94 Mass. 127 (1866).

S. S. & B. Live Poultry Corp. v. Kashruth Association, 285 N. Y. S. 879, 158 Misc. 358 (1936).

Stafford v. State, 154 Ala. 71, 45 So. 673 (1908).

Stahl v. Kansas Educational Association, 54 Kan. 1, 37 Pac. 135 (1894).

State v. Amana Society, 132 Iowa 304, 109 N. W. 894 (1906).

State v. Ancker, 2 Rich. Law. (S. C.) 245 (1846).

State, the Church of the Redeemer, Prosecutor v. Axtell, 41 N. J. L. 114 (1879).

State v. Baltimore & Ohio Railroad Co., 15 W. Va. 362 (1879).

State v. Barlow, 107 Utah 292, 153 P. (2d) 647 (1944); appeal dismissed 324 U. S. 829, 65 Sup. Ct. 916, 89 L. Ed. 1396 (1945); rehearing denied 324 U. S. 891, 65 Sup. Ct. 1026, 89 L. Ed. 1438 (1945).

State v. Barnes, 22 N. D. 18, 132 N. W. 215 (1911).

State v. Beal, 199 N. C. 278, 154 S. E. 604 (1930).

State v. Bird, 253 Mo. 569, 162 S. W. 119 (1913).

State v. Board of Public Instruction, 139 Fla. 43, 190 So. 815 (1939).

State v. Branner, 149 N. C. 559, 63 S. E. 169 (1908).

State v. Brown, 36 Del. 181 (1938).

State v. Brown, 95 Iowa 381, 64 N. W. 277 (1895).

State v. Cantwell, 126 Conn. 1, 8 A (2d) 533 (1939).

State v. Cate, 58 N. H. 240 (1878).

State v. Chandler, 2 Harr. (Del.) 553 (1837).

State v. Chenewith, 163 Ind. 94, 71 N. E. 197 (1904).

State v. Chicago, B. & Q. Railroad Co., 246 Mo. 512, 143 S. W. 785 (1912).

State v. Church of Advent, 208 Ala. 632, 95 So. 3 (1923).

State v. Collector, 24 N. J. Law 108 (1853).

State v. Cooper, 2 Tenn. 96 (1807).

State v. Davis, 80 N. C. 412 (1879).

State v. Delaney, 122 Atl. 890 (1923).

State v. Dilley, 95 Neb. 527, 145 N. W. 999 (1914).

State v. District Board, 76 Wisc. 177, 44 N. W. 967 (1890).

State v. District Board, 162 Wisc. 482, 156 N. W. 477 (1916).

State v. Drew, 192 Atl. 629 (1937).

State v. Dudicoff, 109 Conn. 711, 145 Atl. 655 (1929).

State v. Estabrook, 162 Ore. 476, 91 P. (2d) 838 (1939).

State v. Frazier, 102 Wash. 369, 173 Pac. 35 (1918).

State v. Gehner, 320 Mo. 1172, 11 S. W. (2d) 30 (1928).

State v. Hall, 225 Iowa 1316, 283 N. W. 414 (1939).

State v. Hand, 1 Ohio Dec. 238 (1848).

State v. Howard, 120 La. 311, 45 So. 260 (1908).

State v. Hundley, 195 N. C. 377, 142 S. E. 330 (1928).

State v. Hutterische Bruder Gemeinde, 46 S. D. 189, 191 N. W. 635 (1922).

State v. Jackson, 156 Iowa 588, 137 N. W. 1034 (1912).

State v. Jasper, 15 N. C. 323 (1833).

State v. Jones, 53 Mo. 486 (1873).

State v. Jones, 77 S. C. 385 (1907).

State v. Kirby, 108 N. C. 772, 12 S. E. 1045 (1891).

State v. Kramer, 49 S. D. 56, 206 N. W. 468 (1925).

State v. Leuch, 198 Wash. 331, 88 P. (2d) 440 (1939).

State v. Levine, 109 N. J. L. 503, 162 Atl. 909 (1932).

State v. Levy, 187 N. C. 581, 122 S. E. 386 (1924).

State v. Linkhaw, 69 N. C. 214 (1873).

State v. Mancini, 91 Vt. 507, 101 Atl. 581 (1917).

State v. Matheny, 101 S. E. 661 (1919).

State v. Miller, 59 N. D. 286, 299 N. W. 569 (1930).

State v. Milquet, 180 Wisc. 109, 192 N. W. 392 (1923).

State v. Mockus, 120 Me. 84, 113 Atl. 39 (1921).

State v. Morehouse, 117 Atl. 296 (1922).

State v. Morris, 28 Idaho 599, 155 Pac. 296 (1916).

State v. Neitzell, 69 Wash. 567, 125 Pac. 939 (1912).

State v. Norris, 59 N. H. 536 (1880).

State v. Phillips, 277 N. W. 609 (1938).

State v. Powell, 56 Ohio 784, 50 N. E. 900 (1898).

State v. Ramsey, 78 N. C. 448 (1877).

State v. Richardson, 197 Wisc. 390, 222 N. W. 222 (1928).

State v. Ringer, 6 Blackf. (Ind.) 109 (1841).

State v. Rozell, 225 S. W. 931 (1920).

State v. Sandford, 99 Me. 441, 59 Atl. 597 (1905).

State v. Scheve, 65 Neb. 853, 91 N. W. 846 (1902).

State v. Schieneman, 64 Mo. 386 (1877).

State v. Second Church of Christ, Scientist, 185 Minn. 242, 240 N. W. 532 (1932).

State v. Simpson, 297 S. W. 993 (1927).

State v. Solomon, 33 Ind. 450 (1870).

State v. Southern Publishing Association, 84 S. W. 580 (1904).

State v. St. Louis Young Men's Christian Association, 259 Mo. 233, 168 S. W. 589 (1914).

State v. Stuth, 11 Wash, 423, 39 Pac. 665 (1895).

State v. Swink, 20 N. C. 492 (1839).

State v. Taylor, 122 Neb. 454, 240 N. W. 573 (1932).

State v. Trustees of Westminster College, 175 Mo. 52, 74 S. W. 990 (1903).

State v. Union Congregational Church, 173 Minn. 40, 216 N. W. 326 (1927).

State v. Verbon, 167 Wash. 140, 8 P. (2d) 1083 (1932).

State v. Walker, 36 Kans. 297 (1887).

State v. Washington, 49 La. Ann. 1602, 22 So. 841 (1897).

State v. White, 64 N. H. 48, 5 Atl. 828 (1886).

State v. Wright, 41 Ark. 410 (1883).

Stegall v. Stegall, 151 Miss. 875, 119 So. 802 (1928).

Stein v. Brown, 211 N. Y. S. 822, 125 Misc. 692 (1925).

Stewart v. State, 31 Ga. 232 (1860).

Stogner v. Laird, 145 S. W. 644 (1912).

Stoker v. Schwab, 1 N. Y. 425, 56 Super. 122 (1888).

Stone v. Bogue, 181 S. W. (2d) 187 (1944).

Stovall v. State, 163 So. 504 (1935).

Stump v. Sturm, 254 Fed. 535 (C. C. A., 1918).

Summerhill v. Wilkes, 63 Tex. Civ. App. 456, 133 S. E. 492 (1910).

Sunday School Union of African Methodist Episcopal Church v. Walden, 121 F. (2d) 719 (C. C. A., 1941).

Syracuse Center of Jehovah's Witnesses v. City of Syracuse, 297 N. Y. S. 587, 163 Misc. 535 (1937).

Tanner v. State, 126 Ga. 77, 54 S. E. 914 (1906).

Taylor v. Mississippi, 319 U. S. 583, 63 Sup. Ct. 1200, 87 L. Ed. 1600 (1943).

Terpening v. Gull Lake Assembly of Michigan Conference of Methodist Protestant Church, 298 Mich. 510, 299 N. W. 165 (1941).

Territory v. Evans, 2 Idaho 651, 23 Pac. 232 (1890).

Theta XI Building Association of Iowa City v. Board of Review, 217 Iowa 1181, 251 N. W. 76 (1933).

Thomas v. Collins, 323 U. S. 516, 65 Sup. Ct. 315, 89 L. Ed. 430 (1945); rehearing denied 323 U. S. 819, 65 Sup. Ct. 557, 89 L. Ed. 630 (1945).

Thomas v. Lewis, 224 Ky. 307, 6 S. W. (2d) 255 (1928).

Thompson v. West, 59 Neb. 677, 82 N. W. 13 (1900).

Thurmond v. Cedar Rapids Baptist Church, 110 Ga. 816, 36 S. E. 211 (1900).

Town of Irvington v. Schneider, 120 N. J. Law 460, 200 Atl. 799 (1938).

Town of Irvington v. Schneider, 121 N. J. Law 542, 3 A. (2d) 609 (1939).

Town of Londonderry v. Town of Chester, 2 N. H. 268 (1820).

Trinity Methodist Episcopal Church v. San Antonio, 201 S. W. 669 (1918).

Trustees of Delaware Annual Conference v. Ennis, 29 A. (2d) 374 (1942).

Trustees of East Norway Lake Evangelical Lutheran Church v. Halvorsen, 42 Minn. 503, 44 N. W. 663 (1890).

Trustees of the First Congregational Church of Ionia v. Webber, 54 Mich. 571, 20 N. W. 542 (1884).

Trustees of Griswold College v. State, 46 Iowa 275 (1877).

Trustees of the Methodist Church v. Ellis, 38 Ind. 3 (1871).

Trustees of New Hampshire Conference of the Methodist Episcopal Church v. Sandown, 87 N. H. 47, 173 Atl. 805 (1934).

Trustees of Young Men's and Young Women's Hebrew Association v. State Board of Tax Appeals, 119 N. J. 504, 197 Atl. 372 (1938).

Tsenoff v. Nakoff, 326 Pa. 549, 192 Atl. 873 (1937).

Tucker v. Paulk, 148 Ga. 228, 96 S. E. 339 (1919).

Tucker v. Reil, 51 Ariz. 357, 77 P. (2d) 203 (1938).

Tucker v. Texas, 326 U. S. 517, 66 Sup. Ct. 274, 90 L. Ed. 274 (1946).

Tufts v. Tufts, 8 Utah, 142, 30 Pac. 309 (1892).

Turbeville v. Morris, 26 S. E. (2d) 821 (1943).

United Mine Workers v. Coronado Coal Co., 259 U. S. 344, 42 Sup. Ct. 570, 66 L. Ed. 975 (1922).

United States v. Ballard, 322 U. S. 78, 64 Sup. Ct. 882, 88 L. Ed. 1148 (1944).

United States v. Bassett, 5 Utah 131, 13 Pac. 237 (1887).

United States v. Brooks, 4 Cranch 427, 24 Fed. Cas. No. 14655 (C. C., 1834).

United States v. Brooks, 54 F. Supp. 995 (D. C., 1944); affirmed 147 F. (2d) 134 (C. C. A., 1945); certiorari denied 324 U. S. 878, 65 Sup. Ct. 1027, 89 L. Ed. 1430 (1945).

United States ex rel. Trainin v. Cain, 144 F. (2d) 944 (C. C. A., 1944); certiorari denied 323 U. S. 795, 65 Sup. Ct. 439, 89 L. Ed. 635 (1945); rehearing denied 323 U. S. 819, 65 Sup. Ct. 559, 89 L. Ed. 650 (1945).

United States v. Carruthers, 152 F. (2d) 512 (C. C. A., 1945); certiorari denied 327 U. S. 787, 66 Sup. Ct. 805, 90 L. Ed. 1014 (1946); rehearing denied 327 U. S. 817, 66 Sup. Ct. 816, 90 L. Ed. 1041 (1946).

United States v. Chatwin, 56 F. Supp. 890 (D. C., 1944); affirmed 146 F. (2d) 730 (C. C. A., 1945); reversed on other grounds 326 U. S. 455, 66 Sup. Ct. 233, 90 L. Ed. 198 (1946).

United States v. Domres, 142 F. (2d) 477 (C. C. A., 1944).

United States v. Hillyard, 52 F. Supp. 612 (D. C., 1943).

United States v. Kennedy, 26 Fed. Cas. 761 (D. C., 1843).

United States v. Lee, 26 Fed. Cas. 908 (C. C., 1824).

United States v. Macintosh, 283 U. S. 605, 51 Sup. Ct. 570, 75 L. Ed. 1302 (1931).

United States v. Mroz, 136 F. (2d) 221 (C. C. A., 1943).

United States v. Mroz, 320 U. S. 805, 64 Sup. Ct. 23, 88 L. Ed. 486 (1943).

United States ex rel. Zucker v. Osborne, 54 F. Supp. 984 (D. C.,

1944); affirmed 147 F. (2d) 135 (C. C. A., 1945); certiorari denied 325 U. S. 881, 65 Sup. Ct. 1574, 89 L. Ed. 1997 (1945).

United States v. Parson, 22 F. Supp. 149 (D. C., 1938).

United States v. Pitt, 144 F. (2d) 169 (C. C. A., 1944).

United States v. Reid, 12 How. 361, 13 L. Ed. 1023 (1851).

United States v. Schwimmer, 279 U. S. 644, 49 Sup. Ct. 80, 73 L. Ed. 558 (1929).

United States v. Stephens, 245 Fed. 956 (D. C., 1917).

United States v. Williams, 126 Fed. 253 (C. C., 1903).

University Club v. Lanier, 119 Fla. 146, 161 So. 78 (1935).

University of Maryland v. Coale, 165 Md. 224, 167 Atl. 54 (1933).

Updegraph v. Commonwealth, 11 Serg & R. (Pa.) 394 (1832).

Van Bibber v. United States, 151 F. (2d) 444 (C. C. A., 1945).

Van Vliet v. Vander Haald, 290 Mich. 365, 287 N. W. 564 (1939).

Vaughan v. Maynard, 294 Ky. 38, 170 S. W. (2d) 897 (1943).

Verser v. Ford, 37 Ark. 27 (1878).

Vidal v. Girard's Executor, 43 U. S. 127, 2 How. 127, 11 L. Ed. 205 (1844).

Vonnegut v. Baun, 206 Ind. 172, 188 N. E. 677 (1934).

Wakefield v. Ross, 28 Fed. Cas. 1346 (C. C., 1827).

Walker Memorial Baptist Church v. Saunders, 17 N. Y. S. (2d) 842, 173 Misc. 455 (1940).

Walker Memorial Baptist Church v. Saunders, 285 N. Y. 462, 35 N. E. (2d) 42 (1941).

Walker v. State, 103 Ark. 336, 146 S. W. 862 (1912).

Wall v. Lee, 34 N. Y. 141 (1865).

Warren v. Pulitzer Publishing Co., 336 Mo. 184, 78 S. W. (2d) 404 (1934).

Washburn College v. Commissioners, 8 Kan. 344 (1871).

Watson v. Avery, 2 Bush. (Ky.) 332 (1869).

Watson v. Garvin, 54 Mo. 353 (1873).

Watson v. United States, 80 U. S. 679, 20 L. Ed. 666 (1871).

Watson v. Jones, 13 Wall. 679, 20 L. Ed. 666 (1871).

Weigel v. Reintjes, 154 S. W. (2d) 412 (1941).

Weir v. Harley, 99 Mo. 484, 12 S. W. 798 (1889)

Wesley Foundation v. King County, 185 Wash. 12, 52 P. (2d) 1247 (1936).

West v. State, 28 Tenn. 66 (1848).

West v. State, 105 Ark. 175, 150 S. W. 695 (1912).

Westminster Presbyterian Church v. Presbytery of New York, 127 N. Y. S. 836, 142 App. Div. 855 (1911).

West Virginia State Board of Education v. Barnette, 319 U. S. 624, 63 Sup. Ct. 1178, 87 L. Ed. 1628 (1943).

Whalen v. Olmstead, 61 Conn. 263, 23 Atl. 964 (1891).

Wheaton v. Cutler, 84 Vt. 476, 79 Atl. 1091 (1911).

Whitmore v. Fourth Congregational Society of Plymouth, 68 Mass. 306 (1854).

Wilkerson v. City of Rome, 152 Ga. 762, 110 S. E. 895 (1921).

Wilkins v. Wardens of St. Marks Protestant Episcopal Church, 52 Ga. 352 (1874).

Williams v. Board of Trustees, 173 Ky. 708, 191 S. W. 507 (1917).

Williams v. Concord Congregational Church, 193 Pa. 120, 44 Atl. 272 (1899).

Williams v. State, 83 Ala. 68, 3 So. 790 (1887).

Williamson v. Carroll, 16 N. J. L. 217 (1837).

Wilson v. Evangelical Lutheran Church of the Reformation, 230 N. W. 708 (1930).

Wilson v. Presbyterian Church of Johns Island, 2 Rich. Eq. (N. J.) 192 (1846).

Winnard v. State, 30 S. W. 555 (1895).

Winter v. Winter, 102 Pa. Super. 300, 156 Atl. 603 (1931).

Wolfe v. United States, 291 U. S. 7, 54 Sup. Ct. 279, 78 L. Ed. 617 (1934).

Wood v. State, 11 Tex. A. 318 (1882).

Woodal v. State, 4 Ga. App. 783, 62 S. E. 485 (1908).

Woodstock v. Retreat, 125 Conn. 52, 3 A. (2d) 232 (1938).

Woodward v. State, 173 Ark. 906, 293 S. W. 1010 (1927).

Wright v. State, 135 So. 636 (1931).

Wyath v. State, 56 Tex. Crim. 50, 119 S. W. 1147 (1909).

Wyatt v. Stillman Institute, 303 Mo. 94, 260 S. W. 73 (1924).

Yeary v. White, 268 Ky. 471, 105 S. W. (2d) 609 (1937).

Young v. *State,* 122 Ga. 725, 50 S. E. 996 (1905).

Young v. *State,* 271 Pac. 426 (1928).

Young Men's Christian Association v. *Douglas County,* 60 Neb. 642, 83 N. W. 924 (1900).

Young Men's Christian Association v. *Lancaster County,* 106 Neb. 1, 182 N. W. 593 (1921).

Young Men's Christian Association v. *Paterson,* 61 N. J. L. 420, 39 Atl. 655 (1898).

Zeisweiss v. *James,* 63 Pa. 465 (1870).

Zoularian v. *New England Sanatorium,* 230 Mass. 102, 119 N. E. 686 (1918).

Index

Alienation of affections, as grounds for divorce, 213-214

Antenuptial agreements, 226-229; common law rule, 226; persuasive nature of, 227-228

Assembly, religious, 148-170; legal status of right of, 148-151; common law rule, 148; state statutes, 149-150; theory of, 150; time of beginning and ending, 151-154; place of, 154-155; number protected, 155-156; secondary religious purpose of meeting, 166-167; commercial restrictions, 167-169

Assessments, special, 194-196

Association of religious societies, 106-108; contrast with merger, 106; effects of, 106-108

Bequests, see devises

Bible reading in public schools, 244-249

Blasphemy, 58-60

Cemetery lands, 194

Child control, religious rights in parental conflicts over, 216-231; historical background, 216-218; doctrine of coequality, 218-220; limitation of doctrine, 220-222; supremacy of father, 222-224; non-interference with state custody, 224; non-interference at age of discretion, 224; guardians as public officers, 225-226; antenuptial agreements, 226-229; neglect of medical care, 229-231

Christianity, relation of to American law, 31-35

Civil authority, role of in finality of administrative decisions of religious societies, 118

Colonies, religious situation in, 4-5

Commerce power, as limitation upon religious freedom, 37-38

Constitutions, early state, 14-17; U. S., 17-26, 28-31; revised state, 27-28

Court trials, religious rights in, 277-306; competency of witnesses, 277-283; credibility of testimony, 283-286; witnesses in federal courts, 286-291; children as witnesses, 291-294; aspersions on religion of parties, 294-295; competency of jurors, 295-299; dying declarations, 299-302; privileged communications, 302-304

Delegated power as limitation upon religious freedom, 37-46; commerce power, 37-38; naturalization power, 38-41; postal power, 41-43; military power, 43-46

Devises and bequests for religious purposes, 307-323; character of grants, 307-308; liberal construction favored, 308; indefiniteness of beneficiaries, 308-311; purposes of trusts, 311-313; trusts contrary to public policy, 313-314; effect of incorporation, 314-315; diversion of trusts, 316-317; bequests for the saying of Masses, 318-319; restraints on religious practices, 319-322; peculiar religious beliefs of testator as grounds for avoiding will, 322-323

Distribution of literature: solicitation, 64-76

Disturbance of religious assembly, 151-166; nature of, 151; wilful intent, 156-159; location of disturber, 159-162; member as disturber, 162-166; removal of disturber, 166

Divorce, religious rights in, 207-214; procedure, 210-212; religious oppression as grounds for, 210-212; refusal to cohabit as grounds for, 212-213; alienation of affections, 213-214

Dying declarations, 299-302

Educational practices involving right of religious freedom, 233-276; non-sectarianism in public education, 233-234; public aid, 234-244; reading the Bible in public schools, 244-249; compulsory flag salute, 249-256; compulsory dancing lessons, 257-258; admission, 258; wearing distinctive garb, 258-260; use of school for religious purposes, 260-262; use of religious property for public school, 262-264; excusing students for religious instruction, 264-267; teaching of evolution, 267-268; teachers' views as to war, 268; vaccination, 268-270; language restriction, 270-271; legality of sectarian schools, 271-272; validity of private school regulations, 272-274

English colonies, 8-14

First Amendment to U. S. Constitution, 24-26

Flag salute, as educational practice, 249-256

Fourteenth Amendment to U. S. Constitution, 28-31

Fraud, 60-64

French settlements, 8

Guardians as public officers, 225-226

Health regulation as limitation upon religious freedom, 76-80

Historical analysis of religious freedom in America, 3-36; religious situation in colonies, 4-5; Spanish settlements, 5-8; French settlements, 8; English colonies, 8-14; early state constitutions, 14-17; U. S. Constitution, 17-18; Article VI, U. S. Constitution, 18-24; First Amendment, 24-26; state control, 26-27; revised state constitutions, 27-28; Fourteenth Amendment, U. S. Constitution, 28-31; relation of Christianity to American law, 31-35; role of judiciary, 35-36

Incorporation of religious societies, 89-101; forms of, 89-90; powers of, 95-101

Judiciary, role of, 35-36

Jurors, competency of, 295-299

Leased land, 191-192

Liability of religious societies, 90-95

Marriage, religious rights in, 198-207; early procedure regulating, 198; validity of, 199-203; polygamy, 203-207

Medical care, neglect of, 229-231

Members, relations to religious society, 125-133; contractual relationship, 125-126; voluntary nature, 126-128; lack of civil jurisdiction, 128-133

Merger of religious societies, 102-106; requirement of legislative assent, 102; compliance with statutory mandates, 103; effect of consolidation, 103; attitude of judiciary toward, 105

Military power, as limitation upon religious freedom, 43-46

Naturalization power, as limitation upon religious freedom, 38-41

Oppression, religious, as grounds for divorce, 210-212

Parental conflicts over child control, religious rights in, 216-231
Police power, as limitation upon religious freedom, 46-80; public safety and order, 47-51; Sunday laws, 51-58; blasphemy, 58-60; fraud, 60-64; distribution of literature: solicitation, 64-76; health, 76-80
Polygamy, 203-207
Postal power, as limitation upon religious freedom, 41-43
Powers of incorporated societies, 95-101; general court viewpoint, 95-96; legal rights of religious corporations, 96; *ultra vires* activities, 99-100
Privileged communications, 302-304
Property, religious, used for public school, 262-264
Public aid, 108-112, 234-244; to religious societies, 108-112; for sectarian schools, 234-244; prohibition in form of money or use of public property, 234-236; sectarian orphan asylum, 236-237; teachers' salaries, 237; transportation of pupils to non-secular schools, 237-241; textbooks, 241-243; payment of tuition fees, 244
Public safety and order, 47-51

Religious controversy, 118-123; elements of, 118-121; agency having final ecclesiastical jurisdiction, 121-123
Religious instruction, excusing students for, 264-267
Religious societies, 82-146; nature of, 82-84; society and corporation distinguished, 84-85; acquisition of legal status, 85-89; forms of incorporation, 89-90; liability of religious societies, 90-95; powers of incorporated societies, 95-101; termination of life of religious corporation, 101-102; merger, 102-106; associations, 106-108; public aid to, 108-112; religious corporations distinguished from charitable and educational corporations, 112-115; role of civil authority in affairs of, 118; elements of religious controversy, 118-121; agency having final ecclesiastical jurisdiction, 121-123; procedure in making decisions, 123-125; relation of members to, 125-133; finality of decisions involving property rights, 133-142; temporalities of, not used in accordance with procedural rules, 142-143; activity contrary to civil law, 143-146.

Schools, 260-262, 271-272; nonsectarian used for religious purposes, 260-262; sectarian, legality of, 271-272
Solicitation: distribution of literature, 64-76
Spanish settlements, 5-8
Suggestions for greater religious freedom, 326-331
Sunday laws, 51-58

Taxation, exemption of church property from, 171-197; development of concept, 171-175; construction of legal provisions, 175-176; scope of exemption, 176-178; beginning of exemption, 178-181; exclusive use, 181-185; primary religious use, 185-186; primary secular use, 186-189; doctrine of divisibility, 189-191; ownership as test, 191; leased land, 191-192; property devoted to private worship, 192-194; cemetery lands, 194; special assessments, 194-196

Textbooks, as public aid, 241-243

Transportation of pupils to non-secular schools, 237-241

Trusts, see devises

Use, as determinant in exemption of religious property from txation, 181-191; exclusive use, 181-185; primary religious use, 185-186; primary secular use, 186-189; doctrine of divisibility, 189-191

Vaccination, as educational practice, 268-270

Wearing distinctive garb by teachers, 258-260

Wills, see devises

Witnesses, 277-294; competency of, 277-283; common law disqualification, 277; early American decisions, 278; modification of common law disqualification, 278-281; declaration, 281; affirmation, 282; credibility of, 283-286; in federal courts, 286-291; children as, 291-294